W0009908

STREET ATLAS
Oxfordshire

First published 1992 by

Philip's, a division of
Octopus Publishing Group Ltd
2–4 Heron Quays, London E14 4JP

Second colour edition 2002
Second impression 2002

ISBN 0-540-08108-6 (hardback)
ISBN 0-540-08109-4 (spiral)

© Philip's 2002

OIS Ordnance Survey®

This product includes mapping data licensed
from Ordnance Survey® with the permission of
the Controller of Her Majesty's Stationery Office.
© Crown copyright 2002. All rights reserved.
Licence number 100011710

Printed and bound in Spain
by Cayfosa-Quebecor

Contents

Digital Data

The exceptionally high-quality mapping found in this atlas is available as digital data in TIFF format, which is easily convertible to other bit mapped (raster) image formats.

The index is also available in digital form as a standard database table. It contains all the details found in the printed index together with the National Grid reference for the map square in which each entry is named.

For further information and to discuss your requirements, please contact Philip's on 020 7531 8440 or ruth.king@philips-maps.co.uk

Symbol	Description	Symbol	Description
(22a)	**Motorway** with junction number	⇄ Walsall	**Railway station**
	Primary route – dual/single carriageway	🚂	**Private railway station**
	A road – dual/single carriageway		**Bus, coach station**
	B road – dual/single carriageway	◆	**Ambulance station**
	Minor road – dual/single carriageway	◆	**Coastguard station**
	Other minor road – dual/single carriageway	◆	**Fire station**
– – –	**Road under construction**	◆	**Police station**
	Pedestrianised area	✚	**Accident and Emergency entrance to hospital**
DY7	**Postcode boundaries**	H	**Hospital**
–·–·–	**County and unitary authority boundaries**	+	**Place of worship**
	Railway	🅸	**Information Centre** (open all year)
– – – –	**Railway under construction**	P	**Parking**
	Tramway, miniature railway	P&R	**Park and Ride**
	Rural track, private road or narrow road in urban area	PO	**Post Office**
⊢	**Gate or obstruction to traffic** (restrictions may not apply at all times or to all vehicles)	𝝠	**Camping site**
– – –	**Path, bridleway, byway open to all traffic, road used as a public path**	🚐	**Caravan site**
		▶	**Golf course**
	The representation in this atlas of a road, track or or path is no evidence of the existence of a of a right of way	⊠	**Picnic site**
174 **94** ▶	**Adjoining page indicators**	Prim Sch	**Important buildings, schools, colleges, universities and hospitals**
		River Medway	**Water name**
			River, stream
		◁	**Lock, weir**
			Water
			Tidal water
			Woods
			Houses
		Church	**Non-Roman antiquity**
		ROMAN FORT	**Roman antiquity**

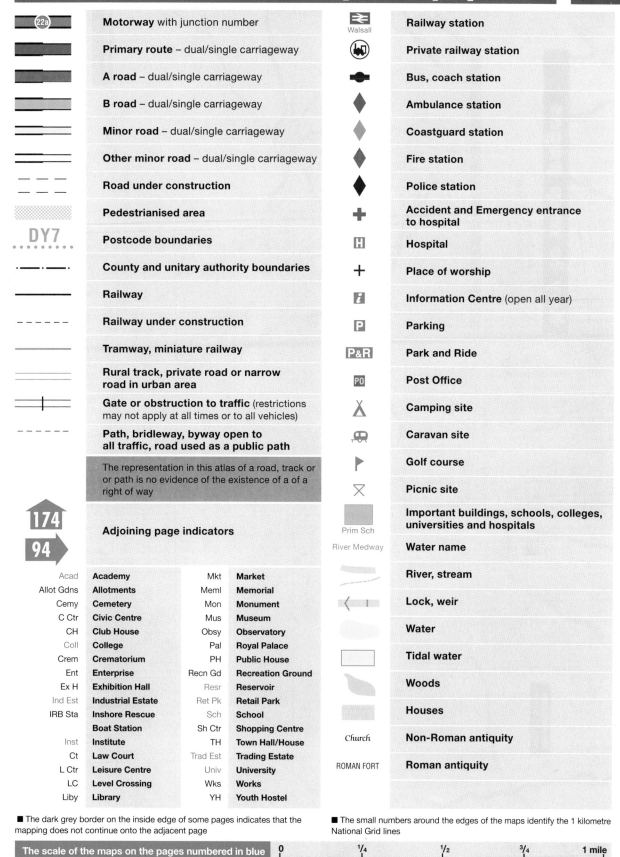

Acad	**Academy**	Mkt	**Market**
Allot Gdns	**Allotments**	Meml	**Memorial**
Cemy	**Cemetery**	Mon	**Monument**
C Ctr	**Civic Centre**	Mus	**Museum**
CH	**Club House**	Obsy	**Observatory**
Coll	**College**	Pal	**Royal Palace**
Crem	**Crematorium**	PH	**Public House**
Ent	**Enterprise**	Recn Gd	**Recreation Ground**
Ex H	**Exhibition Hall**	Resr	**Reservoir**
Ind Est	**Industrial Estate**	Ret Pk	**Retail Park**
IRB Sta	**Inshore Rescue Boat Station**	Sch	**School**
		Sh Ctr	**Shopping Centre**
Inst	**Institute**	TH	**Town Hall/House**
Ct	**Law Court**	Trad Est	**Trading Estate**
L Ctr	**Leisure Centre**	Univ	**University**
LC	**Level Crossing**	Wks	**Works**
Liby	**Library**	YH	**Youth Hostel**

■ The dark grey border on the inside edge of some pages indicates that the mapping does not continue onto the adjacent page

■ The small numbers around the edges of the maps identify the 1 kilometre National Grid lines

The scale of the maps on the pages numbered in blue is 5.52 cm to 1 km • 3¹/₂ inches to 1 mile • 1: 18103

0	¹/₄	¹/₂	³/₄	1 mile
0	250 m	500 m	750 m	1 kilometre

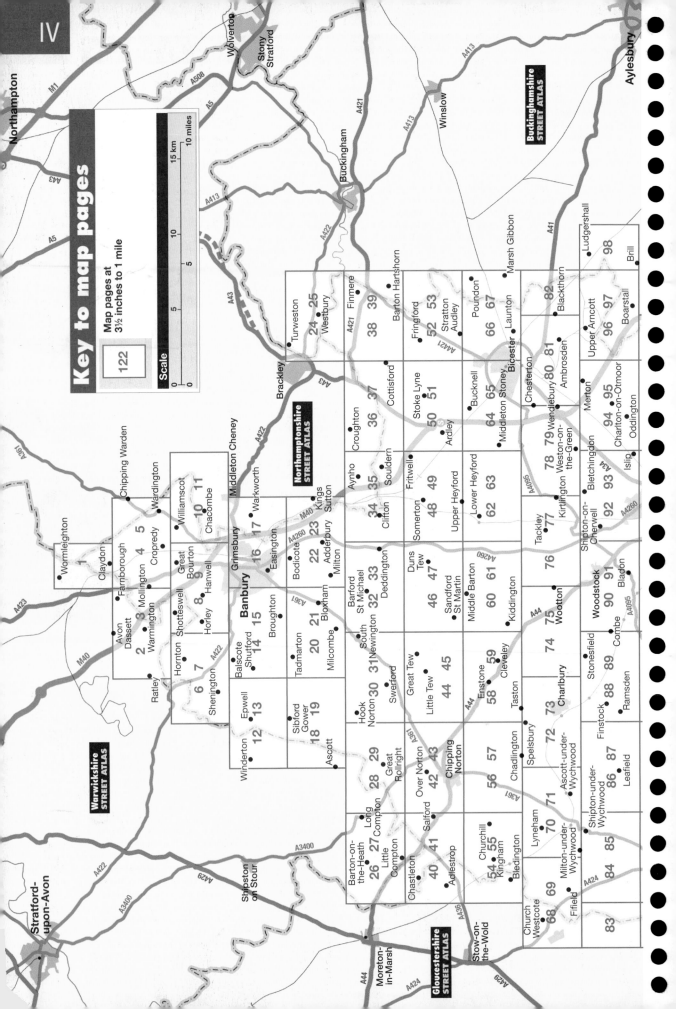

V

Great Barrington
Westwell
Taynton
99
100 101 Burford
Eastleach Martin
113
131 Southrop
Lechlade-on-Thames
Kelmscott
150 151
Buscot
170 171
Highworth
190 191
Bishopstone
Watchfield
208 209
Bourton
227
245
Swindon

North Leigh
Crawley 104 105
102 103 Minster Lovell
Witney
Carterton
Shilton
114 115
Alvescot
132 133 Black Bourton
Langford
Clanfield
152 153
Littleworth
172 173
Faringdon
Great Coxwell
192 193
Longcot
Shrivenham
210 211
Woolstone
Uffington
228 229
Ashbury
Baydon

Freeland
106 107
Cassington
Curbridge
116 117
Brize Norton
South Leigh
118 119
Ducklington
Cumnor
138 139
134 135
Aston
Bampton
136 137
Standlake
Cote
154 155
Hinton Waldrist
Buckland
174 175
Charney Bassett
Stanford in the Vale
194 195
Denchworth
212 213
Sparsholt
Childrey
Letcombe Bassett
230 231
246

Horton-cum-Studley
112
Kidlington
Yarnton
108 109
Marston
Oxford
122 123
Botley
North Hinksey
140 141
Kennington
Northmoor
Sandford-on-Thames
160 161
Radley
Wootton
158 159
Marcham
178 179
Drayton
Appleton
156 157
Longworth
Kingston Bagpuize
176 177
Garford
West Hanney
East Hanney
196 197
Grove
Wantage
214 215
Ardington
Letcombe Regis
232 233
West Ilsley
234 235

Noke
110 111
Beckley
Stanton St John
124 125
Horspath
142 143
Garsington
Little Milton
162 163
Stadhampton
Berinsfield
182 183
Dorchester
Long Wittenham
180 181
Culham
Sutton Courtenay
200 201
Didcot
Milton
198 199
Steventon
Milton Hill
216 217
East Hendred
Harwell
Chilton
218 219
Aston Upthorpe
Aston Tirrold
236 237
Upton
Blewbury
238 239

Haddenham
130
Thame
Towersey
148 149
Long Crendon
128 129
Shabbington
Tiddington
146 147
Wheatley
144 145
Cuddesdon
Great Haseley
164 165
Stoke Talmage
Chalgrove
184 185
Brightwell Baldwin
Warborough
204 205
Ewelme
Benson
202 203
Brightwell-cum-Sotwell
Wallingford
220 221
Crowmarsh Gifford
222 223
Nuffield
Cholsey
Moulsford
South Stoke
240 241
Woodcote
Goring
248 249

Princes Risborough
Henton
Chinnor
168 169
Sydenham
166 167
Aston Rowant
Lewknor
186 187
Watlington
Greenfield
206 207
Stoke Row
224 225
Nettlebed
Whitchurch Hill
250 251
Pangbourne
256 257

Bledlow Ridge
188 189
Beacon's Bottom
Kingston Blount
Stokenchurch
Fawley
226
Lower Assendon
Middle Assendon
242 243
Shepherd's Green
244
Henley-on-Thames
254 255
Shiplake
Tokers Green
252 253
Sonning Common
258 259
Wargrave
Twyford
Sonning
260
Caversham
Reading

Berkshire STREET ATLAS

Wiltshire STREET ATLAS

A418 A4129 A40 M40 A4074 A4130 A4155 A4130 A329 A340 M4 A338 A361 A417 A420 A415 A4185 A346 A419

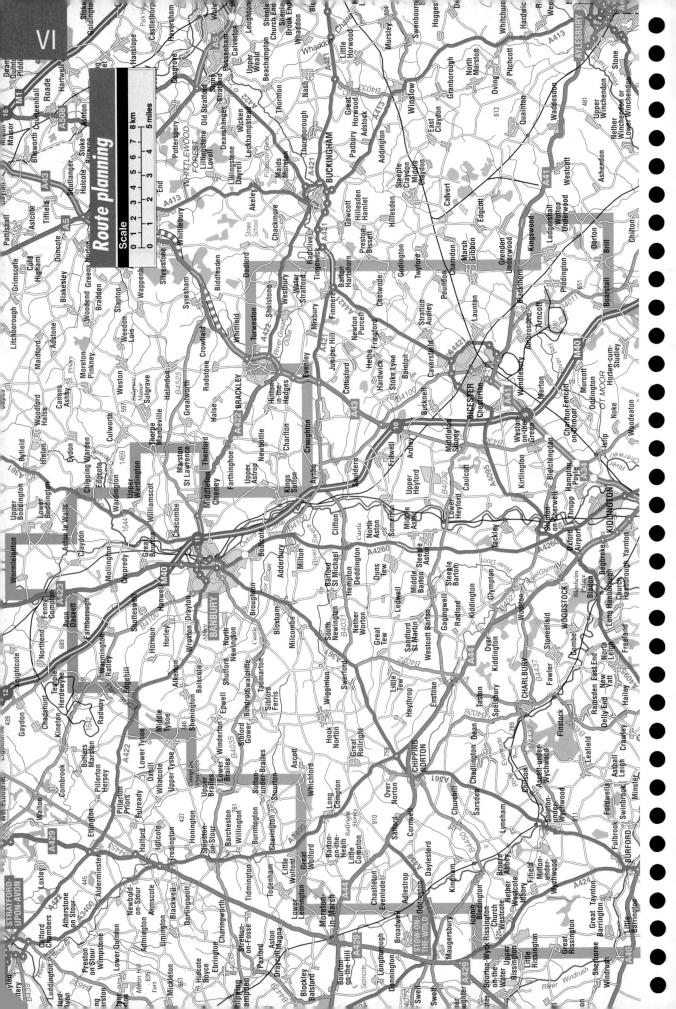

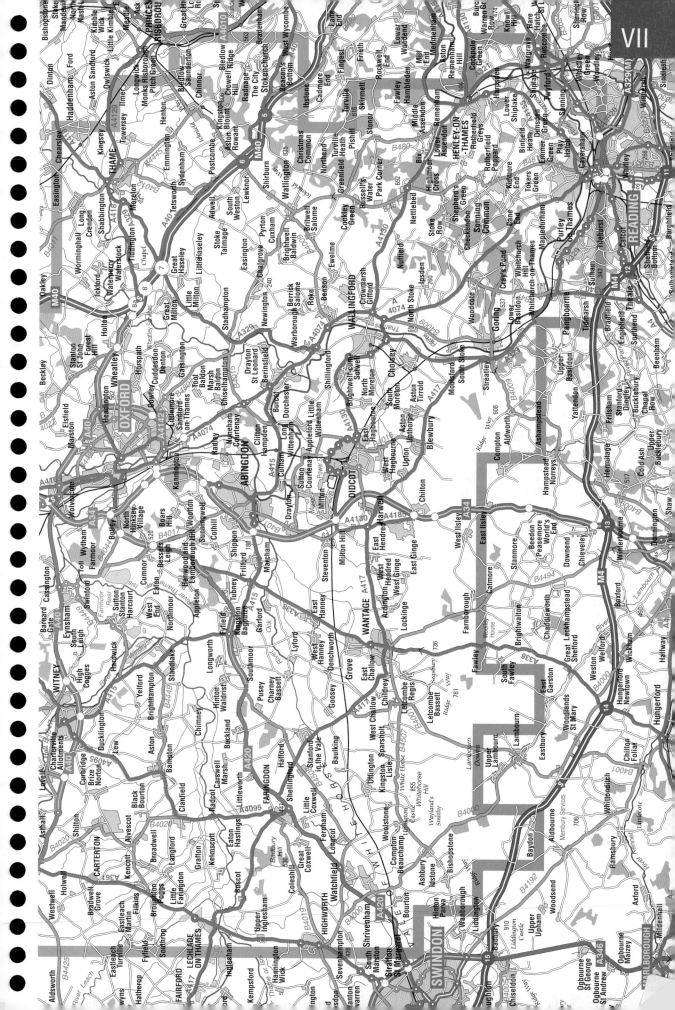

Major administrative and Postcode boundaries

	County and unitary authority boundaries
	District boundaries
	Postcode boundaries
	Area covered by this atlas

Scale

0   5   10   15 km
0   5   10 miles

Warwickshire

Northamptonshire

Mollington

OX17

OX16
Banbury

OX15
Bloxham

Hook Norton

Westbury

CV36

GL56
Adlestrop

Aynho

NN13

Chipping Norton

Fringford

OX27

OX25

Cherwell

Gloucester-shire

OX7

Upper Heyford

West Oxfordshire

Bicester

OX26

Tackley

Charlbury

OX20

OX25 Ambrosden

Ludgershall

GL 54

Woodstock

Stonesfield

OX5

Kidlington

HP18

Burford

OX28

Buckinghamshire

Witney

Eynsham

OX3

Shabbington

OX29

OX33

Wheatley

OX18

Oxford

Carterton

OX2

Oxford

Thame

GL7

Bampton

OX1   OX4

OX9

HP27

SP

Lechlade-on-Thames

Garsington

Chinnor

SP

OX44

OX39

SU

Stadhampton

SU

OX13

Abingdon

HP14
Stokenchurch

Marcham

Watlington

Faringdon

SN7

OX14

Dorchester

OX49

Highworth

Vale of White Horse

South Oxfordshire

Didcot

OX10

SN6

Uffington

Harwell

Wallingford

Shrivenham

OX12 Wantage

OX11

Nettlebed

Chilton

RG9

Bishopstone

Henley-on-Thames

Swindon

RG17

RG20

Woodcote

Sonning Common

RG 10

SN4

Goring

RG8

RG4

SN8

Reading

Wiltshire

West Berkshire

Reading

Wokingham

O x f o r d s h i r e

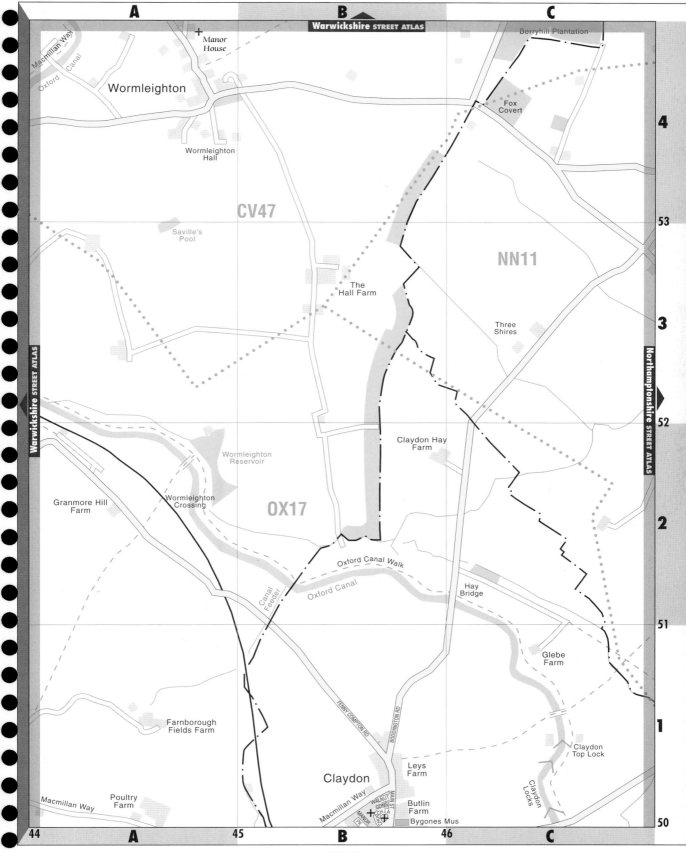

A   B   **Warwickshire** STREET ATLAS   C

Macmillan Way

Oxford Canal

Manor House

Wormleighton

Berryhill Plantation

Fox Covert

Wormleighton Hall

4

CV47

Saville's Pool

53

NN11

The Hall Farm

Three Shires

3

Warwickshire STREET ATLAS

Northamptonshire STREET ATLAS

52

Wormleighton Reservoir

Claydon Hay Farm

Granmore Hill Farm

Wormleighton Crossing

OX17

2

Oxford Canal Walk

Canal Feeder

Oxford Canal

Hay Bridge

51

Glebe Farm

Farnborough Fields Farm

FENNY COMPTON RD

BODDINGTON RD

1

Claydon Top Lock

Claydon Locks

Leys Farm

Macmillan Way

Poultry Farm

Macmillan Way

Claydon

WALNUT GDNS   MAIN ST   SCH LA

MANOR PK

Butlin Farm

Bygones Mus

50

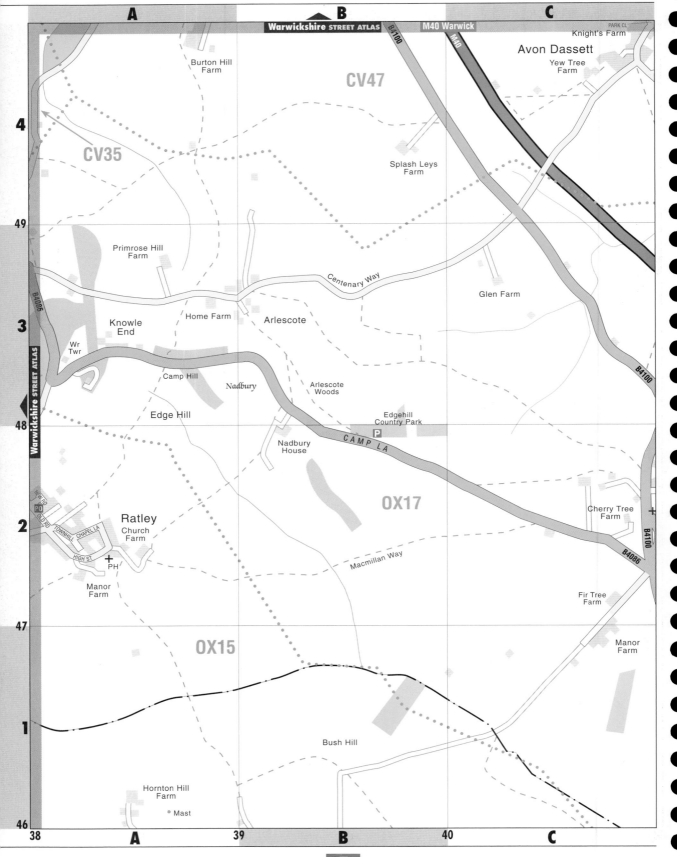

Warwickshire STREET ATLAS

M40 Warwick

PARK CL
Knight's Farm

Avon Dassett

Yew Tree
Farm

CV47

Splash Leys
Farm

CV35

4

49

Primrose Hill
Farm

Centenary Way

Glen Farm

Knowle
End

Home Farm

Arlescote

3

Wr
Twr

Camp Hill

Nadbury

Arlescote
Woods

B4100

Edge Hill

Edgehill
Country Park

P

48

Nadbury
House

CAMP LA

Cherry Tree
Farm

Ratley

Church
Farm

PO

OLD RD

NEW RD

TOWNHILL

CHAPEL LA

HIGH ST

PH

Manor
Farm

OX17

B4086

B4100

Macmillan Way

Fir Tree
Farm

2

47

Manor
Farm

OX15

1

Bush Hill

Hornton Hill
Farm

Mast

46

38

A

39

B

40

C

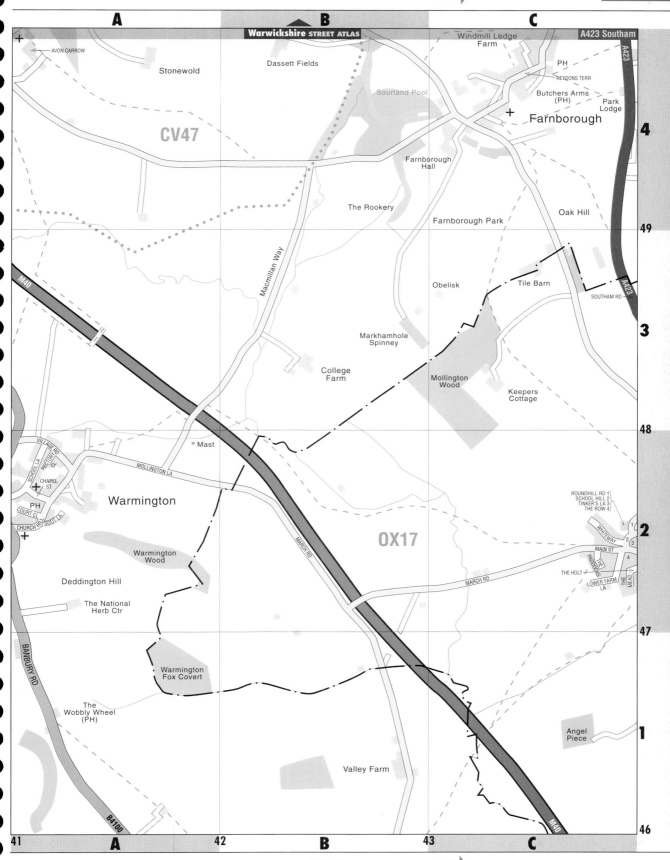

Warwickshire STREET ATLAS

A423 Southam

Column A:
+ Avon Carrow
Stonewold
CV47

M40

VILLAGE RD
RECTORY CT
SCHOOL LA
CHAPEL ST
PH
COURT CL
SCOTT LA
CHURCH HILL
+
Warmington
Deddington Hill
The National Herb Ctr
BANBURY RD
Warmington Wood
Warmington Fox Covert
The Wobbly Wheel (PH)
B4100

Column B:
Dassett Fields
Sourland Pool
Farnborough Hall
The Rookery
Macmillan Way
Mast
MOLLINGTON LA
College Farm
Markhamhole Spinney
MARCH RD
OX17
MARCH RD
Valley Farm

Column C:
Windmill Lodge Farm
PH
HEYDONS TERR
Butchers Arms (PH)
Park Lodge
+ Farnborough
Farnborough Park
Oak Hill
A423
Obelisk
Tile Barn
SOUTHAM RD
A423
Mollington Wood
Keepers Cottage
ROUNDHILL RD 1
SCHOOL HILL 2
TINKER'S LA 3
THE ROW 4
WHITEWAY
MAIN ST
THE PADDOCKS
THE HOLT
LOWER FARM LA
THE MEAD
Angel Piece
M40

Grid references (right side): 4, 49, 3, 48, 2, 47, 1, 46

Grid references (top): A, B, C

Grid references (bottom): 41, A, 42, B, 43, C

Navigation arrows: 4, 8, 4

A   B   C

Farnborough Hill Farm

Macmillan Way

Claydon Crossing

MANOR PK

Manor Farm

BIGNOLDS CL

Filter Bed

Claydon Locks

Macmillan Way

4

Farnborough Hill

Lawn Hill

Firs Farm

49

Clattercote

Oxford Canal Walk

Oxford Canal

Towing Path

3

A423

Oathill Farm

Clattercote Reservoir

Cropredy Lawn

Lambert's Barn

OX17

48

Beecham's Cottages

CLAYDON RD

ROUNDHILL RD

SOUTHAM RD

Mollington

2

ROUNDHILL RD

CHURCH

CHURCHLEY

BLACKSMITHS LA

THE HOLLOWAY

MAIN ST

ORCHARD PIECE

IVY LA

CHESTNUT RD

Manor Farm

Mill Farm

OXHEY HILL

47

Cropredy Hill

Oxhay Farm

Cemy

CREAMPOT CRES

KYETS CNR

CREAMPOT LA

CHAPEL ROW 1
NEW PL 2
VICARAGE FLATS 3

ORCHARD VIEW

HIGH ST

CHAPEL LA

PO

RED LION ST

CHURCH LA

1

Cropredy

PH

DIP AND SAUCER

CHERRY FIELDS

VICARAGE GDNS

THE PLANTATION

STATION RD

Oxford Canal

River Cherwell

Cropredy CE Prim Sch

46

44   45   46

A   B   C

Thickthorn Farm

A423

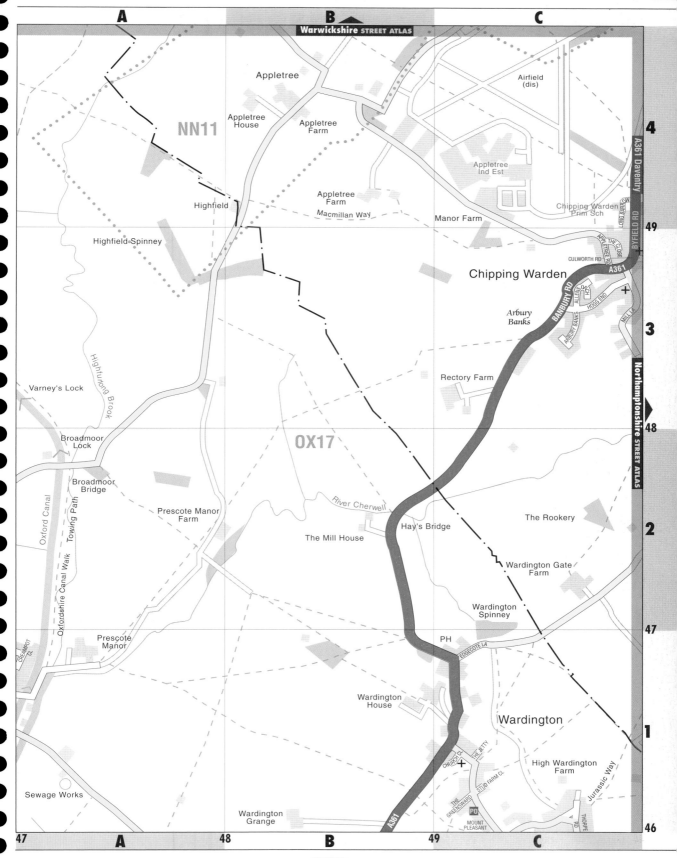

Warwickshire STREET ATLAS

A B C

Appletree

NN11

Appletree House

Appletree Farm

Appletree

Airfield (dis)

Appletree Ind Est

Highfield

Appletree Farm

Macmillan Way

Manor Farm

Chipping Warden Prim Sch

4

49

Highfield Spinney

CULWORTH RD

A361

Chipping Warden

LONG BARROW

BYFIELD RD

A361 Daventry

THE CLOSE

APPLETREE RD

Varney's Lock

Highfurlong Brook

Arbury Banks

BANBURY RD

ARBURY BANKS

ALLENS CL

SCH

HODGE END

MILL K

3

Broadmoor Lock

OX17

Rectory Farm

48

Northamptonshire STREET ATLAS

Broadmoor Bridge

Prescote Manor Farm

River Cherwell

The Mill House

Hay's Bridge

The Rookery

2

Oxford Canal

Oxfordshire Canal Walk

Towing Path

Wardington Gate Farm

Wardington Spinney

47

PH

CREAMPOT CL

Prescote Manor

EDGECOTE LA

Wardington House

Wardington

1

Sewage Works

Wardington Grange

CHURCH CL

THE JETTY

STUD FARM CL

High Wardington Farm

Jurassic Way

THE GREENSWARD

PO

MOUNT PLEASANT

THORPE RD

A361

46

47 A 48 B 49 C

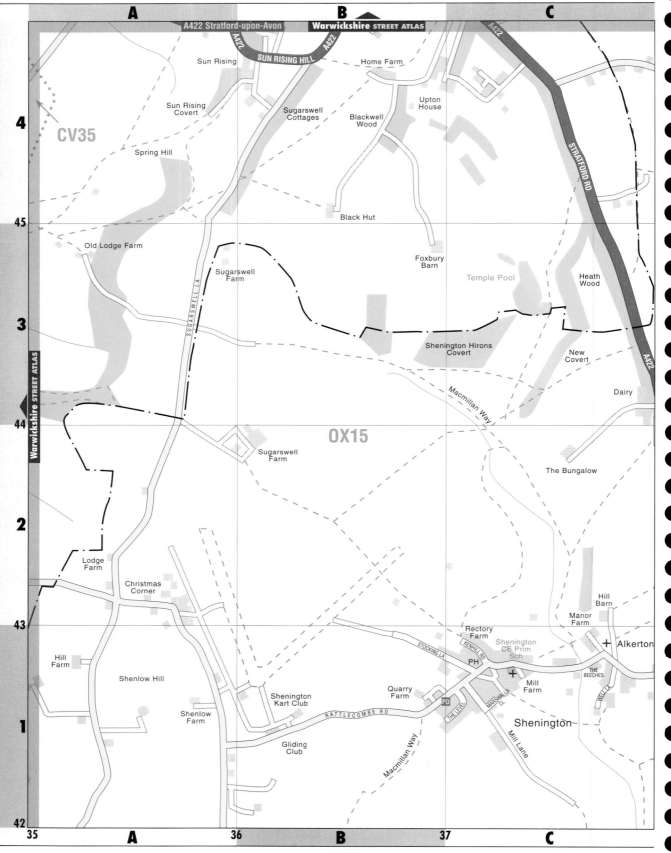

A

B

C

4

CV35

Sun Rising

SUN RISING HILL

Home Farm

Upton House

Sun Rising Covert

Sugarswell Cottages

Blackwell Wood

Spring Hill

45

Black Hut

Old Lodge Farm

Sugarswell Farm

Foxbury Barn

Temple Pool

Heath Wood

3

SUGARSWELL LA

Shenington Hirons Covert

New Covert

Macmillan Way

Dairy

44

OX15

Sugarswell Farm

The Bungalow

2

Lodge Farm

Christmas Corner

Hill Barn

Manor Farm

43

Rectory Farm

Shenington CE Prim Sch

Alkerton

Hill Farm

Shenlow Hill

STOCKING LA

KENHILL RD

PH

THE BEECHES

WELL LA

Quarry Farm

Mill Farm

Shenington Kart Club

RATTLECOMBE RD

PO

MARSHALLS CL

1

Shenlow Farm

THE LEVER

Mill Lane

Shenington

Gliding Club

Macmillan Way

42

35

A

36

B

37

C

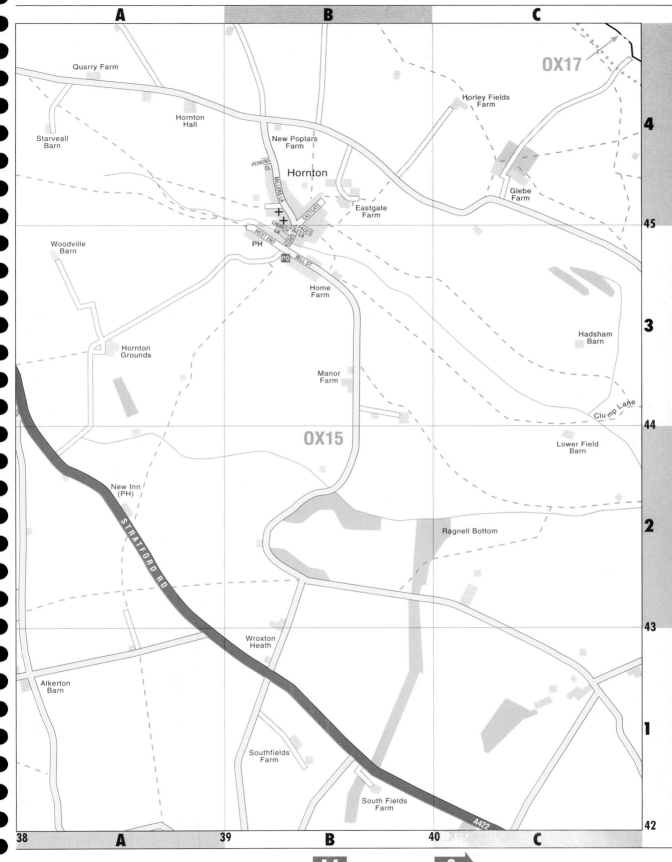

7
3

A   B   C

B4100

M40

Slated Barn

Slade Barn

Laurel Farm

MOLLINGTON RD

BACK HILL

SNUFF LA

MIDDLE LA

BAKEHOUSE LA

BURY CT LA

CHAPEL LA

NEW

CORONATION LA

CHURCH LA

Bury Court Farm

Shotteswell

4

Sor Brook

45

Hadsham House Manor Farm

3

OX17

Water Tower

Clump Lane

Horley House

OX15

44

Hanwell

HANWELL CT

SPRINGFIELD

MAIN ST

PARK CL

MANOR ORCH

LANE CL

PH

GULLIVER S CL

Bramshill Barn

Horley

CHURCH LA

SACKVILLE CL

GULLICOTE LA

Hanwell Castle

THE OLD COUNCIL HOS

THE COUNCIL HOS

Park Farm

2

43

Oxfordshire Cycleway

WARWICK RD

Drayton Lodge

CH

Cemy

1

Lord's Spinney

WINSTON D

ELLISON DR

RYE CL

KING CHELSEA CL

BARCOMBE CL

FIRTREE CL

HADWICK PARK

HIGHLANDS

CHEVIOT WAY

HORLEY PATH RD

HORSHAM CL

SUSSEX DR

ROMNEY RD

QUEEN'S CRES

B4100

OX16

42

A422

41   A   42   B   43   C

7
15

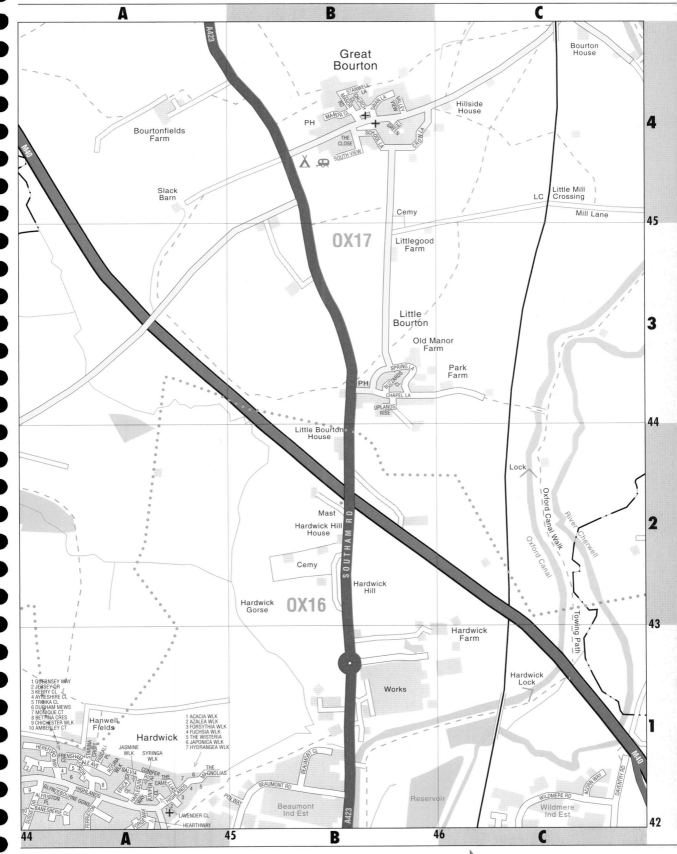

Great
Bourton

Bourton
House

STANWELL LA
CHURCH LA
MANOR CL
SWAN LA
VALLEY VIEW
THE GREEN
CROW LA

Hillside
House

PH
MANOR RD

SCHOOL LA

THE
CLOSE

SOUTH VIEW

Bourtonfields
Farm

Slack
Barn

Cemy

LC

Little Mill
Crossing

Mill Lane

OX17

45

Littlegood
Farm

Little
Bourton

Old Manor
Farm

Park
Farm

SPRING LA

PH

BUZZARDS CL

CHAPEL LA

UPLANDS RISE

Little Bourton
House

3

44

Lock

Oxford Canal Walk

Oxford Canal

River Cherwell

Mast

Hardwick Hill
House

Cemy

SOUTHAM RD

Hardwick
Hill

Hardwick
Gorse

OX16

Hardwick
Farm

2

Towing Path

43

Hardwick
Lock

Works

1 GUERNSEY WAY
2 JERSEY DR
3 KERRY CL
4 AYRESHIRE CL
5 TROIKA CL
6 DURHAM MEWS
7 MONIQUE CT
8 BETTINA CRES
9 CHICHESTER WLK
10 AMBERLEY CT

1 ACACIA WLK
2 AZALEA WLK
3 FORSYTHIA WLK
4 FUCHSIA WLK
5 THE WISTERIA
6 JAPONICA WLK
7 HYDRANGEA WLK

Hanwell
Fields

Hardwick

JASMINE WLK
SYRINGA WLK
STARINA
CROFT
PASCALI PL
RISINA WLK
SALVIA CL
CONIFER RISE
THE HIGHLANDS
JUNIPER CL

THE MAGNOLIAS

HEREFORD WAY
DALE AVE
FRENSHAM CL
ERICA CL
HALEQUIN WAY

BEAUMONT CL

BEAUMONT RD

PEN WAY

Beaumont
Ind Est

A423

Reservoir

Wildmere
Ind Est

WILDMERE RD
ACORN WAY
DAVENTRY RD

1

M40

GLYNDEBOURNE GDNS
ALFRISTON PL
BANESBERIE CL
SUSSEX DR
FERRISTON
FOXWAY
LAVENDER CL
HEARTHWAY

HIGHLANDS

42

A423

A423

M40

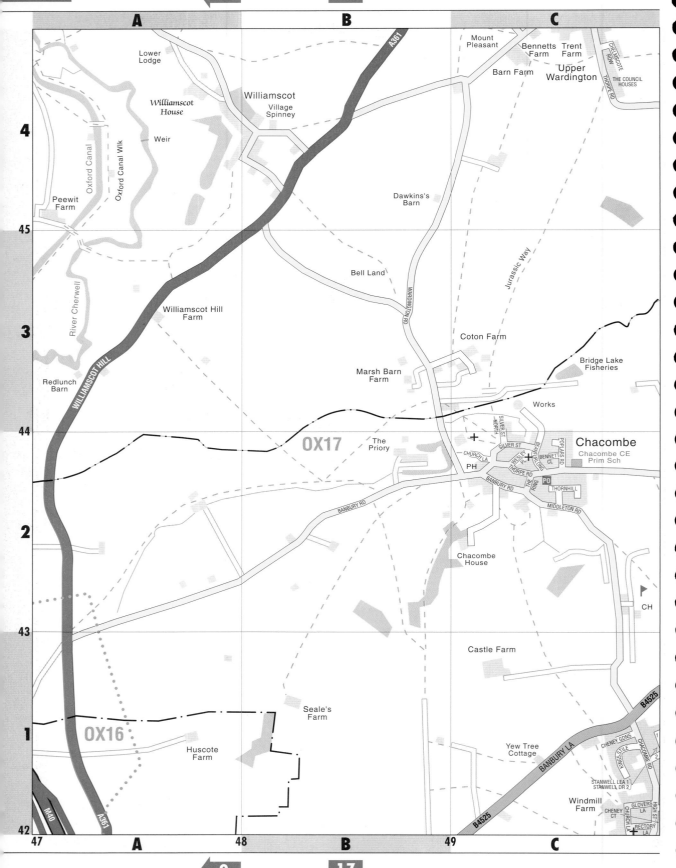

A B C

4

45

3

44

2

43

1

42

47 A 48 B 49 C

Lower Lodge

Williamscot House

Williamscot

Village Spinney

Williamscot

A361

Mount Pleasant

Bennetts Farm

Trent Farm

Barn Farm

Upper Wardington

CHELMSCOTE ROW

THORPE RD

THE COUNCIL HOUSES

Weir

Oxford Canal

Oxford Canal Wlk

Peewit Farm

River Cherwell

Williamscot Hill Farm

WILLIAMSCOT HILL

Redlunch Barn

Dawkins's Barn

Bell Land

WARDINGTON RD

Jurassic Way

Coton Farm

Bridge Lake Fisheries

Marsh Barn Farm

Works

OX17

The Priory

SILVER ST

SILVER ST NORTH

Chacombe

Chacombe CE Prim Sch

CHURCH LA

WESLEY PL

BEAUFURLONG

BENNETTS CL

POPLARS RD

PH

THORPE RD

BANBURY RD

THE RING

PO

Thornhill

MIDDLETON RD

BANBURY RD

Chacombe House

Castle Farm

CH

B4525

Seale's Farm

OX16

Huscote Farm

Yew Tree Cottage

BANBURY LA

CHENEY GDNS

STILE

CHACOMBE RD

STANWELL LEA 1
STANWELL DR 2

GLOVERS LA

HIGH ST

M40

A361

B4525

CHENEY CT

Windmill Farm

CHURCH LA

RECTORY LA

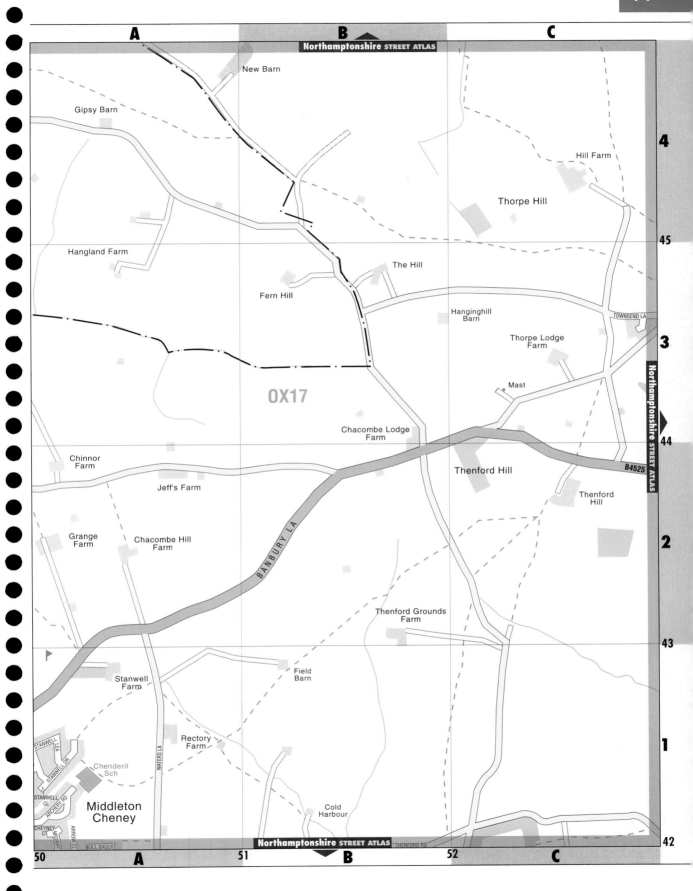

A

B

C

New Barn

Gipsy Barn

Hill Farm

4

Thorpe Hill

45

Hangland Farm

The Hill

Fern Hill

Hanginghill Barn

TOWNSEND LA

Thorpe Lodge Farm

3

Mast

OX17

Chacombe Lodge Farm

44

Chinnor Farm

Thenford Hill

B4525

Jeff's Farm

Thenford Hill

Grange Farm

Chacombe Hill Farm

2

BANBURY LA

Thenford Grounds Farm

43

Stanwell Farm

Field Barn

Rectory Farm

STANWELL LEA

WATERS LA

1

STANWELL DR

Chenderit Sch

STANWELL CL

ARCHER RD

Middleton Cheney

Cold Harbour

CHEYNEY CT

MIDWAY

ARROW CL

BULL BAULK

THENFORD RD

42

50

A

51

B

52

C

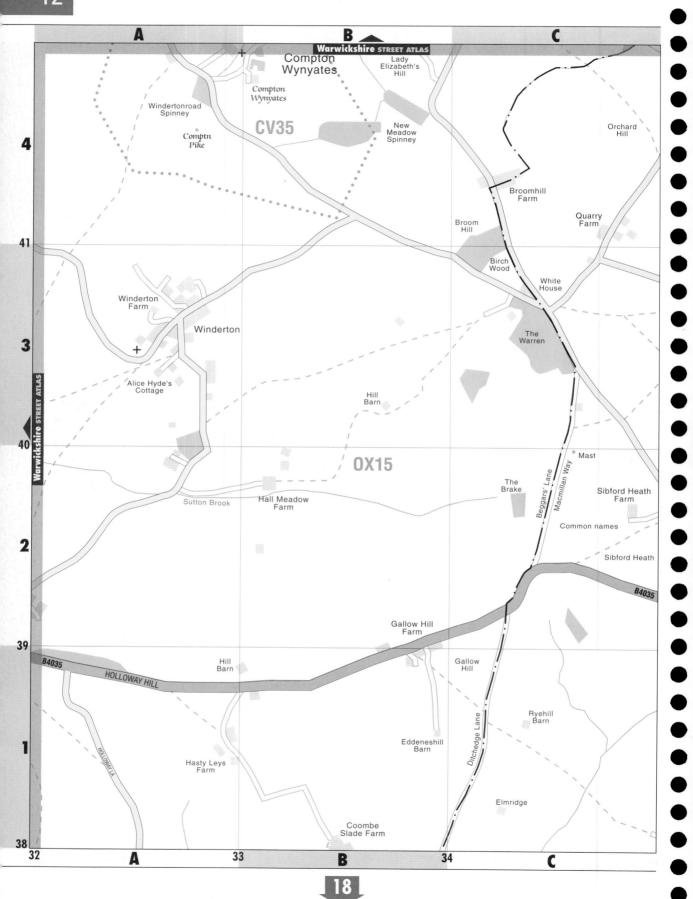

A

B

C

Compton
Wynyates

Lady
Elizabeth's
Hill

*Compton
Wynyates*

Windertonroad
Spinney

CV35

New
Meadow
Spinney

Orchard
Hill

*Comptn
Pike*

Broomhill
Farm

4

Quarry
Farm

Broom
Hill

41

Birch
Wood

White
House

Winderton
Farm

Winderton

The
Warren

3

Alice Hyde's
Cottage

Hill
Barn

40

OX15

Mast

The
Brake

Sibford Heath
Farm

Beggars' Lane

Macmillan Way

Common names

Sutton Brook

Hall Meadow
Farm

Sibford Heath

2

B4035

Gallow Hill
Farm

39

Gallow
Hill

B4035

HOLLOWAY HILL

Hill
Barn

Ryehill
Barn

HOLLOWAY LA

Ditchedge Lane

1

Hasty Leys
Farm

Eddeneshill
Barn

Elmridge

38

Coombe
Slade Farm

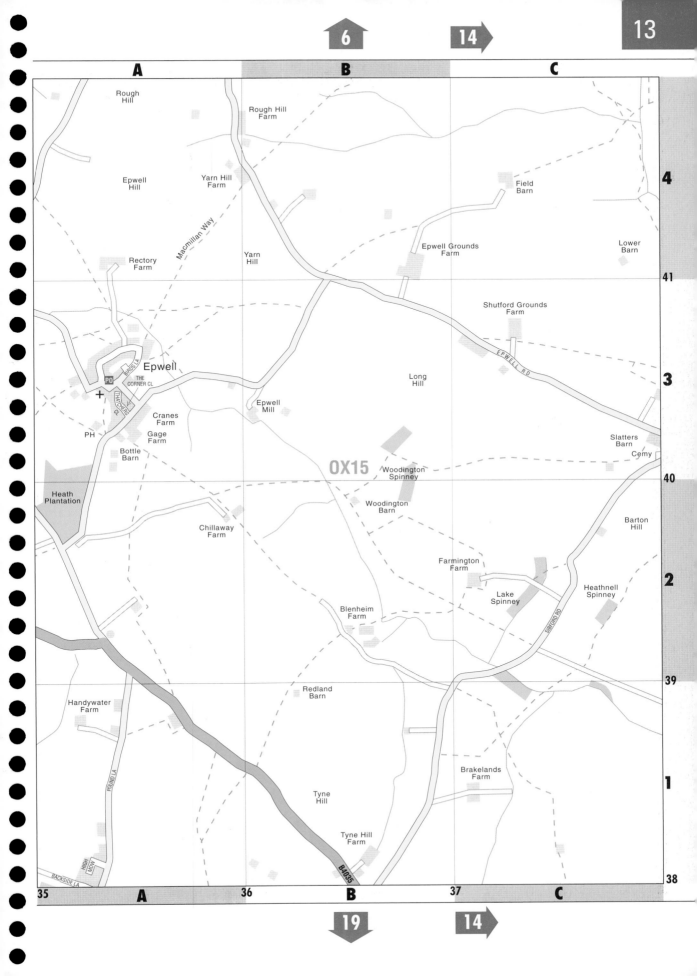

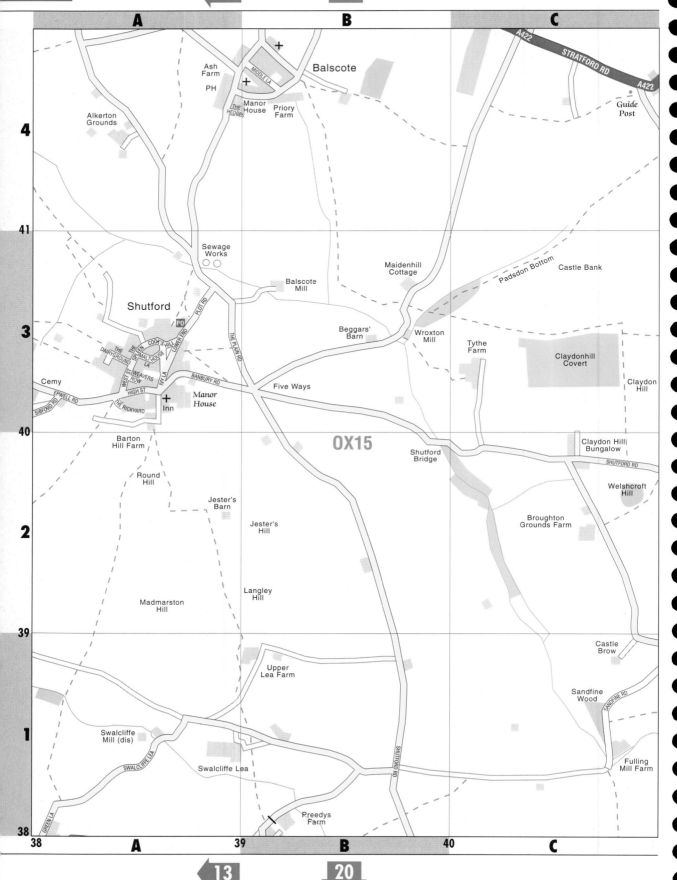

A B C

4

41

3

40

2

39

1

38

38 39 40

Ash Farm
Balscote
PH
MIDDLE LA
Manor House
Priory Farm
THE HEDGES
Alkerton Grounds

A422
STRATFORD RD
A422
Guide Post

Sewage Works

Maidenhill Cottage
Padsdon Bottom
Castle Bank

Balscote Mill
PLOT RD
Shutford
PO
THE PLAIN RD
Beggars' Barn
Wroxton Mill
Tythe Farm
Claydonhill Covert
Claydon Hill

COOK'S HILL
LOWER END
THE GREEN
SMALL
MALT HOUSE LA
DAIRY GROUND
THE
WEST ST
WEAVERS ROW
IVY LA
BANBURY RD
Five Ways
Cemy
EPWELL RD
HIGH ST
SIBFORD RD
THE RICKYARD
Inn
Manor House

OX15

Shutford Bridge
Claydon Hill Bungalow
SHUTFORD RD

Barton Hill Farm
Welshcroft Hill

Round Hill

Jester's Barn
Jester's Hill
Broughton Grounds Farm

Langley Hill

Madmarston Hill

Castle Brow

Upper Lea Farm

Sandfine Wood
SANDFINE RD

Swalcliffe Mill (dis)

SWALCLIFFE LEA
Swalcliffe Lea
SHUTFORD RD
Fulling Mill Farm

GREEN LA
Preedys Farm

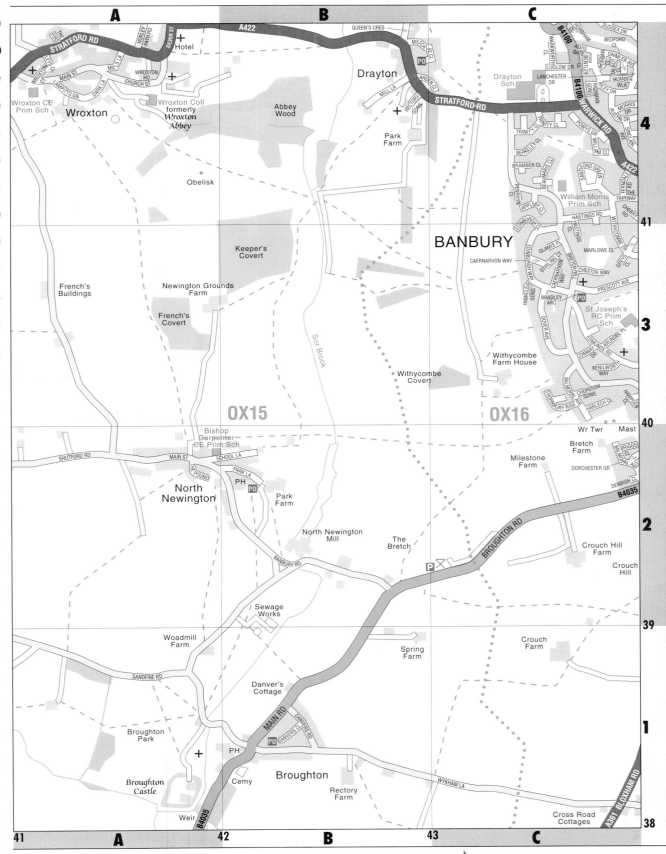

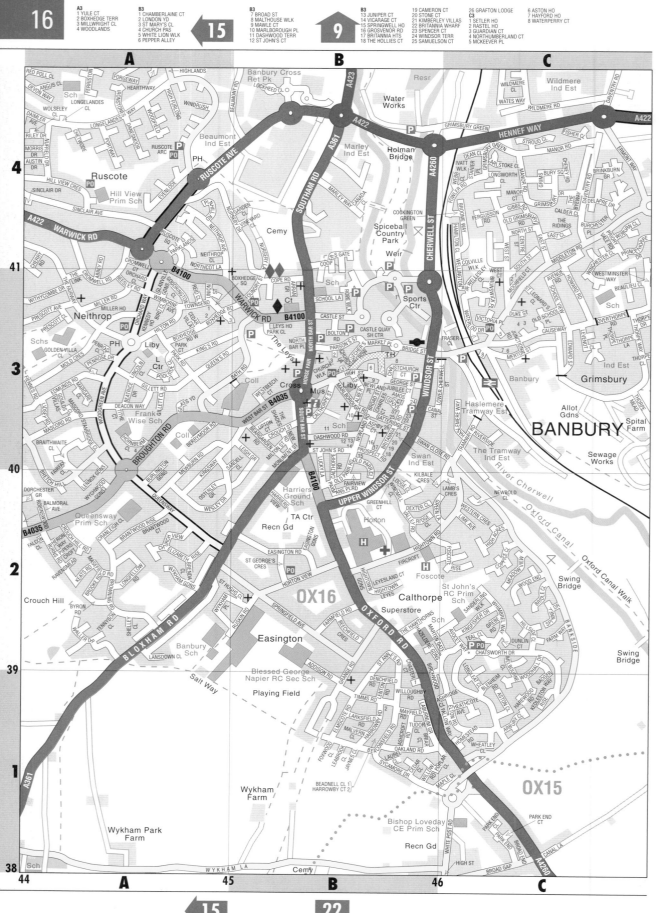

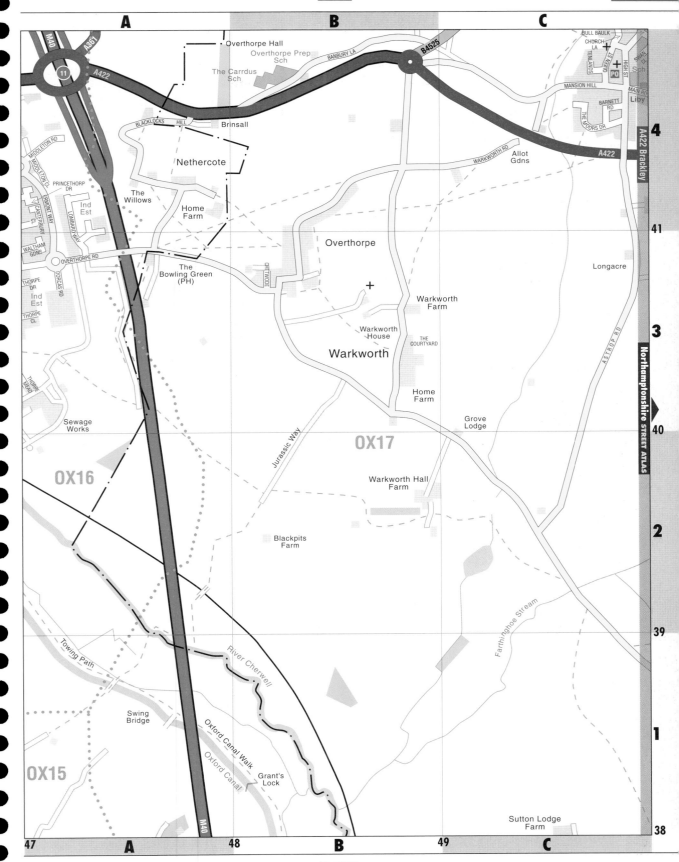

A B C

M40
A361
A422
11
A422

Overthorpe Hall
Overthorpe Prep Sch
The Carrdus Sch
BANBURY LA
B4525

BULL BAULK
CHURCH LA
QUEEN ST
TENLANDS
HIGH ST
PO
Sch
MANSION HILL
Liby
BARNETT RD
THE MOORS DR
A422 Brackley

BLACKLOCKS HILL
Brinsall

Nethercote

MIDDLETON RD
MIDDLETON CL
PRINCETHORPE DR
EMONT WAY
CANTERBURY CL
LOMBARD WAY
WALTHAM GDNS
Ind Est
The Willows
Home Farm

OVERTHORPE RD
The Bowling Green (PH)
THORPE DR
Ind Est
DORCAS RD
THORPE CL
THORPE MEAD

CHETWODE

Overthorpe

Warkworth Farm
Warkworth House
THE COURTYARD
Warkworth
Home Farm
Grove Lodge

WARKWORTH RD
Allot Gdns
Longacre
ASTROP RD

4

41

3

40

Northamptonshire STREET ATLAS

Sewage Works

OX16

Jurassic Way

OX17

Warkworth Hall Farm

Blackpits Farm

2

39

Farthinghoe Stream

Towing Path
River Cherwell
Swing Bridge
Oxford Canal Walk
Oxford Canal
Grant's Lock

OX15

M40

Sutton Lodge Farm

1

38

47 A 48 B 49 C

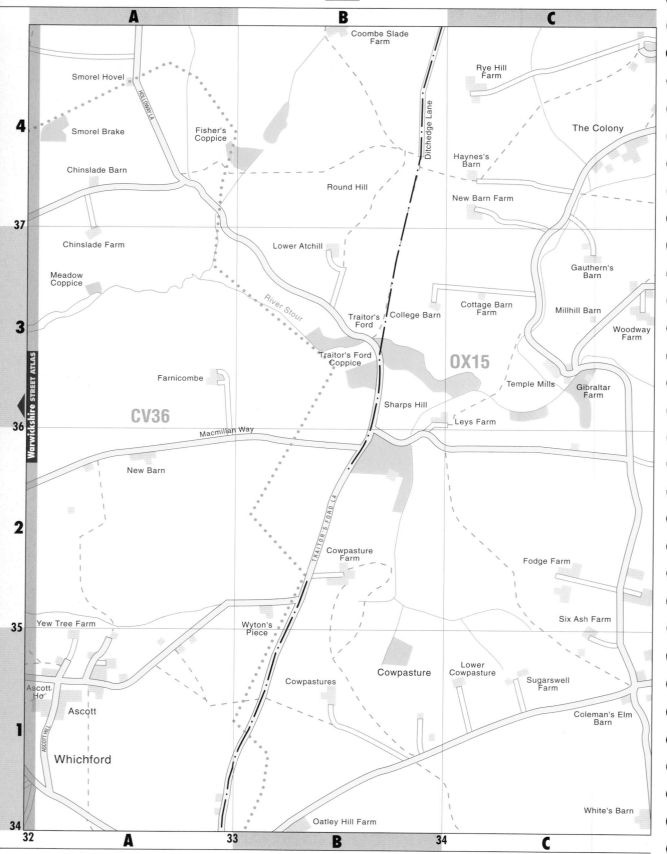

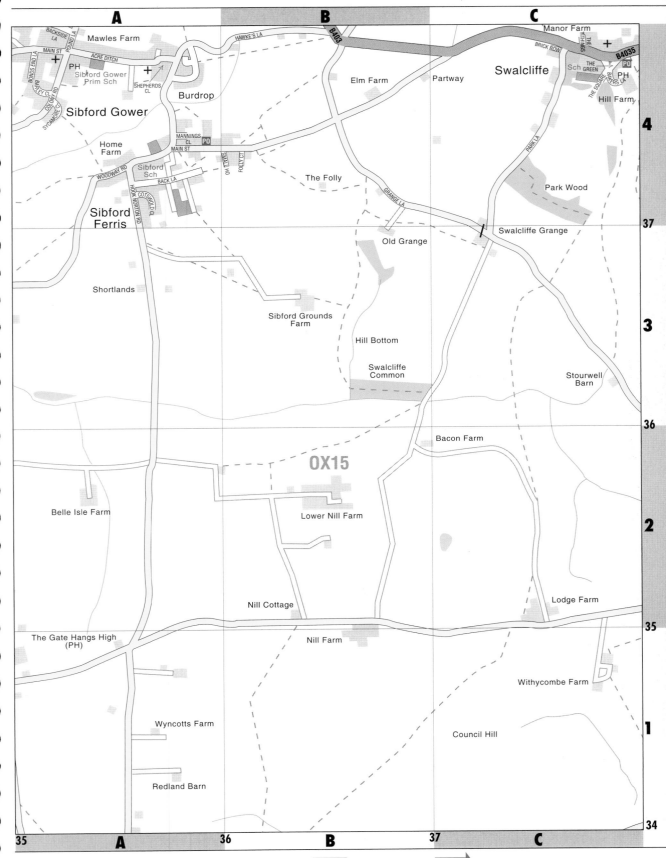

19
14

A   **B**   **C**

B4035

SWALCLIFFE RD

GREEN LA

PH

BAKERS LA

PO

OLD GLEBE

Home Farm

Brick Farm

CHURCH
FURLONG

Tadmarton

Austins
Farm

MAIN ST

BROOKFIELD
RISE

SHUTFORD RD

Five
Acres

B4035

4

Drift Acre

High
Meadow
Farm

Lower
Tadmarton

Ushercombe Barn

37

Ushercoombe Copse

Lower Tadmarton
Farm

3

36

Tadmarton
Heath

Ushercombe
Farm

OX15

CH

Rye
Hill

2

Highways
Farm

Wigginton
Heath

Fern
Hill

CH

Ryehill
Barn

35

Cedar
Bungalow

THE
OLD COUNCIL HOS
THE
GREEN
PH
HEATH
CL

1

Resr

Lessor
Farm

Waterfowl Sanctuary
& Children's Farm

Brickfield
Farm

34

38   **A**   39   **B**   40   **C**

19
31

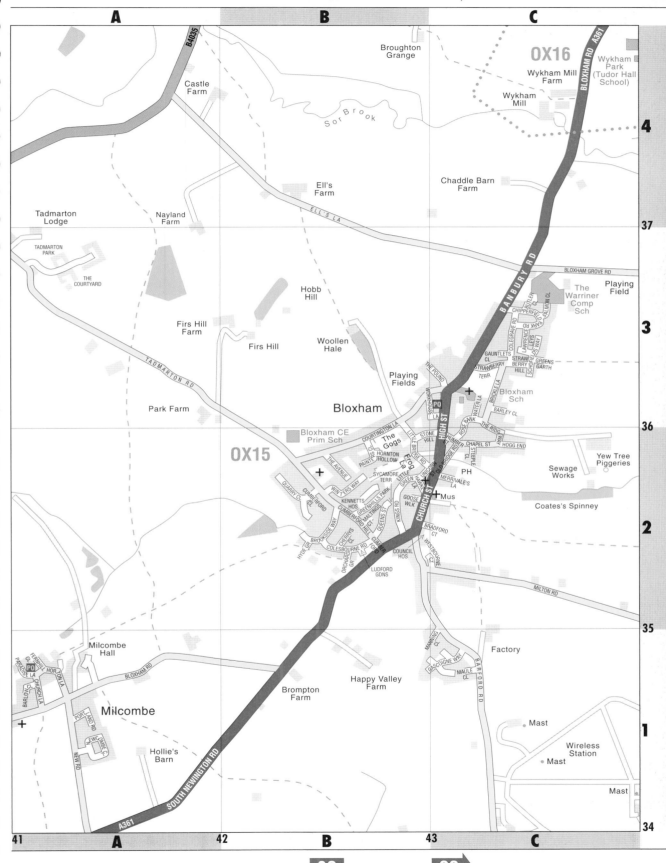

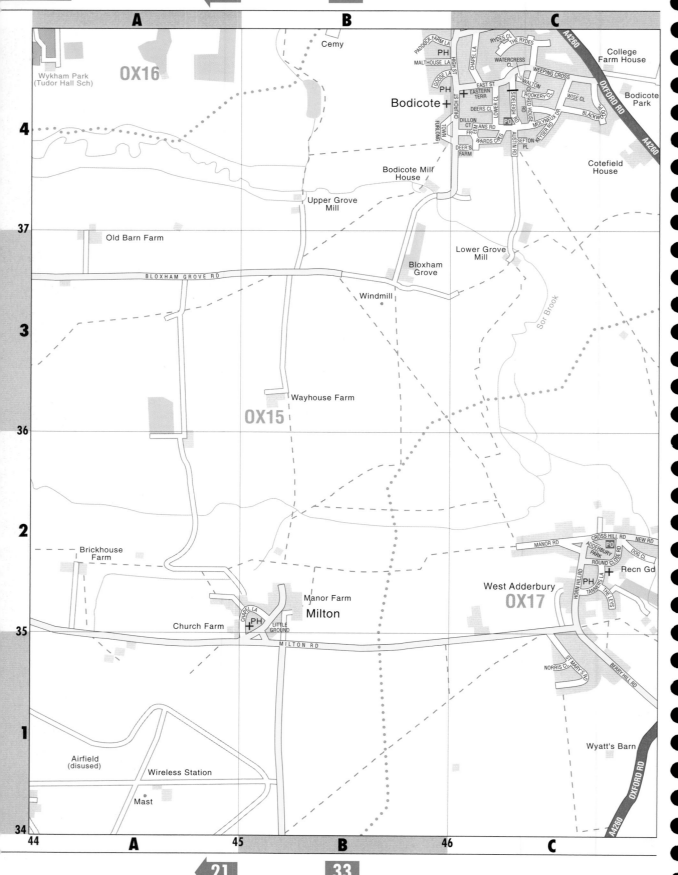

A **B** **C**

Wykham Park
(Tudor Hall Sch)

OX16

Cemy

PADDOCK FARM LA

RYDES CL   THE RYDES

MALTHOUSE LA

CHAPEL LA

HIGH ST

WATERCRESS
CL

WEEPING CROSS

College
Farm House

LOOSE LA

EAST ST
EASTERN
TERR

WALTON
CL

RED
HOUSE

WISE CL

PH

CHURCH ST

RED
HOUSE

ROOKERY CT

BLACKW

Bodicote
Park

Bodicote +

DEERS CL

DILLON
CT

LOWER R CL

MOLYNEUX DR

Cotefield
House

TOWN
FURLONG

FREE

ANS RD

AUSTIN RD

SIDELEIGH

PO

SEFTON
PL

DEER'S
FARM

WARDS CRS

Bodicote Mill
House

Upper Grove
Mill

37

Old Barn Farm

Lower Grove
Mill

BLOXHAM GROVE RD

Bloxham
Grove

Sor Brook

Windmill

3

OX15

Wayhouse Farm

36

2

Brickhouse
Farm

MANOR RD

CROSS HILL RD   NEW RD

ADDERBURY
PARK

PO

DOG CL

HORN HILLRD

ROUND CLOSE RD

Recn Gd

West Adderbury

OX17

Manor Farm

PH

TANNERS LA

THE LEYS

Milton

CHAPEL LA

PH

LITTLE
GROUND

Church Farm +

BERRY HILL RD

35

MILTON RD

NORRIS CL   ST MARY'S R

1

Airfield
(disused)

Wireless Station

Wyatt's Barn

OXFORD RD

Mast

A4260

34

44 **A** 45 **B** 46 **C**

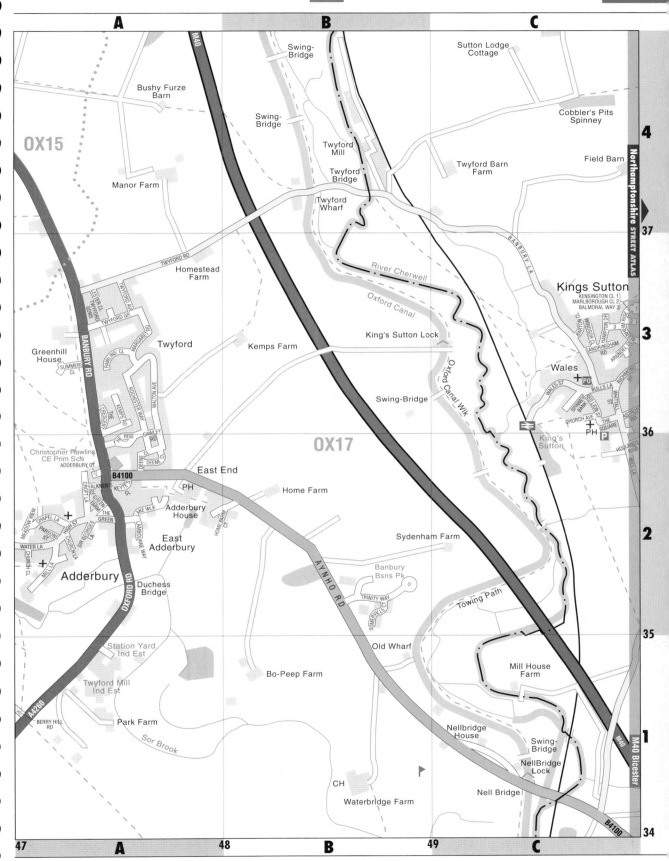

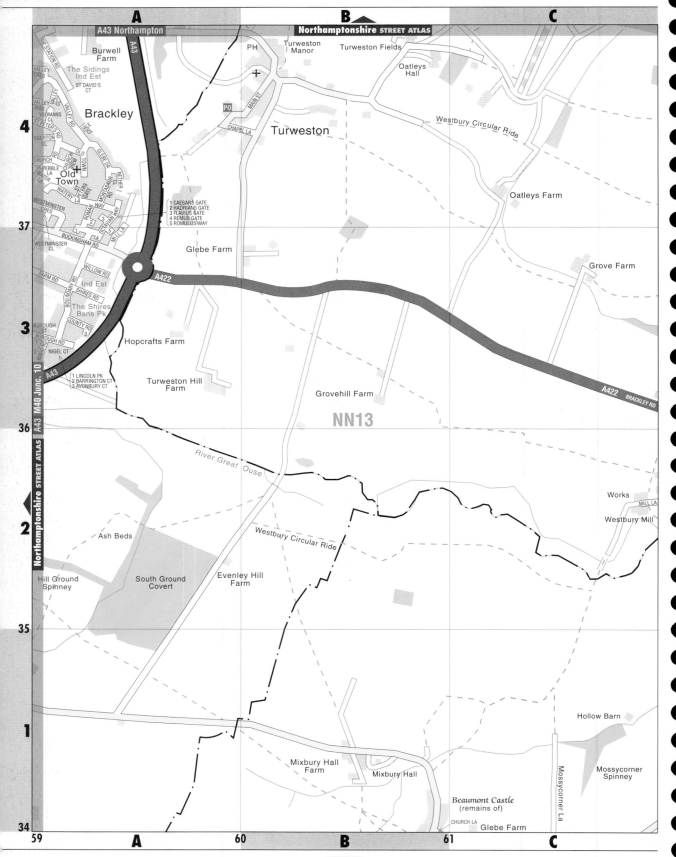

Burwell
Farm

The Sidings
Ind Est
ST DAVID'S
CT

PH

Turweston
Manor

Turweston Fields

Oatleys
Hall

Westbury Circular Ride

PO

Brackley

CHAPEL LA

Turweston

4

Old
Town

1 CAESARS GATE
2 HADRIANS GATE
3 FLAVIUS GATE
4 REMUS GATE
5 ROMULUS WAY

Oatleys Farm

37

WESTMINSTER
CRES

BUCKINGHAM RD

Glebe Farm

Grove Farm

WESTMINSTER
CL

A422

FARM RD

Ind Est

SHIRES RD

The Shires
Bsns Pk

3

BOROUGH
CT

BOROUGH RD

COUNTY RD

Hopcrafts Farm

NIGEL CT

1 LINCOLN PK
2 BARRINGTON CT
3 AVONBURY CT

Turweston Hill
Farm

Grovehill Farm

A422 BRACKLEY RD

NN13

36

River Great Ouse

Works

MILL LA

Westbury Mill

2

Ash Beds

Westbury Circular Ride

Hill Ground
Spinney

South Ground
Covert

Evenley Hill
Farm

35

Hollow Barn

1

Mixbury Hall
Farm

Mixbury Hall

Mossycorner La

Mossycorner
Spinney

Beaumont Castle
(remains of)

CHURCH LA

Glebe Farm

34

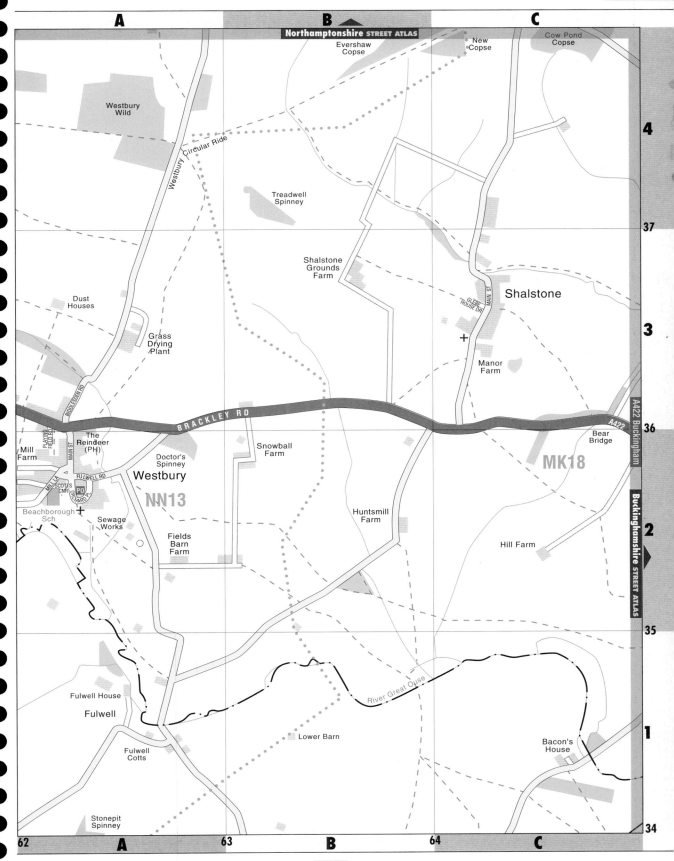

A

B

C

4

37

3

36

A422 Buckingham

A422

Buckinghamshire STREET ATLAS

2

35

1

34

Westbury Wild

Evershaw Copse

New Copse

Cow Pond Copse

Westbury Circular Ride

Treadwell Spinney

Shalstone Grounds Farm

GLEBE HOUSE DRI

MAIN ST

Shalstone

Dust Houses

Grass Drying Plant

Manor Farm

BRACKLEY RD

Mill Farm

BIDDLESDEN RD

PLAYING FIELD RD

MAIN ST

The Reindeer (PH)

Doctor's Spinney

FULWELL RD

Snowball Farm

Bear Bridge

MK18

Westbury

MILL LA

SCOTTS CNR

ORCHARD PL

PO

NN13

Huntsmill Farm

Hill Farm

Beachborough Sch

Sewage Works

Fields Barn Farm

Fulwell House

Fulwell

River Great Ouse

Lower Barn

Bacon's House

Fulwell Cotts

Stonepit Spinney

62

A

63

B

64

C

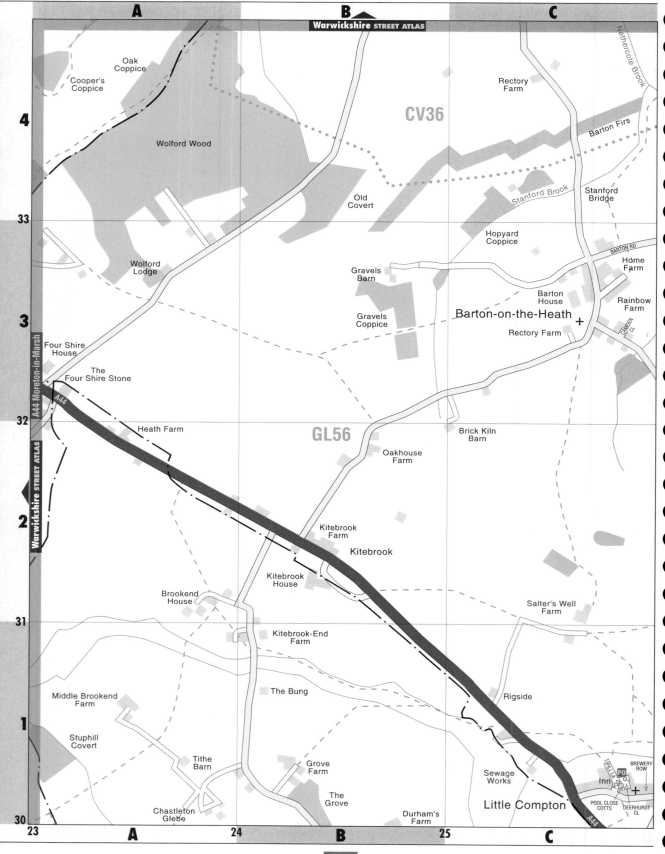

A B C

4

CV36

Oak Coppice

Cooper's Coppice

Wolford Wood

Rectory Farm

Barton Firs

Old Covert

Nethercote Brook

Stanford Brook

Stanford Bridge

33

Wolford Lodge

Hopyard Coppice

BARTON RD

Home Farm

Gravels Barn

Barton House

Rainbow Farm

Gravels Coppice

Barton-on-the-Heath

CAMDEN CL

3

Four Shire House

Rectory Farm

A44 Moreton-in-Marsh

The Four Shire Stone

Warwickshire STREET ATLAS

A44

32

Heath Farm

GL56

Brick Kiln Barn

Oakhouse Farm

2

Kitebrook Farm

Kitebrook

Salter's Well Farm

Kitebrook House

Brookend House

31

Kitebrook-End Farm

Rigside

Middle Brookend Farm

The Bung

1

Stuphill Covert

Sewage Works

BREWERY ROW

PO

Inn

POOL CL

Tithe Barn

Grove Farm

DEERHURST CL

Chastleton Glebe

The Grove

Durham's Farm

Little Compton

POOL CLOSE COTTS

A44

30

23 A 24 B 25 C

28

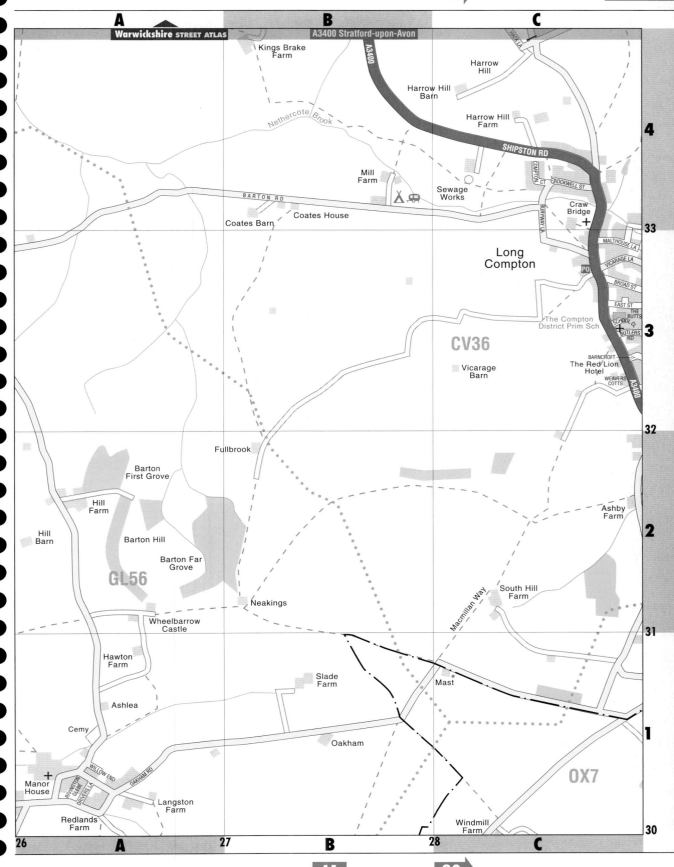

A Warwickshire STREET ATLAS

B A3400 Stratford-upon-Avon

C

Kings Brake Farm

Harrow Hill

Harrow Hill Barn

Harrow Hill Farm

SHIPSTON RD

4

Nethercote Brook

Mill Farm

Sewage Works

BARTON RD

COMPTON CT

CROCKWELL ST

BURYWAY LA

Craw Bridge

Coates House

Coates Barn

33

MALTHOUSE LA

Long Compton

VICARAGE LA

PO

BROAD ST

EAST ST

THE BUTTS

SCHOOL CL

BUTLERS RD

The Compton District Prim Sch

CV36

3

Vicarage Barn

BARNCROFT

The Red Lion Hotel

WEAVERS COTTS

A3400

32

Fullbrook

Barton First Grove

Ashby Farm

Hill Farm

2

Hill Barn

Barton Hill

Barton Far Grove

GL56

South Hill Farm

Neakings

Macmillan Way

Wheelbarrow Castle

31

Hawton Farm

Slade Farm

Mast

Ashlea

Cemy

Oakham

1

WILLOW END

OAKHAM RD

RIVINGTON GLEBE

DRIVERS LA

OX7

Manor House

Langston Farm

Redlands Farm

Windmill Farm

30

26

A

27

B

28

C

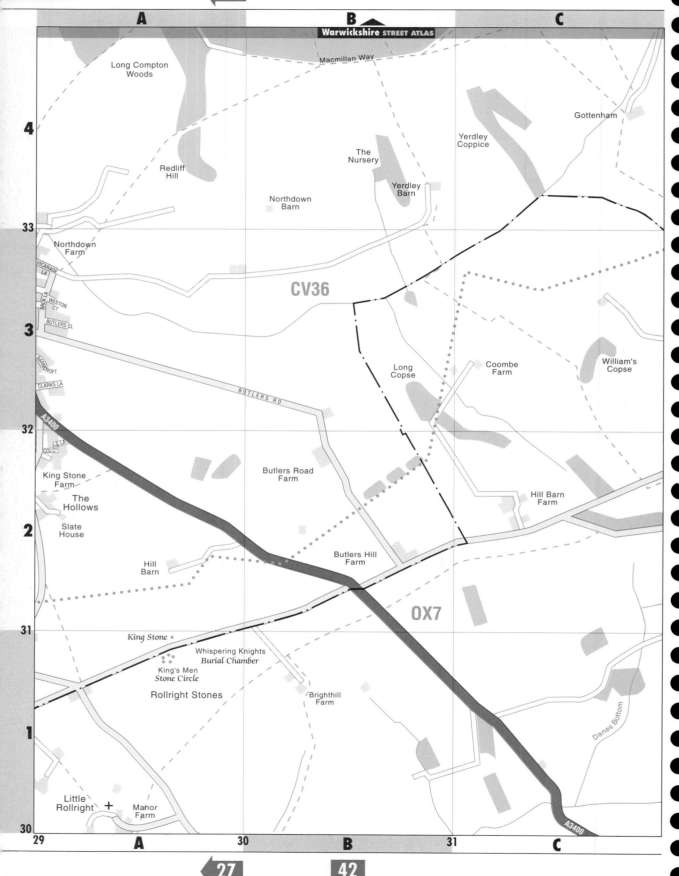

Warwickshire STREET ATLAS

A · B · C

Long Compton
Woods

Macmillan Way

Gottenham

Yerdley Coppice

The
Nursery

Yerdley
Barn

4

Redliff
Hill

Northdown
Barn

33

Northdown
Farm

VICARAGE LA
BACK LA
WESTON CT
BUTLERS CL

CV36

Long
Copse

Coombe
Farm

William's
Copse

3

BARNCROFT

CLARKS LA

BUTLERS RD

A3400

32

COLDS LA

King Stone
Farm

Butlers Road
Farm

Hill Barn
Farm

The
Hollows

2

Slate
House

Hill
Barn

Butlers Hill
Farm

31

King Stone

Whispering Knights
Burial Chamber

OX7

Danes Bottom

King's Men
Stone Circle

Rollright Stones

Brighthill
Farm

1

Little
Rollright

Manor
Farm

A3400

30

29 · A · 30 · B · 31 · C

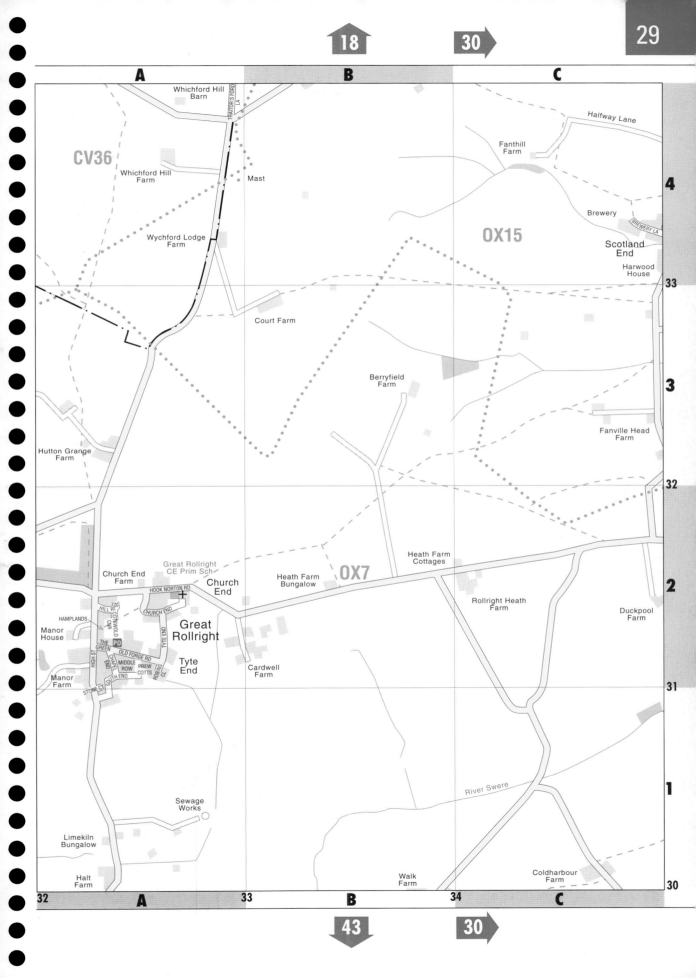

A B C

Whichford Hill Barn

TRAITOR'S FORD

CV36

Whichford Hill Farm

Mast

Halfway Lane

Fanthill Farm

OX15

Brewery

BREWERY LA

Scotland End

Harwood House

4

Wychford Lodge Farm

33

Court Farm

Berryfield Farm

3

Fanville Head Farm

Hutton Grange Farm

32

Heath Farm Cottages

OX7

Church End Farm

Great Rollright CE Prim Sch

HOOK NORTON RD

Church End

CHURCH END

Heath Farm Bungalow

Rollright Heath Farm

Duckpool Farm

2

HAMPLANDS

HILL RD

COTSWOLD CNR

Great Rollright

Manor House

THE GREEN

PO

OLD FORGE RD

MIDDLE ROW

HIGH ST

CHAPEL END

PREW COTTS

ROBINS CL

TYTE END

TYTE END

Tyte End

Cardwell Farm

31

Manor Farm

STONE CT

Sewage Works

River Swere

1

Limekiln Bungalow

Halt Farm

Walk Farm

Coldharbour Farm

30

32 A 33 B 34 C

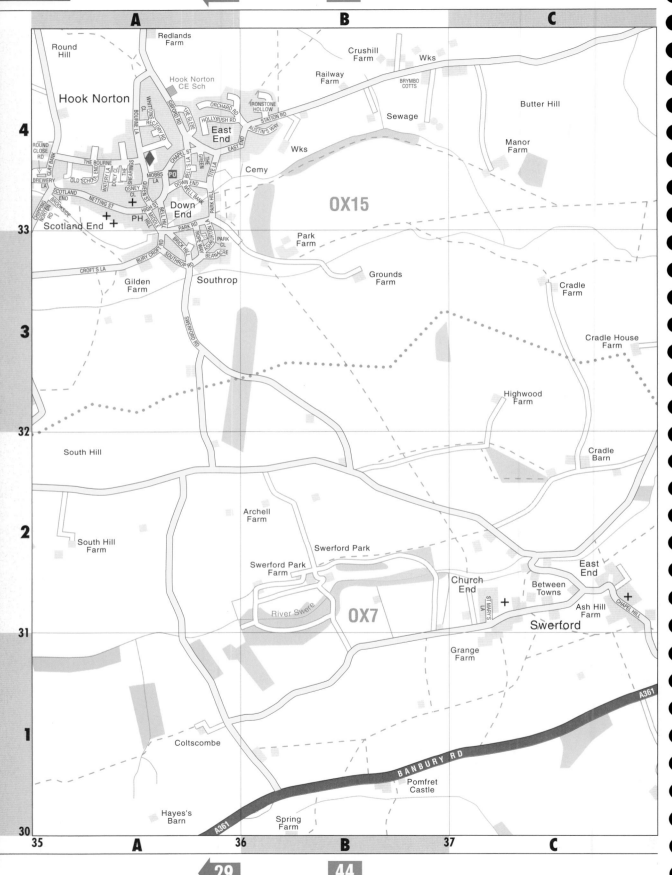

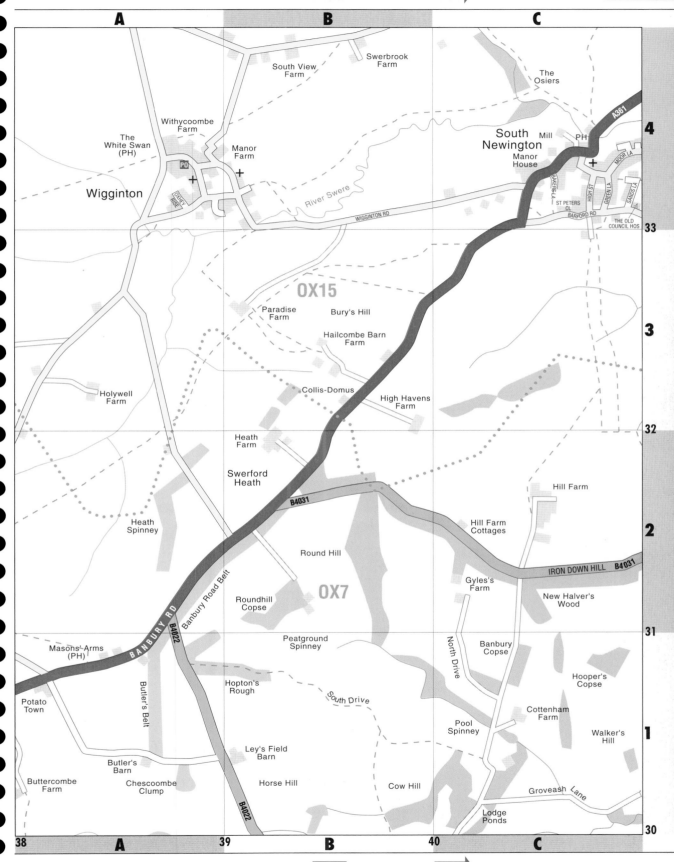

A   B   C

A361

A361

The Baulk

MOOR LA

River Swere

BARFORD RD

BLOXHAM RD

4

Barford St John

MEAD RD

Mead Farm

Manor Farm

33

BARFORD RD

Rignell Farm

Rignell Hall

SOUTH NEWINGTON RD

The Manor House

PO

PH

LOWER ST

BISHOPS CL

THE ROCK

SUMMER LEY

HORN HILL

Barford Lodge

Buttermilk Farm

3

Barford St Michael

CHURCH ST

THE GREEN

ROBINS CL

HIGH ST

College Farm

OX15

BROAD CL

TOWNSEND

THE COUNCIL HOS

Spring Hill Farm

NETHERWORTON RD

32

STEEPNESS HILL

B4031

Irondown Farm

Iron Down

2

IRON DOWN HILL

B4031

Black Jane Farm

Ilbury Farm

Upper Grove Ash Farm

Irondown Spinney

31

Lower Grove Farm

Raven Hill

OX7

Hawk Hill

1

Nether Worton

The Boltons

Manor Farm

Nether Worton House

30

41   A   42   B   43   C

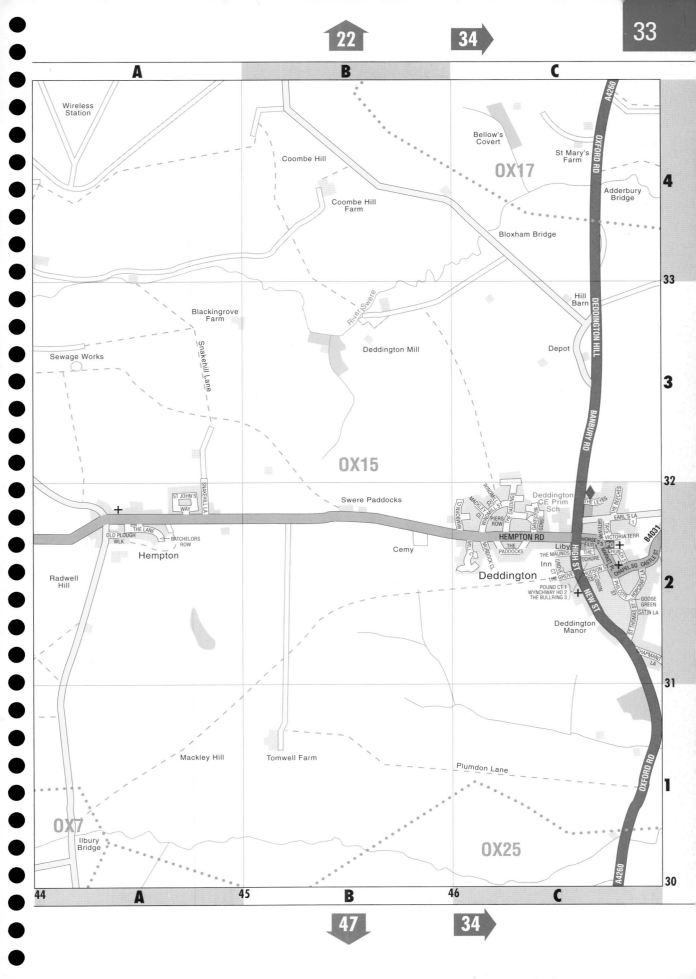

A

B

C

Wireless
Station

Coombe Hill

Bellow's
Covert

St Mary's
Farm

OX17

Oxford RD

A4260

Adderbury
Bridge

Coombe Hill
Farm

Bloxham Bridge

4

33

Blackingrove
Farm

River Swere

Hill
Barn

Deddington Mill

Depot

DEDDINGTON HILL

BANBURY RD

Sewage Works

Snakehill Lane

3

OX15

Swere Paddocks

Windmill St

Deddington
CE Prim
Sch

THE LEYES

THE BEECHES

32

St John's
Way

SNAKEHILL LA

WIMBORN CL

MACKLEY CL

WINDMILL ST

PIERS
ROW

THE DAEDINGS

GAVESTON
GDNS

EARL'S LA

B4031

THE LANE

OLD PLOUGH
WLK

BATCHELORS
ROW

Cemy

MILL CL

MURDOCK CL

HEMPTON RD

THE
PADDOCKS

Liby

HORSE
FAIR

TAYS
GATEWAY

THE
CHURCHE

VICTORIA TERR

MARKET PL

CHURCH ST

PO

CHAPEL SQ

CASTLE ST

Hempton

Inn

THE MAUNDS

THE GROVE

GROVE LA

HIGH ST

HUDSON ST

PHILCOTE ST

Radwell
Hill

Deddington

POUND CT 1
WYNCHWAY HO 2
THE BULLRING 3

NEW ST

ST THOMAS ST

HOPCRAFT LA

GOOSE
GREEN

SATIN LA

2

Deddington
Manor

CHAPMANS
LA

31

Mackley Hill

Tomwell Farm

Plumdon Lane

OXFORD RD

1

OX7

OX25

A4260

Ilbury
Bridge

44

A

45

B

46

C

30

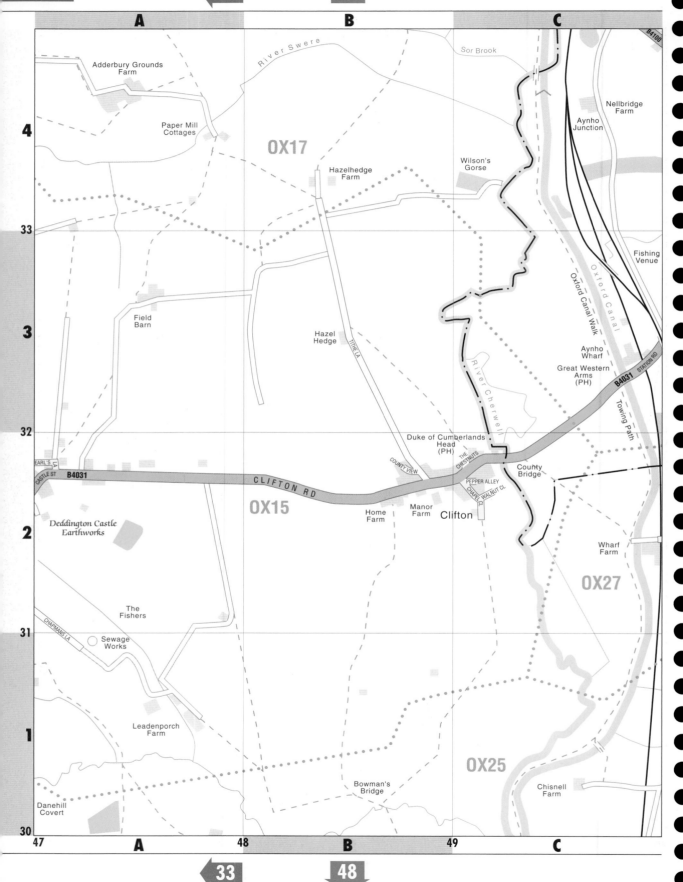

A **B** **C**

River Swere

Sor Brook

Adderbury Grounds Farm

Nellbridge Farm

OX17

Paper Mill Cottages

Wilson's Gorse

Aynho Junction

4

Hazelhedge Farm

Fishing Venue

33

Oxford Canal Walk

Oxford Canal

Field Barn

Hazel Hedge

Aynho Wharf

3

TITHE LA

Great Western Arms (PH)

B4031 STATION RD

River Cherwell

Towing Path

32

Duke of Cumberlands Head (PH)

EARL'S LA

CASTLE ST

B4031

COUNTY VIEW

THE CHESTNUTS

County Bridge

CLIFTON RD

PEPPER ALLEY

CHAPEL CL WALNUT CL

OX15

Home Farm

Manor Farm

Clifton

2

Deddington Castle Earthworks

Wharf Farm

OX27

CHAPMANS LA

The Fishers

31

Sewage Works

1

Leadenporch Farm

OX25

Bowman's Bridge

Chisnell Farm

Danehill Covert

30

47 48 49

A **B** **C**

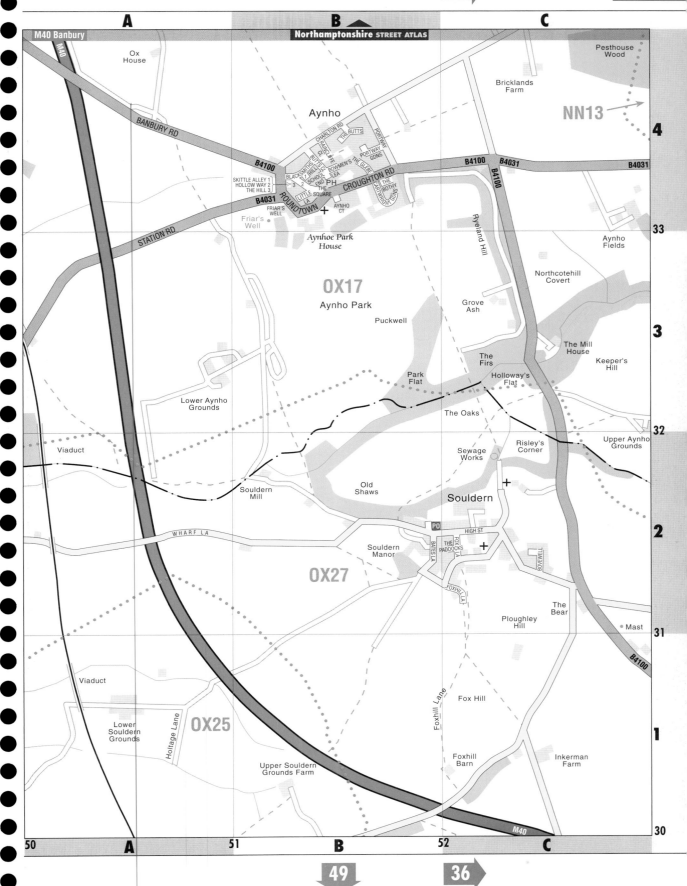

36

Northamptonshire STREET ATLAS

M40 Banbury

Ox House

BANBURY RD

B4100

B4031

STATION RD

Aynho

CHARLTON RD

THE BUTTS

PORTWAY

PORTWAY GDNS

CROUGHTON RD

B4100

B4031

B4031

NN13

Bricklands Farm

Pesthouse Wood

B4100

B4031

BLACKSMITHS

BUTTS

HILL

SCHOOL

BOWMEN'S

END

PH

THE SQUARE

LITTLE LA

ROUNDTOWN

THE GLEBE

CARTWRIGHT

THE BOTHY

GDNS

SKITTLE ALLEY 1
HOLLOW WAY 2
THE HILL 3

FRIAR'S WELL

Friar's Well

AYNHO CT

Aynho Fields

33

OX17

Aynhoe Park House

Aynho Park

Puckwell

Ryeland Hill

Grove Ash

Northcotehill Covert

3

The Firs

The Mill House

Keeper's Hill

Park Flat

Holloway's Flat

The Oaks

Lower Aynho Grounds

Viaduct

Sewage Works

Risley's Corner

32

Upper Aynho Grounds

Old Shaws

Souldern Mill

Souldern

WHARF LA

Souldern Manor

OX27

PO

BATES LA

THE PADDOCKS

FOX LA

HIGH ST

BOVEWELL

2

The Bear

Mast

Ploughley Hill

31

B4100

FOXHILL LA

Viaduct

Lower Souldern Grounds

Holtage Lane

OX25

Upper Souldern Grounds Farm

Foxhill Lane

Fox Hill

Foxhill Barn

Inkerman Farm

1

M40

50

51

52

30

A   B   C

4

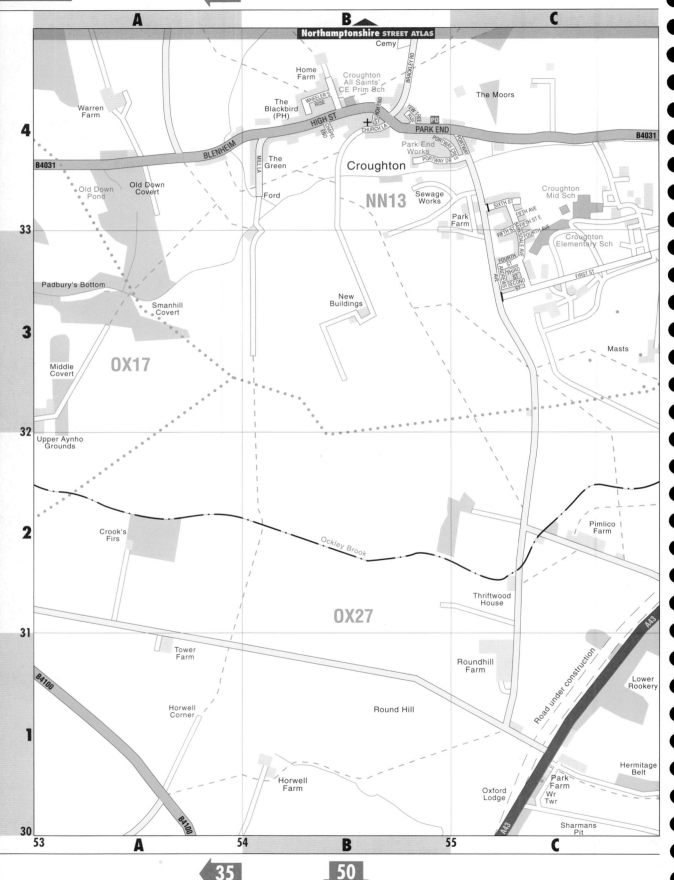

Northamptonshire STREET ATLAS

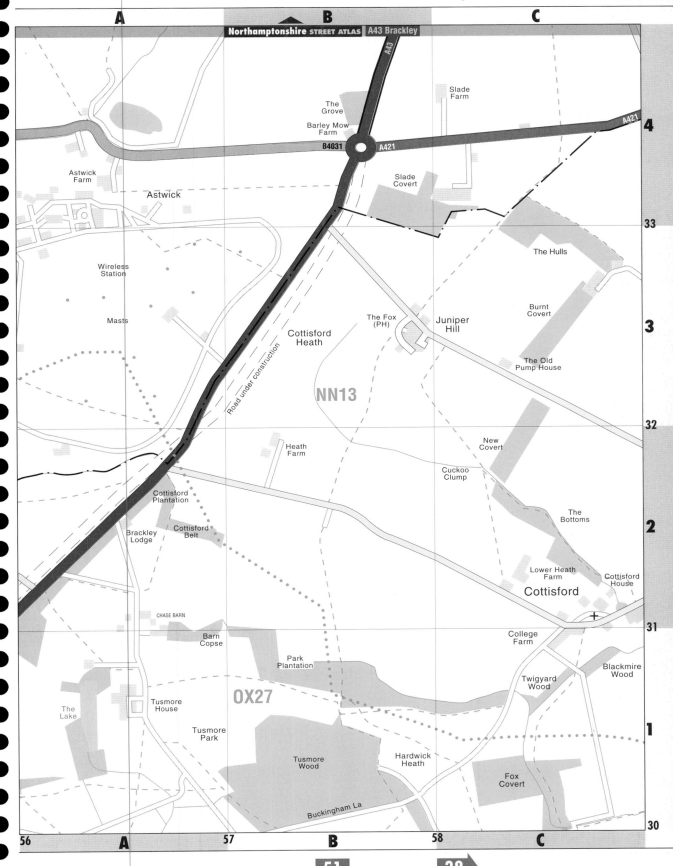

Northamptonshire STREET ATLAS | A43 Brackley

A43

B4031 ● A421

A421

The Grove

Barley Mow Farm

Slade Farm

Slade Covert

Slade Covert

Astwick Farm

Astwick

The Hulls

Burnt Covert

Wireless Station

The Fox (PH)

Juniper Hill

The Old Pump House

Masts

Cottisford Heath

Road under construction

NN13

New Covert

Cuckoo Clump

Heath Farm

The Bottoms

Cottisford Plantation

Brackley Lodge

Cottisford Belt

Lower Heath Farm

Cottisford House

Cottisford

CHASE BARN

Barn Copse

Park Plantation

College Farm

Twigyard Wood

Blackmire Wood

OX27

The Lake

Tusmore House

Tusmore Park

Tusmore Wood

Hardwick Heath

Fox Covert

Buckingham La

4

33

3

32

2

31

1

30

56 · 57 · 58

	A	B	C

Barrow Hill

Mixbury

MIXBURY

CHURCH LA

The Bowling Green

A421

4

Monk's House

Mixbury Lodge Farm

A421

Monk's House Barn

33

Mixbury Plantation

The Pits

Middle Farm

NN13

FEATHERBED LA

3

Park Thorns

Diggings Wood

32

Coldharbour Farm

MK18

2

Wr Twr

LAKE VIEW

Cottisford Pond

Shelswell Plantation

Pondhead

HETHE RD

The View

31

The Belt

Shelswell Park

Home Farm

Spilsmere Wood

Windmill Hook

The Cut

Shelswell

OX27

1

Hethe Spinney

30

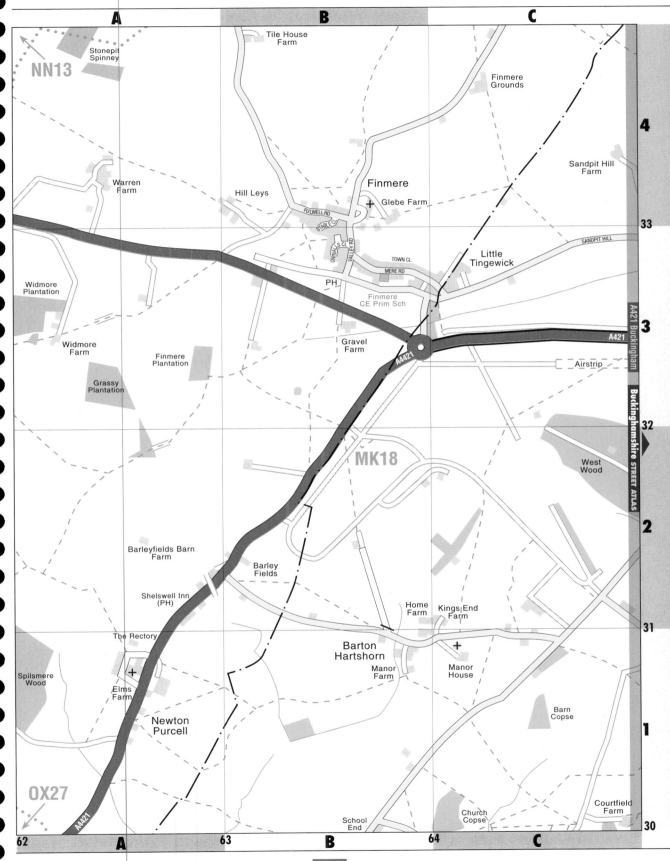

A B C

NN13

Stonepit
Spinney

Tile House
Farm

Finmere
Grounds

4

Sandpit Hill
Farm

Warren
Farm

Hill Leys

Finmere

Glebe Farm

FULWELL RD

STABLE CT

33

CHINALLS CL

VALLEY RD

Little
Tingewick

SANDPIT HILL

A421 Buckingham

Widmore
Plantation

TOWN CL

MERE RD

PH

Finmere
CE Prim Sch

3

A421

Buckinghamshire STREET ATLAS

Widmore
Farm

Finmere
Plantation

Gravel
Farm

A4421

Airstrip

Grassy
Plantation

32

West
Wood

MK18

2

Barleyfields Barn
Farm

Barley
Fields

Home
Farm

Kings End
Farm

31

Shelswell Inn
(PH)

The Rectory

Barton
Hartshorn

Manor
Farm

Manor
House

Spilsmere
Wood

Elms
Farm

Barn
Copse

Newton
Purcell

1

OX27

A4421

School
End

Church
Copse

Courtfield
Farm

30

62 A 63 B 64 C

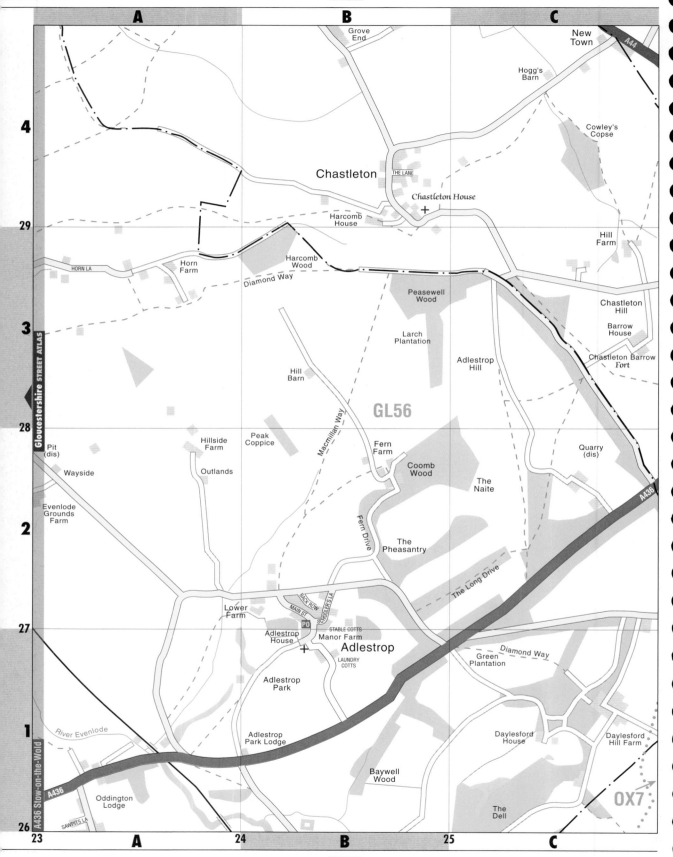

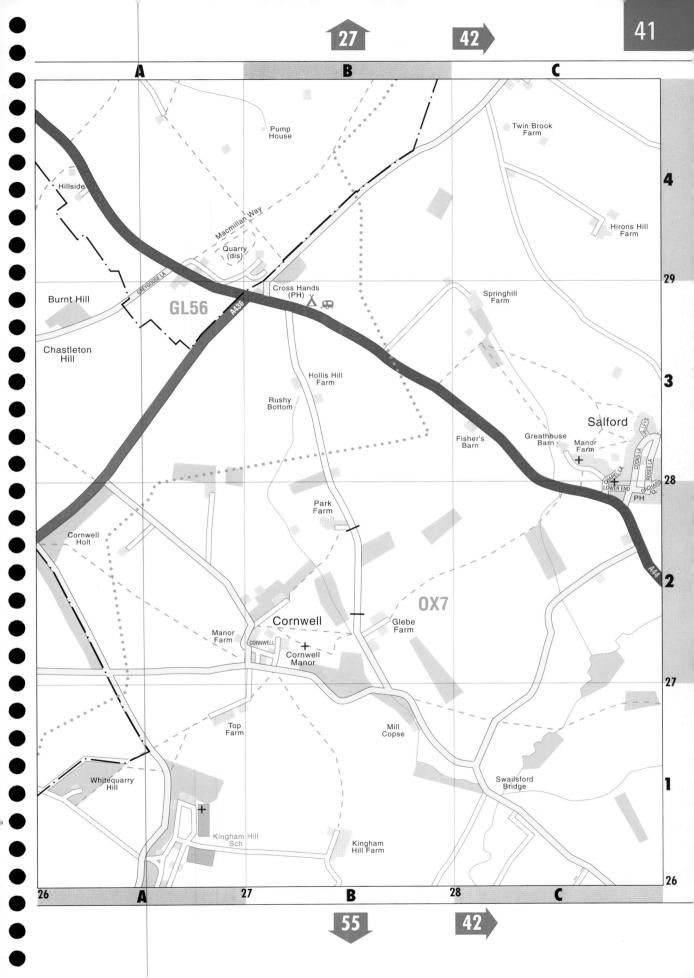

A
B
C

Pump House

Hillside

Macmillan Way

Quarry (dis)

4

Cross Hands (PH)

29

Burnt Hill

GREYGOOSE LA

GL56

A436

Springhill Farm

Twin Brook Farm

Hirons Hill Farm

Chastleton Hill

Hollis Hill Farm

3

Rushy Bottom

Fisher's Barn

Greathouse Barn

Salford

THE LEYS

Manor Farm

COOKS LA

ROSES LA

CHAPEL LA

LOWER END

ORCHARD CL

28

PH

Cornwell Holt

Park Farm

OX7

A44

2

Manor Farm

CORNWELL

Cornwell

Glebe Farm

Cornwell Manor

27

Top Farm

Mill Copse

Swailsford Bridge

1

Whitequarry Hill

Kingham Hill Sch

Kingham Hill Farm

26

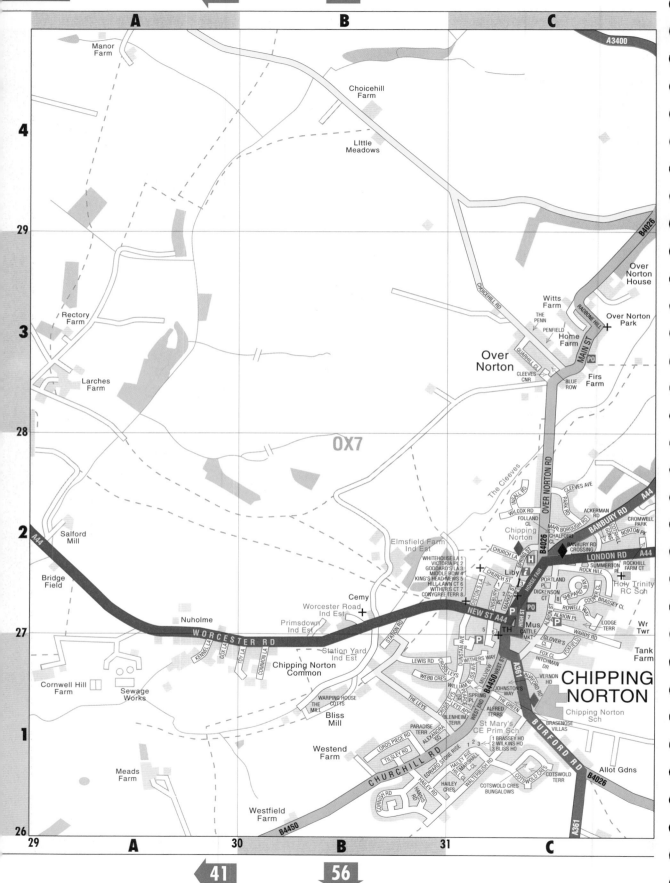

A
B
C

Priory Mill

Walk Farm

Walk Gorse

Caroline Colyear Cottages

Hull Farm

Kiteney Copse

The Bungalows

B4026

Sandfields Farm

A361

4

Over Norton Common

29

Merryweather Farm

BANBURY RD

Banbury Lodge

Over Norton Park

Wynmere Farm

A3400

Hide Wood

3

Resr

A361

Chapel House

Priory Farm

Hit or Miss Farm

Chapel House Farm

A44

The Warren

28

OX7

Black Knap

Priory Wood

Cromwell Park

Park Farm

2

Fowler's Barn

LONDON RD

Ovens Gorse

Wks

27

Southcoombe

CH

New Chalford Farm

Chalford Oaks Farm

Glyme Farm

1

River Glyme

Chalford Oaks

B4026

A44

26

43
30

A   B   C

A361

A361

4

Cherwell
Barn

The
Meetings

Showell
Bungalow

Showell
Farm

Showell
Copse

29

River Dorn

Magpie
Farm

3

GREEN LA

Dunthrop

Chivelcorner
Plantation

Chivel
Farm

28

OX7

Heythrop

Little Tew
Grounds Farm

+

Wheatfield
Copse

2

Deerpen
Wood

Iron's
Copse

Foxberry
Wood

West
Wood

27

Harris's
Bottom

Heythrop Park

Fattingfield
Copse

1

Broadstone
Hill

Heythrop Park
Staff Training College

Kite
Grove

The
Wilderness

26

35   A   36   B   37   C

43
58

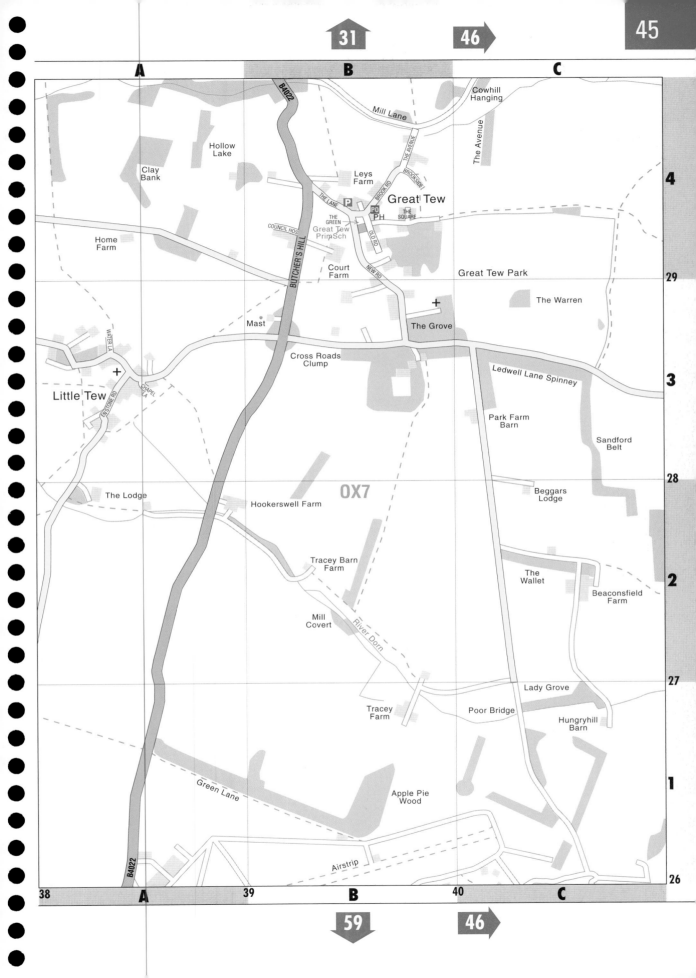

45 32

A B C

4

Newhouse Farm

Flighthill Farm

Over Worton

Grange Farm

Worton House

Rest Hill Farm

Flighthill Cottage

Hobbshole Farm

29

Lark Rise

The Bungalow

3

Brae

Hangman's Hill

Cockley Brook

Heath Farm

Ledwell

Close Farm

28

OX7

Worton Wood

Conygree Wood

2

Parkend Cottages

Heath Cottage Farm

Cricket Ground

High Ley

27

Down Hill Farm

Park Farm

Sandford Park

River Dorn

Sandford St Martin

1

Mill

Brandon Farm

Manor House

Manor Farm

MANOR RD

SANDFORD ST MARTIN RD

ORCHARD WAY

HILLSIDE RD

WORTON RD

HOLLIERS CRES

BALLARD CL

Manor House

26

41 A 42 B 43 C

45 60

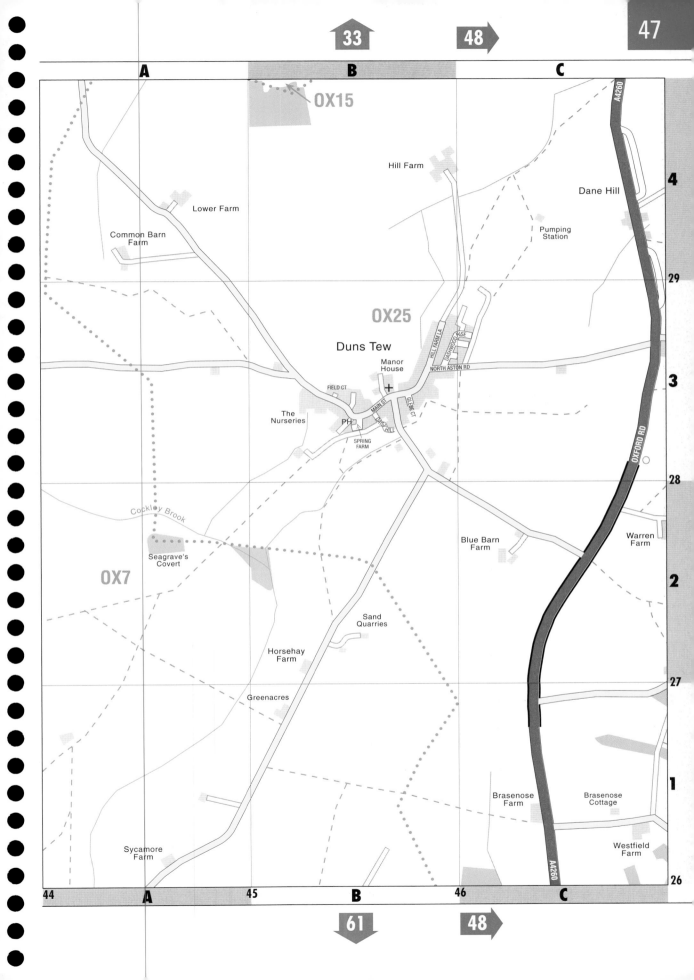

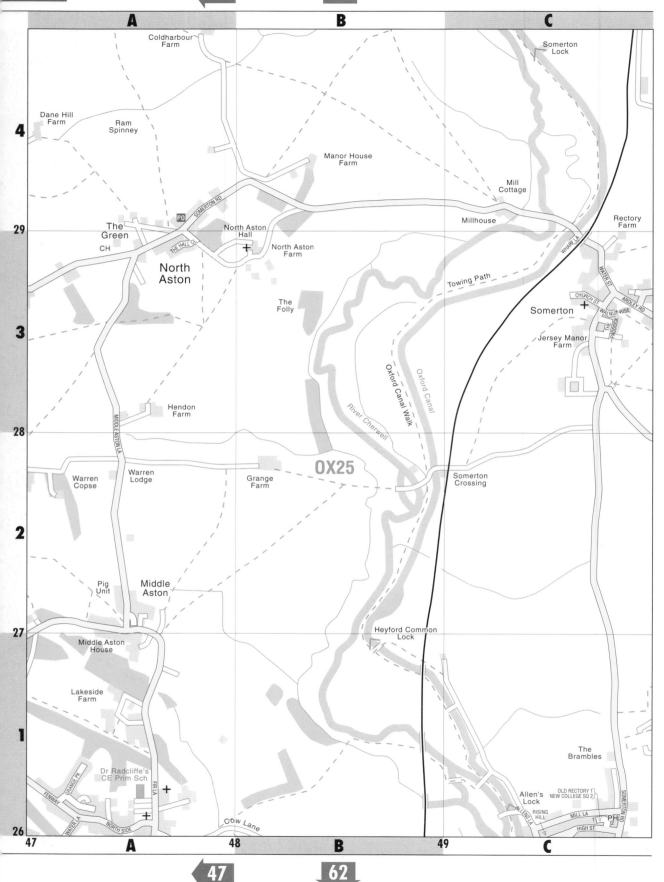

A   B   C

Coldharbour
Farm

Dane Hill
Farm

Ram
Spinney

4

Manor House
Farm

Somerton
Lock

Mill
Cottage

SOMERTON RD

PO

The
Green

CH

North Aston
Hall

Millhouse

Rectory
Farm

29

North Aston
Farm

WHARF LA

WATER ST

North
Aston

THE HALL CL

North Aston
Farm

Towing Path

CHURCH ST

Somerton

ARDLEY RD

The Folly

WALNUT RISE

3

THE PADDOCK

Jersey Manor
Farm

Oxford Canal Walk

Oxford Canal

River Cherwell

MIDDLE ASTON LA

Hendon
Farm

28

OX25

Warren
Copse

Warren
Lodge

Grange
Farm

Somerton
Crossing

2

Pig
Unit

Middle
Aston

Heyford Common
Lock

27

Middle Aston
House

Lakeside
Farm

1

The
Brambles

GRANGE PK

FENWAY

FIR LA

Dr Radcliffe's
CE Prim Sch

Allen's
Lock

OLD RECTORY 1
NEW COLLEGE SQ 2

SOMERTON RD

RISING
HILL

PH

ALLEN'S LA

WATER LA

NORTH SIDE

Cow Lane

MILL LA

HIGH ST

26

47   A   48   B   49   C

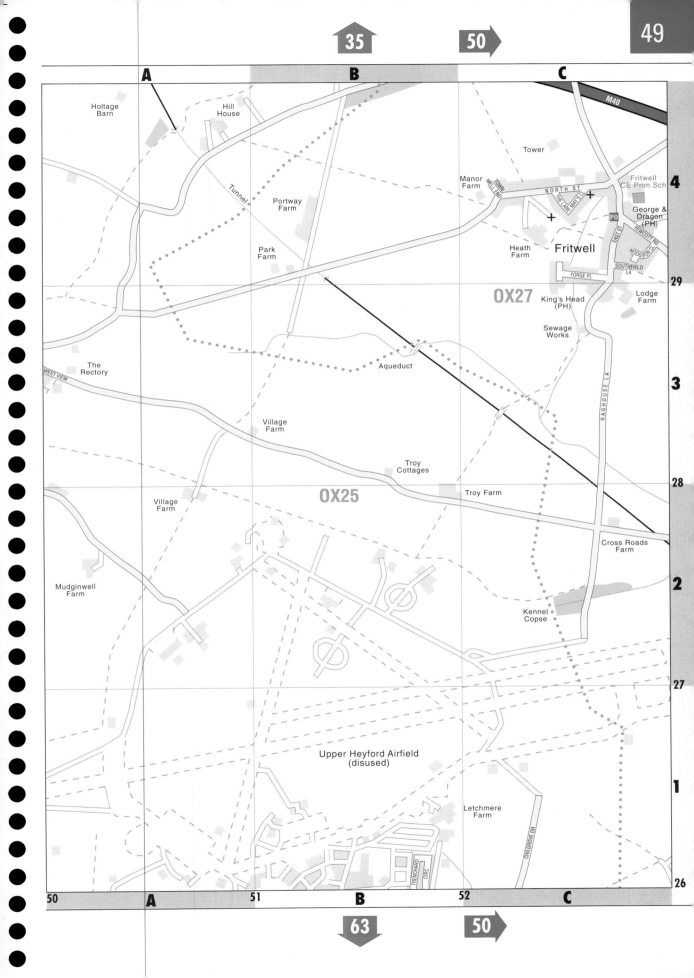

A

Holtage
Barn

Hill
House

Tunnel

Portway
Farm

Park
Farm

B

Tower

Manor
Farm

TOWN
WELL END

NORTH ST

THE LANE

MAY'S CL

Fritwell
CE Prim Sch

4

George &
Dragon
(PH)

EAST ST

FEWCOTT RD

HODGSON CL

PO

Heath
Farm

Fritwell

FORGE PL

SOUTHFIELD
LA

29

OX27

King's Head
(PH)

Lodge
Farm

Sewage
Works

C

M40

WEST VIEW

The
Rectory

Village
Farm

Troy
Cottages

Troy Farm

OX25

Aqueduct

RAGHOUSE LA

3

28

Village
Farm

Cross Roads
Farm

Mudginwell
Farm

Kennel
Copse

2

27

Upper Heyford Airfield
(disused)

Letchmere
Farm

CHILGROVE DR

TRENCHARD
CIRC

1

26

A **B** **C**

B4100

M40

Horwell

Green
Farm

4

Baynards Green
Farm

Baynard's
Green

A43

Park Farm Belt

Medkre

Baynard
House

29

Road under construction

Lone
Barn

3

OX27

Sycamore
Grove

Cherwell
Valley
Services

Fewcott

Manor
Farm

Fewcott
Farm

Sewage
Works

A43

28

FRITWELL RD

PLOUGHLEY
CL

WATER LA

KEEY'S
CL

RUSSET RD

ARDLEY RD

B430

10

Nature
Trail

Stoke
Wood

B4100

PADDOCK RD

PO ORCHARD
RD

Ardley

Woodbine
Cottage

SOMERTON RD

CASTLE
FIELDS

2

Ardley
Wood

Manor
Farm

PH

ST MARY'S
WLK

CHURCH RD

Kilby's
Barn

STATION RD

ARDLEY RD

27

Kilby's
Copse

1

Nevilles
Farm

M40

Ashgrove
Farm

Digging
Copse

Woodlands
Farm

26

B430

Ardley Fields
Farm

53 **A** **54** **B** **55** **C**

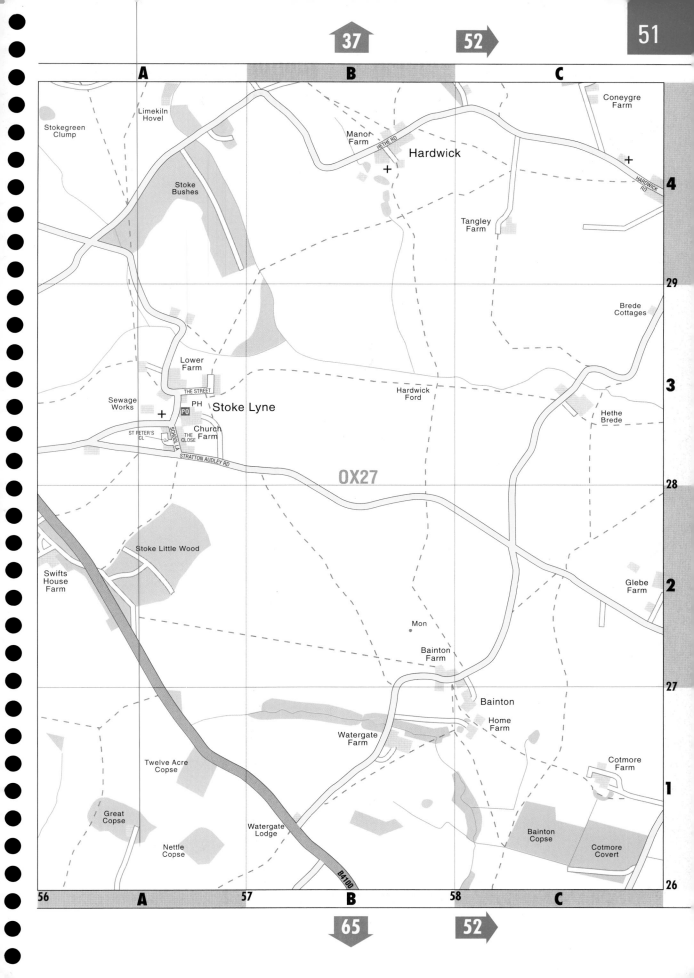

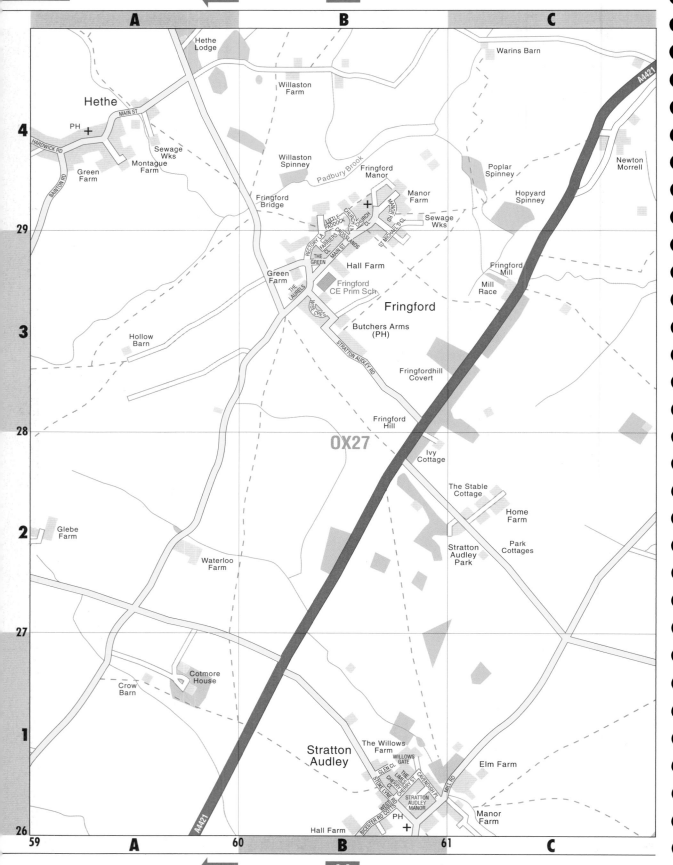

A   B   C

Hethe Lodge

Warins Barn

Willaston Farm

A4421

Hethe
PH
Main St
Green Farm
Montague Farm
Sewage Wks

Willaston Spinney

Padbury Brook

Fringford Manor

Manor Farm

Poplar Spinney

Newton Morrell

4

Barton Rd

Hardwick Rd

Fringford Bridge

Hopyard Spinney

Sewage Wks

29

Rectory La
Larriers Cl
Priors Cl
Main St
Church Cl
Church La
Little Paddock
The Green
Sands
St Michael's Cl
Manor Rd

Fringford Mill

Green Farm
The Laurels

Hall Farm

Fringford CE Prim Sch

Mill Race

Wise Cres

Fringford

3

Hollow Barn

Butchers Arms (PH)

Stratton Audley Rd

Fringfordhill Covert

28

Fringford Hill

OX27

Ivy Cottage

The Stable Cottage

Home Farm

2

Glebe Farm

Waterloo Farm

Stratton Audley Park

Park Cottages

27

Cotmore House

Crow Barn

A4421

1

Stratton Audley

The Willows Farm
Willows Gate
Glen Cl
Stoke Lyne
The Limes
Cherry St
Bicester Rd Cotts
West Rd
Gatehouse Pl
Cherry St
PH
Stratton Audley Manor
Mill Rd

Elm Farm

Manor Farm

26
Hall Farm

59   A   60   B   61   C

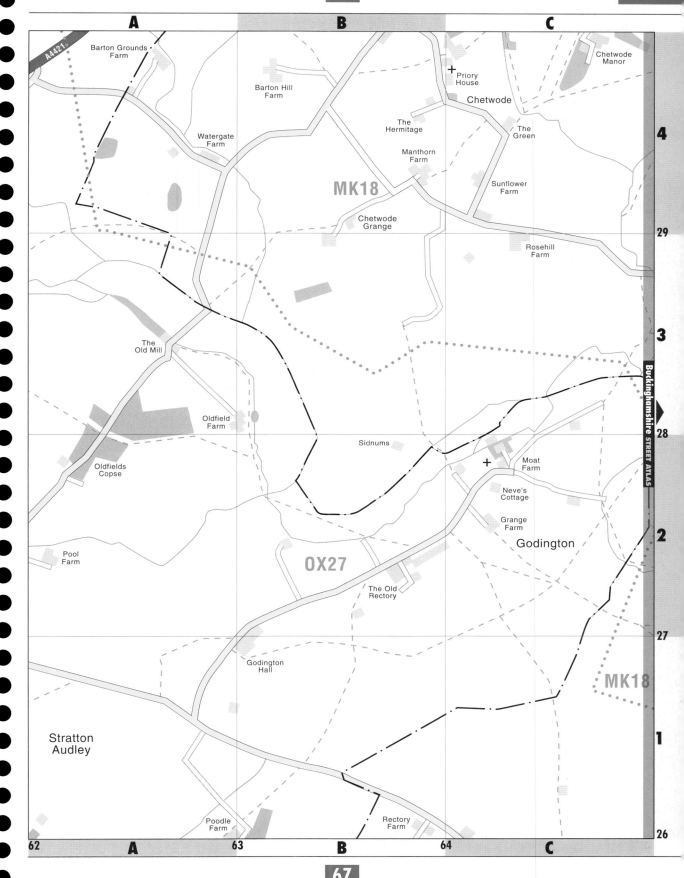

A4421

A

B

C

Barton Grounds
Farm

Barton Hill
Farm

Priory
House

Chetwode
Manor

Chetwode

Watergate
Farm

The Hermitage

The
Green

Manthorn
Farm

4

MK18

Sunflower
Farm

Chetwode
Grange

29

Rosehill
Farm

The
Old Mill

3

Oldfield
Farm

Sidnums

Buckinghamshire STREET ATLAS

Oldfields
Copse

Moat
Farm

28

Neve's
Cottage

Grange
Farm

2

Pool
Farm

OX27

Godington

The Old
Rectory

27

Godington
Hall

MK18

Stratton
Audley

1

Poodle
Farm

Rectory
Farm

26

40

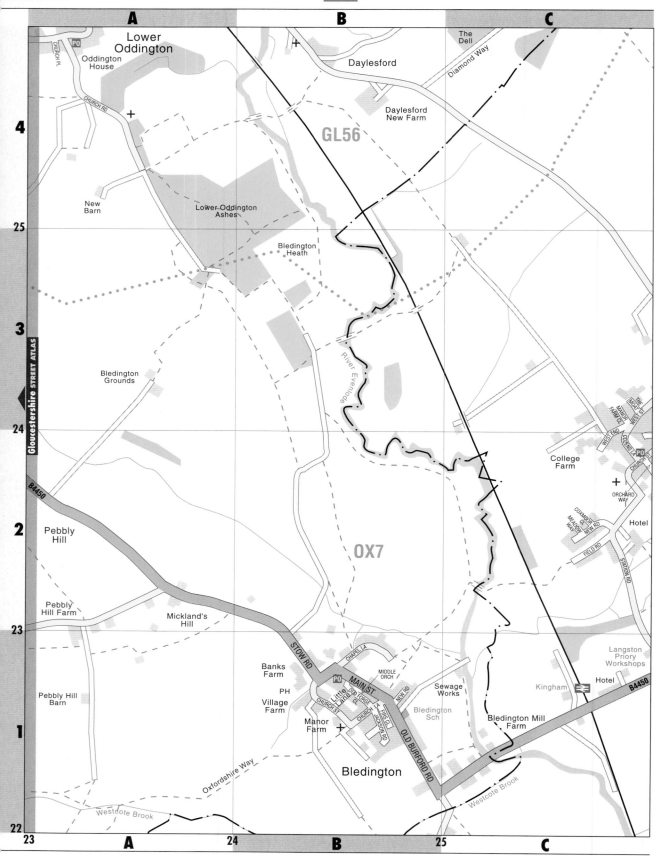

69

Gloucestershire STREET ATLAS

A **B** **C**

Lower Oddington

Daylesford

The Dell

Diamond Way

Oddington House

CHURCH RD

CHURCH PL

PO

Daylesford New Farm

GL56

New Barn

Lower Oddington Ashes

Bledington Heath

River Evenlode

Bledington Grounds

OX7

The Moat St
West End
Manor Farm Cl
Cotswold La

College Farm

West End
Church La
PO

ORCHARD WAY

B4450

Pebbly Hill

Coxmoor Cl
Meadow Way
New Rd
Field Rd

Hotel

Station Rd

Pebbly Hill Farm

Mickland's Hill

Pebbly Hill Barn

Langston Priory Workshops

Kingham

Hotel

B4450

STOW RD

Chapel La

Banks Farm

MAIN ST

PO

MIDDLE ORCH

Little Lane
Old Forge Cl

NEW RD

Sewage Works

PH
Village Farm

CHURCH ST

FIRS CL
JACKSON RD

Bledington Sch

Bledington Mill Farm

Manor Farm

CHURCH RD

OLD BURFORD RD

Bledington

Oxfordshire Way

Westcote Brook

Westcote Brook

23 24 25

A **B** **C**

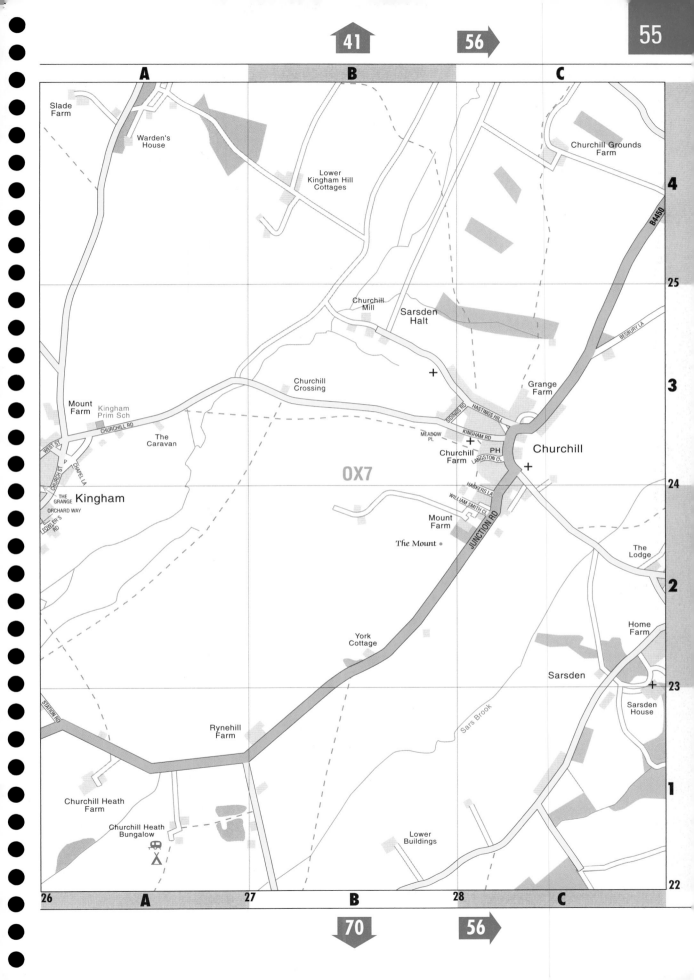

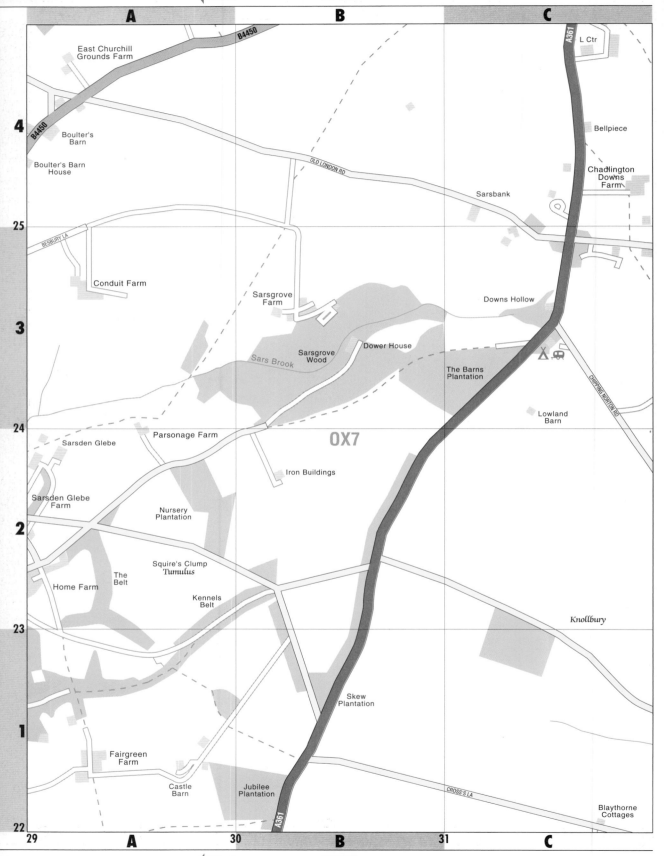

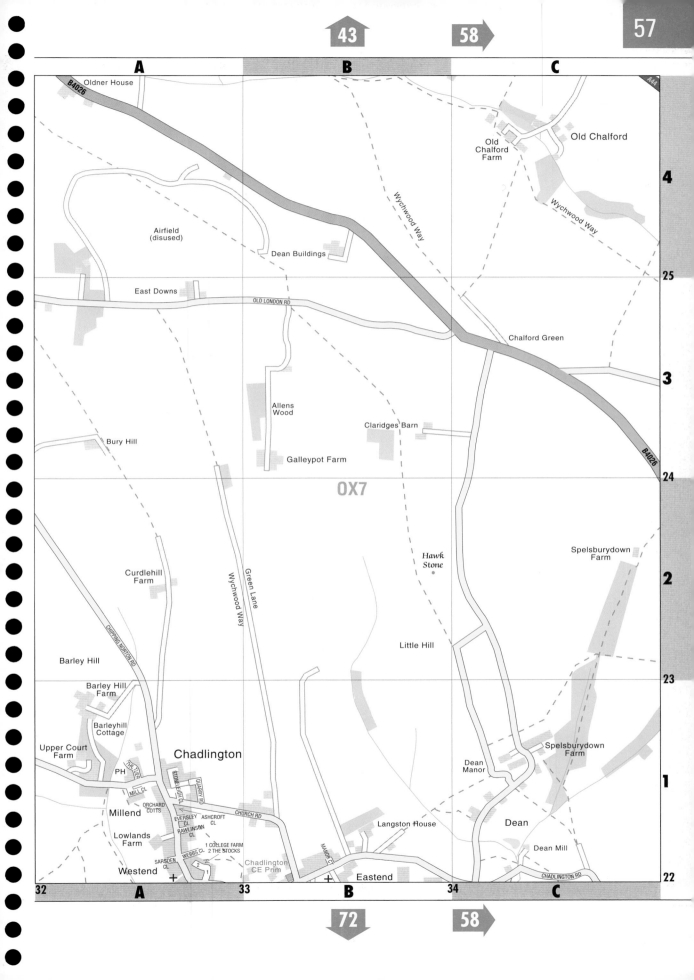

A B C

A44

Leys Farm

Broadstone Plantation

Long Firs

Mast

Manor Farm

Sewage Works

Church Enstone

PH

B4030

4

Stone Farm

Lidstone

Hill Farm

Lidstone Bottom

River Glyme

BICESTER RD

Stoney Bridge

CLAY HILL CL

B4030

PH

THE DRIVE

Enstone

25

3

CHAPEL LA

KEENS CL

OXFORD RD

Neat Enstone

LITCHFIELD CL

MANOR CL

WOODFORD CL

Enstone Cty Prim Sch

FENVELL CL

CLEVELEY RD

Litchfield Farm

OX7

THE SPINNEYS

BRAYBROOKE CL

COX'S LA

PH

A44

QUARRY CL

B4022

24

B4026

Hoar Stone
Burial Chamber

Enstone Firs

2

Fulwell Farm

Fulwell

Wychwood Way

Fulwell Brake North

23

The Warren

Henley Knapp

Resr

Henel Buildings

1

Henel

Taston

Laurel Corner

B4026

TASTON RD

Middle Farm Plantation

B4022

David's Plantation

22

35

A

36

B

37

C

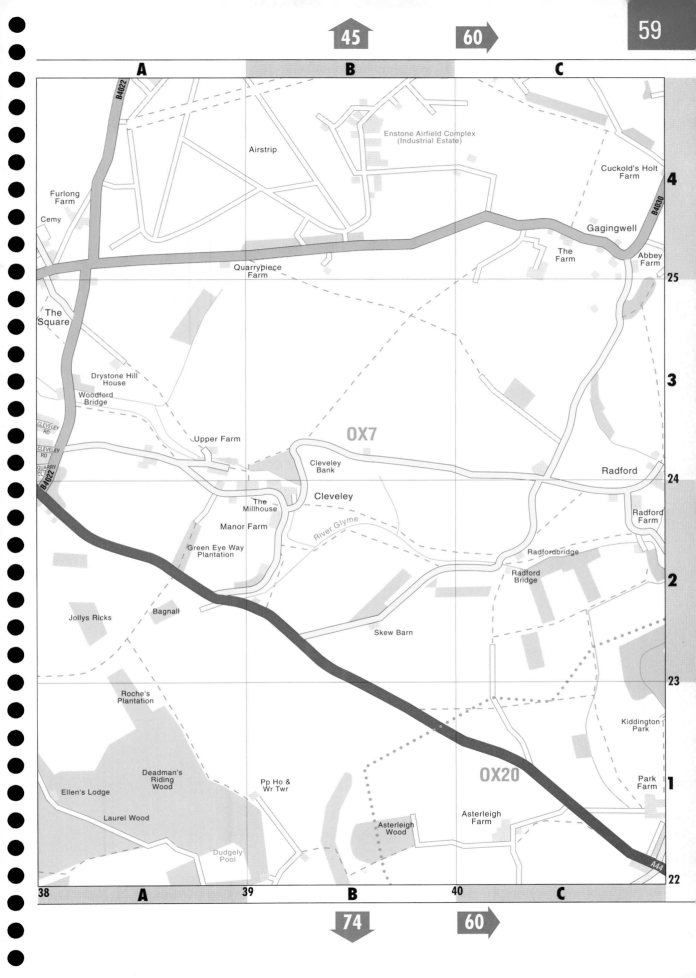

A
B
C

B4022

Airstrip

Enstone Airfield Complex
(Industrial Estate)

Cuckold's Holt
Farm

4

Furlong
Farm

Cemy

Gagingwell

The
Farm

B4030

Abbey
Farm

Quarrypiece
Farm

25

The
Square

Drystone Hill
House

3

Woodford
Bridge

CLEVELEY
RD

OX7

CLEVELEY
RD

Upper Farm

Cleveley
Bank

Radford

QUARRY
CL

B4022

24

Cleveley

The
Millhouse

Radford
Farm

Manor Farm

River Glyme

Radfordbridge

Green Eye Way
Plantation

Radford
Bridge

2

Jollys Ricks

Bagnall

Skew Barn

23

Roche's
Plantation

Kiddington
Park

Deadman's
Riding
Wood

Pp Ho &
Wr Twr

OX20

Park
Farm

1

Ellen's Lodge

Asterleigh
Farm

Laurel Wood

Asterleigh
Wood

Dudgely
Pool

A44

22

38
A
39
B
40
C

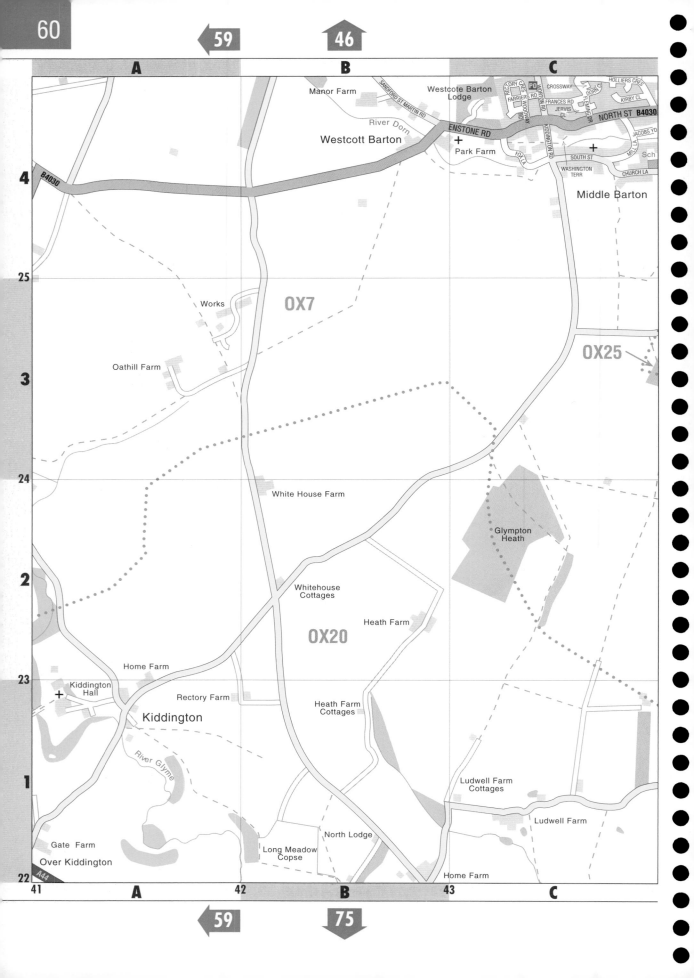

A B C

Manor Farm

Westcote Barton
Lodge

RECTORY CRES
FARRIERS RD
WOODWAY
WORTON RD
RECTORY RD
CROSSWAY
FRANCES RD
JERVIS CL
HOLLIERS CRES
KIRBY CL
DORN CL
FLEMING DR
NORTH ST B4030

River Dorn

ENSTONE RD

Westcott Barton

Park Farm

FOX LA
KIDDINGTON RD
SOUTH ST
WASHINGTON TERR
CHURCH LA
JACOBS YD
MILL LA
Sch

Middle Barton

B4030

4

Works

OX7

OX25

Oathill Farm

3

White House Farm

Glympton
Heath

24

Whitehouse
Cottages

2

Heath Farm

OX20

Home Farm

23

Kiddington
Hall

Rectory Farm

Heath Farm
Cottages

Kiddington

River Glyme

Ludwell Farm
Cottages

Ludwell Farm

1

Gate Farm

Over Kiddington

Long Meadow
Copse

North Lodge

Home Farm

22

A44

41 A 42 B 43 C

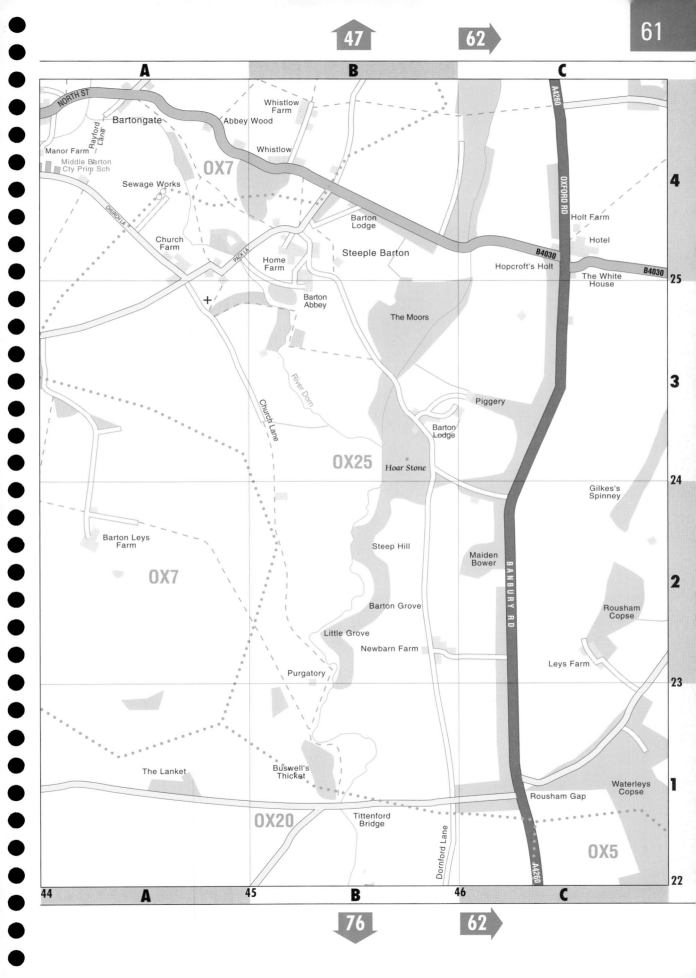

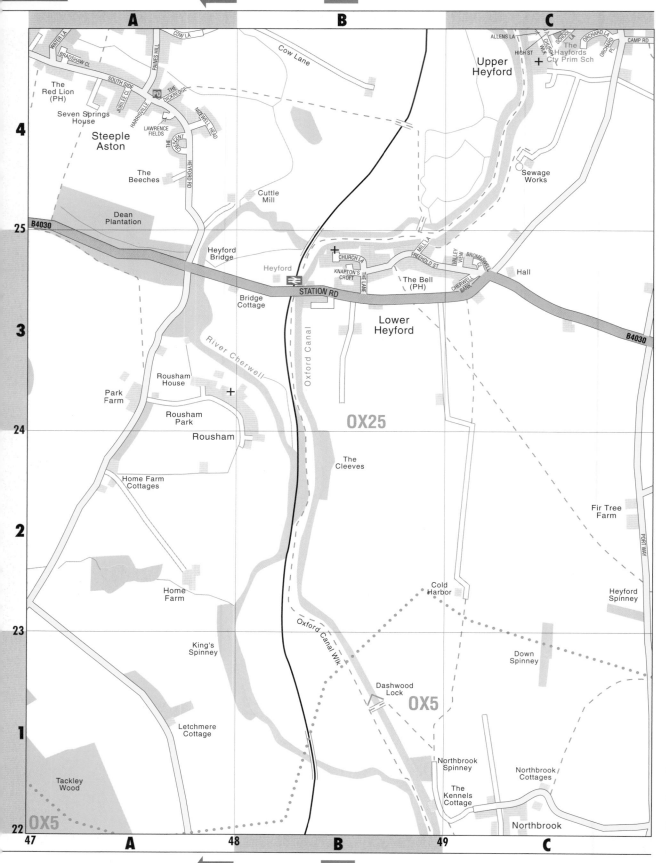

A

B

C

COW LA

WATER LA

BRADSHAW CL

PARKES HILL

SOUTH SIDE

HUBBLE CL

HARRISVILLE

The Dickredge

PO

THE CRESCENT

HEYFORD RD

NEWELL HEAD

LAWRENCE FIELDS

Cow Lane

ALLENS LA

HIGH ST

SCHOOL LA

CHURCH WLK

The Hayfords Cty Prim Sch

ORCHARD LA

ORCHARD PL

CAMP RD

Upper Heyford

The Red Lion (PH)

Seven Springs House

Steeple Aston

The Beeches

Cuttle Mill

Sewage Works

4

Dean Plantation

B4030

Heyford Bridge

Heyford

MILL LA

CHURCH LA

KNAPTON'S CROFT

THE LANE

FREEHOLD ST

VALLEY VIEW

BROMESWELL

CHERWELL BANK

Hall

25

Bridge Cottage

STATION RD

The Bell (PH)

B4030

River Cherwell

Lower Heyford

3

Rousham House

Park Farm

Rousham Park

Rousham

Oxford Canal

OX25

24

Home Farm Cottages

The Cleeves

Fir Tree Farm

2

Home Farm

Cold Harbor

Heyford Spinney

PORT WAY

Oxford Canal Wlk

King's Spinney

Down Spinney

23

Dashwood Lock

OX5

1

Letchmere Cottage

Northbrook Spinney

Northbrook Cottages

The Kennels Cottage

Tackley Wood

OX5

Northbrook

22

47

A

48

B

49

C

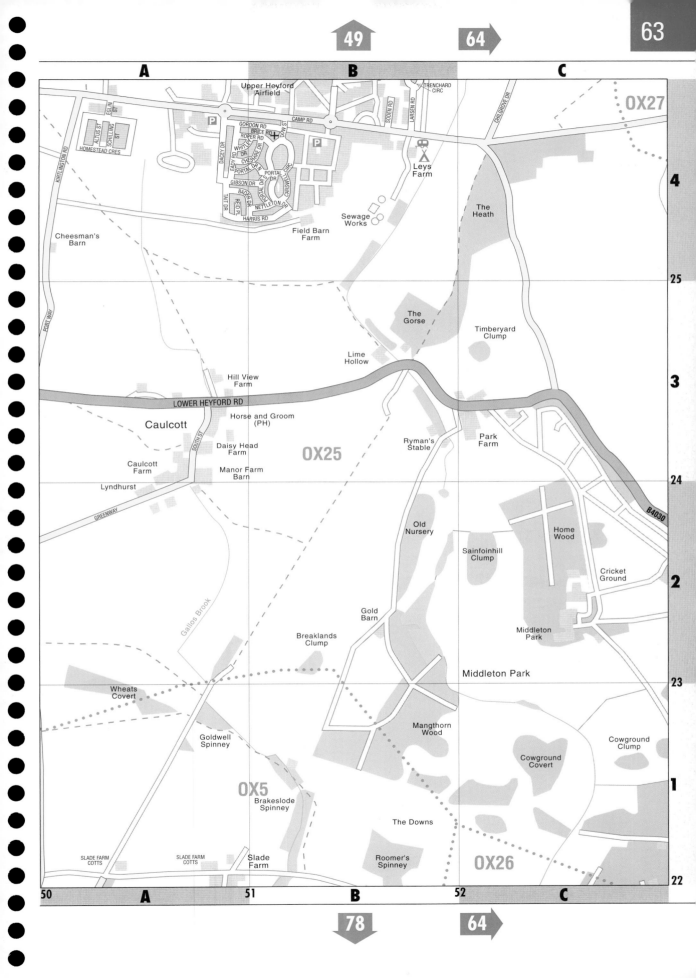

A   B   C

OX27

Upper Heyford
Airfield

TRENCHARD
CIRC

CAMP RD

SODEN RD

LARSEN RD

CHILGROVE DR

P
GORDON RD
BRICE RD
ROPER RD
DOW ST
EADY RD
WHITLEY
DR
CHESHIRE DR
PORTAL DR
GIBSON DR
DUXFORD
DR
CARSWELL CIRC
BADEN DR
NETTLETON DR
TAIT DR
RED PL
HARRIS RD
PORTAL DR

P

KIRTLINGTON RD

EGLIN ST
ALTUS ST
SCHILLING ST
HOMESTEAD CRES

DACEY DR

Leys
Farm

4

Cheesman's
Barn

Field Barn
Farm

Sewage
Works

The
Heath

PORT WAY

25

The Gorse

Timberyard
Clump

Lime
Hollow

Hill View
Farm

3

LOWER HEYFORD RD

Caulcott

Horse and Groom
(PH)

Ryman's
Stable

Park
Farm

B4030

SOUTH ST

Daisy Head
Farm

OX25

Caulcott
Farm

Manor Farm
Barn

Lyndhurst

Old
Nursery

Home
Wood

24

GREENWAY

Sainfoinhill
Clump

Cricket
Ground

2

Gallos Brook

Gold
Barn

Breaklands
Clump

Middleton
Park

Middleton Park

23

Wheats
Covert

Mangthorn
Wood

Cowground
Clump

Goldwell
Spinney

Cowground
Covert

OX5

1

Brakeslode
Spinney

The Downs

SLADE FARM
COTTS

SLADE FARM
COTTS

Slade
Farm

Roomer's
Spinney

OX26

22

50   A   51   B   52   C

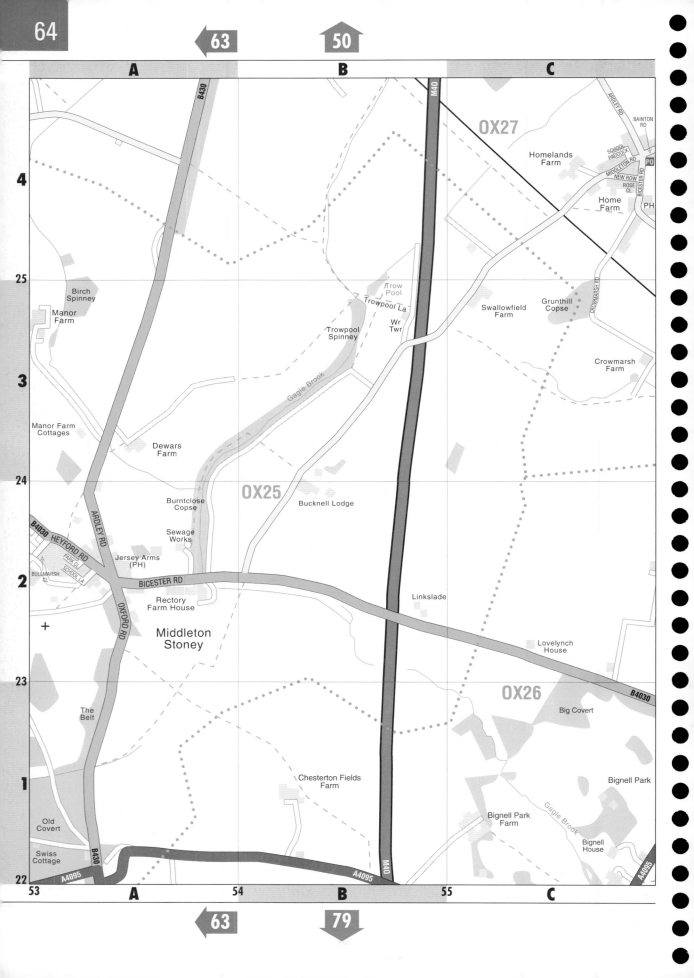

A   B   C

B430

OX27

Homelands Farm

ARDLEY RD

BAINTON RD

SCHOOL PADDOCK

MIDDLETON RD

BICESTER RD

NEW ROW

ROSE CL

PO

Home Farm

PH

4

Birch Spinney

Manor Farm

25

Trow Pool

Trowpool La

Wr Twr

Swallowfield Farm

Grunthill Copse

CROWMARSH RD

Trowpool Spinney

Crowmarsh Farm

Gagle Brook

3

Manor Farm Cottages

Dewars Farm

24

Burntclose Copse

OX25

Bucknell Lodge

B4030

HEYFORD RD

ARDLEY RD

PARK CL

SCHOOL LA

Sewage Works

BULLMARSH CL

Jersey Arms (PH)

2

BICESTER RD

Linkslade

Rectory Farm House

OXFORD RD

+

Middleton Stoney

Lovelynch House

23

OX26

B4030

The Belt

Big Covert

Chesterton Fields Farm

1

Bignell Park

Old Covert

Bignell Park Farm

Gagle Brook

Bignell House

Swiss Cottage

22

B430

A4095

M40

A4095

A4095

M40

53   A   54   B   55   C

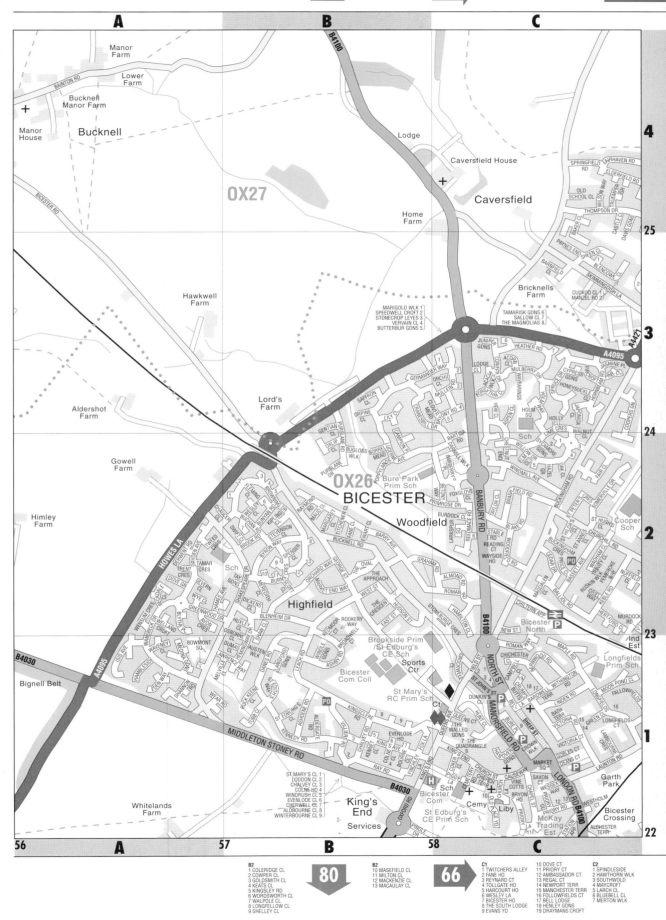

B2
1 COLERIDGE CL
2 COWPER CL
3 GOLDSMITH CL
4 KEATS CL
5 KINGSLEY RD
6 WORDSWORTH CL
7 WALPOLE CL
8 LONGFELLOW CL
9 SHELLEY CL

B2
10 MASEFIELD CL
11 MILTON CL
12 MACKENZIE CL
13 MACAULAY CL

C1
1 TWITCHERS ALLEY
2 FANE HO
3 REYNARD CT
4 TOLLGATE HO
5 HARCOURT HO
6 WESLEY LA
7 BICESTER HO
8 THE SOUTH LODGE
9 EVANS YD
10 DOVE CT
11 PRIORY CT
12 AMBASSADOR CT
13 REGAL CT
14 NEWPORT TERR
15 MANCHESTER TERR
16 FOLLOWFIELDS CT
17 BELL LODGE
18 HENLEY GDNS
19 DRAYMANS CROFT

C2
1 SPINDLESIDE
2 HAWTHORN WLK
3 SOUTHWOLD
4 MAYCROFT
5 LARCH CL
6 BLUEBELL CL
7 MERTON WLK

A	B	C

Dymock's Farm

Fringford Lodge

Hall

The Bradburys

West Farm

LAUNTON RD

Sewage Works

Brashfield House

BICESTER RD

The Kennels

4

FAIRHAVEN RD

WOLSCOTE RD

CHERWOOD HOUSE COTTS

Quarry

OX27

MONTGOMERY RD

HORNE

RAIL CT

THOMPSON DR

BOTT CL

HARMON CL

25

1 GRIFFITHS GDNS
2 MANZEL RD
3 SKIMMINGDISH LA

A4421

TURNPIKE RD

Airfield

3

A4421

SKIMMINGDISH RD

Field Barn

Bardwell Sch

24

ROCHFORD GDNS

CURTISS

BLACKBURN WLK

OTTERSTRAND

DUXFORD GDNS

SUNDERLAND DR

HENDON CL

LINCOLN CL

HARRIER WAY

DUXFORD GDNS

Glory Farm Sch

LEWICK CROFT

BICESTER

Cooper Sch

HART

IPL

FULMAR CT

BOSTON RD

OX26

WELLINGTON

ROY AL HALFAX

BRISTOL

LANCASTER CL

YORK

ANSON WAY

HAMPDEN

DEFIANT RISLEY

WHITLEY RES

BATTLE CL

ANWA UN

FAIRFX

CYPRESS RD

METEOR

MANSTON CL

TANGMERE CL

SCAMPTON CL

2

5

BENSON CL

A2
1 WARWICK CT
2 GAYDON WLK
3 HERALD WAY
4 SHACKLETON CL
5 LYSANDER CL
6 SPITFIRE CL
7 STERLING CL
8 BEAUFORT CL
9 MERTON WLK

Folly Cottage

LC

NUFFIELD WAY

STAN WLK

CHURCHILL RD

WEDGWOOD RD

ARKWRIGHT RD

TELFORD RD

JARVIS LA

LAUNTON RD

STATION RD

23

Launton Bsns Ctr

MURDOCK RD

GRANVILLE WAY

LC

CHARBRIDGE LA

Manor Farm

+

BICESTER RD

Launton CE Prim Sch

THE SPINNEY

THE GLADES

ANCIL AVE

SYCAMORE RD

BLENHEIM DR

Grange Farm

BESSEMER

FALLOWFIELDS

CHARBRIDGE WAY

Ind Est

FOREST CL

SHERWOOD CL

PO

SKINNER RD

LANES END

SHARPEY COTTS

BLACKTHORN RD

Tubb's Crossing

1

WHIMOREL CL

THE BRAMBLINGS

GAVRAY DR

CHARBRIDGE LA

1 MERGANSER DR
2 HERON CT
3 FALCON MEAD
4 SANDPIPER CL
5 THE BUNTINGS
6 GREBE RD

THE POPLARS

PH

THE GREEN

+

CORNFLOWER WAY

MALLARDS WAY

REDWING CL

DUNNOCK CL

Launton

PH

WEST END

WEST END CL

CHESTNUT CL

SISKIN

WOODPECKER CL

HERON DR

OSPREY CL

A4421

22

59	A	60	B	61	C

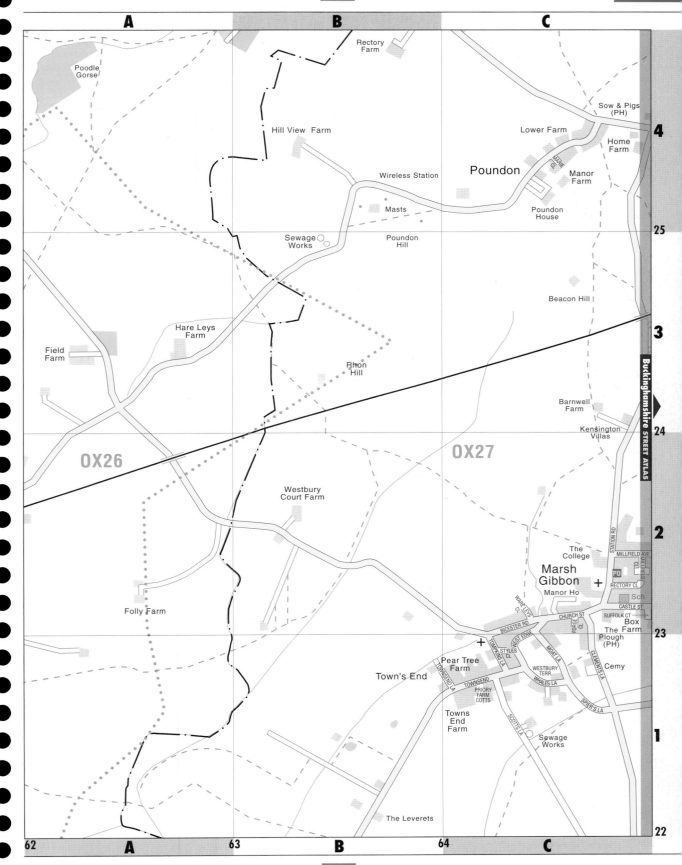

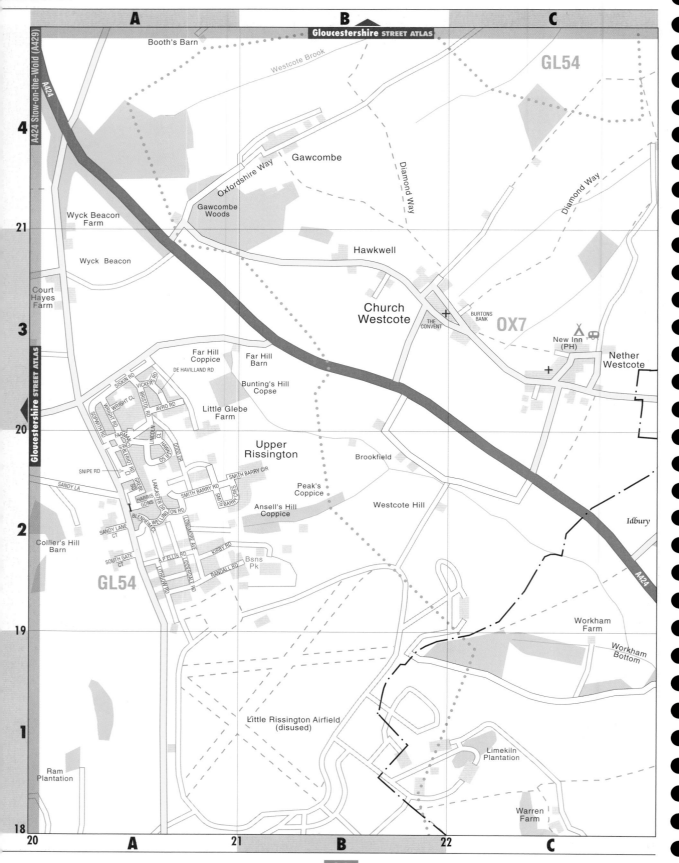

A B C

4

21

3

20

2

19

1

18

GL54

OX7

GL54

Booth's Barn

Westcote Brook

Gawcombe

Oxfordshire Way

Gawcombe Woods

Wyck Beacon Farm

Wyck Beacon

Court Hayes Farm

Diamond Way

Diamond Way

Hawkwell

Church Westcote

THE CONVENT

BURTONS BANK

New Inn (PH)

Nether Westcote

Far Hill Coppice

DE HAVILLAND RD

Far Hill Barn

Bunting's Hill Copse

Little Glebe Farm

SISKIN RD

VICKER RD

WRIGHT CL

BRISTOL RD

AVRO RD

SOPWITH RD

FARMAN

HAWKER CT

DODO DR

DOWDING CT

Upper Rissington

SNIPE RD

SANDY LA

GREBE CRES

BLERIOT RD

HARRIS GDNS

LANCASTER DR

WELLINGTON RD

SMITH BARRY RD

SMITH BARRY CRES

SMITH BARRY CIR

Peak's Coppice

Ansell's Hill Coppice

Brookfield

Westcote Hill

Idbury

A424 Stow-on-the-Wold (A429)

A424

Gloucestershire STREET ATLAS

Collier's Hill Barn

SANDY LANE CT

SOUTH GATE CT

A P ELLIS RD

LONGMORE AVE

BLENHEIM CT

LITHGOW RD

LUDGERSHALL RD

KIRBY RD

RANDALL RD

Bsns Pk

Workham Farm

Workham Bottom

A424

Little Rissington Airfield (disused)

Limekiln Plantation

Ram Plantation

Warren Farm

20 A 21 B 22 C

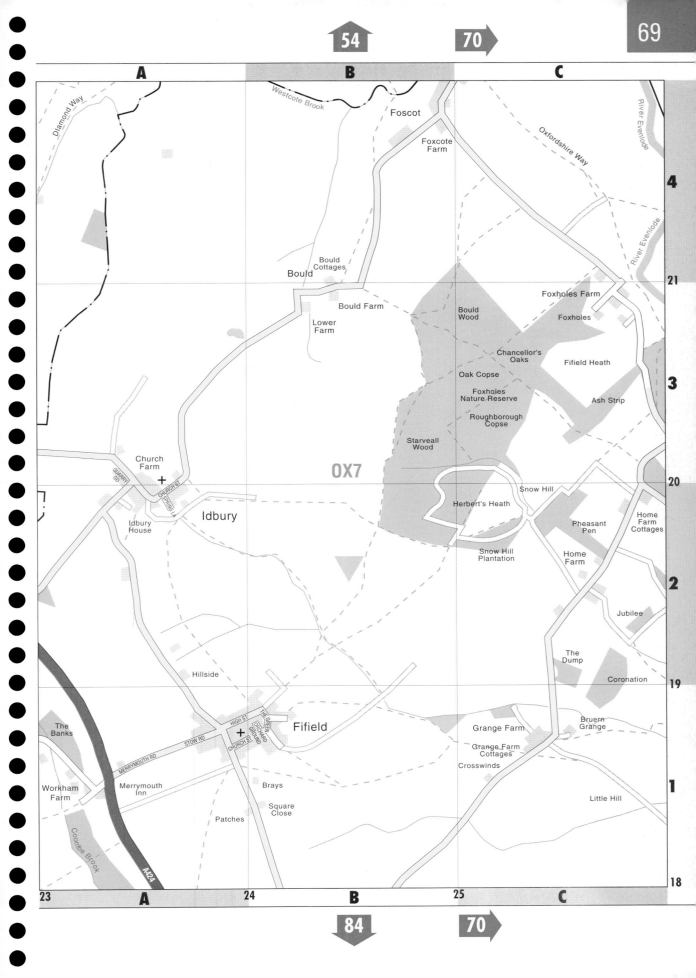

A
B
C

Diamond Way
Westcote Brook
Foscot
Foxcote Farm
Oxfordshire Way
River Evenlode

4

River Evenlode

Bould
Cottages
Bould
Bould Farm
Foxholes Farm
21
Lower
Farm
Bould Wood
Foxholes
Chancellor's
Oaks
Fifield Heath
Oak Copse
Foxholes
Nature Reserve
Ash Strip
3
Roughborough
Copse
Starveall
Wood

Church
Farm
OX7
Snow Hill
20
CHURCH ST
QUARRY RD
SPRING LA
Idbury House
Idbury
Herbert's Heath
Home
Farm
Cottages
Pheasant
Pen
Snow Hill
Plantation
Home
Farm
2
Jubilee

Hillside
The
Dump
Coronation
19

The
Banks
Fifield
Grange Farm
Bruern
Grange
HIGH ST
THE GREEN
ORCHARD
GROUND
Grange Farm
Cottages
STOW RD
CHURCH ST
Crosswinds
Workham
Farm
MERRYMOUTH RD
Merrymouth
Inn
Brays
Little Hill
1
Patches
Square
Close
Coombe Brook
A424

18
23
24
25

A
B
C

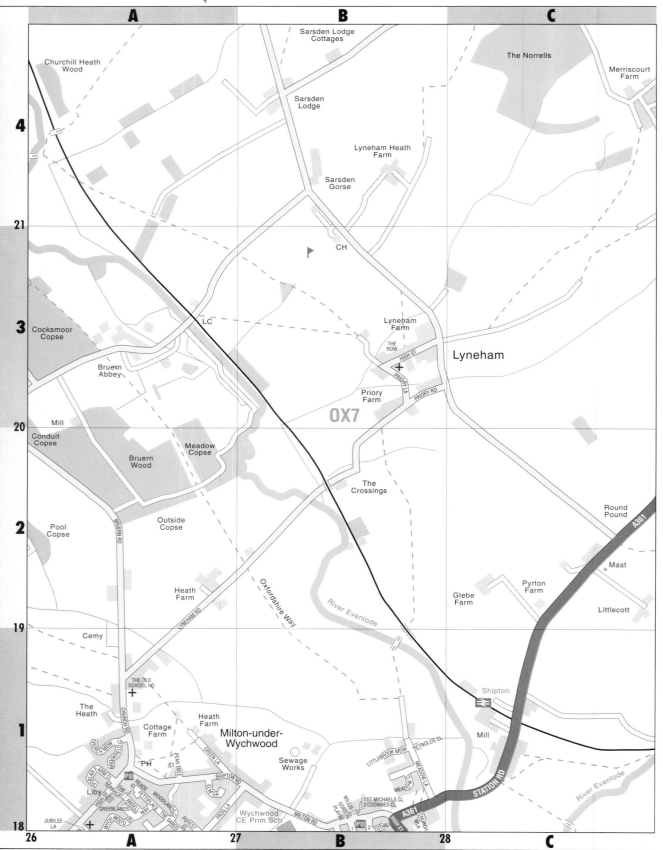

69
55
69
85

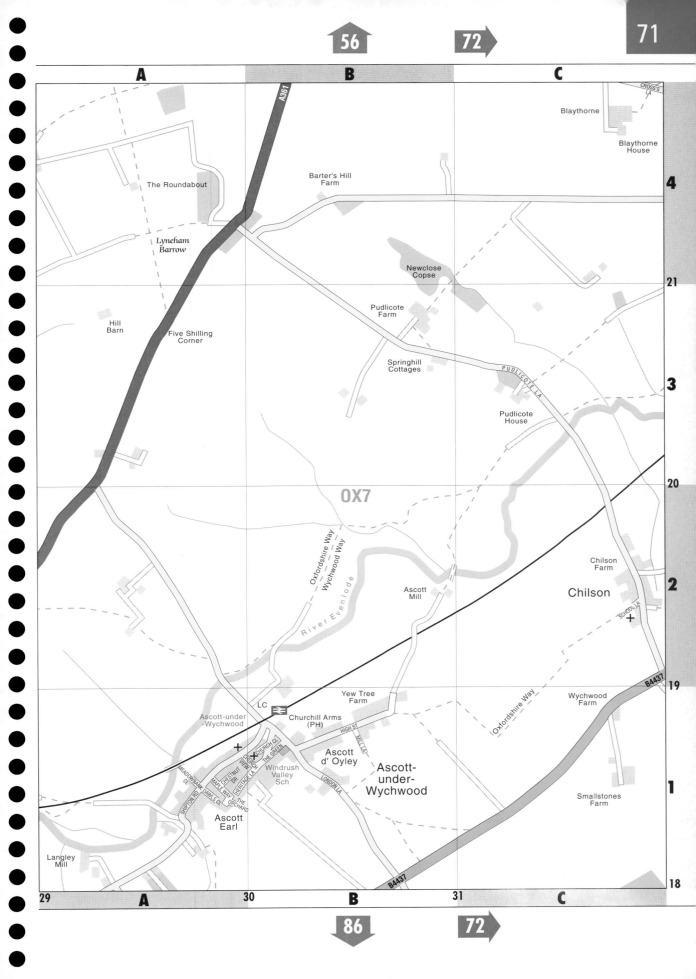

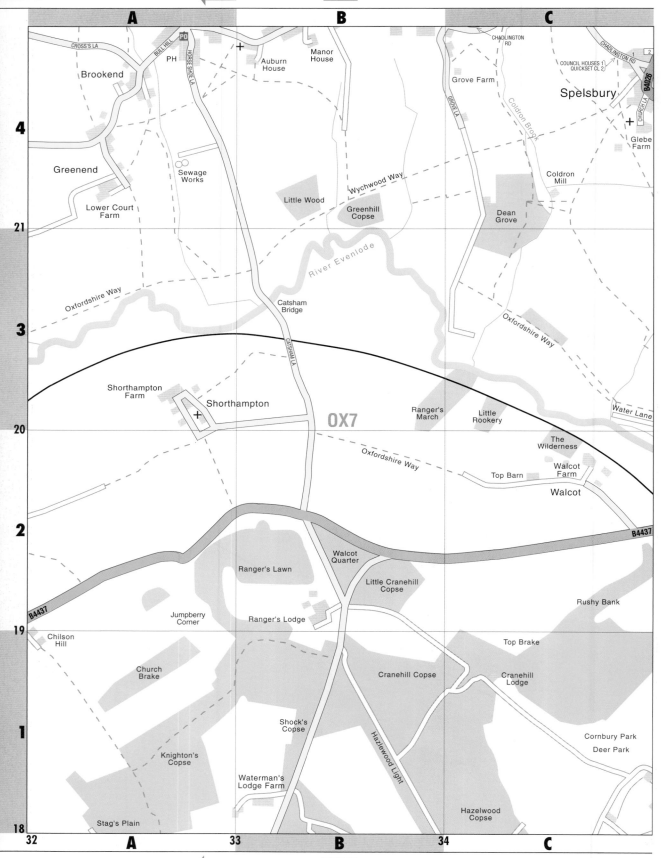

A   B   C

Brookend

CROSS'S LA

BULL HILL

PO

PH

HORSE SHOE LA

Auburn
House

Manor
House

CHADLINGTON
RD

COUNCIL HOUSES 1
QUICKSET CL 2

Grove Farm

Spelsbury

CHADLINGTON RD

B4026

CHURCH LA

B4026

Glebe
Farm

4

Greenend

Sewage
Works

Coldron Brook

GROVE LA

Coldron
Mill

Little Wood

Wychwood Way

Greenhill
Copse

Dean
Grove

21

Lower Court
Farm

River Evenlode

Oxfordshire Way

Catsham
Bridge

Oxfordshire Way

3

CATSHAM LA

Shorthampton
Farm

Shorthampton

OX7

Ranger's
March

Little
Rookery

Water Lane

20

The
Wilderness

Oxfordshire Way

Top Barn

Walcot
Farm

Walcot

2

Ranger's Lawn

Walcot
Quarter

Little Cranehill
Copse

Rushy Bank

B4437

B4437

Jumpberry
Corner

Ranger's Lodge

19

Chilson
Hill

Top Brake

Church
Brake

Cranehill Copse

Cranehill
Lodge

1

Shock's
Copse

Hazelwood Light

Cornbury Park
Deer Park

Knighton's
Copse

Waterman's
Lodge Farm

Hazelwood
Copse

18

Stag's Plain

32   A   33   B   34   C

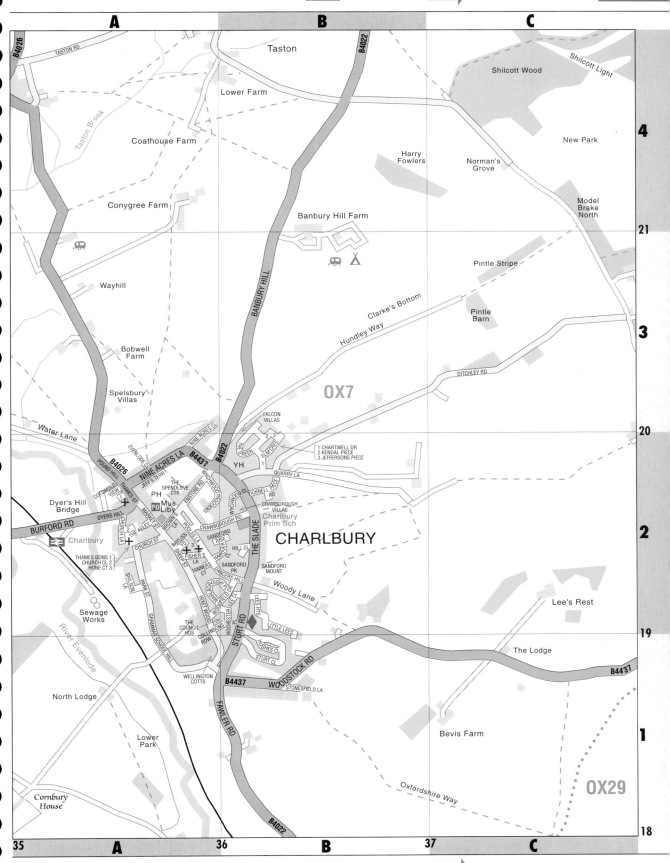

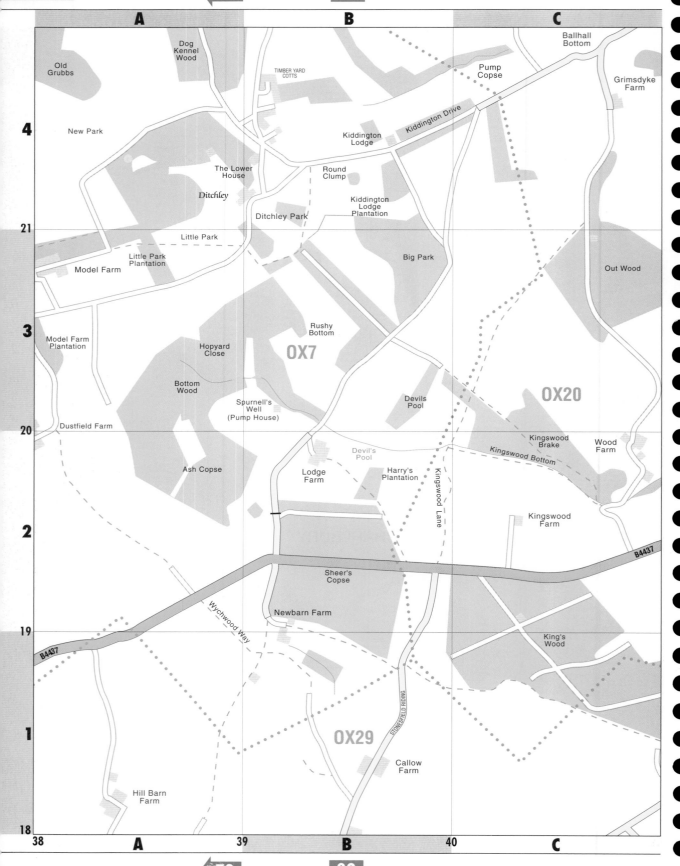

A
B
C

4

Old Grubbs

Dog Kennel Wood

TIMBER YARD COTTS

New Park

Pump Copse

Ballhall Bottom

Grimsdyke Farm

Kiddington Lodge

Kiddington Drive

The Lower House

Round Clump

Ditchley

Kiddington Lodge Plantation

21

Ditchley Park

Little Park

Big Park

Out Wood

Little Park Plantation

Model Farm

3

Model Farm Plantation

Rushy Bottom

Hopyard Close

OX7

Bottom Wood

Spurnell's Well (Pump House)

Devils Pool

OX20

20

Dustfield Farm

Kingswood Brake

Wood Farm

Ash Copse

Lodge Farm

Devil's Pool

Kingswood Bottom

Harry's Plantation

Kingswood Lane

Kingswood Farm

2

B4437

Sheer's Copse

Wychwood Way

Newbarn Farm

19

B4437

King's Wood

STONESFIELD RIDING

1

OX29

Callow Farm

Hill Barn Farm

18

38
A
39
B
40
C

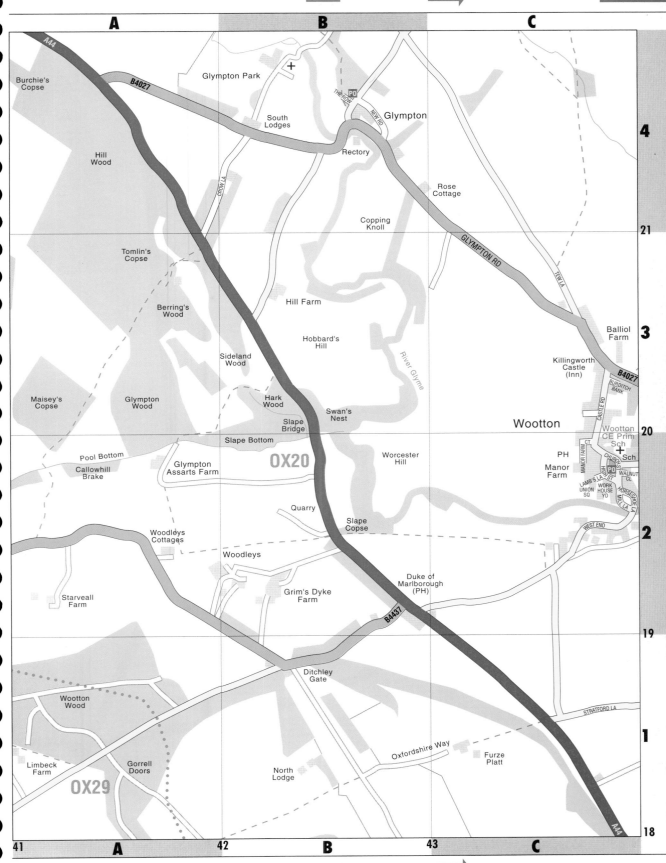

75
61

A   B   C

4

21

3

20

OX20

OX5

2

19

1

18

44   A   45   B   46   C

Woottondown Farm

Upper Dornford Farm

Upper Dornford Cottages

Woottondown Cottages

Tackley Heath

Old Man Leys Cottage

Old Man Leys

Holly Bank

River Dorn

Lower Dornford Farm

Dornford Lane

Dornford Grove

B4027

MARRIOTT CL
MILFORD PL
DORN VIEW

Home Farm

Milford Bridge

Snakestail Clump

BANBURY RD

Hordley Farm

River Glyme

Oxfordshire Way

Sturdy's Castle (PH)

Sansoms Cottage

Sansom's Farm

STRATFORD LA

Stratford Bridge

Sansom's Platt

Upper Weaveley Farm

Sansoms Lane

Old Weaveley Farm

B4027

Field Barn

Weaveley Farm

Weaveley Furze

A4260

A4260

BANBURY RD

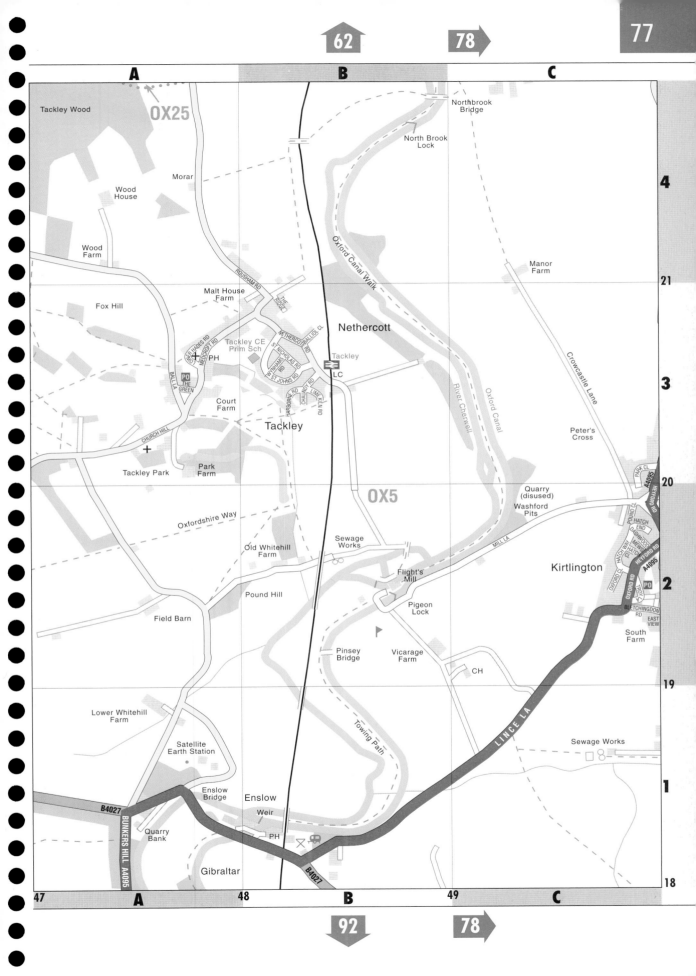

62
78
78

A   B   C

4
21
3
20
2
19
1
18

Tackley Wood

OX25

Morar

Wood House

Wood Farm

Fox Hill

ROUSHAM RD

Malt House Farm

THE RIDGE

NETHERCOTT RD

BALLIOL CL

Nethercott

Northbrook Bridge

North Brook Lock

Oxford Canal Walk

Manor Farm

Crowcastle Lane

LONG HAODS RD

METCROFT RD

Tackley CE Prim Sch

ST NICHOLAS RD

TWYNHAMS RD

ST JOHNS RD

PH

BALL LA

PO THE GREEN

CHURCH HILL

Court Farm

HARBORNE RD

CHAUNDY RD

LIME KILN RD

Tackley
LC

Tackley

River Cherwell

Oxford Canal

Peter's Cross

Park Farm

Tackley Park

Park Farm

Oxfordshire Way

OX5

Old Whitehill Farm

Sewage Works

Quarry (disused)
Washford Pits

PARK CL

A4095

HEYFORD RD

POUND CL

HATCH END

DISHWOOD CL

HATCH WAY

MEADOW CL

HEYFORD RD

A4095

OXFORD CL

OXFORD RD

Kirtlington

PO

Pound Hill

Field Barn

Flight's Mill

MILL LA

BLETCHINGDON RD

EAST VIEW

South Farm

Pigeon Lock

Pinsey Bridge

Vicarage Farm

CH

LINCE LA

Lower Whitehill Farm

Satellite Earth Station

Towing Path

Sewage Works

Enslow Bridge

Enslow

Weir

PH

B4027

BUNKERS HILL A4095

Quarry Bank

Gibraltar

B4027

47   48   49

A   B   C

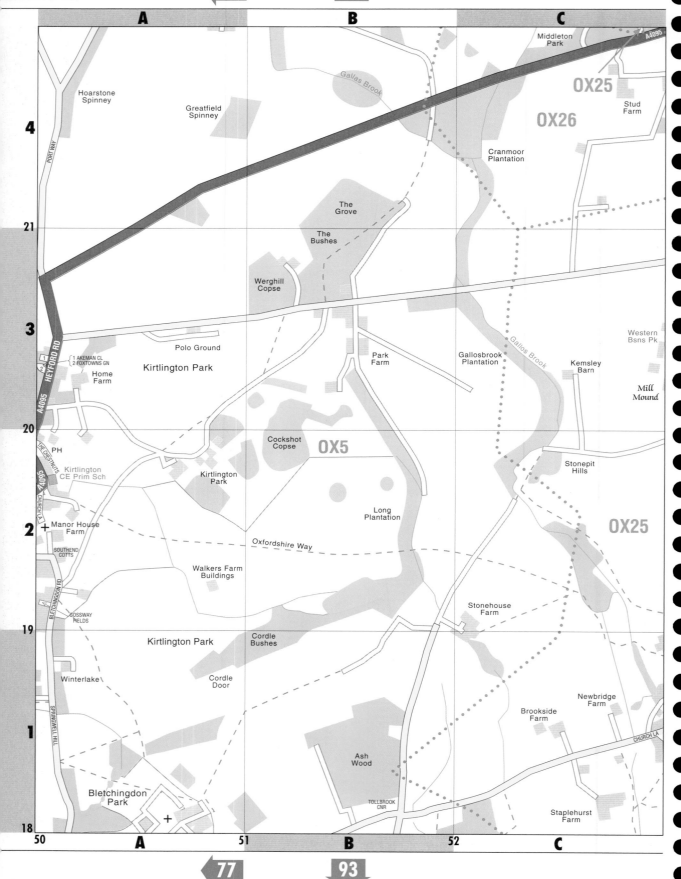

A   B   C

Middleton Park

OX25

OX26

Hoarstone Spinney

Greatfield Spinney

Gallas Brook

Stud Farm

Cranmoor Plantation

4

21

The Grove

The Bushes

Werghill Copse

Western Bsns Pk

3

PORT WAY

HEYFORD RD

Polo Ground

Park Farm

Gallosbrook Plantation

Gallos Brook

Kemsley Barn

Mill Mound

1 AKEMAN CL
2 FOXTOWNS GN

Home Farm

Kirtlington Park

20

A4095

PH

THE CHESTNUTS

A4095

CHURCH LA

Kirtlington CE Prim Sch

Kirtlington Park

Cockshot Copse

OX5

Long Plantation

Stonepit Hills

OX25

2

Manor House Farm

SOUTHEND COTTS

Oxfordshire Way

Walkers Farm Buildings

BLETCHINGDON RD

GOSSWAY FIELDS

19

Kirtlington Park

Cordle Bushes

Stonehouse Farm

Winterlake

Cordle Door

Newbridge Farm

Brookside Farm

1

SPRINGWELL HILL

Ash Wood

CHURCH LA

Bletchingdon Park

TOLLBROOK CNR

Staplehurst Farm

18

50   A   51   B   52   C

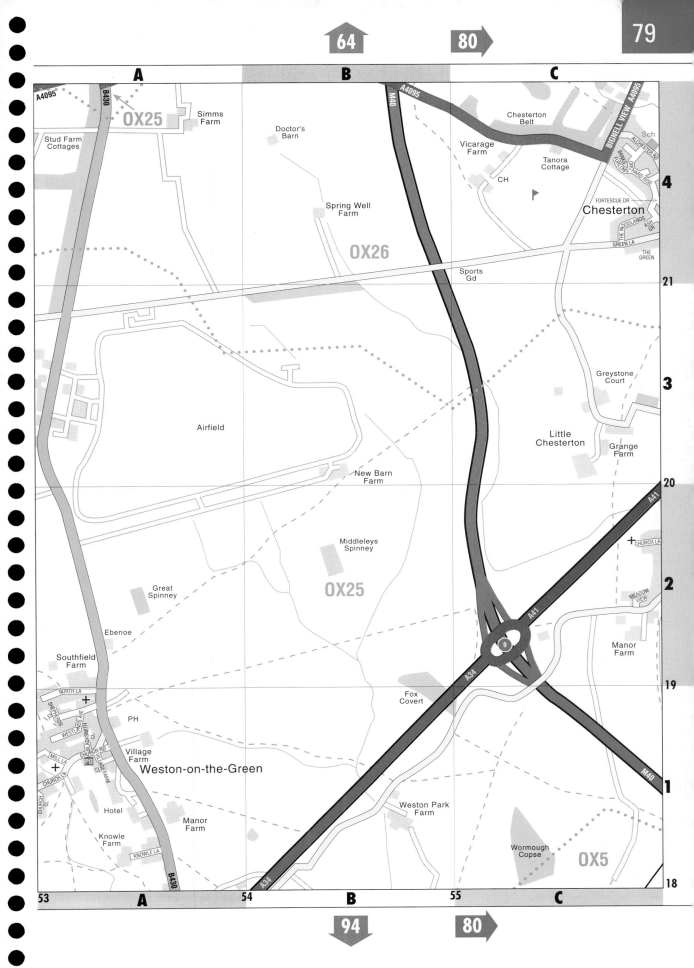

79
65

A

B

C

4

21

OX26

3

20

OX25

2

19

1

OX5

18

Home
Farm

Gagle Brook

ALCHESTER RD

1 TUBBS YD
2 FORTESCUE DR
3 CHESTNUT CL

TUBBS LA

GREEN
LA

The Red
Cow
(PH)

Chesterton
Lodge

Foxey Leys
Copse

OXFORD RD

B4030

A41

PINGLE DR

Recn Gd

McKay
Trad Est

Bicester Village
Ret Park

Bicester
Town

B4100

TALISMAN RD

LONDON RD

The
Talisman
Bsns Ctr

MARTIN CL

A41

Langford
Park
Farm

Rodney
House

Lodge
Farm

Wendlebury
Farm

Works

Promised
Land
Farm

LCs

CIRCULAR RD

Depot

Graven Hill

Gravenhill
Wood

Bowler's
Copse

A41

LC

Langford La

LANGFORD LA

Alchester
ROMAN TOWN
(site of)

RECTORY CL

Old Rectory
Ct

CHURCH LA

Red Lion
(PH)

Elm Tree
Farm

ST GILES
CL

FARRIER'S
MEAD

Wendlebury

College
Farm

Langford Lane

Merton
Grounds

M40

Astley
Bridge
Cottage

56

57

58

A

B

C

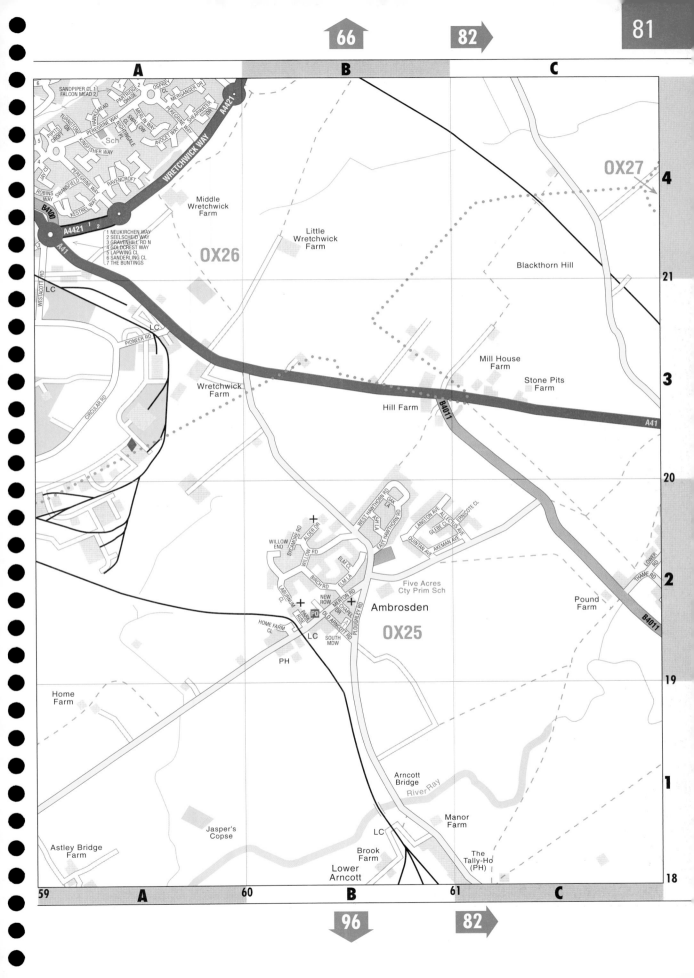

81
67

A **B** **C**

OX26

Marsh-Field
Farm

Yew Elm
Farm

4

Furze
Ground

OX27

21

Essex
Farm

Oakapple
Farm

Grange
Farm

3

Blackthorn

A41

Heath
Bridge

River Ray

Weir
Farm

WEIR LA

20

Westbury
Farm

LOWER R RD

Leaches
Farm

A41

A41 Aylesbury

STATION RD

Elm Tree
Farm

Lower
Cow Leys
Farm

2 BLACKTHORN
CL

EAST VIEW

Shaw's
Farm

Piddington
Cow Leys

THAME RD

Royal Oak
(PH)

OX25

Middle
Cow Leys
Farm

B4011

19

Blackthorn
Bridge

Bridge
Farm

Upper
Cow Leys
Farm

Treadwell's
Barn

1

HP18

New Farm

B4011

18
62 **A** 63 **B** 64 **C**

Buckinghamshire STREET ATLAS

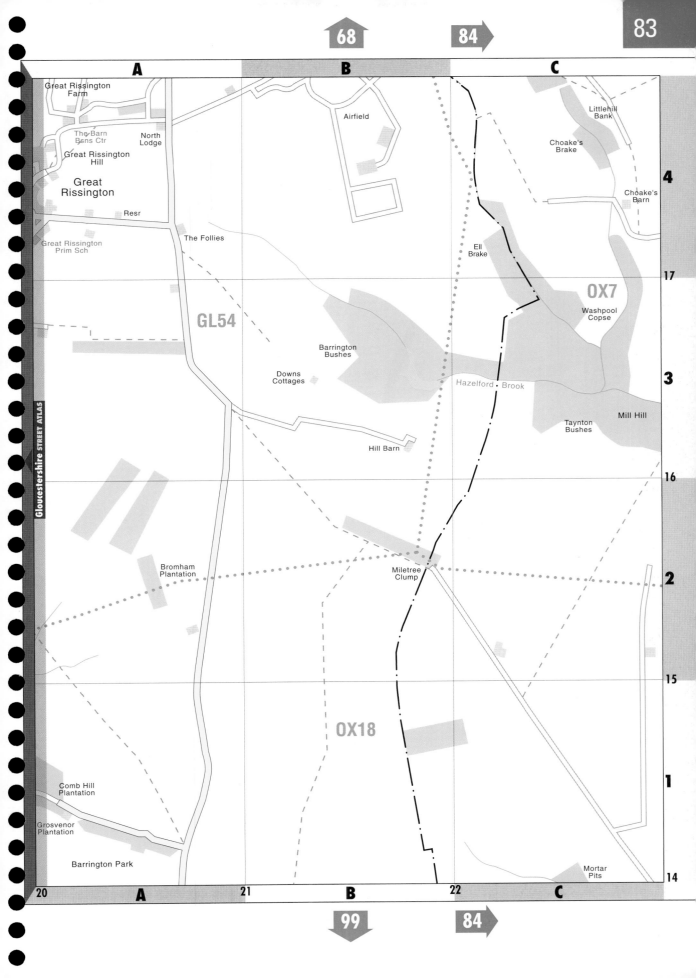

A

B

C

Great Rissington Farm

The Barn Bsns Ctr

North Lodge

Great Rissington Hill

Great Rissington

Resr

Great Rissington Prim Sch

The Follies

Airfield

Littlehill Bank

Choake's Brake

Choake's Barn

4

Ell Brake

17

GL54

OX7

Barrington Bushes

Washpool Copse

Downs Cottages

Hazelford Brook

3

Taynton Bushes

Mill Hill

Hill Barn

16

Bromham Plantation

Miletree Clump

2

15

OX18

Comb Hill Plantation

1

Grosvenor Plantation

Barrington Park

Mortar Pits

14

20

A

21

B

22

C

A B C

4

Coombe's Copse

Barrett's Brake

Tangley Woods

Hill Farm Cottage

Hill Farm

High Lodge Farm

Upper Milton

Manor Farm

17

Tangley Farm

Tangley Farm Cottages

Tangley Hall

Long Copse

Hop Copse

Springhill Farm

3

Habber Gallows Hill

OX7

Camsden Copse

Crow's Castle Hill

Old Quarries Plantation

16

Crow's Castle

Quarry Hill Cottage

Milton Downs Farm

2

Hazelford Bridge

Coombe Brook

Blackheath Clump

Milton Down

Taynton Down

Hill Barn

15

Blackheath Bungalow

1

OX18

Dean Bottom

Lower Farm

A424

14

23 A 24 B 25 C

A424

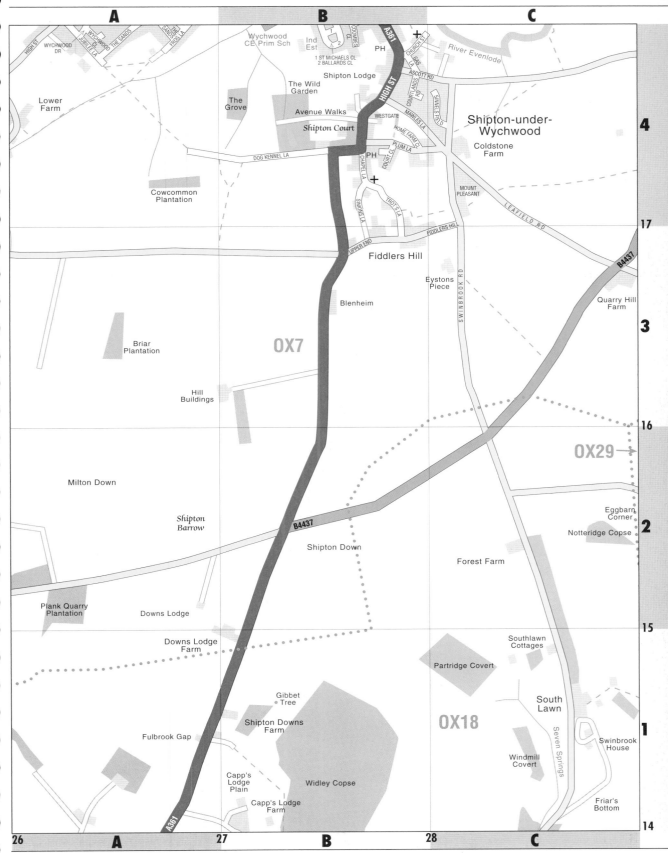

85
71

A   B   C

B4437

Wychwood Manor

Fernhill Farm

Coldwell Brook

OX7

Coldwell Bridge

4

Wychwood Way

Boynal Copse

Kingstanding Farm

Brasswell Corner

B4437

17

Priest Grove

Woefield Green

Kingswood Clump

Fairspear Farm

LEAFIELD RD

3

Langley Holding Cottage

The Grove

Fairspear Farm

Fairspear House

Farfield Corner

Homefield Spinney

Limekiln Spinney

16

OX29

Langley Farm

Mast •

Langley

Leafield Tech Ctr

Chimney-end

Bramington Farm

FAIRSPEAR RD

Mast •

PH

CHAPEL CL

Church Farm

2

Leafield CE Sch

RIDINGS BGLWS

PO

WITNEY LA

Leafield

15

Potter's Hill Farm

Potter's Hill

Ridings Farm

THE RIDING

1

OX18

Buttermilk House

BUTTERMILK LA

Wastidge Spinney

Lowbarrow

Leafield Pig Farm

Hill Farm

Fordwells Farm Barns

PURRANTS LA

14

29   A   30   B   31   C

85
102

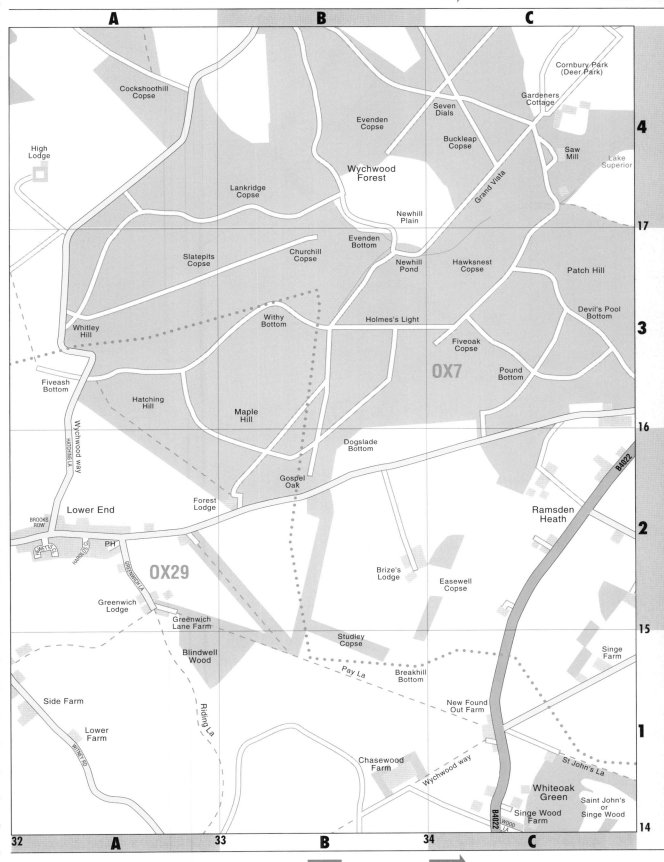

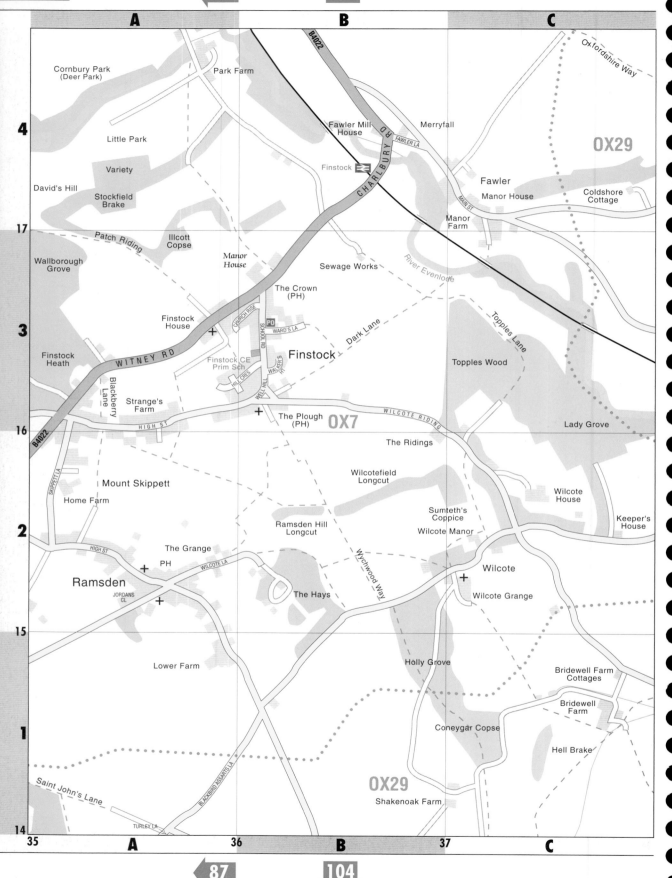

87 73

A   B   C

Cornbury Park
(Deer Park)

Park Farm

B4022

Fawler Mill
House

Merryfall

4

Little Park

FAWLER LA

Fawler

OX29

David's Hill

Variety

Finstock

CHARLBURY RD

Manor House

Coldshore
Cottage

Stockfield
Brake

MAIN ST

Manor
Farm

17

Patch Riding

Illcott Copse

Manor
House

Sewage Works

River Evenlode

Wallborough
Grove

The Crown
(PH)

Topples Lane

3

Finstock House

CHURCH RISE

SCHOOL RD

WARD'S LA

Dark Lane

Finstock
Heath

PO

Finstock

Topples Wood

WITNEY RD

Blackberry
Lane

Finstock CE
Prim Sch

HILL CRES

WELL HILL

WALKER'S

Strange's
Farm

WILCOTE RIDING

16

B4022

HIGH ST

The Plough
(PH)

OX7

Lady Grove

The Ridings

Wilcotefield
Longcut

Wilcote
House

SKIPPETT LA

Mount Skippett

Sumteth's
Coppice

Wilcote Manor

Keeper's
House

2

Home Farm

HIGH ST

The Grange

PH

WILCOTE LA

Ramsden Hill
Longcut

Wychwood Way

Wilcote

Ramsden

JORDANS
CL

The Hays

Wilcote Grange

15

Lower Farm

Holly Grove

Bridewell Farm
Cottages

Bridewell
Farm

1

Coneygar Copse

Hell Brake

BLACKBIRD ASSARTS LA

Saint John's Lane

OX29

Shakenoak Farm

TURLEY LA

14

35   A   36   B   37   C

87 104

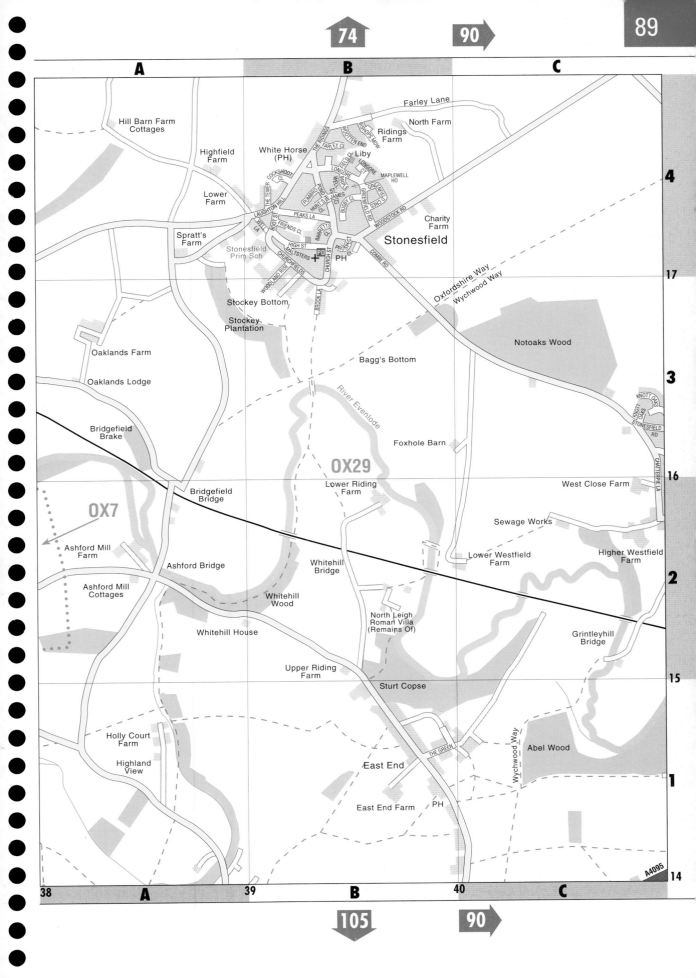

74
90

A B C

Farley Lane

Hill Barn Farm
Cottages

North Farm

Highfield
Farm

Ridings
Farm

White Horse
(PH)

Liby

Lower
Farm

MAPLEWELL
HO

4

Spratt's
Farm

Charity
Farm

Stonesfield
Prim Sch

Stonesfield

17

Stockey Bottom

Oxfordshire Way

Wychwood Way

Stockey
Plantation

Oaklands Farm

Bagg's Bottom

Notoaks Wood

3

Oaklands Lodge

River Evenlode

KNOTT OAKS

Bridgefield
Brake

OX29

Foxhole Barn

STONESFIELD RD

CHATTERPIE LA

16

OX7

Lower Riding
Farm

West Close Farm

Bridgefield
Bridge

Ashford Mill
Farm

Sewage Works

Ashford Bridge

Whitehill
Bridge

Lower Westfield
Farm

Higher Westfield
Farm

2

Ashford Mill
Cottages

Whitehill
Wood

Whitehill House

North Leigh
Roman Villa
(Remains Of)

Grintleyhill
Bridge

Upper Riding
Farm

15

Sturt Copse

Holly Court
Farm

Abel Wood

Wychwood Way

Highland
View

East End

1

East End Farm

PH

A B C

A4095

14

38 39 40

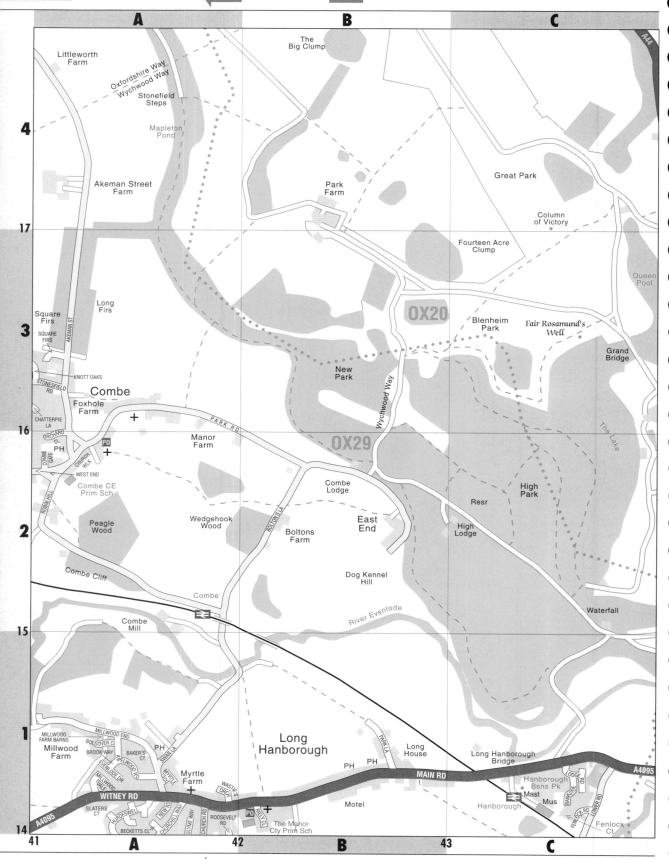

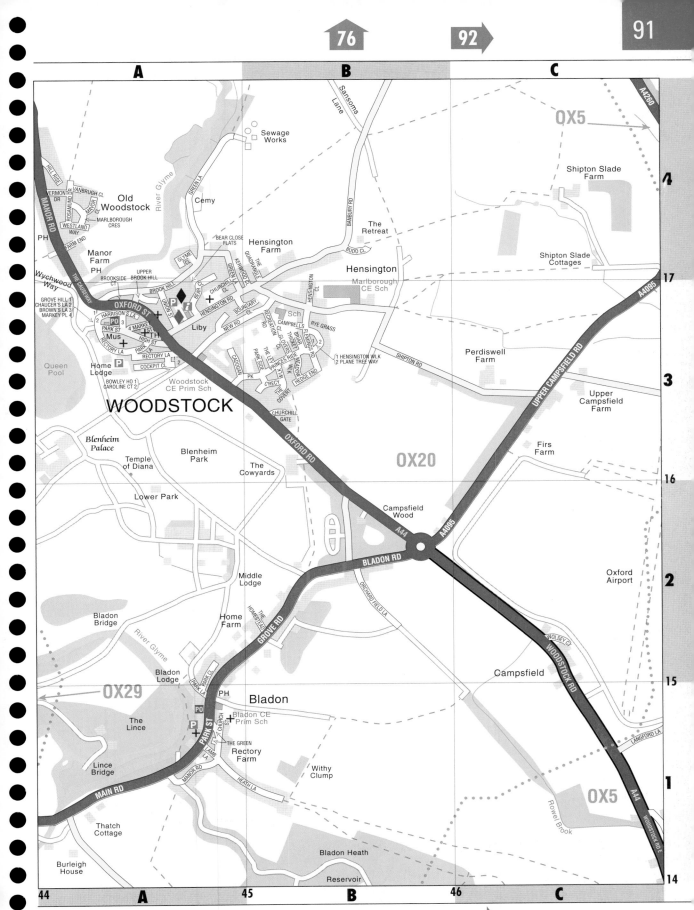

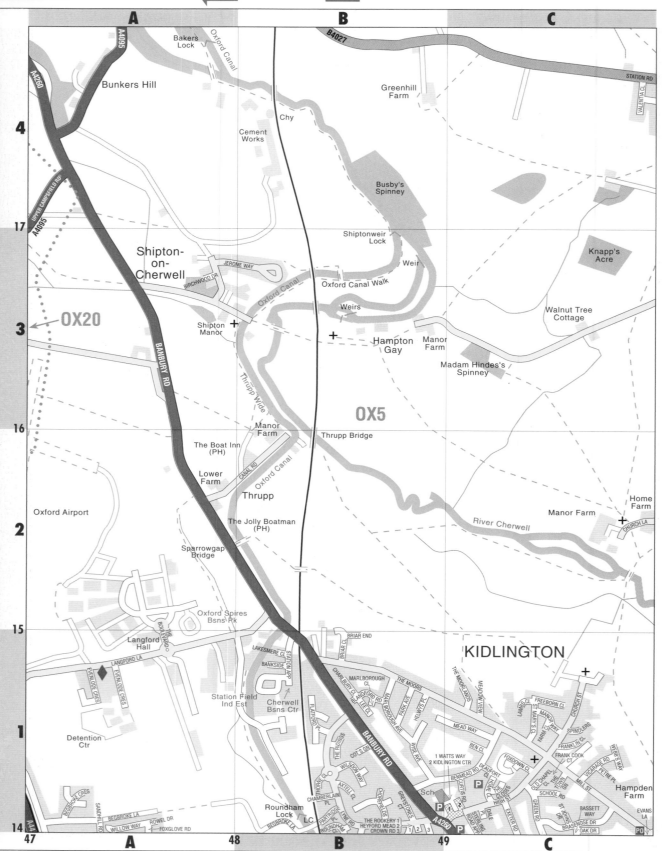

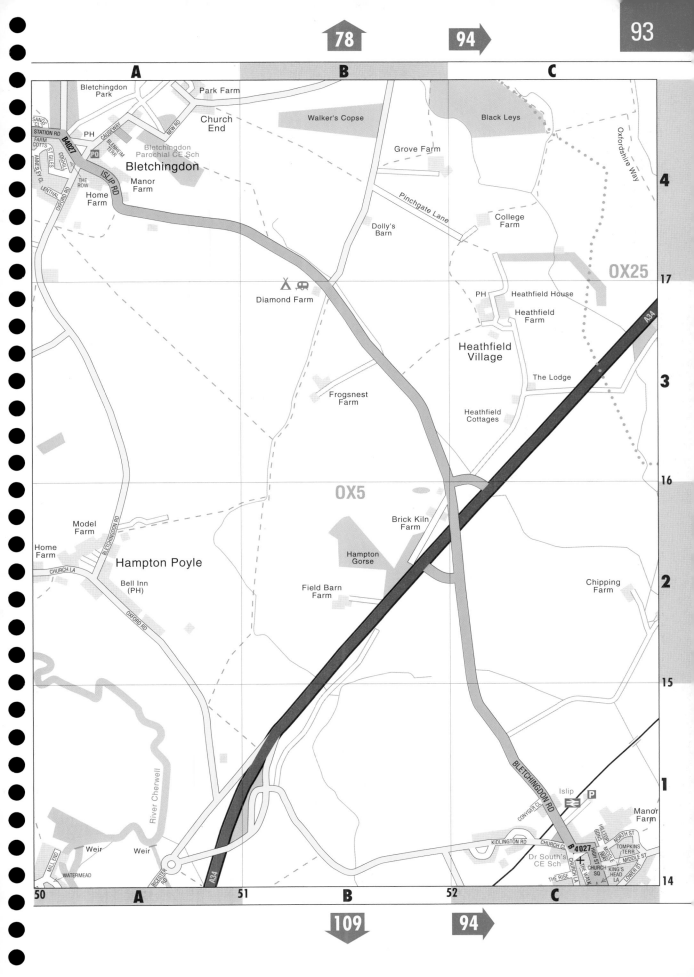

93
79

A   B   C

The Chequers Inn (PH)

B430

A34

Weston Wood

Holts Farm

LC

MANSMOOR RD

4

OX25

Gallos Brook

A34

17

Family Farm

Oddington Wood

Rowles Farm

Oddington Grange

3

Barndon Farm

New House Farm

16

LC

Oxfordshire Way

OX5

RAY VIEW

HIGH ST

2

Brookfurlong Farm

Hillcroft Farm

Otter House

COLLEGE FARM CL

15

Oddington

Rectory Farm   +

New River Ray

1

Logg Farm

River Ray

OX3

14

53   A   54   B   55   C

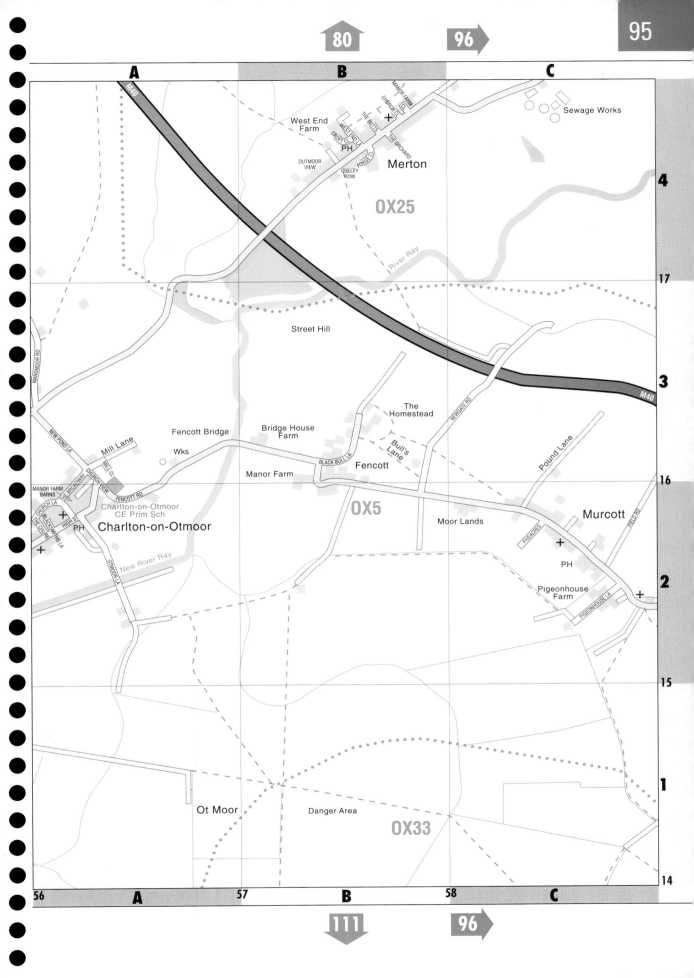

80
96

A   B   C

M40

Sewage Works

MANOR FARM CL
CHURCH CL
West End Farm
THE BUTTS
WEST END LA
CROFT CL
THE ORCHARD
PH
FORGE CL
OUTMOOR VIEW
GULLEY ROW

Merton

OX25

4

River Ray

17

Street Hill

3

M40

The Homestead

NEWGATE RD

Bridge House Farm

Fencott Bridge

BLACK BULL LA

Pound Lane

MANSMOOR RD

NEW POND LA

Mill Lane

Wks

Bull's Lane

Fencott

16

Manor Farm

MILL CL

CHURCH VIEW

FENCOTT RD

OX5

Murcott

FIELD RD

MANOR FARM BARNS
THE BROADWAY
Charlton-on-Otmoor CE Prim Sch

Moor Lands

FIVEACRES

CHURCH LA
BLACKSMITHS LA
HIGH ST
PH
THE CHURE
Charlton-on-Otmoor

PH

Pigeonhouse Farm

PIGEONHOUSE LA

2

OTMOOR LA

New River Ray

15

Ot Moor

Danger Area

1

OX33

56   A   57   B   58   C

14

95
81

A   **B**   **C**

Astley Bridge
Farm

LC

The Plough
(PH)

PALMER AVE

River Ray

LC

LC

Depot

Upper Arncott

Arncott Hill

4

PATRICK HAUGH RD

NORRIS RD

PLOUGHLEY RD

GREEN LA

YALE

MILL HILL

CSIDE CL

BUCHANAN RD

HOPCROFT CL

CONSTABLE'S CROFT

CH

HARPER CL DS

GREENFLDS

WOODPIECE RD

Arncott Hill
Wood

17

LCs

OX25

MURCOTT RD

Arncott Hill
Farm

LC

Depot

LC

LC

ARNCOTT WOOD RD

3

M40

PRRM RD

LC

LC

Boarstall Lane

16

New Park
Farm

Red House
Farm

Murcott

OX5

Oldhouse
Spinney

Marlake
House

Latchmeads

2

Four Winds
Farm

Whitecross Green

Panshill Farms

Pans Hill

15

Manor
Farm

Upper Panshill
Farm

HP18

Whitecross Green Wood
Nature Reserve

1

OX33

M40

Upper
Wood

Oriel Wood

14

59   **A**   60   **B**   61   **C**

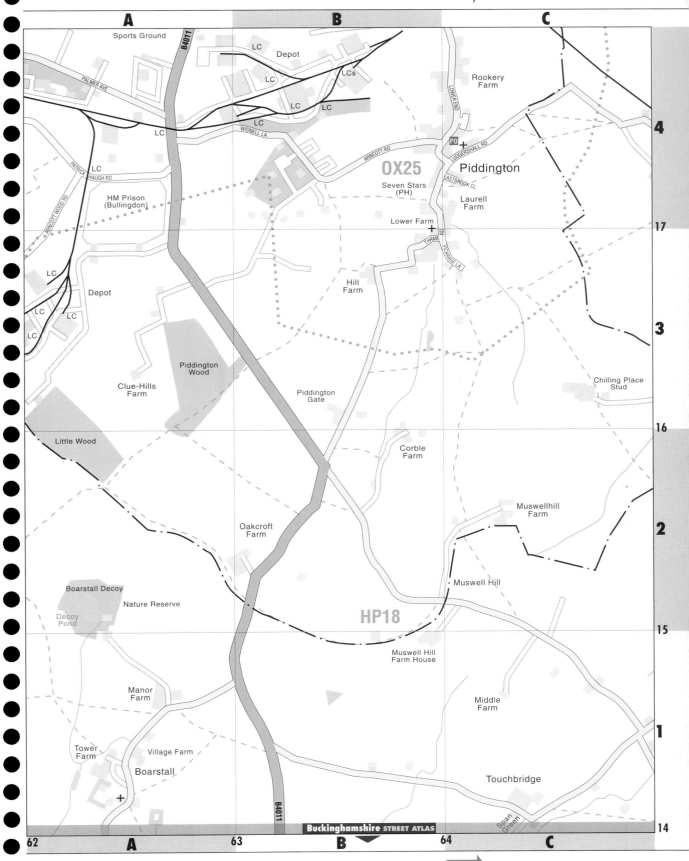

Sports Ground

A

B

C

PALMER AVE

B4011

LC

Depot

LC

LCs

LC

LC

LC

WIDNELL LA

LC

ARNCOTT RD

Rookery Farm

LOWER END

LUDGERSHALL RD

PO

4

PATRICK HAUGH RD

LC

HM Prison
(Bullingdon)

OX25

Seven Stars
(PH)

EASTBROOK CL

Piddington

Laurell
Farm

ARNCOTT WOOD RD

Lower Farm

17

THAME RD

VICARAGE LA

LC

Depot

Hill
Farm

LC

LC

LC

Clue-Hills
Farm

Piddington
Wood

Piddington
Gate

Chilling Place
Stud

3

Little Wood

16

Corble
Farm

Muswellhill
Farm

Oakcroft
Farm

2

Boarstall Decoy

Nature Reserve

Muswell Hill

Decoy
Pond

HP18

15

Muswell Hill
Farm House

Manor
Farm

Middle
Farm

1

Tower
Farm

Village Farm

Boarstall

Touchbridge

Span
Green

14

62

A

63

B4011

B

64

C

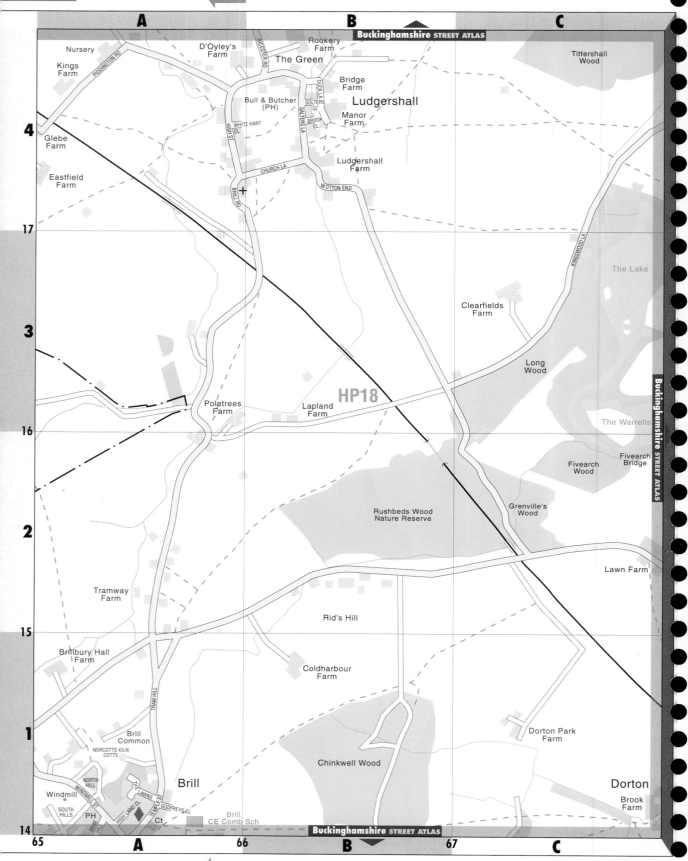

A   B   C

Nursery

Kings Farm

PODINGTON RD

D'Oyley's Farm

BICESTER RD

Rookery Farm

The Green

Bridge Farm

Tittershall Wood

4

Glebe Farm

Bull & Butcher (PH)

HIGH ST

WHITE HART CL

SOLTERS CL

DUCK LA

SALTERS LA

BROOK CL

Ludgershall

Manor Farm

Eastfield Farm

CHURCH LA

BRILL RD

Ludgershall Farm

WOTTON END

17

KINGSWOOD LA

The Lake

Clearfields Farm

3

Long Wood

Poletrees Farm

Lapland Farm

HP18

The Warrells

16

Fivearch Wood

Fivearch Bridge

Rushbeds Wood Nature Reserve

Grenville's Wood

2

Lawn Farm

Tramway Farm

Rid's Hill

15

Brilbury Hall Farm

Coldharbour Farm

TRAM HILL

1

Brill Common

NORCOTTS KILN COTTS

Dorton Park Farm

NORTH HILL

THE LAWNS

TEMPLE ST

GODFREYS CL

Chinkwell Wood

Dorton

Windmill

WINDMILL ST

HIGH LAND QL

SOUTH HILLS

PH

Brill

Brook Farm

Ct

Brill CE Comb Sch

14

65   A   66   B   67   C

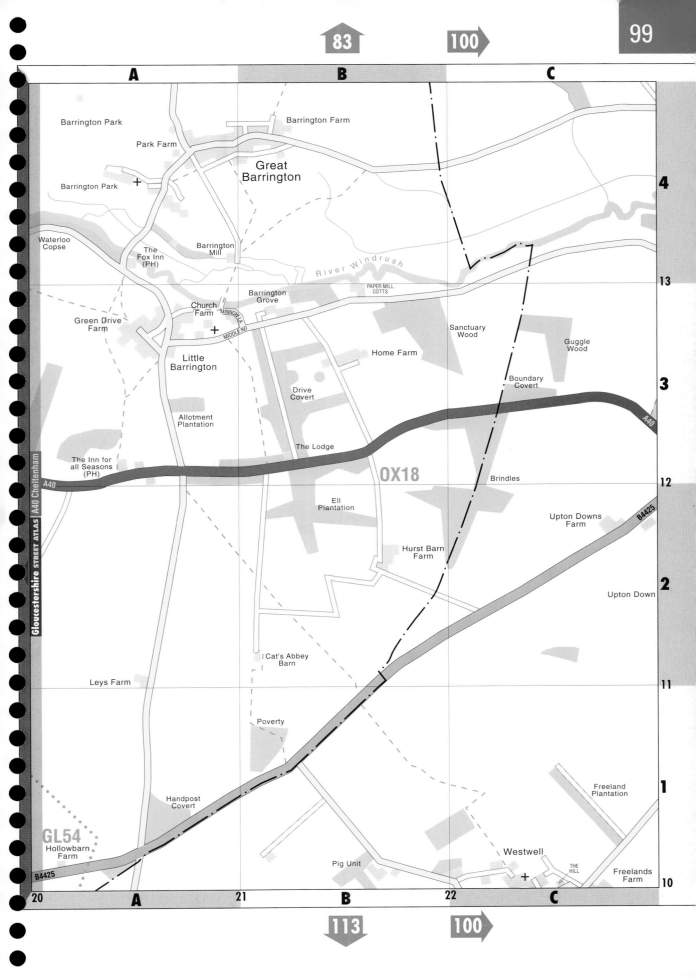

A   **B**   **C**

Barrington Park

Park Farm

Barrington Farm

Barrington Park

Great
Barrington

4

Waterloo
Copse

The
Fox Inn
(PH)

Barrington
Mill

River Windrush

13

PAPER MILL
COTTS

Barrington
Grove

Green Drive
Farm

Church
Farm

MINNOW LA

Sanctuary
Wood

Guggle
Wood

MIDDLE RD

Little
Barrington

Home Farm

Boundary
Covert

3

Drive
Covert

Allotment
Plantation

The Lodge

A40

The Inn for
all Seasons
(PH)

OX18

Brindles

12

A40 Cheltenham

A40

Ell
Plantation

Upton Downs
Farm

B4425

Hurst Barn
Farm

2

Upton Down

Cat's Abbey
Barn

Leys Farm

11

Poverty

Freeland
Plantation

1

Handpost
Covert

GL54

Westwell

THE
HILL

Freelands
Farm

Hollowbarn
Farm

Pig Unit

10

B4425

20   **A**   **21**   **B**   **22**   **C**

Gloucestershire street atlas | A40 Cheltenham

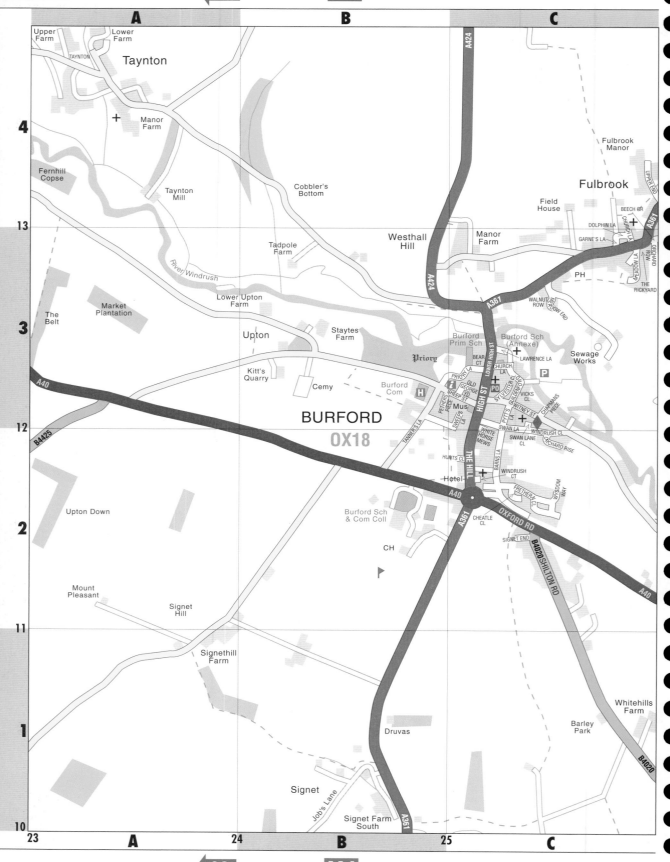

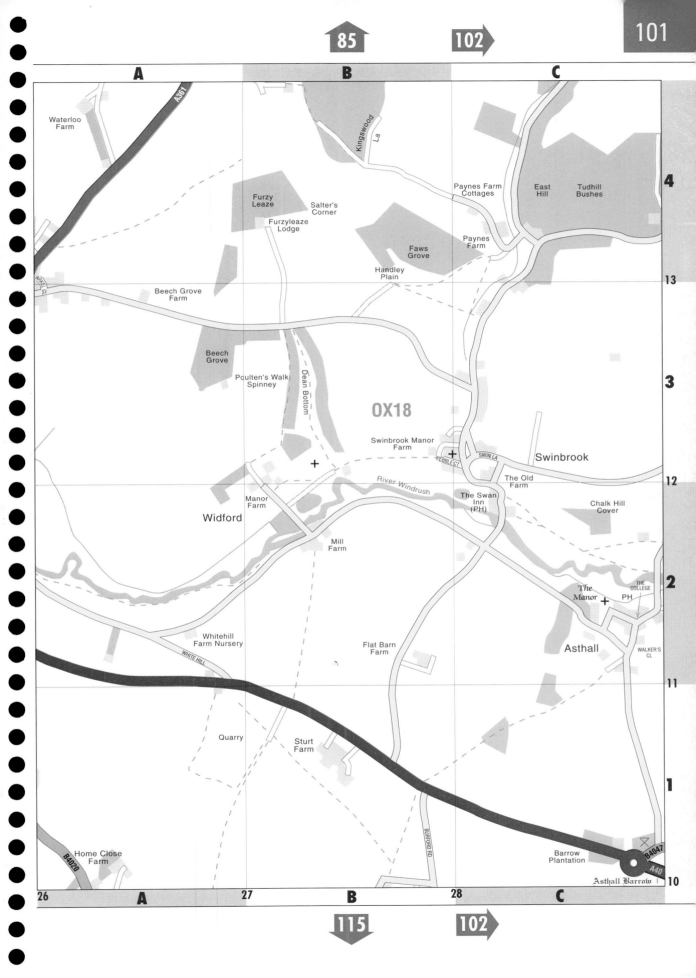

◄ 101   ▲ 86

A   B   C

4

Hens Grove

Roustage

Fordwells

NORTON TERR

Fordwells Farm House

Field Assarts

Home Farm

HOME FARM COTTS

BUTTERMILK LA

MINSTER RIDING

BOCKETT'S CNR

13

Stockley Copse

Wisdom's Bottom

College Farm

Asthall Leigh

Wisdom's Copse

The Olde Farm

Pool's Bottom

The Grove

3

Holywell Barn

Pinnocks Farm

Postern Bottom

Standridge Copse

Worsham Turn Cottage

WORSHAM TURN

Shorthazel Bottom

Bangry Bottom

12

OX18

NINETY CUT HILL

OX29

Kitesbridge Farm

Foxhole Bottom

MINSTER RIDING

Stonefold

Cot Farm

The Grove

2

Asthall Farm

Little Minster

SCHOOL LA

Minster Lovell Mill

The Old Swan Hotel

The Bungalow

Lower Field Farm

LOWER CRES

SCHOOL HILL

11

River Windrush

Folly Farm

WYCHWOOD VIEW

UPPER CRES

PH

B4477

B4047

Minster Lovell

O'CONNORS RD

CHARTERVILLE CL

ST KENELM'S CL

Works

WHITEHALL CL

WENRISC DR

DRYLANDS RD

BRIZE NORTON RD

St Kenelm's CE Prim Sch

Factory
Worsham

LOVELL CL

RIPLEY AVE

COTSWOLD CL

PO

1

Barrow Farm

Charterville Allotments

B4047

B4047

B4477

10

A40

29   A   30   B   31   C

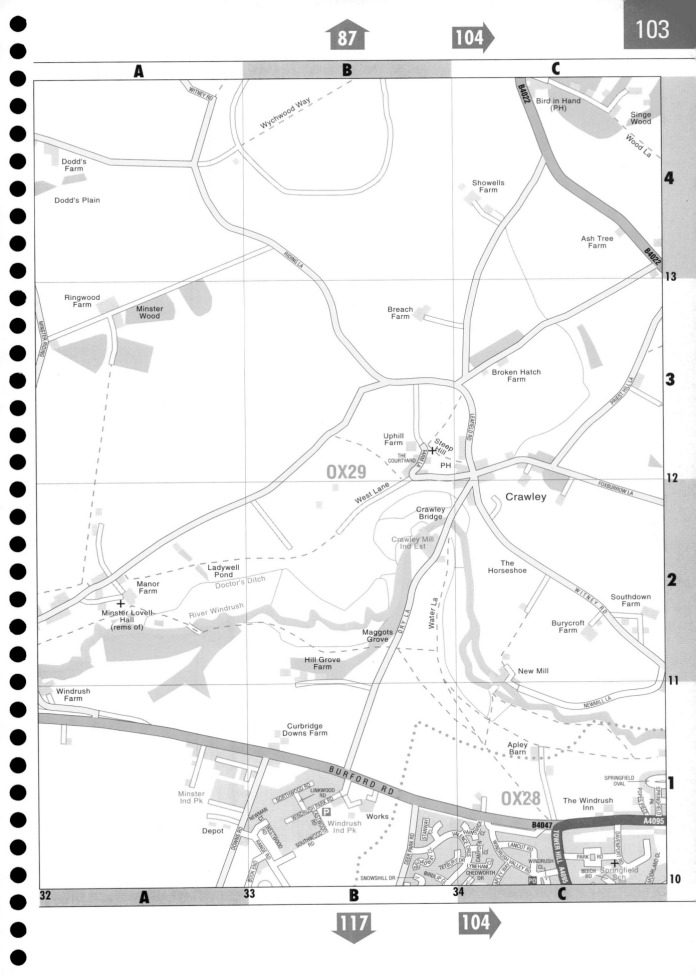

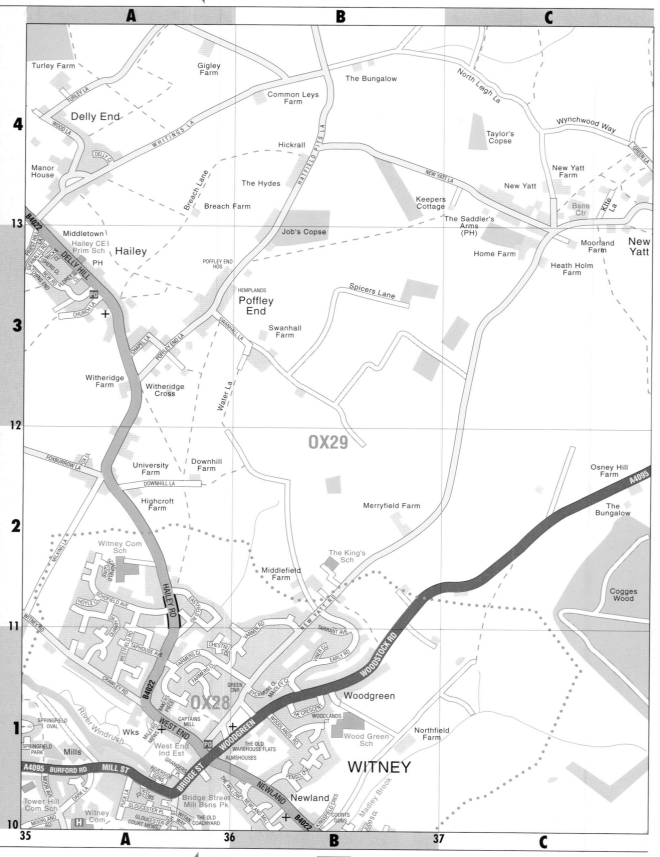

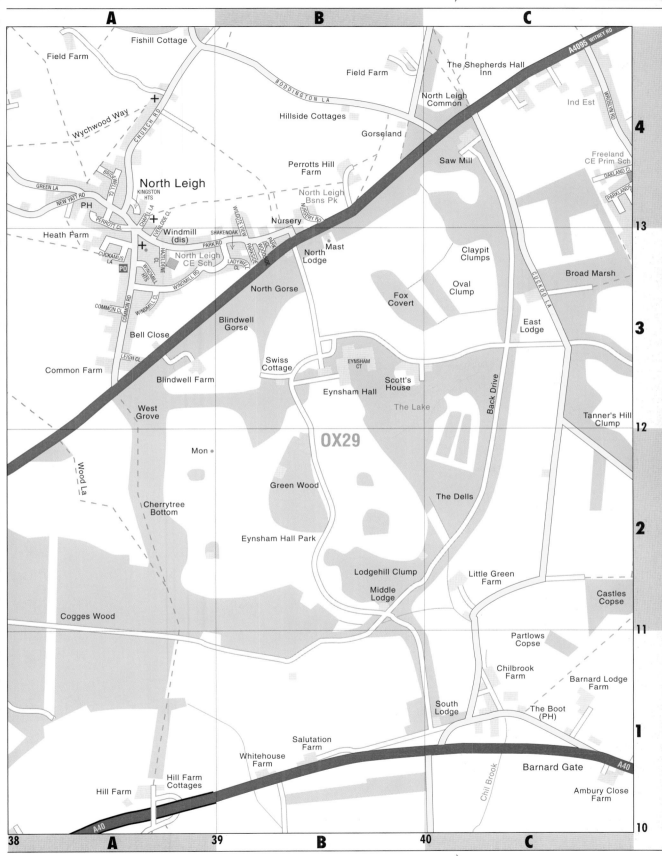

A   B   C

Fishill Cottage
Field Farm
Field Farm
The Shepherds Hall Inn
A4095 WITNEY RD
Wychwood Way
BODDINGTON LA
Hillside Cottages
North Leigh Common
Ind Est
Gorseland
Saw Mill
Freeland CE Prim Sch
OAKLAND CL
PARKLANDS
Perrotts Hill Farm
North Leigh
CHURCH RD
North Leigh Bsns Pk
4
GREEN LA
BRIDEWELL CL
KINGSTON HTS
NEW YATT RD
PERROTT CL
CHAPEL LA
EVENLODE CL
PH
Nursery
NURSERY RD
13
Heath Farm
CUCKAMUS LA
HAZELDENE CL
WILDCOTE VIEW
PARK LA
WOODSIDE
PARKSIDE
Windmill (dis)
SHAKENOAK
North Lodge
Mast
Claypit Clumps
Broad Marsh
CUCKOO LA
PO
North Leigh CE Sch
PARK RD
LADYWELL CL
North Gorse
Fox Covert
Oval Clump
East Lodge
COMMON CL
WINDMILL CL
Bell Close
Blindwell Gorse
3
COMMON RD
WINDMILL RD
WINDMILL HTS
LEIGH CL
Common Farm
Blindwell Farm
Swiss Cottage
EYNSHAM CT
Eynsham Hall
Scott's House
The Lake
Back Drive
Tanner's Hill Clump
West Grove
12
Wood La
Mon
OX29
Cherrytree Bottom
Green Wood
The Dells
2
Eynsham Hall Park
Lodgehill Clump
Little Green Farm
Castles Copse
Middle Lodge
Cogges Wood
Partlows Copse
11
Chilbrook Farm
Barnard Lodge Farm
South Lodge
The Boot (PH)
1
Salutation Farm
Whitehouse Farm
Chil Brook
Barnard Gate
A40
Hill Farm
Hill Farm Cottages
Ambury Close Farm
A40
10

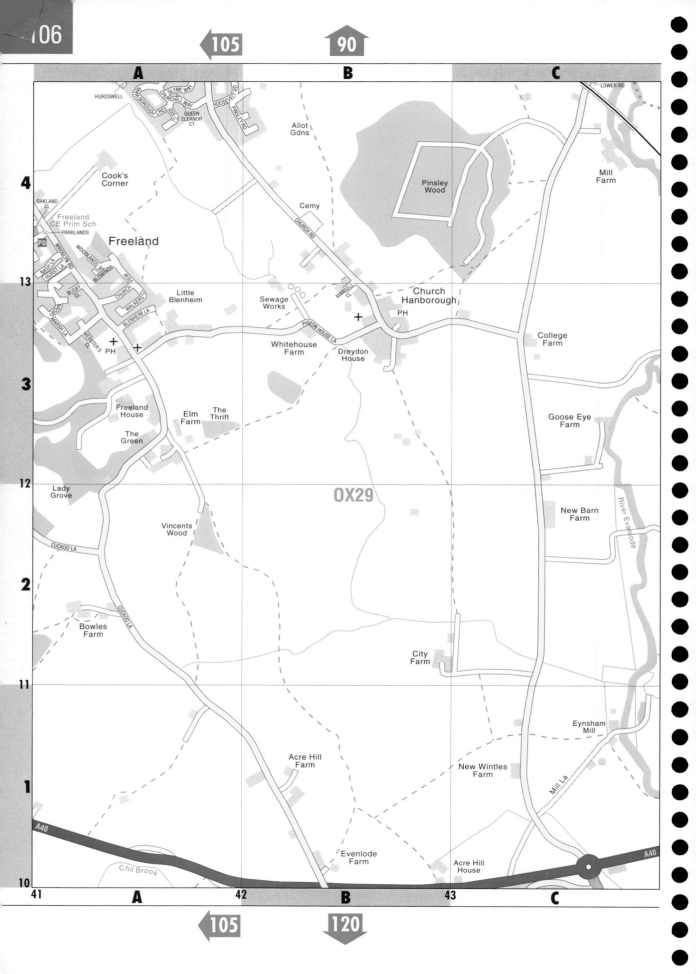

105
90

LOWER RD

HURDSWELL

Cook's
Corner

Mill
Farm

OAKLAND
CL

Freeland
CE Prim Sch

PARKLANDS

Freeland

Pinsley
Wood

Allot
Gdns

Cemy

CHURCH RD

4

13

Little
Blenheim

Sewage
Works

MANSELL CL

Church
Hanborough

PH

PIGEON HOUSE LA

College
Farm

Whitehouse
Farm

Dreydon
House

PH

3

Freeland
House

Elm
Farm

The
Thrift

Goose Eye
Farm

The
Green

12

Lady
Grove

OX29

New Barn
Farm

River Evenlode

Vincents
Wood

CUCKOO LA

2

Bowles
Farm

CUCKOO LA

City
Farm

11

Eynsham
Mill

Acre Hill
Farm

New Wintles
Farm

MILL LA

1

A40

Evenlode
Farm

Acre Hill
House

A40

Chil Brook

10

41

42

43

105
120

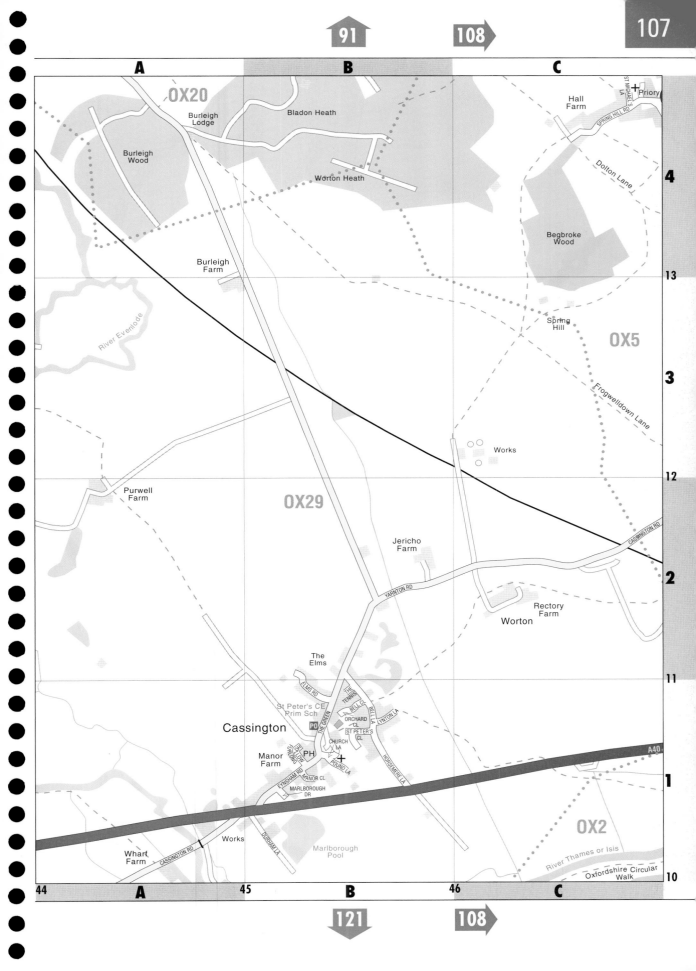

91
108

A
B
C

OX20

Burleigh Lodge

Bladon Heath

St MICHAEL'S LA
Priory
Hall Farm
Spring Hill Rd

Burleigh Wood

Worton Heath

Dolton Lane

4

Begbroke Wood

Burleigh Farm

13

River Evenlode

Spring Hill

OX5

Frogwelldown Lane

3

Works

Purwell Farm

OX29

12

Jericho Farm

Cassington Rd

2

Yarnton Rd

Rectory Farm

Worton

The Elms

11

ELMS RD
St Peter's CE Prim Sch
THE TENNIS
BELL CL
BELL LA
LYNTON LA

Cassington
PO
THE GREEN
ORCHARD CL
ST PETER'S CL

CHURCH LA
Manor Farm
PH
CHELTON FURLONG
MANOR CL
POUND LA
HORSEMERE LA

A40

1

EYNSHAM RD
MARLBOROUGH DR

OX2

Wharf Farm
CASSINGTON RD
Works
DURHAM LA
Marlborough Pool

River Thames or Isis
Oxfordshire Circular Walk

10

44
A
45
B
46
C

121
108

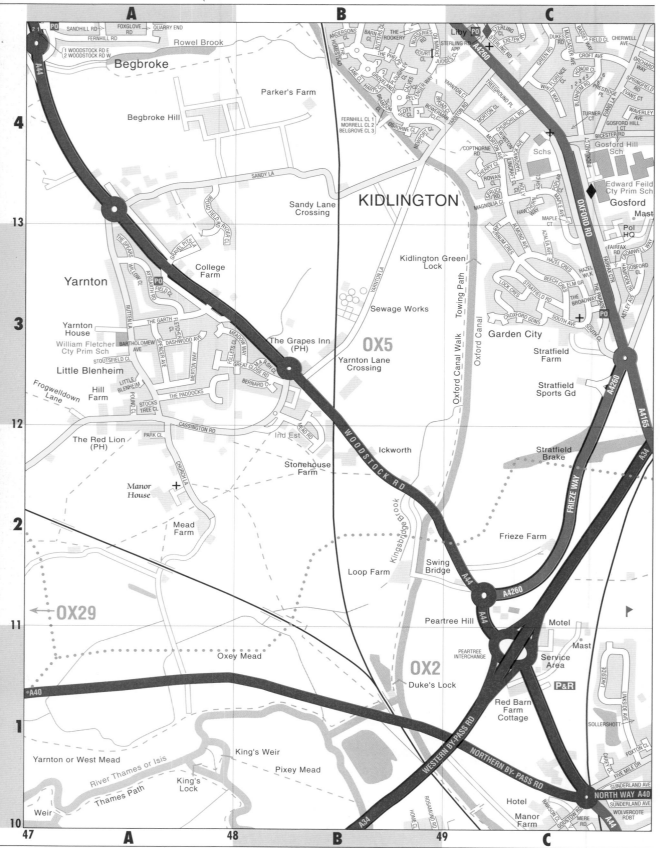

C4
1 ANDOVER CT
2 BLENHEIM CT
3 CLEVEDON CT
4 DORCHESTER CT
5 EXETER CT
6 FARNHAM CT
7 GUILDFORD CT
8 HERTFORD CT

SANDHILL RD
FOXGLOVE RD
QUARRY END
FERNHILL RD
Rowel Brook

1 WOODSTOCK RD E
2 WOODSTOCK RD W

Begbroke

Parker's Farm

Begbroke Hill

SANDY LA

Sandy Lane
Crossing

KIDLINGTON

THE ROOKERY
NURSERIES
THE PHELPS

FERNHILL CL 1
MORRELL CL 2
BELGROVE CL 3

Liby
PO

STERLING RD
EXETER RD
DUKES CT
BASSET AVE
FIELD CL
CHERWELL AVE

A4260

GREEN RD
WHITE WAY
FLORENCE CT
MILCASTER AVE
CROFT AVE
ORCHARD WAY

BLENHEIM RD
PRESTIDGE PL
EVANS CT
TURNER CT
GOSFORD HILL
SPRINGFIELD RD
WAVERLEY AVE

Schs

Bicesterd

Gosford Hill
Sch

Edward Feild
Cty Prim Sch

Gosford
Mast

Pol
HQ

FAIRFAX
RD
CROMWELL WAY
GOSFORD
CT
HAMPDEN DR

Yarnton

College
Farm

Yarnton
House

William Fletcher
Cty Prim Sch

THE SPEARS
WILLOW CL
THE GARTH
FLETCHER CL
BARTHOLOMEW AVE
DASHWOOD AVE
SPENCER AVE

GRAVEL PITS

RYSGARTH RD
FIELD CL

MEADOW WAY

4

13

3

Yarnton Lane
Crossing

OX5

Kidlington Green
Lock

Sewage Works

Oxford Canal Walk
Towing Path
Oxford Canal

CHERRY CL
ROWAN CL
SPRUCE RD
HOLLY
HAWTHORN
MAGNOLIA CL
ALMOND CRES
AZALEA RD
SPANIUM CRES
MAPLE AVE
MAPLE CT
HAZEL CRES
HAZEL GR
ELM GR
BEECH CRES
STRATFIELD RD
LOCK CRES
CROXFORD GDNS
SOUTH AVE

Garden City
Stratfield
Farm

Stratfield
Sports Gd

THE
BROADWAY

OXFORD RD

THE PARADE
ASTLEY AVE

PO

A4260

A4165

Little Blenheim

Frogwelldown
Lane

Hill
Farm

STOUTSFIELD CL
LITTLE
BLENHEIM
POUND CL
STOCKS
TREE CL
THE PADDOCKS

MERTON CL

FOLLETS CL
GREAT CLOSE RD
BERNARD CL
MARSH CL

The Grapes Inn
(PH)

The Red Lion
(PH)

PARK CL

CASSINGTON RD

MEAD RD

Ind Est

Manor
House

Mead
Farm

CHURCH LA

Stonehouse
Farm

Ickworth

WOODSTOCK RD

Stratfield
Brake

12

2

OX29

Oxey Mead

A40

Kingsbridge Brook

Loop Farm

Swing
Bridge

A44

Frieze Farm

FRIEZE WAY

A4260

A34

Motel
Mast

Peartree Hill

PEARTREE
INTERCHANGE

Service
Area

P&R

OX2

Duke's Lock

Red Barn
Farm
Cottage

LAKESIDE
LINKSIDE AVE

SOLLERSHOTT

11

1

Yarnton or West Mead

River Thames or Isis

King's Weir
Pixey Mead

King's
Lock

Thames Path

Weir

WESTERN BY-PASS RD
NORTHERN BY-PASS RD

A34

HOME CL
ROSAMUND RD

GODSTOW BR
RAWSON CL
GOODSTOW RD

Hotel

Manor
Farm

MERE
RD

SUNDERLAND AVE
SUNDERLAND AVE

North Way A40
WOLVERCOTE
RDBT

FOXTOL CL
FIVE MILE DR
CAREY CL

A44
A40

10

47
A
48
B
49
C

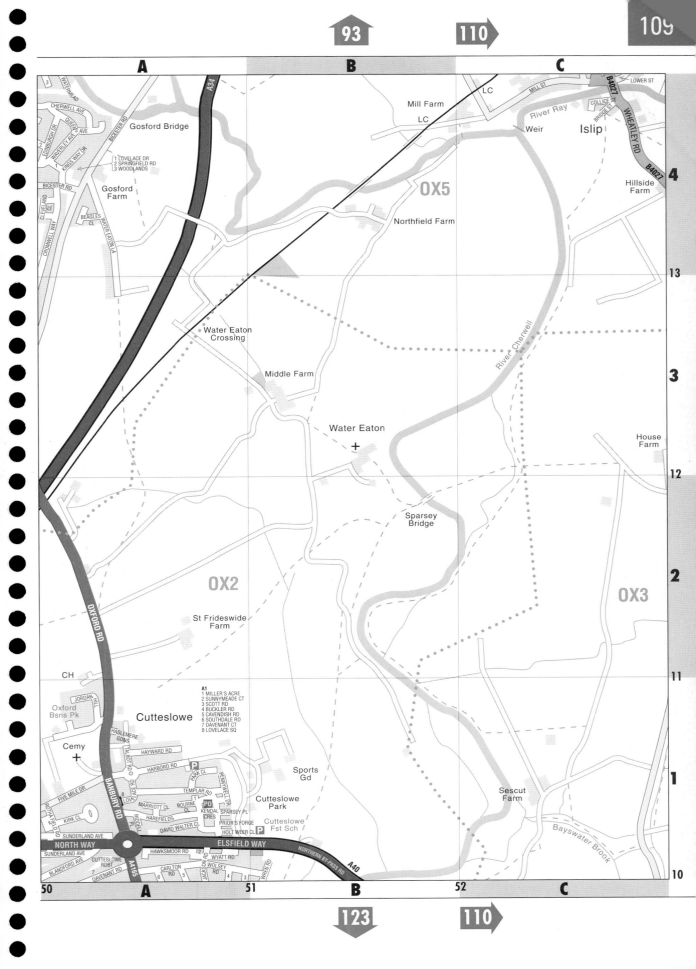

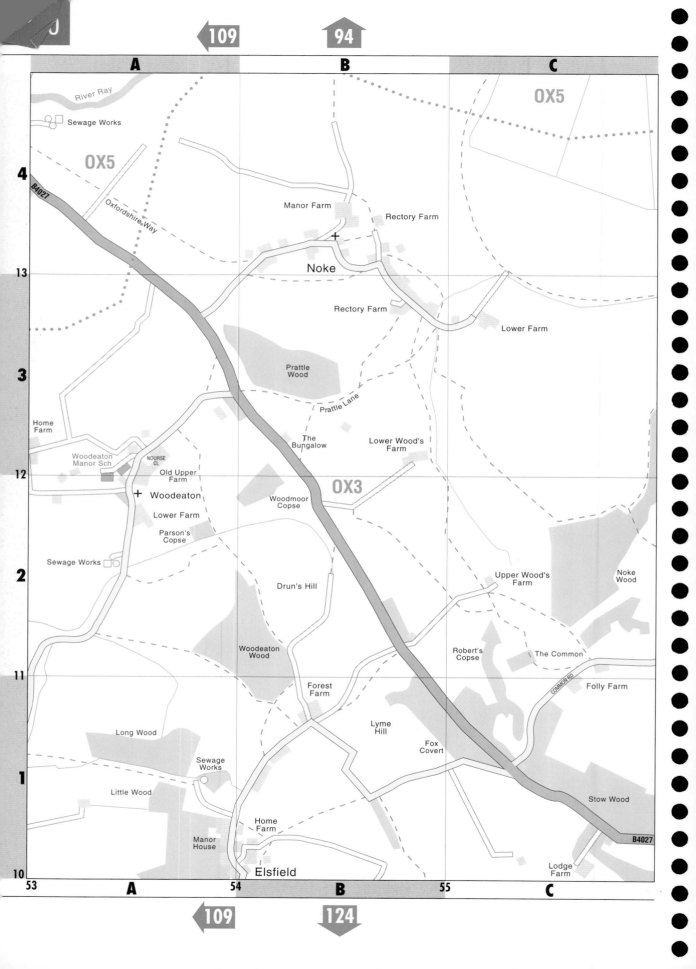

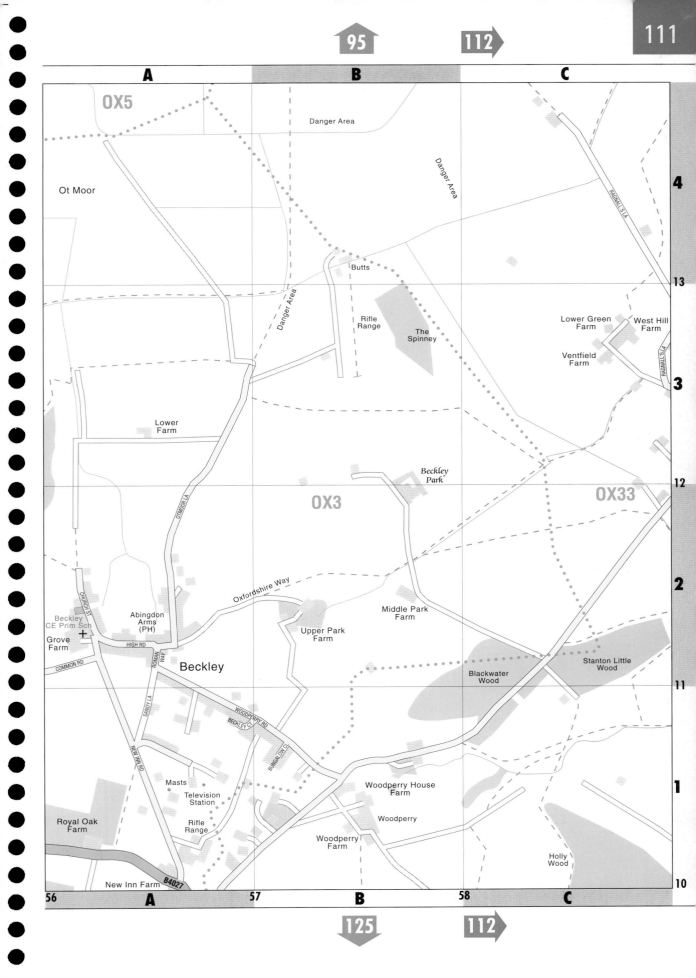

95
112
125
112

OX5

Ot Moor

Danger Area

Danger Area

Danger Area

Danger Area

Butts

Rifle Range

The Spinney

Lower Green Farm

West Hill Farm

Ventfield Farm

RAGNALL'S LA

RAGNALL'S LA

Lower Farm

Beckley Park

OX3

OX33

CHURCH ST

OTMOOR LA

Oxfordshire Way

Middle Park Farm

Stanton Little Wood

Beckley CE Prim Sch

Abingdon Arms (PH)

Grove Farm

Upper Park Farm

Blackwater Wood

HIGH RD

ROMAN WAY

Beckley

COMMON RD

SANDY LA

WOODPERRY RD

BECKLEY CL

BUNGALOW CL

NEW INN RD

Masts

Television Station

Rifle Range

Woodperry House Farm

Woodperry

Royal Oak Farm

Woodperry Farm

Holly Wood

B4027

New Inn Farm

A   56   57   B   58   C

A   B   C

4

13

3

12

2

11

1

10

111
96

A **B** **C**

4

Old Arngrove

Warren
Farm

New Arngrove
Farm

Gardner's
Barn

Tippens
Copse

13

Nursery

Sermin's
Copse

Pasture
Farm

BRILL RD

Studley
Farm

Danes Brook

Horton-cum-Studley

3

+

MILL LA

CHURCH LA

PO

THE GREEN

FORGE CL

The Kings
Arms
(PH)

VENTFIELD
CL

Manor
Farm

New
Farm

*Studley
Priory*

PRIORY
CL

Hotel

Moors
Farm

OAKLEY RD

Sewage
Works

12

CH

OX33

HP18

P

Studley
Wood

Oakley
Wood

Nature Trail

2

Corner
Farm

Nature
Reserve

Shabbington Wood

The Moat

11

Bernwood Forest

York's
Wood

Danesbrook
Farm

Danes Brook

1

Moorbirge Brook

Oxfordshire Way

Hell
Coppice

Beckley

Menmarsh
Guide Post

Moorbirge
Bridge

10

59 **A** **60** **B** **61** **C**

M40 Thame (A418)
Buckinghamshire STREET ATLAS

M40

111
126

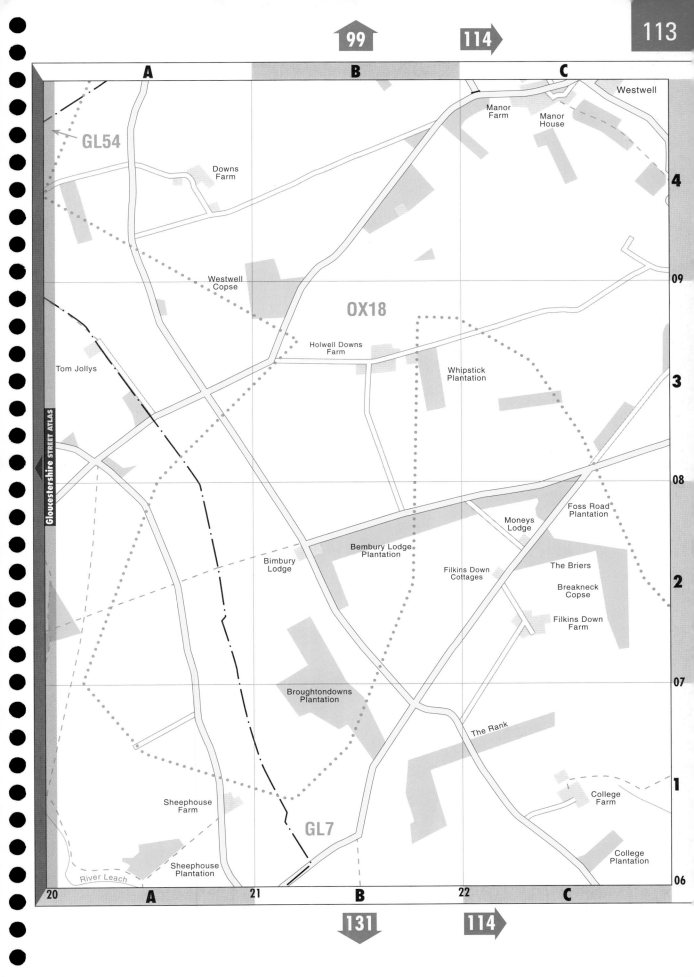

A   B   C

Westwell

GL54

Manor
Farm

Manor
House

Downs
Farm

4

09

Westwell
Copse

OX18

Holwell Downs
Farm

Whipstick
Plantation

Tom Jollys

3

Gloucestershire STREET ATLAS

08

Foss Road
Plantation

Moneys
Lodge

Bembury Lodge
Plantation

Bimbury
Lodge

Filkins Down
Cottages

The Briers

Breakneck
Copse

2

Filkins Down
Farm

Broughtondowns
Plantation

07

The Rank

1

College
Farm

Sheephouse
Farm

GL7

College
Plantation

06

Sheephouse
Plantation

River Leach

20   A   21   B   22   C

A   B   C

Job's Lane

Tansley's Buildings

Shill Brook

Sturt Copse

Mount Zion Bottom

4

Manor Farm

Holwell Plantation

Upper Glissard's Plantation

Porters Buildings

Shilton Downs Farm

Holwell

SYCAMORE PL

HAWTHORN DR

BIRCH DR

WINDSIDE DR

LARCH RD

Old Pits Plantation

09

GLISSARD WAY

Glissard's Wood

Lower Glissard's Plantation

Groveground Plantation

Bradwell Grove

Woodside Farm

Hen and Chicken Wood

3

P

Cotswold Wildlife Park

OX18

THE COTTAGES

Aston Copse

Fishpond Copse

Westfield Farm

The Kennels

08

Home Farm

Bradwell Grove Wood

South Lodge

Bradwell Grove Park

Manor Dairy Farm

Works

Scrubs Farm

2

Furze Ground

07

Pumphouse Plantation

GL7

Hill Plantation

1

Kencot Hill Farm

Furzey Hall Farm

A361

06

23   A   24   B   25   C

A361

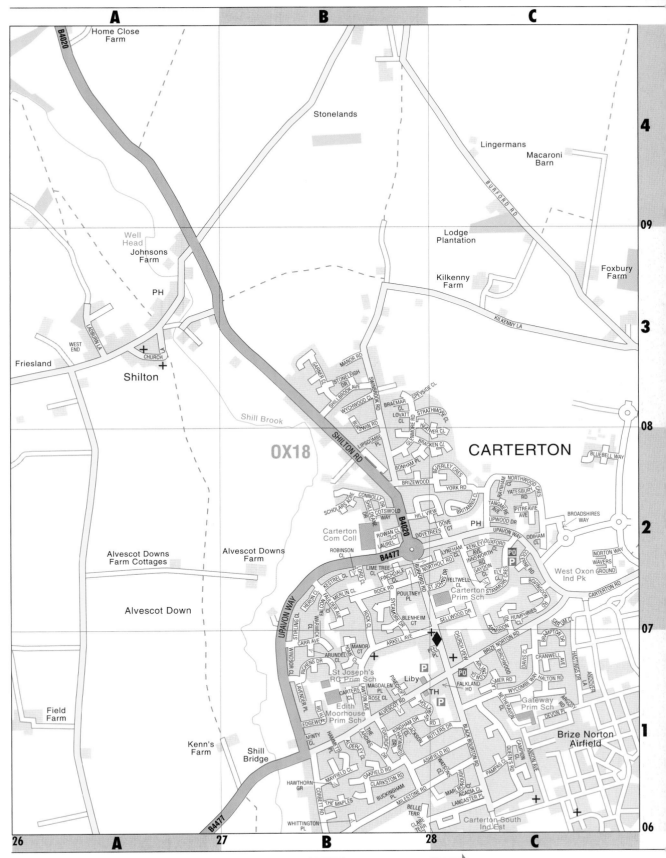

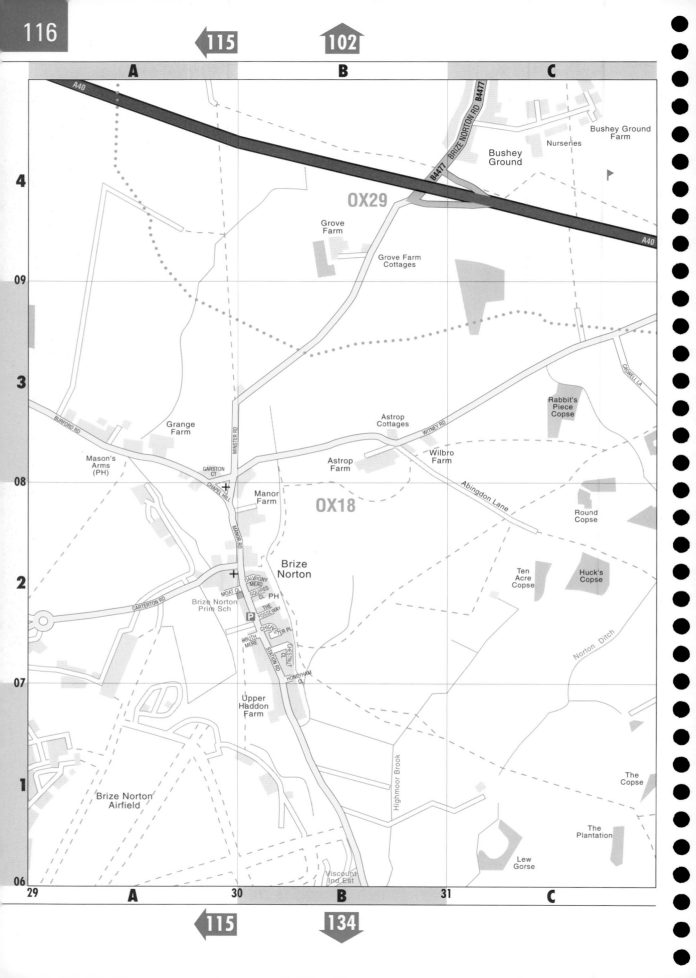

115
102
115
134

A40
B4477
BRIZE NORTON RD
B4477

Bushey Ground Farm
Nurseries
Bushey Ground

OX29

Grove Farm
Grove Farm Cottages

A40

CASWELL LA

Rabbit's Piece Copse

BURFORD RD
Grange Farm

Astrop Cottages
WITNEY RD

Mason's Arms (PH)

MINSTER RD
GARSTON CT
CHAPEL HILL

Astrop Farm

Wilbro Farm

Abingdon Lane

Round Copse

OX18
Manor Farm

MANOR RD

Ten Acre Copse

Huck's Copse

Brize Norton

DALBIGNY MEAD
SQUIRES CL PH
MOAT CL
CARTERTON RD
Brize Norton Prim Sch
P
THE FOSSEWAY
CHICHESTER PL
SOUTH MERE
CHESTNUT CL
STATION RD
HONEYHAM CL

Norton Ditch

Upper Haddon Farm

Highmoor Brook

The Copse

Brize Norton Airfield

The Plantation

Lew Gorse

Viscount Ind Est

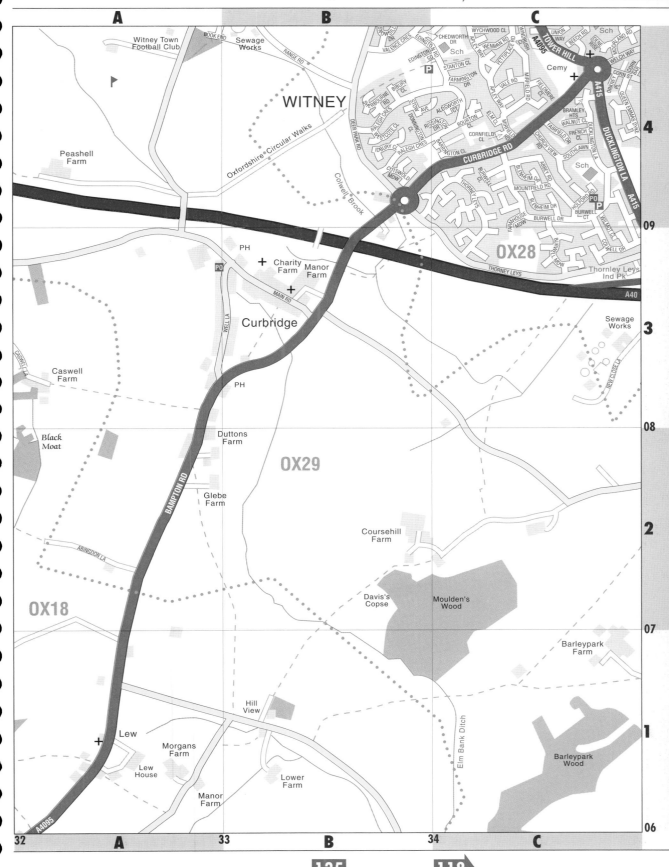

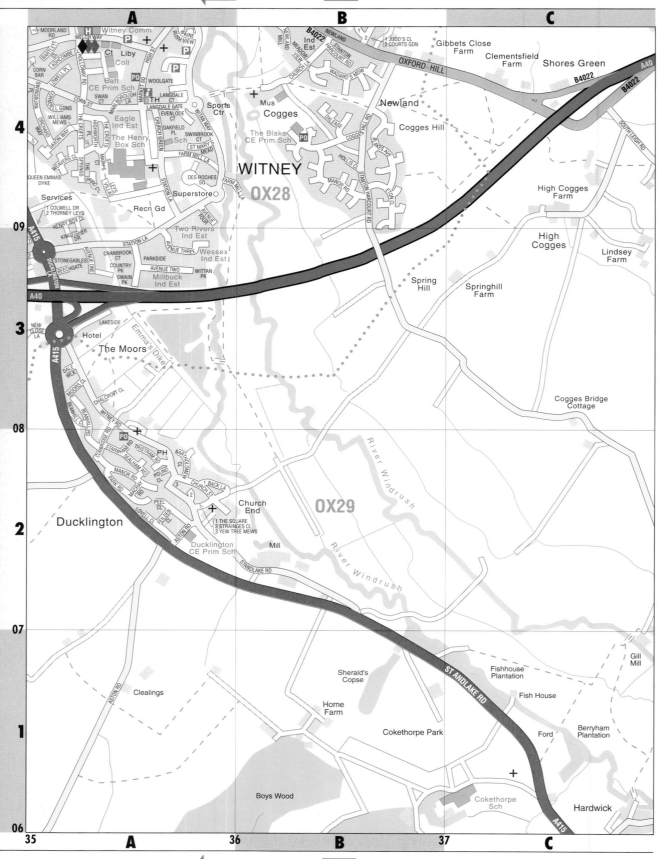

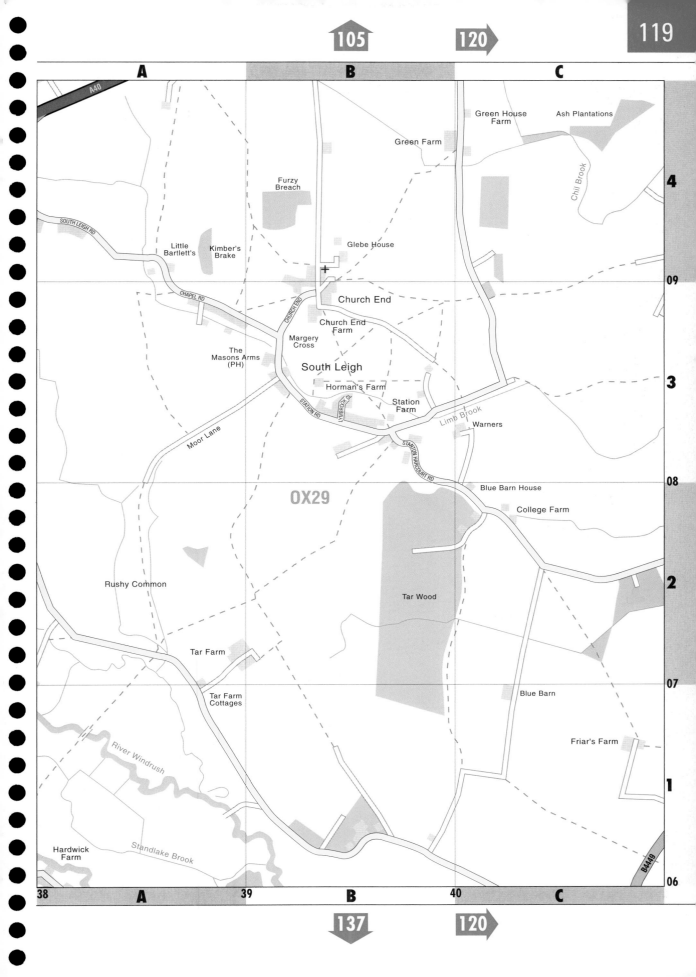

105

120

A   B   C

A40

Green House Farm

Ash Plantations

Green Farm

Chil Brook

4

SOUTH LEIGH RD

Furzy Breach

Little Bartlett's

Kimber's Brake

Glebe House

09

CHAPEL RD

CHURCH END

Church End

Church End Farm

Margery Cross

The Masons Arms (PH)

South Leigh

3

Horman's Farm

STATION RD

LYMBROOK CL

Station Farm

Limb Brook

Warners

Moor Lane

STANTON HARCOURT RD

Blue Barn House

08

College Farm

OX29

Rushy Common

Tar Wood

2

Tar Farm

07

Tar Farm Cottages

Blue Barn

River Windrush

Friar's Farm

1

Hardwick Farm

Standlake Brook

B4449

06

38   A   39   B   40   C

137

120

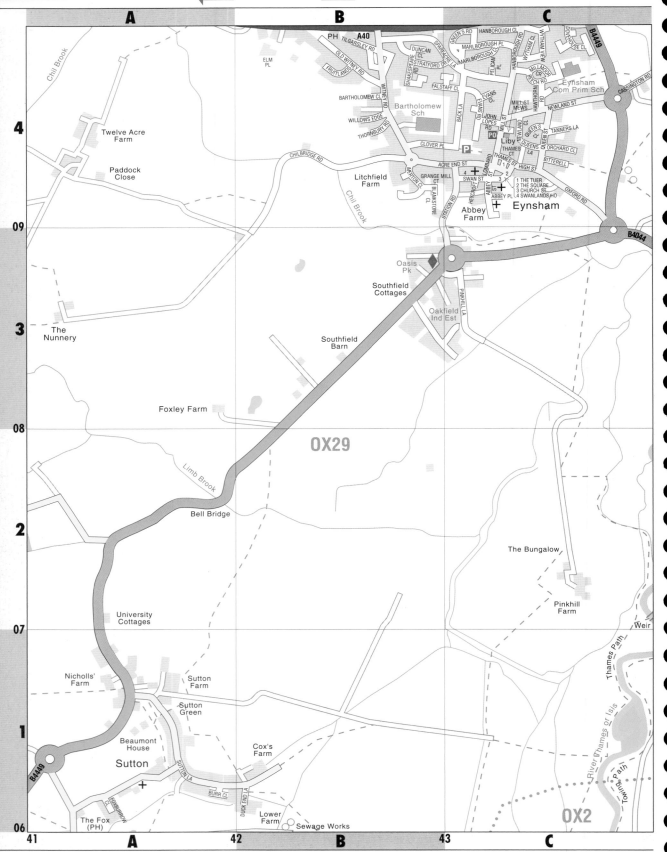

A40
PH
ELM PL
TILGARSLEY RD
OLD WITNEY RD
FRUITLANDS
WITNEY RD
DUNCAN CL
SHAKESPEARE RD
STRATFORD DR
SPRATSCAR LA
FALSTAFF CL
BARTHOLOMEW CL
WILLOWS EDGE
THORNBURY RD
Bartholomew Sch
BACK LA
GREEN S RD
HANBOROUGH CL
MARLBOROUGH PL
MARLBOROUGH CL
PELICAN PL
HANBOROUGH RD
WYTHAM CL
WYTHAM VIEW
DOVEHOUSE CL
B4449
Eynsham Com Prim Sch
CASSINGTON RD
MILLMOOR
BEECH RD
NEWLAND ST
HAWTHORN
EVANS RD
EVANS CL
MILL ST MEWS
JOHN LOPES RD
PO
TANNERS LA
CLOVER PL
Liby
THAMES CT
QUEEN S CL
QUEEN S LA
ORCHARD CL
ACRE END ST
GRANGE MILL CT
MARTON CL
BLANKSTONE CL
STATION RD
SWAN ST
HEDCROFT
4
3
2
1
LOMBARD ST
THAMES ST
HIGH ST
QUEEN ST
BITTERELL
OXFORD RD
Litchfield Farm
1 THE TUER
2 THE SQUARE
3 CHURCH ST
4 SWANLANDS HO
Eynsham
ABBEY PL
ABBEY ST
Abbey Farm
B4044

Chil Brook
Twelve Acre Farm
Paddock Close
CHILBRIDGE RD
Chil Brook
The Nunnery
Oasis Pk
Southfield Cottages
Oakfield Ind Est
PINKHILL LA
Southfield Barn
OX29
Foxley Farm
Limb Brook
The Bungalow
Bell Bridge
Pinkhill Farm
Weir
University Cottages
Thames Path
Nicholls' Farm
Sutton Farm
Sutton Green
River Thames or Isis
Beaumont House
Cox's Farm
Towing Path
Sutton
B4449
SUTTON LA
BURR CL
DUCK END LA
OX2
The Fox (PH)
LECKFORD ROW
Lower Farm
Sewage Works

4

09

3

08

2

07

1

06

41   42   43

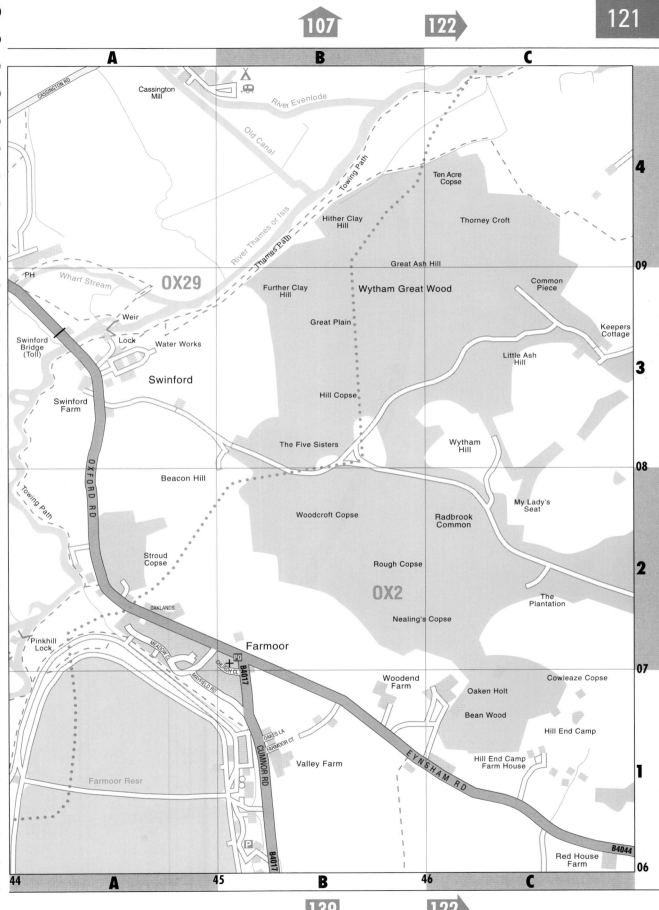

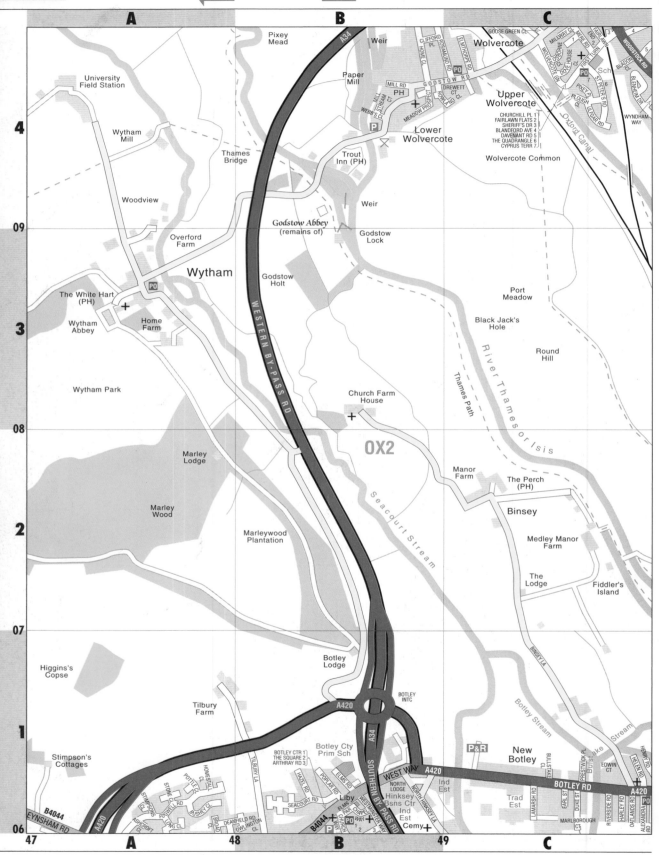

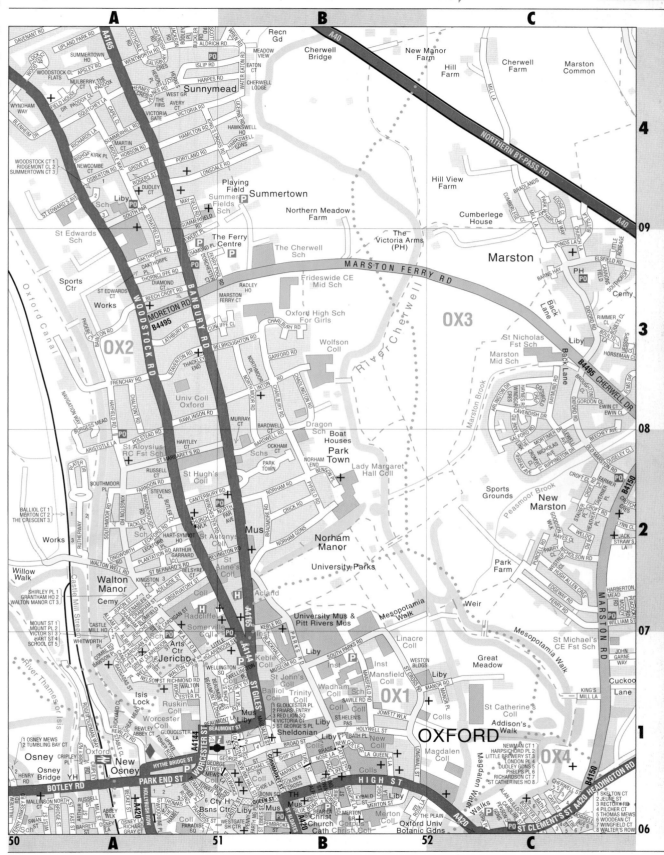

A1
1 CASTLE MEWS
2 THE OLD BAKERY
3 CLEMENT BURROWS HO
4 CHRIST CHURCH OLD BLDGS
5 JACKSON COLE HO
6 ST GEORGES GATE
7 SWAN CT

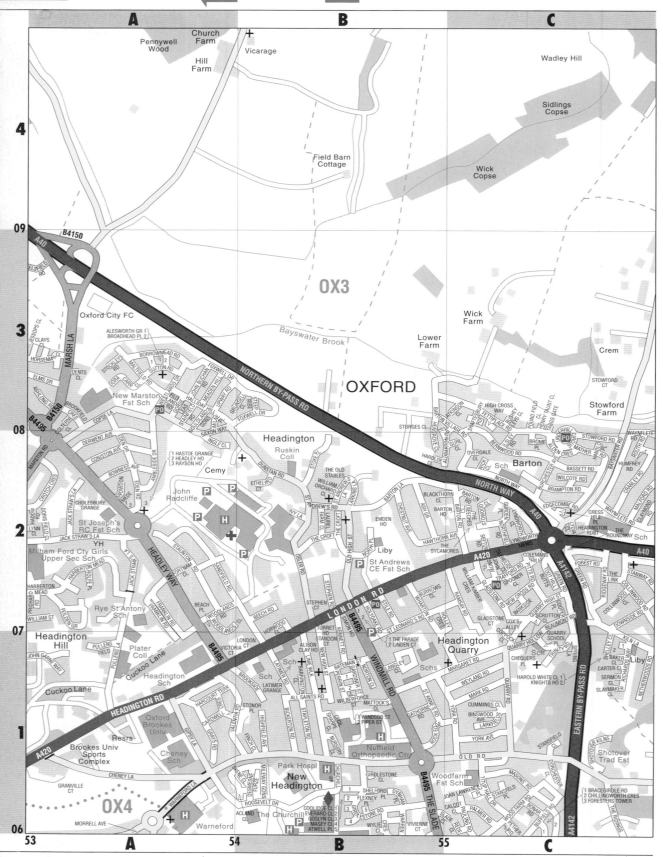

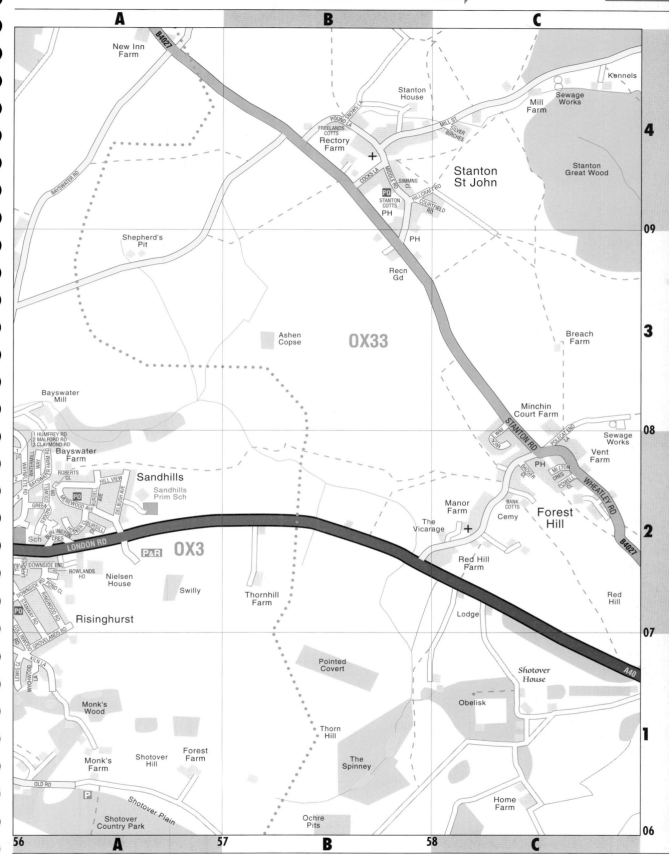

125   112

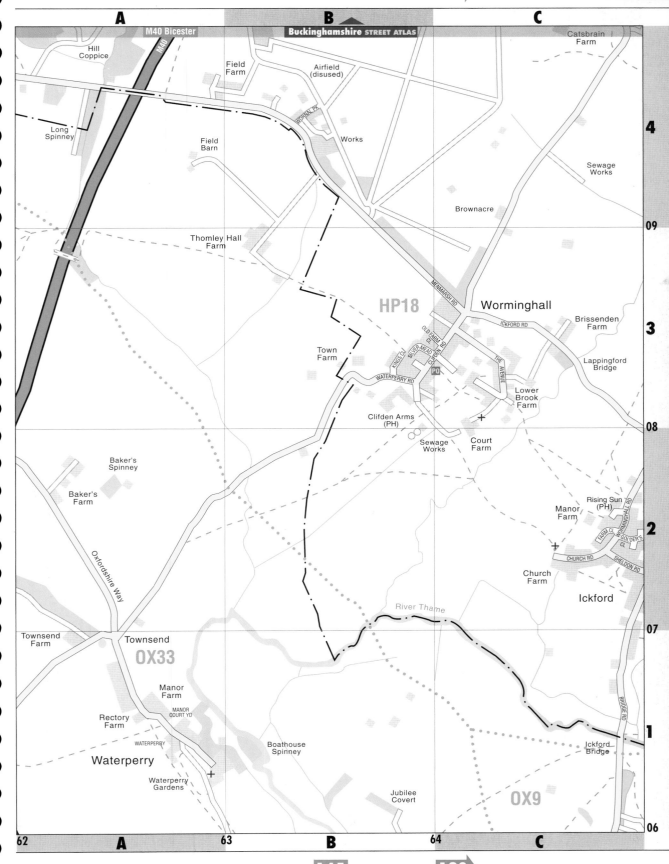

128

A   B   Buckinghamshire STREET ATLAS   C

M40 Bicester

Hill Coppice

Long Spinney

Field Farm

Airfield (disused)

Field Barn

WORNAL PK

Works

Catsbrain Farm

Sewage Works

Brownacre

4

Thomley Hall Farm

09

MENMARSH RD

HP18

Worminghall

ICKFORD RD

Brissenden Farm

3

Town Farm

OLD FARM CL

KINGS CL

SILVER MEAD CL

DUCKLAKE CL

PO

THE AVENUE

Lappingford Bridge

WATERPERRY RD

Lower Brook Farm

Clifden Arms (PH)

Sewage Works

Court Farm

08

Baker's Spinney

Baker's Farm

Rising Sun (PH)

Manor Farm

FARM CL

WOGLER'S CL

WORMINGHALL RD

2

Oxfordshire Way

CHURCH RD

SHELDON RD

Church Farm

Ickford

Townsend Farm

Townsend

OX33

River Thame

07

Manor Farm

MANOR COURT YD

Rectory Farm

WATERPERRY

Boathouse Spinney

BRIDGE RD

Ickford Bridge

1

Waterperry

Waterperry Gardens

Jubilee Covert

OX9

06

62   A   63   B   64   C

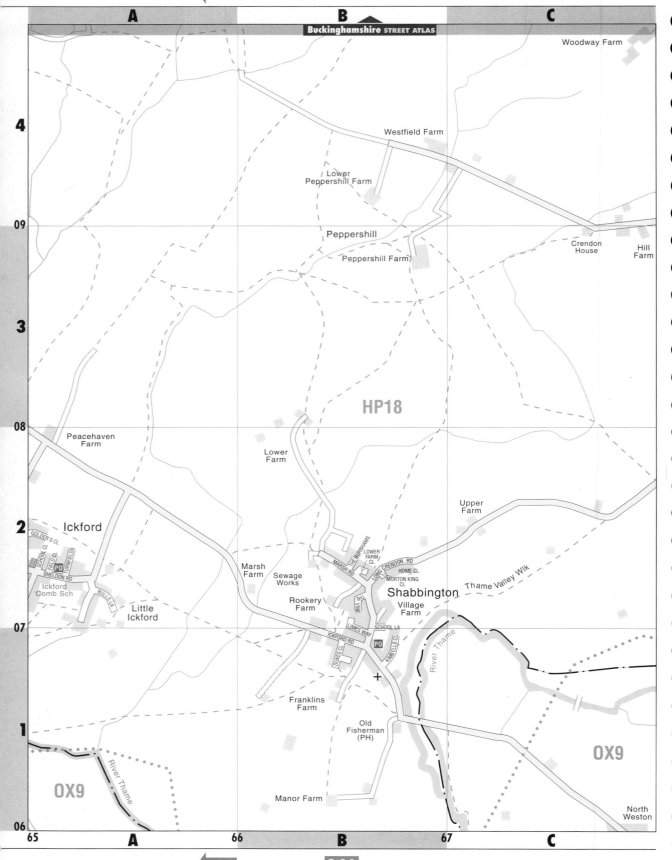

Buckinghamshire STREET ATLAS

Woodway Farm

Westfield Farm

Lower
Peppershill Farm

Peppershill

Peppershill Farm

Crendon
House

Hill
Farm

HP18

Peacehaven
Farm

Lower
Farm

Upper
Farm

Ickford

GOLDER'S CL

SCHOOL CL
FIELD CL
TURNFIELDS
PO
SHELDON RD
BULL'S LA

Ickford
Comb Sch

Little
Ickford

Marsh
Farm

Sewage
Works

THE BURNHAMS
MARSH RD
LOWER FARM CL
LONG CRENDON RD
HOME CL
MORTON KING CL

Shabbington

Rookery
Farm

THE VINE

Village
Farm

Thame Valley Wlk

LIMES WAY

ICKFORD RD
PO
SCHOOL LA
KINGFELLS CL

DUKES CL

River Thame

Franklins
Farm

Old
Fisherman
(PH)

OX9

Manor Farm

OX9

River Thame

North
Weston

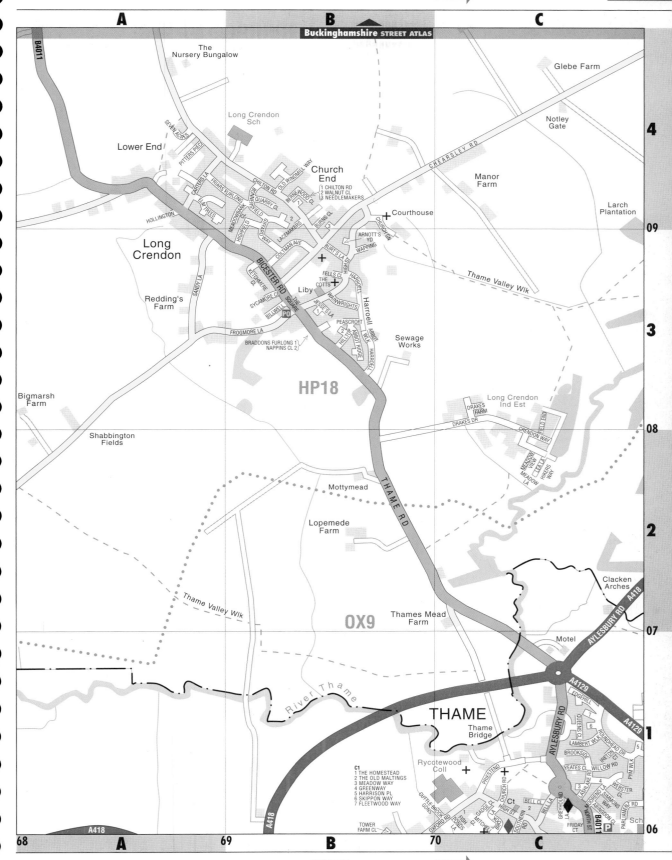

A B C

The Nursery Bungalow

Glebe Farm

Long Crendon Sch

Notley Gate

4

Lower End

Chearsley Rd

Manor Farm

Pitters Piece

Seven Acres

Larch Plantation

Carters La

Chilton Rd

Friars Furlong

Church End

1 CHILTON RD
2 WALNUT CL
3 NEEDLEMAKERS

Hollington

Old Windmill Way

Quarry Cl

Berneywood Cl

Bernewood Cl

Church Gn

Courthouse

09

Long Crendon

Meadowbank

Highfield

Sheard Way

Coltman Ave

Lacemakers

Burns Cl

Arnott's Yd

Wapping

Thame Valley Wlk

Bicester Rd

Square

Ketomere Cl

Burt's La

Fells Cl

The Cotts

Harroell

Redding's Farm

Sandy La

Sycamore Cl

Billwell

PO

Liby

Wainwrights

Jesse's La

Harroell

Abbot Ridge

Abbot

Harroell

3

Peascroft

Frogmore La

BRADDONS FURLONG 1
NAPPINS CL 2

Sewage Works

HP18

Bigmarsh Farm

Long Crendon Ind Est

Drakes Farm

Field End

08

Shabbington Fields

Drakes Dr

Crendon Way

Meadow View

Lea La

Hikers Way

Meadow La

Thame Rd

Mottymead

2

Lopemede Farm

Clacken Arches

Thame Valley Wlk

Aylesbury Rd

A418

OX9

Thames Mead Farm

07

Motel

A4129

River Thame

THAME

A4129

Edgehill

Thame Bridge

Queens Cl

Aylesbury Rd

Roundhead Dr

Lambert Wlk

Brookside

Ireton Cl

Willow Rd

1

C1
1 THE HOMESTEAD
2 THE OLD MALTINGS
3 MEADOW WAY
4 GREENWAY
5 HARRISON PL
6 SKIPPON WAY
7 FLEETWOOD WAY

Rycotewood Coll

Priestend

Yeates Cl

Webster Cl

Lashlake Rd

Doddend La

Simmons Way

Lexington Dr

North St

B4011

Sch

Chinnor Rd

Church Rd

High St

Bell La

Greyhound La

Mitchell

Parliament Rd

P

A418

Oxford Rd

Cuttle Brook Gdns

Ct

Cadge Cl

Potash

Ponds

Bella

Southern Rd

Friday Ct

A418

TOWER FARM CL

68 69 70

A B C

06

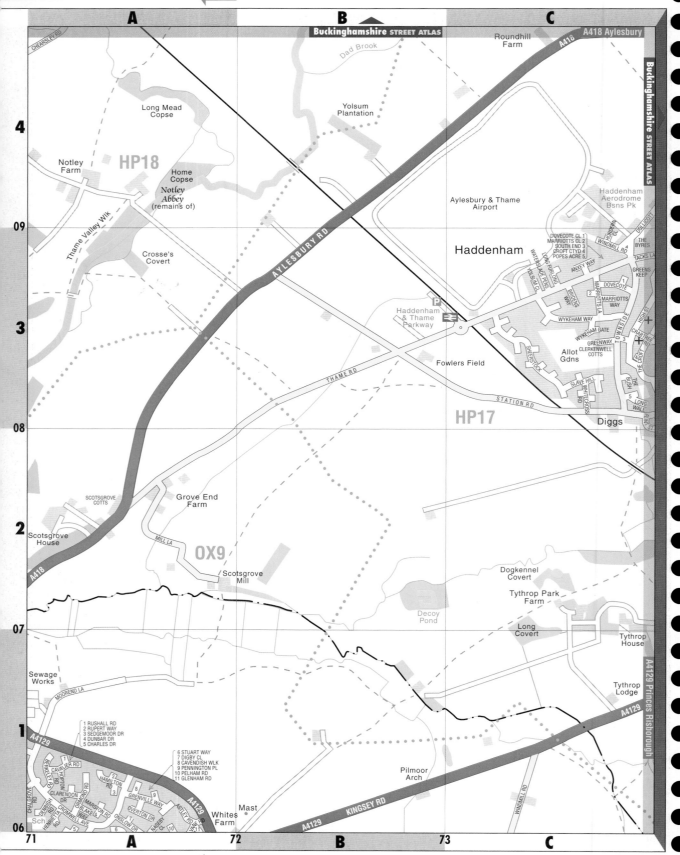
129

Buckinghamshire STREET ATLAS

Buckinghamshire STREET ATLAS

A418 Aylesbury
A418

Roundhill Farm

Dad Brook

Yolsum Plantation

Long Mead Copse

HP18

Notley Farm

Home Copse
Notley Abbey (remains of)

Thame Valley Wlk

Crosse's Covert

AYLESBURY RD

Aylesbury & Thame Airport

Haddenham

Haddenham Aerodrome Bsns Pk

DOVECOTE CL 1
MARRIOTTS CL 2
SOUTH END 3
CROFT CTYD 4
POPES ACRE 5.

WINDMILL RD
NORTHERN
DOLLICOTT
THE BYRES
JACKS LA

WATERSIDE PENS
YOLSUM CL
LONG PIN LONG

ANXEY WAY

BRIDGES WAY

GREENS KEEP
DOVECOTE
MARRIOTTS WAY

TO WILLSIDE
HIGH ST
THE CROSS

WYKEHAM WAY
WYKEHAM GATE
GREENWAY

CRAB TREE RD
THE BUSH

SHEEP STOCK
SLAVE HILL
WHITECROSS RD

GREENWAY
CLERKENWELL COTTS
Allot Gdns

LONG WALL
FUN ST

P

Haddenham & Thame Parkway

Fowlers Field

THAME RD

STATION RD

HP17

Diggs

08

Scotsgrove COTTS

Grove End Farm

Scotsgrove House

MILL LA

OX9

A418

Scotsgrove Mill

Dogkennel Covert

Tythrop Park Farm

Decoy Pond

Long Covert

Tythrop House

07

Sewage Works

MOOREND LA

Tythrop Lodge

A4129 Princes Risborough

1 RUSHALL RD
2 RUPERT WAY
3 SEDGEMOOR DR
4 DUNBAR DR
5 CHARLES DR

6 STUART WAY
7 DIGBY CL
8 CAVENDISH WLK
9 PENNINGTON PL
10 PELHAM RD
11 GLENHAM RD

A4129

1

CAVALIER RD
BERKELEY RD
DENBIGH
CLARENDON DR
HAMPTON RD
HENRIETTA CL
BLAKE L
ORMOND RD
MARSTON RD
GRENVILLE WAY
OVERTON DR
ASTLEY RD
GLEBE RD

HAMILTON RD

Pilmoor Arch

CHALGROVE
CROMWELL AVE
NASEBY CL

Sch

Mast

Whites Farm

WINDMILL RD

A4129 KINGSEY RD

A4129

71

A

72

B

73

C

129

148

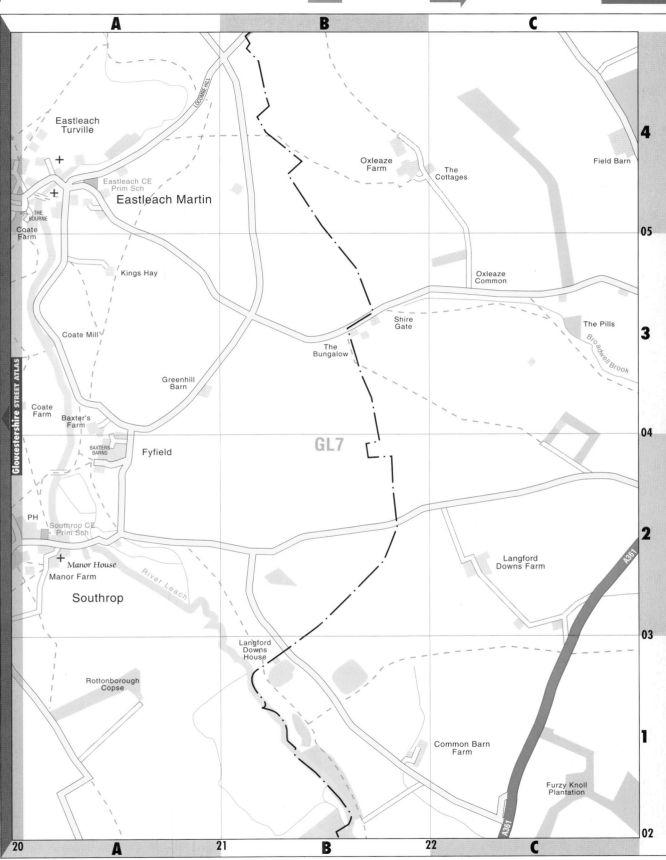

A   B   C

4

Eastleach
Turville

Oxleaze
Farm

The Cottages

Field Barn

Eastleach CE
Prim Sch

Eastleach Martin

05

THE
BOURNE

Coate
Farm

Oxleaze
Common

Kings Hay

The Pills

Broadwell Brook

3

Shire
Gate

Coate Mill

The
Bungalow

Greenhill
Barn

Coate
Farm

Baxter's
Farm

04

GL7

BAXTERS
BARNS

Fyfield

PH

2

Southrop CE
Prim Sch

Langford
Downs Farm

A361

Manor House

Manor Farm

River Leach

Southrop

03

Langford
Downs
House

Rottonborough
Copse

1

Common Barn
Farm

Furzy Knoll
Plantation

A361

02

20   A   21   B   22   C

Gloucestershire STREET ATLAS

A   **B**   **C**

OX18

4

05

Hillview
Farm

B4477

Peartree
Farm

Home
Farm

Filkins

3

Filkins
Farm

CROSS
TREE LA

Asthall
Farm

Filkins
Hall

Kencot

HAZELL ST LA

ROUSE LA

PO

BULLS
CL

Mus

THE
GASSONS

Manor
Farm

Factory

PH

PH

Cemy

GL7

04

B4477

KINGS LA

PH

Manor
Farm

Broadwell

Broughton
Hall

Manor
Farm

Lower
Farm

Broughton
Poggs

2

A361

Filkins
Mill

Broadshire
Bridge

Broadwell Brook

Holly
Cottage

CALCROFT LA

03

FILKINS RD

PH

BROADWELL RD

Langford

Ansells
Farm

LECHLADE RD

Broadwell
Mill

1

St Christopher's CE
Prim Sch

THE ELMS

PH

CHURCH
ROW

CHURCH LA

Lower
Farm

Rectory
Farm

HOOKS CL

Little
Faringdon
Wood

LEYS
VIEW

Hulse Grounds
Farm

02

23   **A**   24   **B**   25   **C**

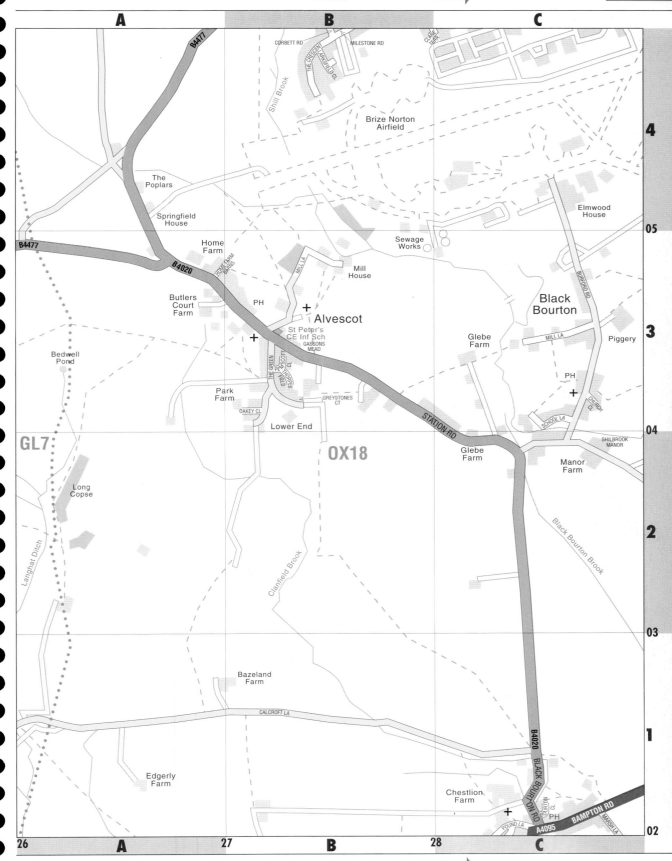

133
116

A **B** **C**

4

05

3

04

OX18

2

03

1

02

29 **A** 30 **B** 31 **C**

Brize Norton
Airfield

Viscount
Ind Est

Lower
Haddon
Farm

Ven
Bridge

Piggery

A4095

Lew Heath
House

Wind
Pump

STATION RD

Deanery
Farm

Garson's
Copse

Hobbs
Buildings

Mill
Farm

The Plantation

The
Windmill

Bampton

Highmoor Brook

Bampton
CE Prim Sch

Field
Cottage

Shill Brook

Cemy

MANOR
VIEW

PEMBROKE PL

NEW RD

WINDSOR COTTS 1
VICTORIA COTTS 2
BELL LA 3
LAVENDER SQ 4

THE LANES

BUSHEY ROW

POCOCKS LA

THE PIECES

FOX CL

SOUTHBY

CALAIS

Liby

CHURCH
ST

TH

BROAD ST

CHEAPSIDE

QUEEN ST

LAVENDER
SQ

OATHURST
EST

AMPNEY ORCH

CHY MEAD

HIGH ST

ASTON RD

BOURTON
COTTS

PH

SHREWSBURY
PL

ROSEMARY
LA

Sch

PO

P

B4449

PH

B4449

MERCURY
CL

Ham
Court

BRIDGE ST

CHENEL LA

MARKET
SQ

The
Grange

BUCKLAND RD

PH

CLANFIELD RD

Shill Brook

COWLEAZE
CNR

Weald
Manor

MILL GREEN
CL

BARN END

PRIMROSE LA

Weald
Manor
Farm

WEALD ST

Backhouse
Farm

A4095

Black Bourton
Brook

Weald
Farm

THE PADDOCKS

Weald

Glebe
Farm

133
153

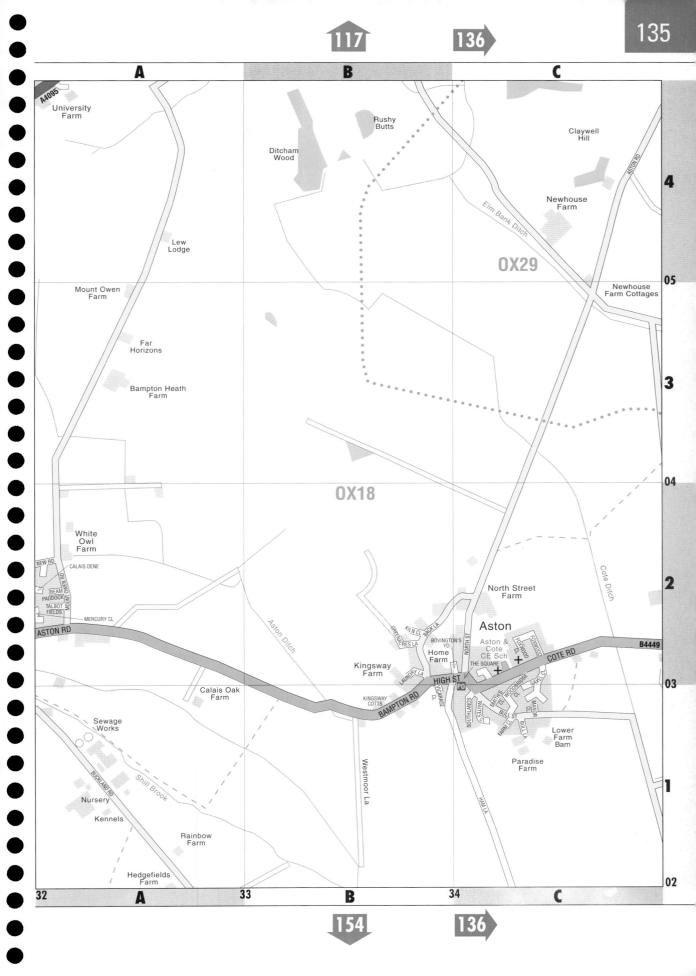

A

B

C

A4095

University Farm

Ditcham Wood

Rushy Butts

Claywell Hill

Lew Lodge

Elm Bank Ditch

Newhouse Farm

4

OX29

Mount Owen Farm

Newhouse Farm Cottages

05

Far Horizons

Bampton Heath Farm

3

OX18

04

White Owl Farm

NEW RD

CALAIS DENE

UNION HAND RD

BEAM PADDOCK

TALBOT FIELDS

MERCURY CL

Cote Ditch

North Street Farm

2

ASTON RD

Aston Ditch

Kingsway Farm

KILN CL

GREEN LA

RES LA

BACK LA

BOVINGTON'S YD

Home Farm

NORTH ST

Aston

Aston & Cote CE Sch

THE SQUARE

FOXWOOD

FOXWOOD CL

COTE RD

B4449

Calais Oak Farm

LAUNDRY LA

HIGH ST

PO

VICARAGE CL

SOUTH SIDE

SMITH'S CL

WAITES CL

BULL ST

FARM CL

WOODBRIDGE CL

SACK CL

MANOR CL

BULL LA

03

KINGSWAY COTTS

BAMPTON RD

Sewage Works

BUCKLAND RD

Shill Brook

Westmoor La

Lower Farm Barn

Paradise Farm

HAM LA

1

Nursery

Kennels

Rainbow Farm

Hedgefields Farm

02

32

A

33

B

34

C

ASTON RD

135
118

A **B** **C**

ASTON RD

Boys Wood

Long Train

Cokethorpe Park

A415

B4449

FAIRFIELDS

Hardwick

Home Wood

STANDLAKE RD

A415

4

Claywell Farm

Rickless Hill

Breach Farm
Cottage

05

Manor Farm

Westfield
Farm

Hawthorn
Farm

Yelford

College
Farm

CALAIS LA

3

OX29

04

Brighthampton Cut

Cote Lodge
Farm

2

New Shifford
Farm

B4449

Green
Acres

New Shifford
Cottages

ASTON RD

03

B4449

OX18

Cote

South Farm

Chicken
Hatchery

New
Cottages

1

Cote
Bungalow

Cote House

Cote House
Farm

Shifford

02

35 **A** 36 **B** 37 **C**

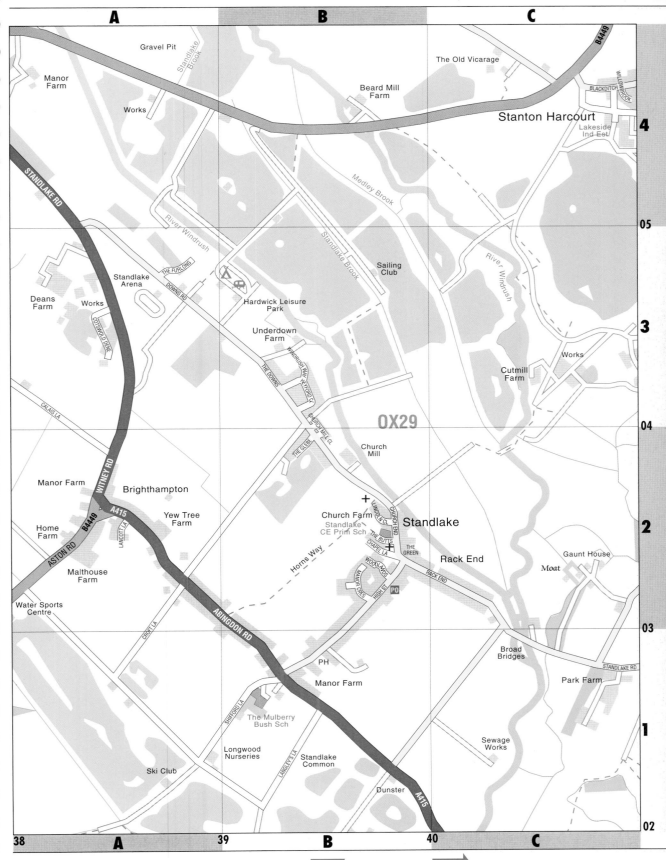

137
120

A

B

C

Stanton Harcourt
CE Prim Sch

Chapel
&
Pope's Tower

Blackditch

Stanton
Harcourt

STEADY'S LA

Steady's
Farm

MANOR
COTTS

Cemy

4

Stanton
Harcourt
Ind Est

OX2

Tawney's
Farm

05

Pimm
Farm

Gravel Pits

Whitley
Copse

Linch Hill
Cottages

3

Elms Farm

Payne's Farm

The Ferryman
Inn

West End

Bablock Hythe

Linch Hill
Leisure Park

Stoneacres
Lake

04

OX29

Lower Farm

Thames Path

River Thames or Isis

BABLOCK HYTHE RD

Towing Path

Mast

Watkins Farm

2

Manor Farm

Mount
Pleasant

CHAPEL LA

Pencots

Long
Meadow

Pinnocks Farm

GRIFFITHS CL

Ferryman
Farm

OX13

03

Brook
Farm

The Dun Cow
(PH)

Clarks Farm

Northmoor

STANDLAKE RD

The Red Lion
(PH)

Church
Farm

Rectory
Farm

Eaton
Plantation

Fairacre Farm

NORTHMOOR
PK

1

Northmoor
Lock

Ash Copse

Weir

02

41

42

43

A

B

C

A   B   C

4

05

3

04

2

03

1

02

Tower
Farmoor Resr

Filchampstead

Jumpers

Denman's Farm

Denman's Copse

Saddle Copse

Lower Whitley Farm

Bushy Leaze Copse

Autumn Lodge

Fox Covert

Whitley Brake

Smith Hill Copse

Tumbledowns

CHAWLEY LA

Physic Well

Upper Whitley Farm

New Farm

OX2

Cumnor CE Prim Sch

NORREYS RD

BERTIE RD

Long Leys Farm

LEYS RD

PO

College Farm

OXFORD RD

CUMNOR HILL

Long Leys House

Cumnor

PH

PH

THE GLEBE

PH

Cut's End

APPLETON RD

THE WINDYARDS

THE PARK

FORSTER LA

Eaton Heath

KENILWORTH RD

ROBSART PL

Cross Roads Farm

Manor Farm

Jackman's Copse

BABLOCK HYTHE RD

PH

West Farm

Eaton

OX13

Wayside

St John's Cottages

Spring Farm

Bradley Farm

Bradley Cottages

Caps Lodge

EATON RD

FARINGDON RD

Works

Rockley Cottages

OX1

B4017

Hengrove Wood

Hengrove

Rockley Heath

Rockley Copse

A420

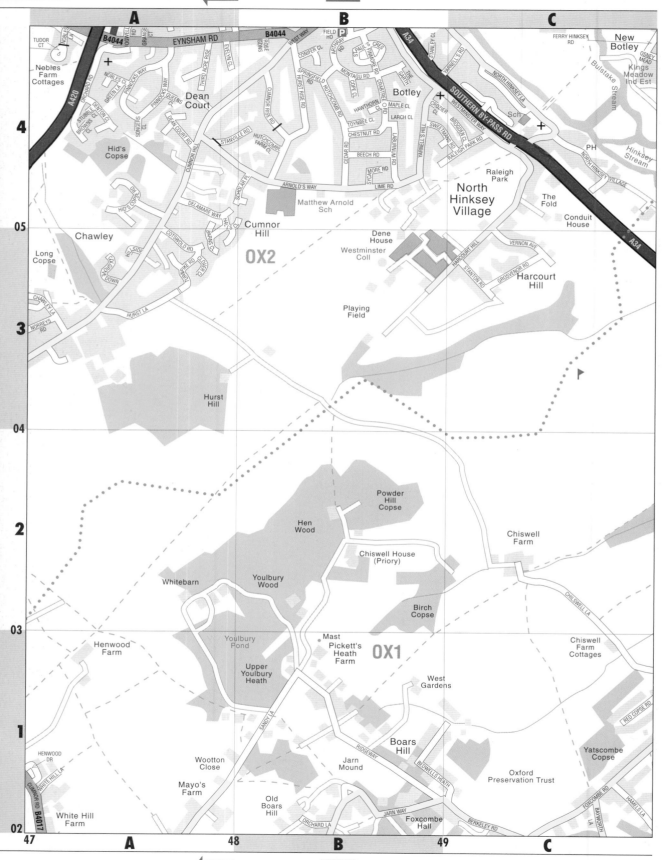

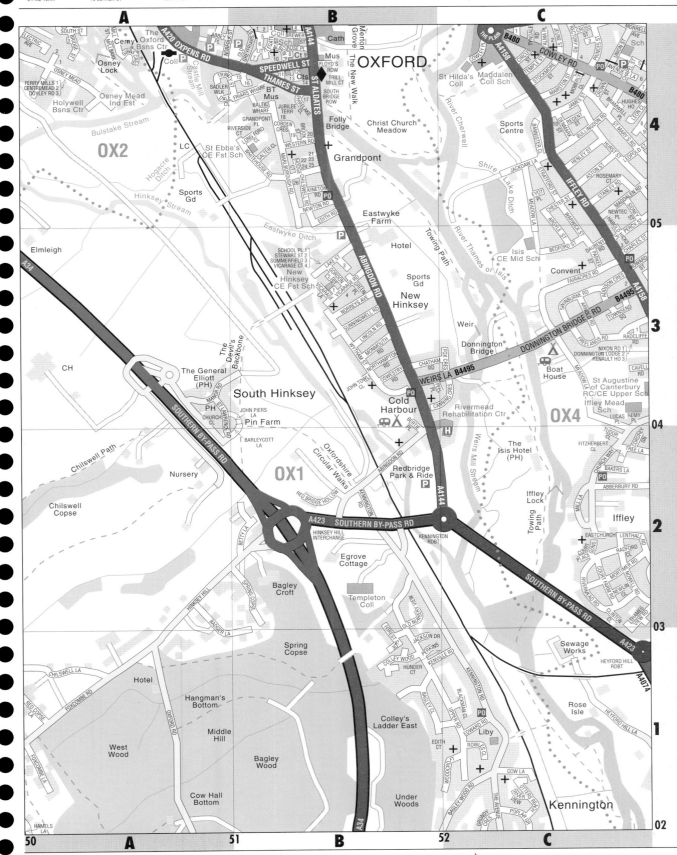

B4
1 WESTGATE SH CTR
2 ROGER BACON LA
3 ST EBBES ST
4 PEMBROKE SQ
5 TURN AGAIN LA
6 PIKE TERR
7 FAULKNER ST
8 CAMBRIDGE TERR
9 CLARK'S ROW
10 BROOKS TAYLOR CT
11 BUTTERWYKE PL
12 CROMWELL ST
13 LUTHER CT
14 STEPHENSON HO
15 BLACKFRIARS RD
16 PREACHERS LA
17 FOLLY BRIDGE CT
18 THAMES CT
19 BUCKINGHAM ST
20 WATERMANS REACH
21 THE CLOISTERS
22 BURFORD LODGE
23 PEGASUS CT
24 STREATLEY LODGE
25 GORING LODGE
26 OLNEY CT

C4
1 DAWSON ST
2 JEUNE HALL
3 GRANTS MEWS
4 PEMBROKE CT
5 COLLINS ST
6 SOUTH PARK CT
7 EAST AVE
8 RANDOLPH ST
9 HAWKINS ST
10 MONARD TERR

123
142
160
142

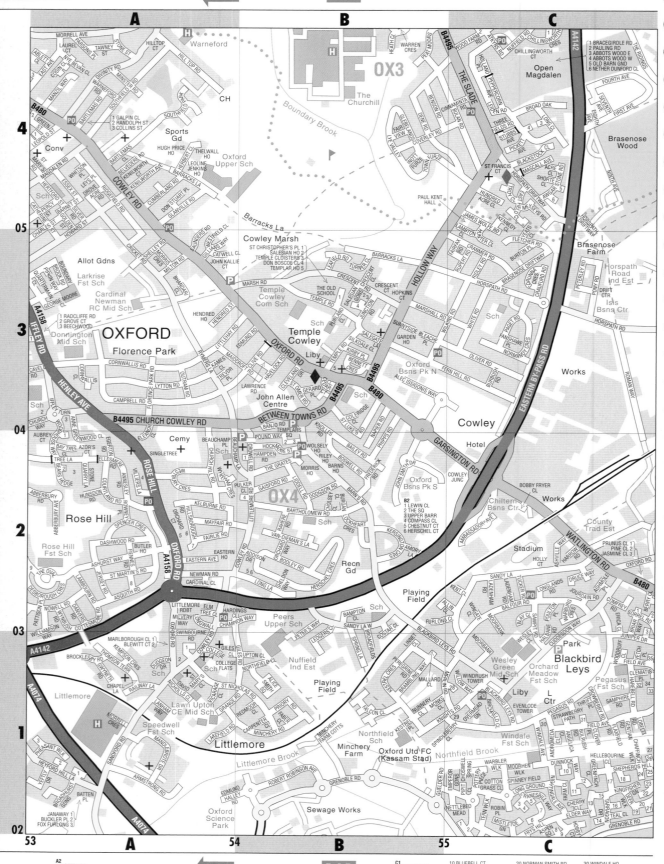

A   B   C

OX3

Warneford

The Churchill

Boundary Brook

Open
Magdalen

Brasenose
Wood

1 BRACEGIRDLE RD
2 PAULING RD
3 ABBOTS WOOD D
4 ABBOTS WOOD W
5 OLD BARN GND
6 NETHER DUNFORD CL

1 GALPIN CL
2 RANDOLPH ST
3 COLLINS ST

Sports
Gd

CH

Conv

Oxford
Upper Sch

St Francis
Ct

Brasenose
Farm

Horspath
Road
Ind Est

Isis
Bsns Ctr

Allot Gdns

Larkrise
Fst Sch

Cowley Marsh

St Christopher's Pl 1
Salesian Ho 2
Temple Cloisters 3
Don Bosco Cl 4
Templar Ho 5

Barracks La

Cardinal
Newman
RC Mid Sch

1 RADCLIFFE RD
2 GROVE CT
3 BEECHWOOD

The Old
School

Temple
Cowley
Com Sch

OXFORD

Donnington
Mid Sch

Florence Park

Temple
Cowley

Liby

Oxford
Bsns Pk N

Works

John Allen
Centre

Cowley

Cemy

John Allen
Centre

Cowley
Hotel

Rose Hill

Rose Hill
Fst Sch

OX4

Oxford
Bsns Pk S

Cowley
Junc

Works

County
Trad Est

B2
1 LEWIN CL
2 THE SQ
3 UPPER BARR
4 COMPASS CL
5 CHESTNUT CT
6 HERSCHEL CL

Stadium

Recn
Gd

Chiltern
Bsns Ctr

Littlemore
RDBT

Peers
Upper Sch

Playing
Field

Blackbird
Leys

Nuffield
Ind Est

Wesley
Green
Mid Sch

Orchard
Meadow
Fst Sch

Liby
L
Ctr

Pegasus
Fst Sch

Littlemore

Playing
Field

Lawn Upton
CE Mid Sch

Speedwell
Fst Sch

Minchery
Sch

Littlemore

Minchery
Farm

Oxford Utd FC
(Kassam Stad)

Northfield Brook

Windale
Fst Sch

Littlemore Brook

Oxford
Science
Park

Sewage Works

53   54   55

A   B   C

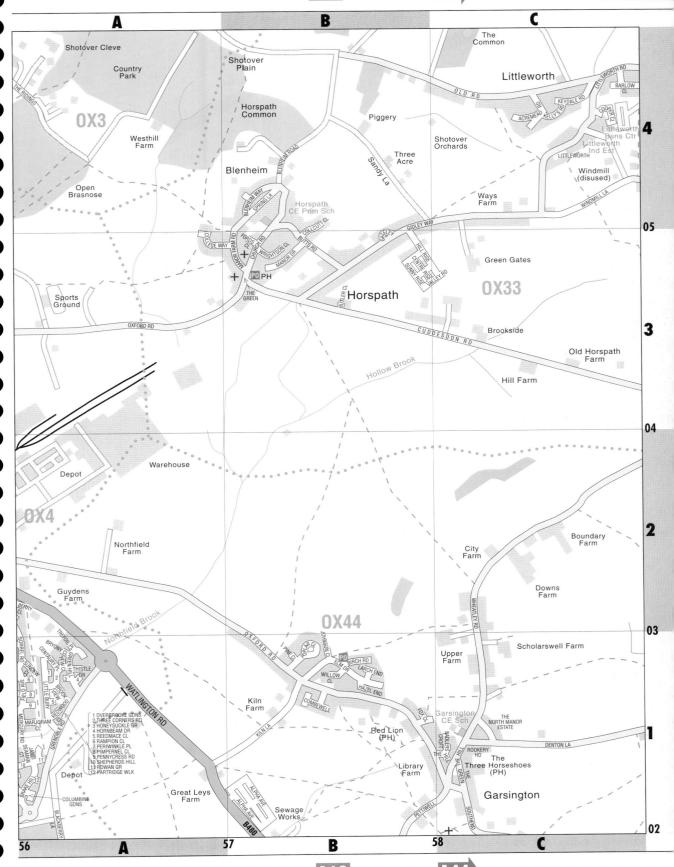

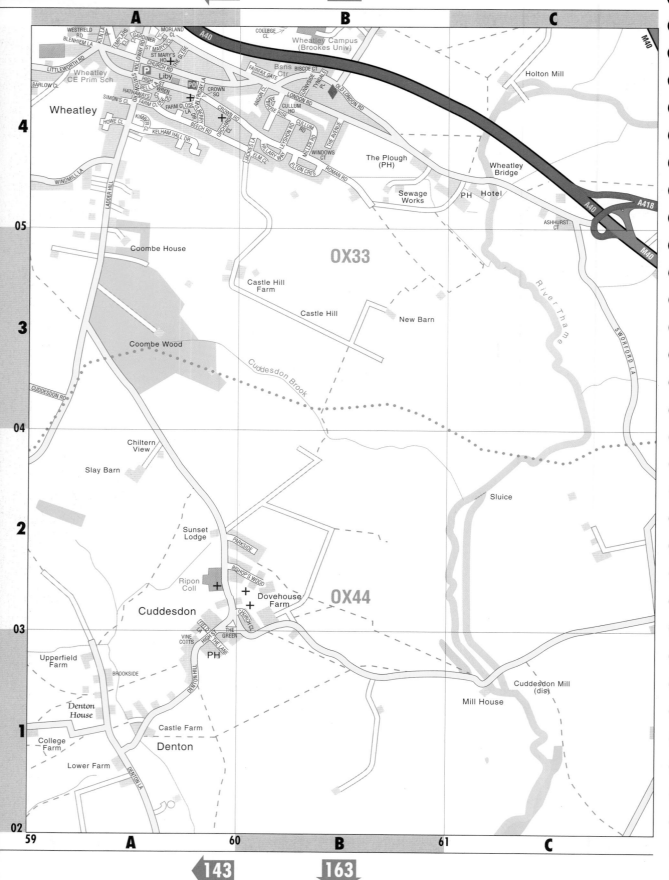

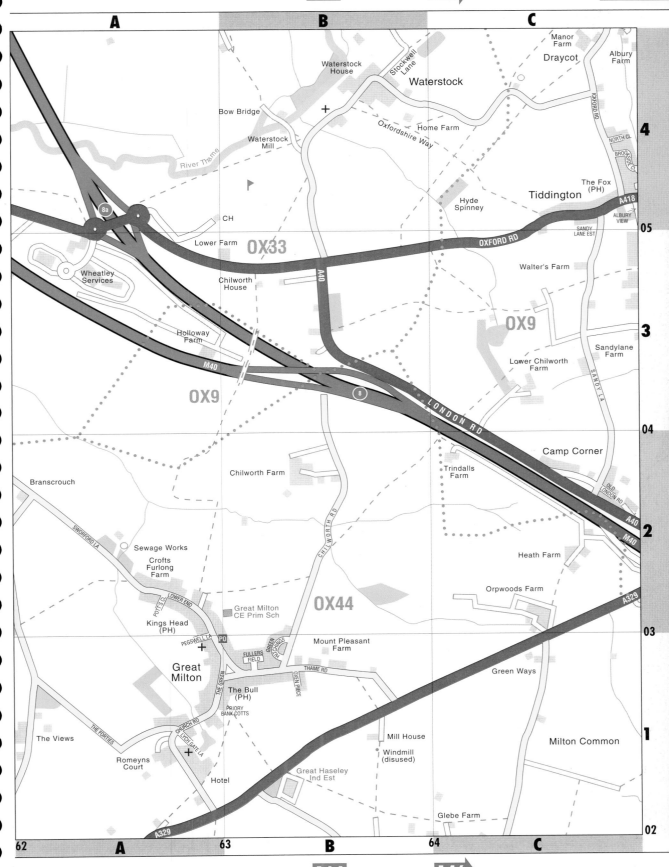

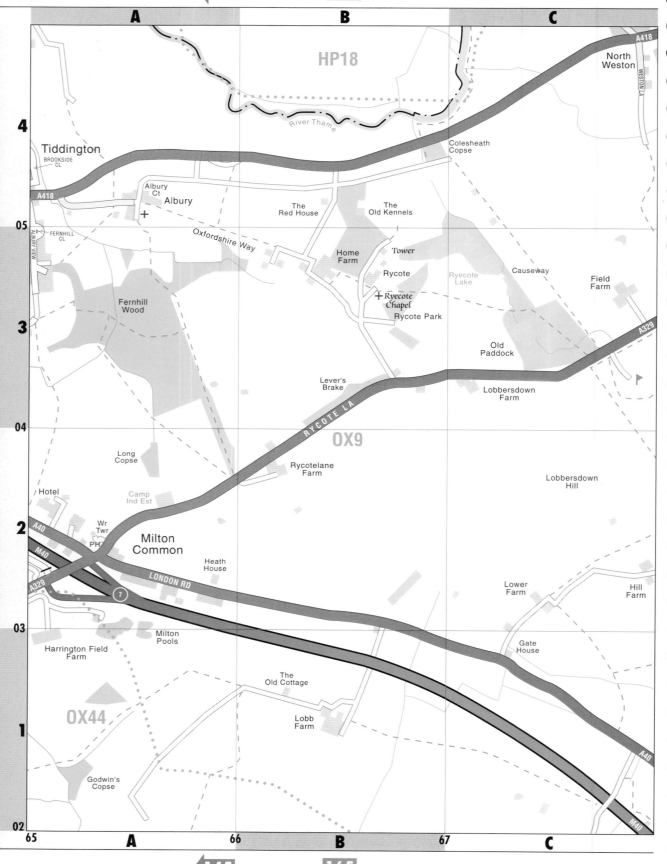

A   B   C

HP18

A418

North Weston

WESTON LA

River Thame

4

Tiddington

Colesheath Copse

BROOKSIDE CL

A418

Albury Ct

Albury

The Red House

The Old Kennels

05

FERNHILL CL

ALBURY VIEW

Oxfordshire Way

Home Farm

Tower

Rycote

Rycote Lake

Causeway

Field Farm

Fernhill Wood

+ Rycecote Chapel

Rycote Park

3

Old Paddock

A329

Lever's Brake

Lobbersdown Farm

RYCOTE LA

Long Copse

OX9

04

Rycotelane Farm

Lobbersdown Hill

Hotel

Camp Ind Est

A40

Wr Twr

PH

Milton Common

Heath House

2

M40

LONDON RD

Lower Farm

Hill Farm

A329

7

03

Milton Pools

Gate House

Harrington Field Farm

The Old Cottage

OX44

Lobb Farm

1

A40

Godwin's Copse

M40

02

65   A   66   B   67   C

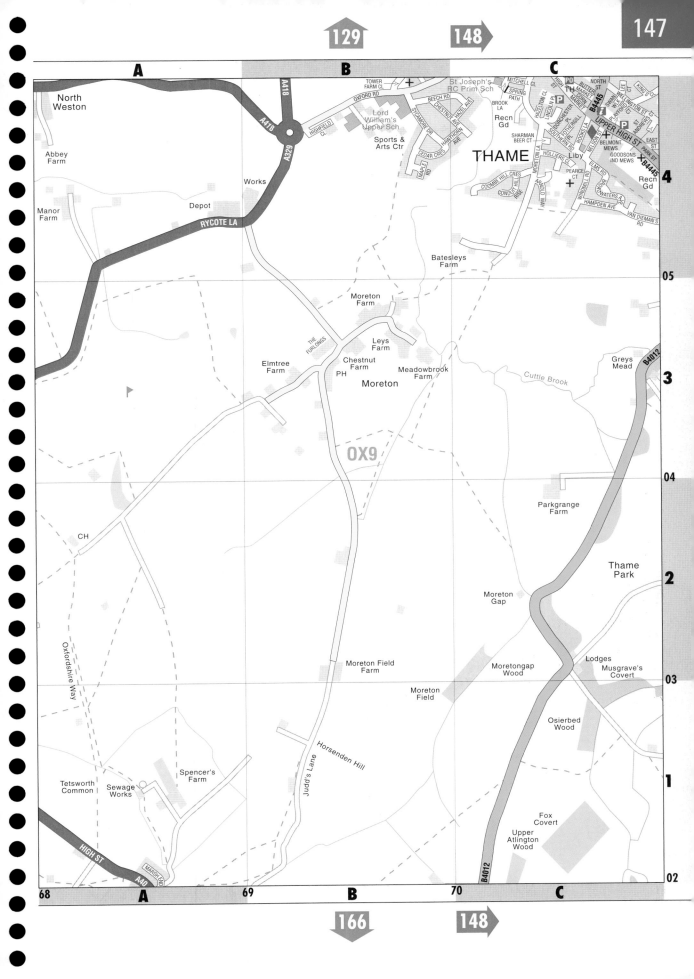

129
148

A
B
C

North Weston

A418

Abbey Farm

A329

HIGHFIELD CL

OXFORD RD

TOWER FARM CL

Lord William's Upper Sch

Sports & Arts Ctr

St Joseph's RC Prim Sch

SPRING PATH

BROOK LA

Recn Gd

MITCHELL CL

HAZELTON CL

LINCOLN PL

SHARMAN BEER CT

CHESTNUT AVE

HAZEL AVE

BEECH RD

SYCAMORE DR

HAWTHORN AVE

CEDAR CRES

MAPLE RD

THAME

COOMBE HILL CRES

COND. RISE

COOMBE HILL

MORETON LA

HOLLIERS

ARNOLD WAY

WINDMILL RD

SOUTHERN RD

PEARCE CT

NORTH ST

MARKET

CORN MARKET

SWAN WLK

WELLINGTON ST

PLAYFORD CT

ROOKS LA

NELSON ST

BELMONT MEWS

GOODSONS IND MEWS

UPPER HIGH ST

B4445

HIGH ST

KING'S RD

EAST ST

FAIR ST

Liby

Recn Gd

ELMS RD

BACKSWATERS

HAMPDEN AVE

VAN DIEMAN'S RD

B4445

4

Manor Farm

Works

Depot

RYCOTE LA

Batesleys Farm

05

Moreton Farm

THE FURLONGS

Leys Farm

Elmtree Farm

Chestnut Farm

PH

Moreton

Meadowbrook Farm

Cuttle Brook

Greys Mead

B4012

3

OX9

04

Parkgrange Farm

CH

Oxfordshire Way

Thame Park

2

Moreton Gap

Moreton Field Farm

Moretongap Wood

Lodges

Musgrave's Covert

03

Moreton Field

Judd's Lane

Horsenden Hill

Osierbed Wood

Tetsworth Common

Sewage Works

Spencer's Farm

Fox Covert

1

Upper Atlington Wood

HIGH ST

MARSH END

A40

B4012

02

68
A
69
B
70
C

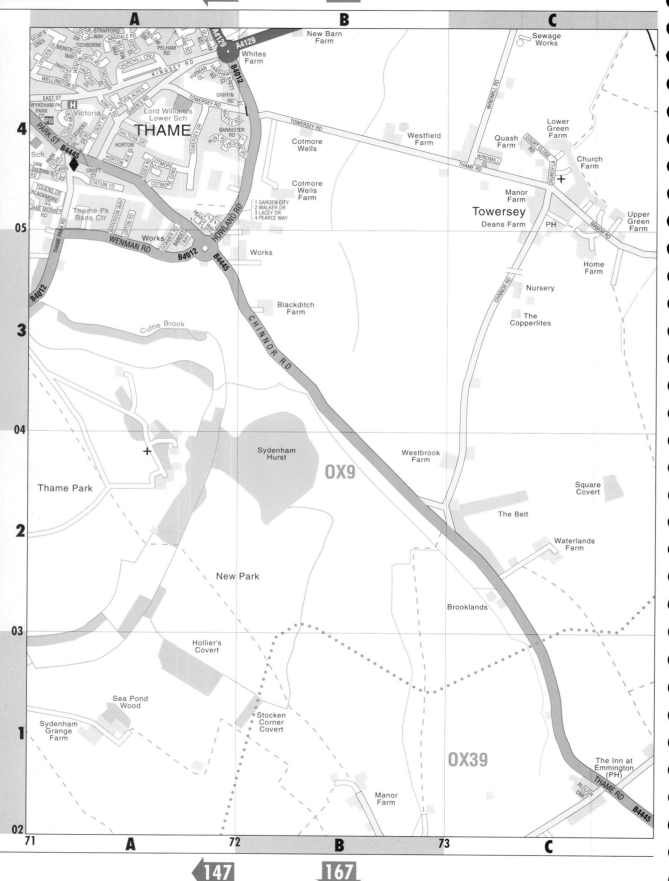

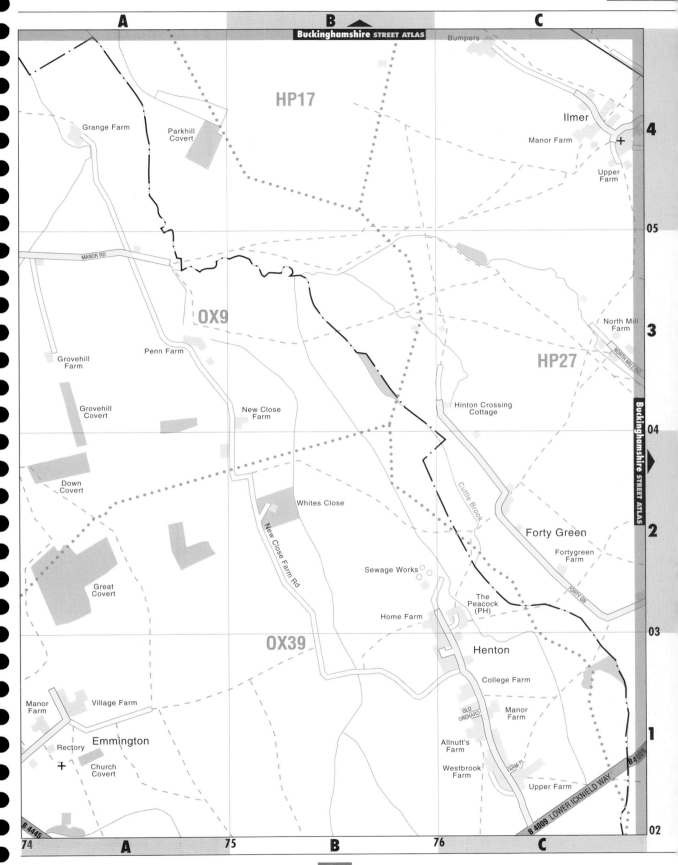

Buckinghamshire STREET ATLAS

Buckinghamshire STREET ATLAS

A B C

Bumpers

HP17

Ilmer

Grange Farm

Parkhill Covert

Manor Farm

Upper Farm

MANOR RD

05

OX9

North Mill Farm

Grovehill Farm

Penn Farm

HP27

Grovehill Covert

New Close Farm

Hinton Crossing Cottage

04

Down Covert

Whites Close

Cuttle Brook

Forty Green

New Close Farm Rd

Fortygreen Farm

Great Covert

Sewage Works

FORTY GN

The Peacock (PH)

Home Farm

2

OX39

03

Henton

College Farm

Manor Farm

Village Farm

OLD ORCHARD

Manor Farm

Allnutt's Farm

Emmington

FARM PL

1

Rectory

Church Covert

Westbrook Farm

Upper Farm

LOWER ICKNIELD WAY

B 4445

B 4009

02

74 A 75 B 76 C

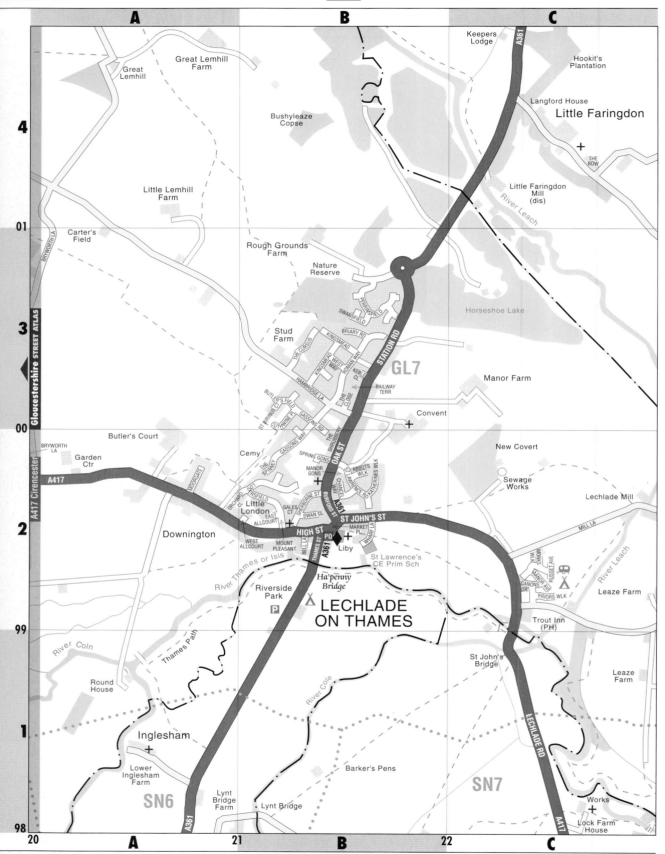

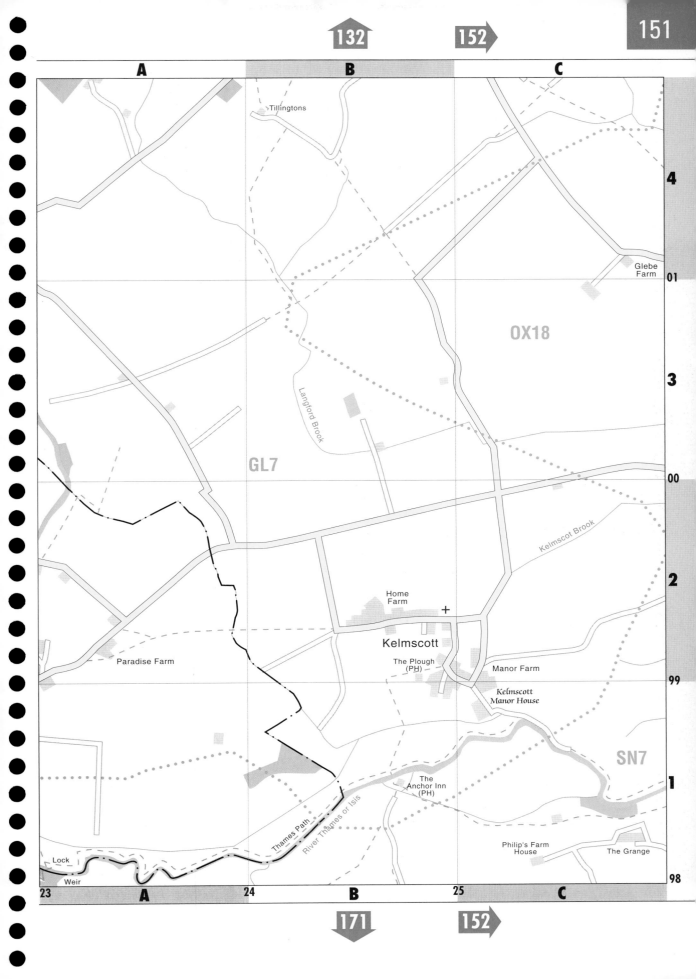

132
152

A
B
C

4

Tillingtons

Glebe
Farm

01

OX18

3

Langford Brook

GL7

00

Kelmscot Brook

2

Home
Farm

Kelmscott

Paradise Farm

The Plough
(PH)

Manor Farm

99

Kelmscott
Manor House

SN7

1

The
Anchor Inn
(PH)

Thames Path

River Thames or Isis

Philip's Farm
House

The Grange

Lock

Weir

98

23
A
24
B
25
C

171
152

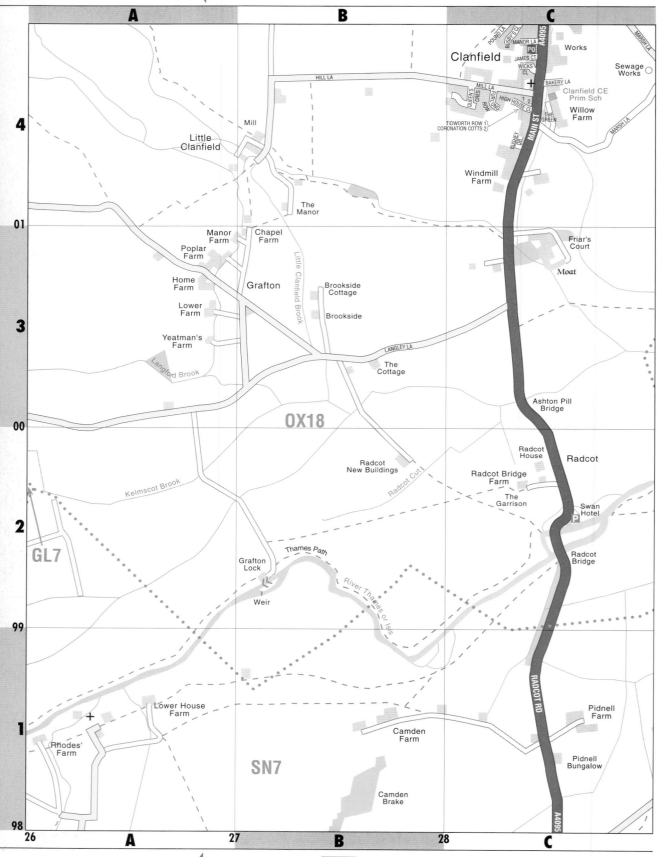

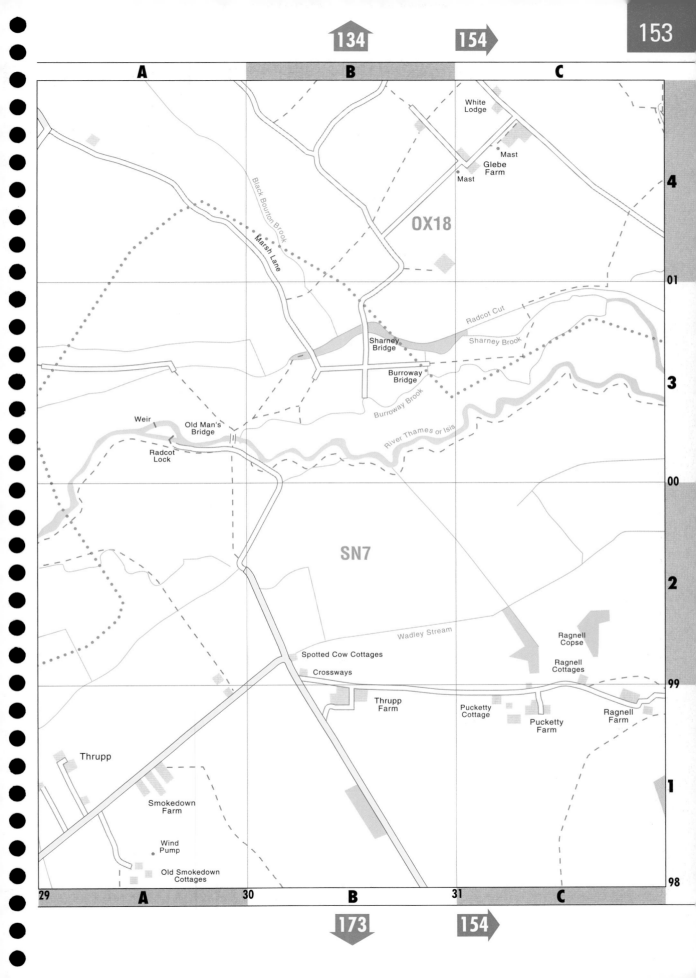

A
B
C

White Lodge

Mast
Glebe
Farm
Mast
Mast

OX18

Black Bourton Brook

Marsh Lane

4

01

Radcot Cut

Sharney Brook

Sharney
Bridge

Burroway
Bridge

3

Burroway Brook

Weir

Old Man's
Bridge

River Thames or Isis

Radcot
Lock

00

SN7

2

Wadley Stream

Ragnell
Copse

Spotted Cow Cottages

Ragnell
Cottages

Crossways

99

Thrupp
Farm

Pucketty
Cottage

Pucketty
Farm

Ragnell
Farm

Thrupp

Smokedown
Farm

1

Wind
Pump

Old Smokedown
Cottages

98

153
135

A **B** **C**

Meadow Arch
Bridge

Meadow Farm
Cottages

Shill Brook

HAM LA

OX18

Meadow Brook

BUCKLAND RD

4

Great Brook

01

Hoskins
Barn

Meadow
Farm

Isle Of Wight
Bridge

3

Tadpole
Bridge

Tadpole

The Trout Inn
(PH)

Rushey
Lock

River Thames or Isis

Weir

00

Buckland
Marsh

2

Buckland Marsh
Farm

SN7

Carswell Marsh

Gore Farm

99

Marriage
Hill

The
Lakes

Weir

Vicar's
Copse

1

Deer Park

Manor
House

Sewage
Works

CARSWELL LA

Middle
Brake

Rivey
Brake

Buckland
House

Buckland

BUCKLAND
RD

Rivey
Copse

Arch
Plantation

ST GEORGE'S RD

ORCHARD
RD

98

32 **A** 33 **B** 34 **C**

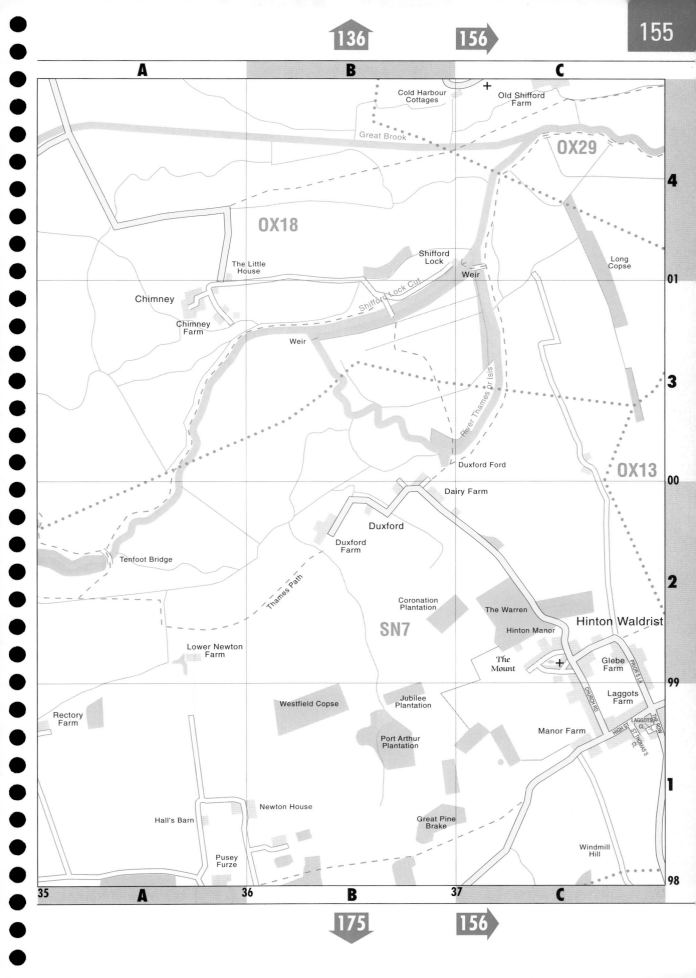

A B C

Cold Harbour Cottages

Old Shifford Farm

Great Brook

OX29

4

OX18

Shifford Lock

The Little House

Weir

01

Chimney

Shifford Lock Cut

Chimney Farm

Weir

River Thames or Isis

3

Long Copse

Duxford Ford

OX13

00

Dairy Farm

Duxford

Tenfoot Bridge

Duxford Farm

Thames Path

Coronation Plantation

The Warren

Hinton Waldrist

2

Hinton Manor

SN7

Lower Newton Farm

The Mount

Glebe Farm

99

Rectory Farm

Westfield Copse

Jubilee Plantation

Laggots Farm

PRIORS LA

THE ROW

LAGGOTS CL

Port Arthur Plantation

Manor Farm

CHURCH RD

HIGH ST

ST THOMAS'S CL

1

Hall's Barn

Newton House

Great Pine Brake

Windmill Hill

Pusey Furze

98

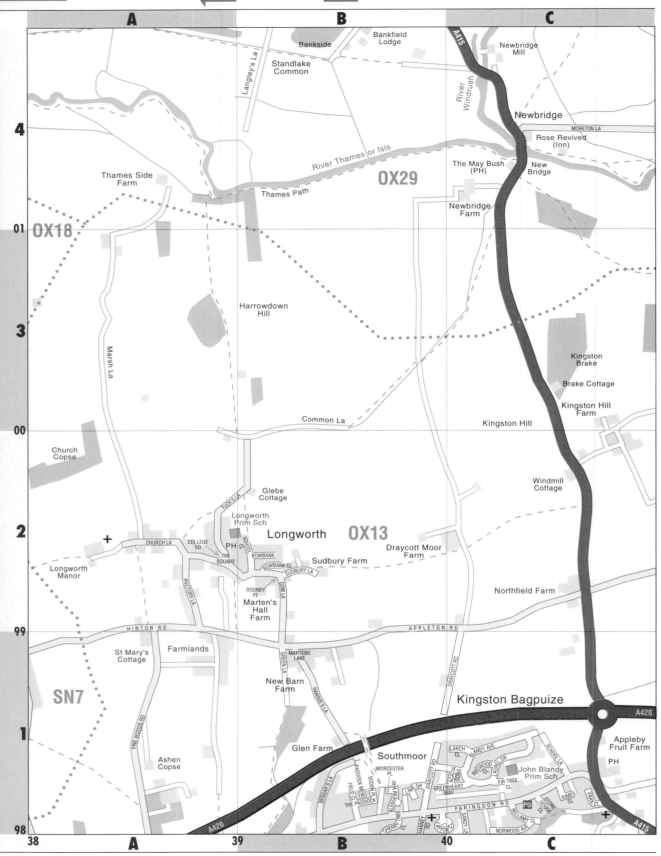

A   B   C

4

Bankside
Bankfield
Lodge
Langley's La
Standlake
Common

Newbridge
Mill

A415

River Windrush

Newbridge

MORETON LA

Rose Revived
(Inn)

River Thames or Isis

OX29

The May Bush
(PH)

New
Bridge

Thames Side
Farm

Thames Path

Newbridge
Farm

01

OX18

Harrowdown
Hill

Kingston
Brake

Brake Cottage

3

Marsh La

Kingston Hill
Farm

Common La

Kingston Hill

00

Church
Copse

Windmill
Cottage

Glebe
Cottage

TUCK'S LA

Longworth
Prim Sch

Longworth

OX13

Draycott Moor
Farm

2

+

CHURCH LA

COLLEGE
SQ

PH
THE
SQUARE

SCHOOL CL

BOWBANK

BOWBANK CL

Sudbury Farm

Longworth
Manor

SUDBURY LA

Northfield Farm

RECTORY LA

RODNEY
PL

COW LA

Marten's
Hall
Farm

HINTON RD

APPLETON RD

99

St Mary's
Cottage

Farmlands

GREEN LA

MARTENS
LAKE

DRAYCOTT RD

SN7

New Barn
Farm

HARRIS'S LA

Kingston Bagpuize

A420

1

Glen Farm

Southmoor

Appleby
Fruit Farm

PNE WOODS RD

Ashen
Copse

LARCH
CL

BLANDY AVE

REDWOOD
CL

LAUREL DR

SCHOOL LA

PH

WORCESTER
PL

DRAYCOTT RD

ACACIA
GDNS

FIR TREE
CL

John Blandy
Prim Sch

RIMES
CL

FRAY CL

BEGGAR'S LA

SODEN RD

THE PADDOCK

FIELD CL

PADDOCK MEWS

BLENHEIM WAY

LIME GR

GREENHEART
WAY

FARINGDON RD

STONE
HOUSE
CL

PO

BELLAMY CL

98

CHERRY
CL

HANNEY
RD

SAXTON
RD

SANDY LA

NORWOOD AVE

+

A420

A415

+

38   A   39   B   40   C

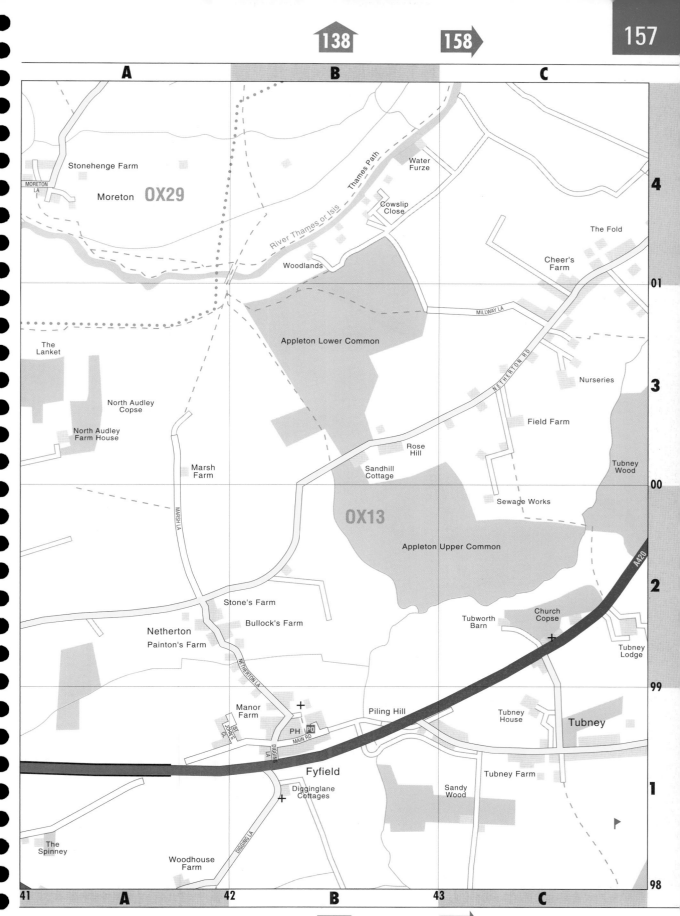

A | B | C

4

01

3

00

2

99

1

98

Stonehenge Farm

MORETON LA

Moreton OX29

Water Furze

Thames Path

River Thames or Isis

Cowslip Close

Woodlands

The Fold

Cheer's Farm

MILLWAY LA

NETHERTON RD

Nurseries

The Lanket

Appleton Lower Common

Field Farm

North Audley Copse

Rose Hill

Tubney Wood

North Audley Farm House

Sandhill Cottage

Marsh Farm

OX13

MARSH LA

Sewage Works

Appleton Upper Common

A420

Stone's Farm

Bullock's Farm

Church Copse

Tubworth Barn

Netherton

Tubney Lodge

Painton's Farm

NETHERTON LA

Manor Farm

Piling Hill

Tubney House

Tubney

ST JOHN'S CL

PH PO

MAIN RD

DIGGINS LA

Fyfield

Tubney Farm

Digginglane Cottages

Sandy Wood

DIGGING LA

The Spinney

Woodhouse Farm

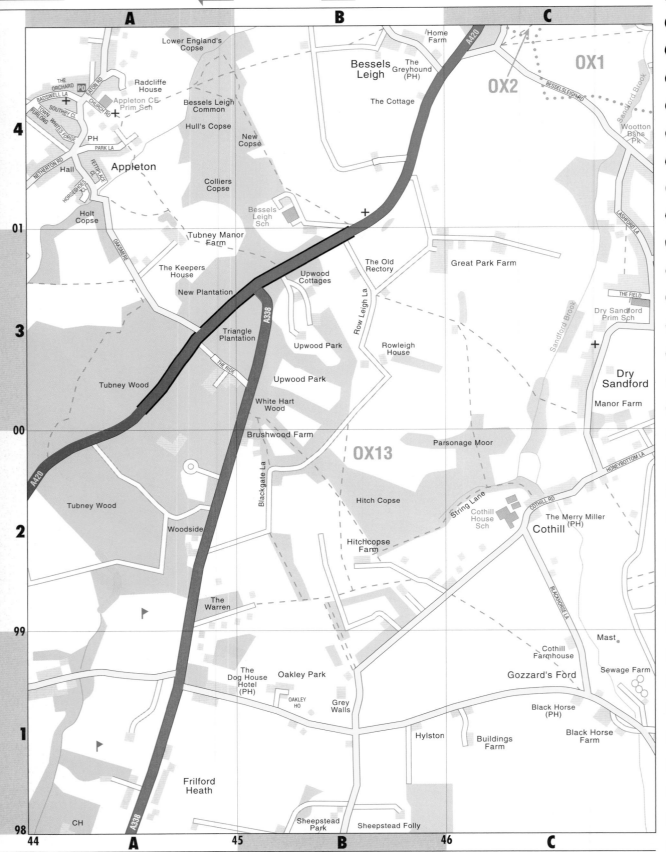

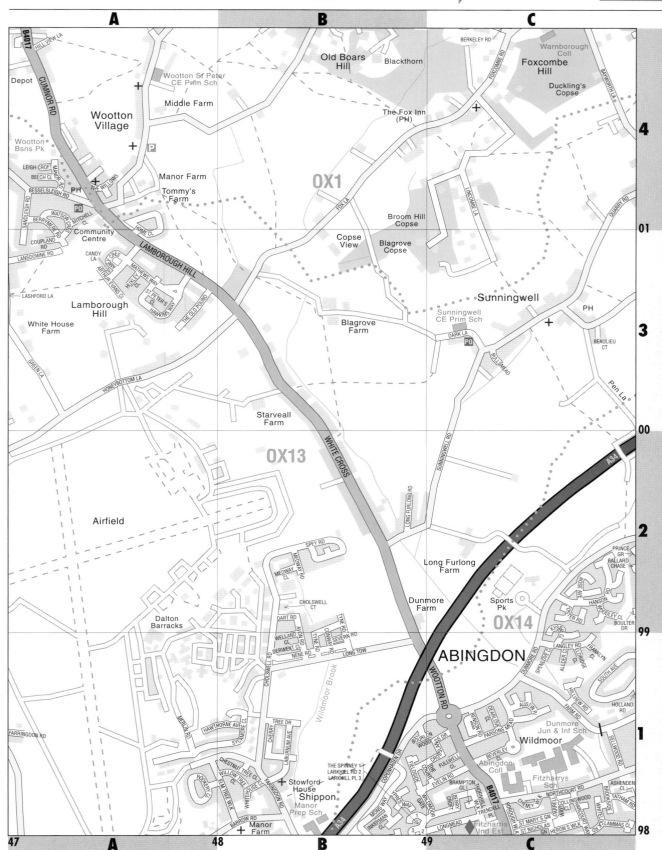

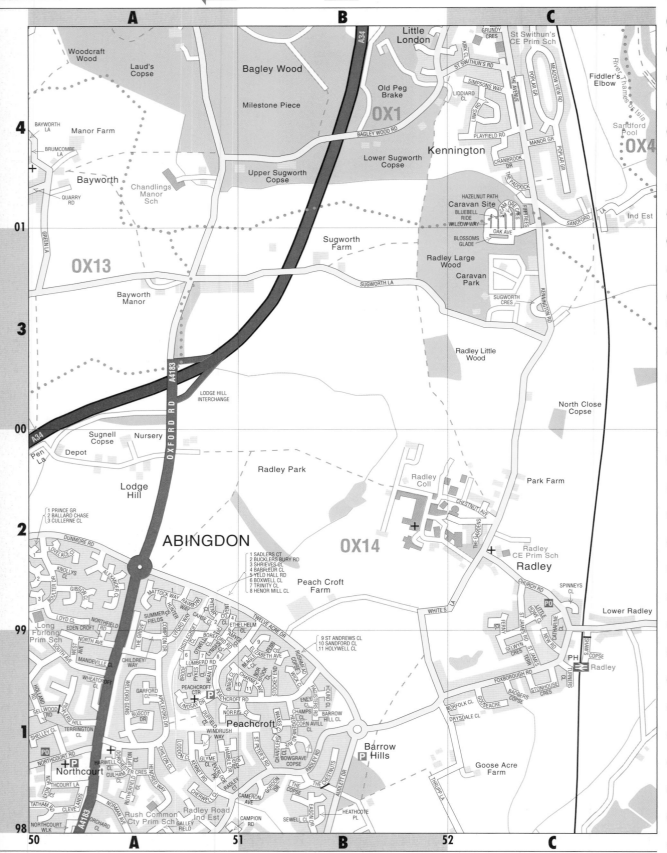

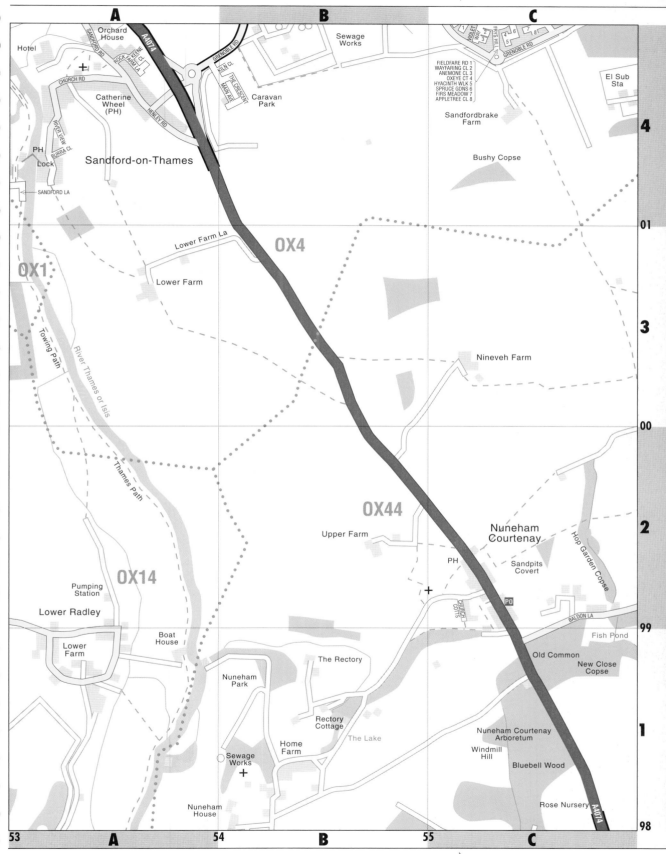

A B C

Orchard House
Hotel
CHURCH RD
Catherine Wheel (PH)
RIVER VIEW
BURRA CL
PH
Lock
Sandford-on-Thames
SANDFORD LA
SANDFORD RD
ROCK FARM LA
PARK CL
KEENE CL
A4074
HENLEY RD
GRENOBLE RD
KILN CL
MAIN AVE
THE CRESCENT
Caravan Park

Sewage Works

GRENOBLE RD
FRY'S HILL
FIELDFARE RD 1
WAYFARING CL 2
ANEMONE CL 3
OXEYE CT 4
HYACINTH WLK 5
SPRUCE GDNS 6
FIRS MEADOW 7
APPLETREE CL 8
Sandfordbrake Farm
El Sub Sta

Bushy Copse

4

OX1
Lower Farm La
OX4
Lower Farm

01

Towing Path
River Thames or Isis

Nineveh Farm

3

Thames Path

00

OX44
Upper Farm
Nuneham Courtenay
Hop Garden Copse
Sandpits Covert

2

OX14
Pumping Station
Lower Radley
PH
+
CHURCH COTTS
PO
BALDON LA

Lower Farm
Boat House
Nuneham Park
The Rectory
Old Common
Fish Pond
New Close Copse

99

Rectory Cottage
The Lake
Home Farm
Nuneham Courtenay Arboretum
Windmill Hill
Bluebell Wood

1

Sewage Works
+
Nuneham House
Rose Nursery
A4074

98

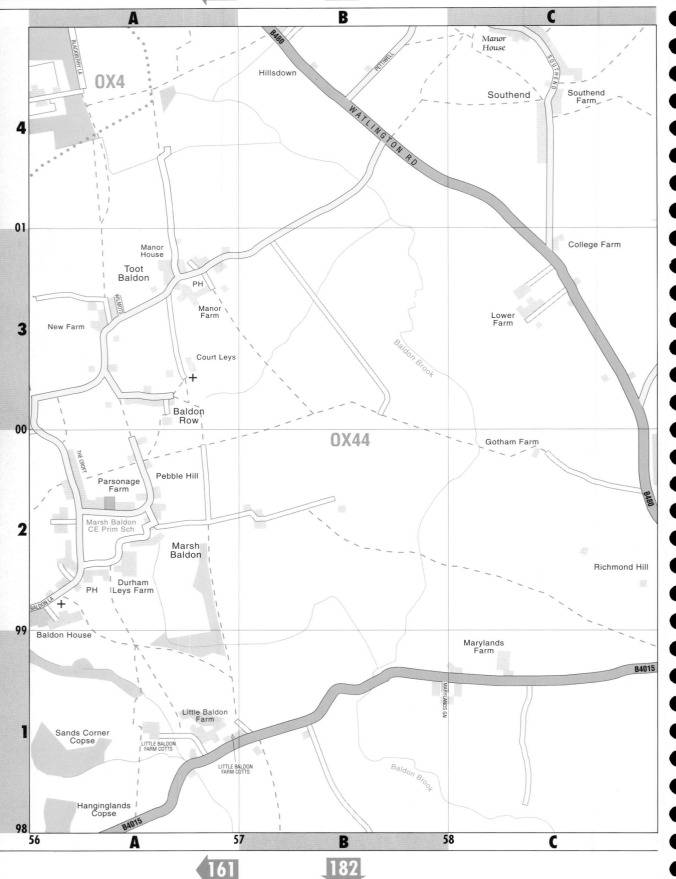

A B C

4

01

3

00

2

99

1

98

56 A 57 B 58 C

OX4

B480

Hillsdown

PETTIWELL

Manor House

Southend

SOUTHEND

Southend Farm

WATLINGTON RD

College Farm

Manor House

Toot Baldon

PH

Manor Farm

New Farm

WILMOTS

Court Leys

Lower Farm

Baldon Brook

Baldon Row

OX44

Gotham Farm

THE CROFT

Pebble Hill

Parsonage Farm

B480

Marsh Baldon CE Prim Sch

Marsh Baldon

Richmond Hill

PH

Durham Leys Farm

BALDON LA

Baldon House

Marylands Farm

B4015

Little Baldon Farm

Sands Corner Copse

LITTLE BALDON FARM COTTS

MARYLANDS GN

LITTLE BALDON FARM COTTS

Baldon Brook

Hanginglands Copse

B4015

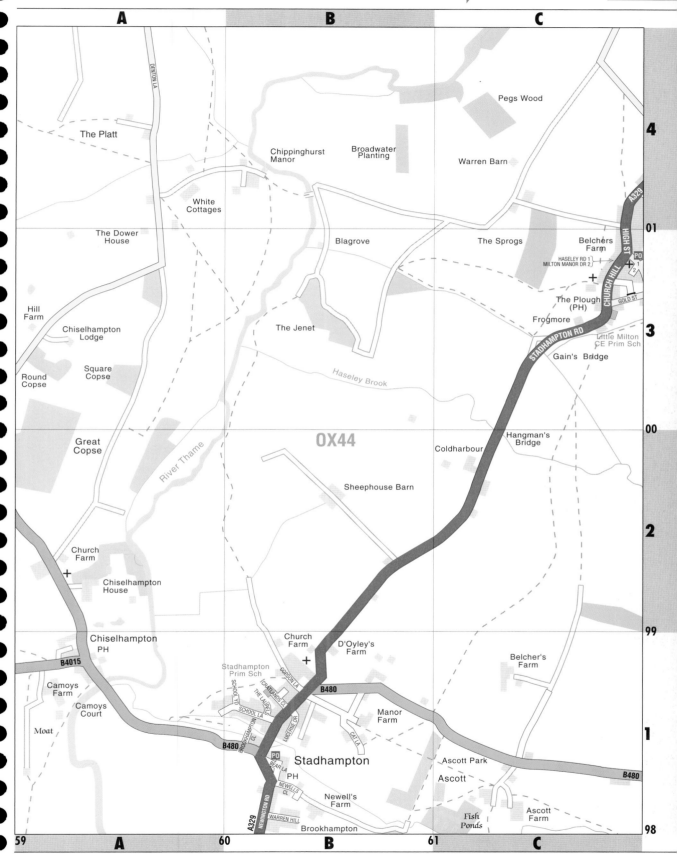

DENTON LA

The Platt

Chippinghurst Manor

Broadwater Planting

Pegs Wood

Warren Barn

White Cottages

The Dower House

Blagrove

The Sprogs

Belchers Farm

A329

HIGH ST

01

HASELEY RD 1
MILTON MANOR DR 2

PO

Hill Farm

CHURCH HILL

The Plough (PH)

GOLD ST

Chiselhampton Lodge

The Jenet

Frogmore

3

Little Milton CE Prim Sch

STADHAMPTON RD

Square Copse

Gain's Bridge

Round Copse

Haseley Brook

Great Copse

OX44

00

Coldharbour

Hangman's Bridge

River Thame

Sheephouse Barn

2

Church Farm

Chiselhampton House

99

Chiselhampton PH

Church Farm

D'Oyley's Farm

Belcher's Farm

B4015

Stadhampton Prim Sch

GAPSON LA

GRASSLANDS CL

Camoys Farm

SCHOOL YD

THE LAURELS

B480

Manor Farm

Camoys Court

SCHOOL LA

BROOKHAMPTON CL

LUCERNE DR

CAT LA

Moat

B480

PO

Stadhampton

Ascott Park

1

BEAR LA

PH

Ascott

B480

NEWELLS CL

NEWINGTON RD

A329

WARREN HILL

Newell's Farm

Ascott Farm

Fish Ponds

98

Brookhampton

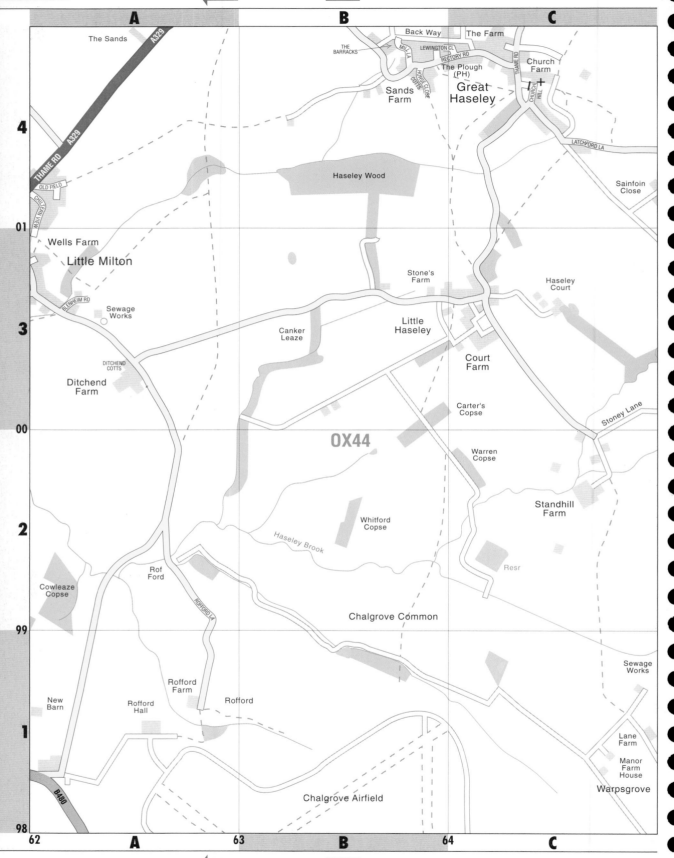

A

B

C

The Sands

A329

Back Way

The Farm

THE BARRACKS

MILL LA

LEWINGTON CL

RECTORY RD

THAME RD

Church
Farm

The Plough
(PH)

Sands
Farm

HORSE CLOSE
COTTS

Great
Haseley

CHURCH HILL

4

THAME RD

A329

Haseley Wood

LATCHFORD LA

Sainfoin
Close

OLD FIELD

CHILTERN VIEW

01

Wells Farm

Stone's
Farm

Haseley
Court

Little Milton

3

BLENHEIM RD

Sewage
Works

Canker
Leaze

Little
Haseley

DITCHEND
COTTS

Court
Farm

Ditchend
Farm

Carter's
Copse

Stoney Lane

00

OX44

Warren
Copse

Standhill
Farm

2

Whitford
Copse

Resr

Haseley Brook

Cowleaze
Copse

Rof
Ford

99

ROFFORD LA

Sewage
Works

Rofford
Farm

Chalgrove Common

New
Barn

Rofford

Rofford
Hall

Lane
Farm

1

Manor
Farm
House

B480

Warpsgrove

98

Chalgrove Airfield

62

A

63

B

64

C

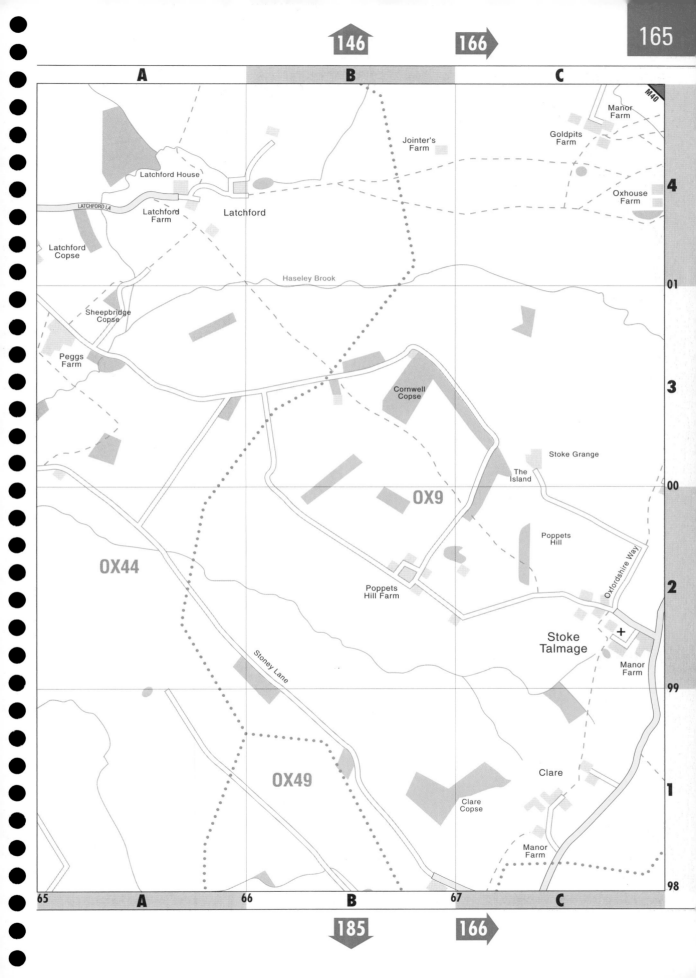

A
B
C

M40

Manor Farm

Goldpits Farm

Jointer's Farm

Oxhouse Farm

4

Latchford House

Latchford

LATCHFORD LA

Latchford Farm

Latchford Copse

Haseley Brook

01

Sheepbridge Copse

Peggs Farm

Cornwell Copse

Stoke Grange

3

The Island

OX9

00

Poppets Hill

OX44

Oxfordshire Way

2

Poppets Hill Farm

Stoke Talmage

Manor Farm

Stoney Lane

99

OX49

Clare

1

Clare Copse

Manor Farm

98

65
A
66
B
67
C

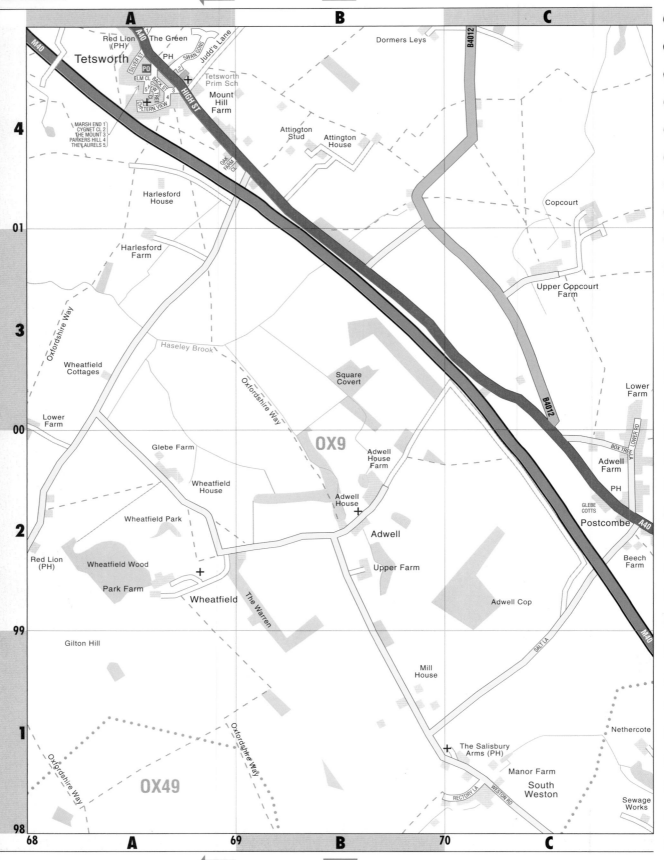

165
147
165
186

A   B   C

4
01
3
00
2
99
1
98

68   A   69   B   70   C

M40

Tetsworth
Red Lion (PH)
The Green
PH
Judd's Lane
PO
HIGH ST
SILVER ST
SWAN GDNS
BACK ST
YEW TREE
ELM CL
CHILTERN VIEW
Tetsworth Prim Sch
Mount Hill Farm

MARSH END 1
CYGNET CL 2
THE MOUNT 3
PARKERS HILL 4
THE LAURELS 5

Dormers Leys

B4012

Attington Stud
Attington House

Copcourt

Upper Copcourt Farm

Harlesford House

OAK PARK CL

Harlesford Farm

Oxfordshire Way

Haseley Brook

Wheatfield Cottages

Oxfordshire Way

Square Covert

Lower Farm

OX9

Lower Farm

B4012

Glebe Farm

Wheatfield House

Adwell House Farm

Adwell Farm

LOWER RD

BOX TREE LA

PH

A40

GLEBE COTTS

Wheatfield Park

Adwell House

Postcombe

Red Lion (PH)

Wheatfield Wood

Adwell

Beech Farm

Park Farm

Wheatfield

The Warren

Upper Farm

Adwell Cop

M40

Gilton Hill

Mill House

SALT LA

Oxfordshire Way

Nethercote

Oxfordshire Way

The Salisbury Arms (PH)

OX49

Manor Farm

South Weston

Sewage Works

RECTORY LA

WESTON RD

148 168

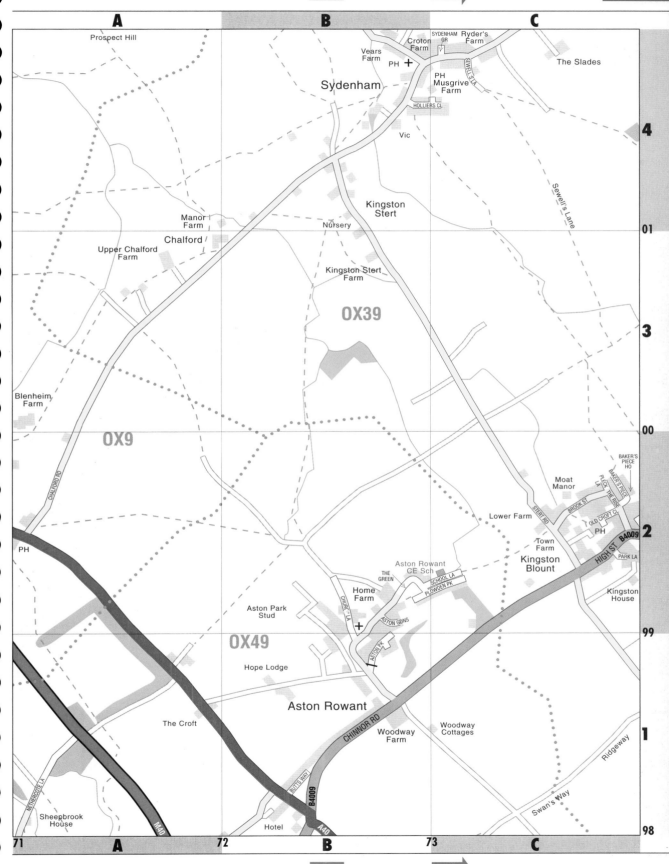

A B C

Prospect Hill

SYDENHAM GR
Croton Farm
Vears Farm
PH
Sydenham
PH Musgrive Farm
HOLLIERS CL
Ryder's Farm
The Slades
SEWELL'S LA

Vic

4

Kingston Stert

Manor Farm

Nursery

Sewell's Lane

Chalford
Upper Chalford Farm

Kingston Stert Farm

OX39

01

3

Blenheim Farm

OX9

00

BAKER'S PIECE HO

Moat Manor
BAKER'S PIECE
PLECK THE RISE
BROOK ST

Lower Farm
STERT RD
OLD CROFT CL
PH

PH

Town Farm

Kingston Blount
B4009

2

CHALFORD RD

Aston Rowant CE Sch
THE GREEN
SCHOOL LA
PLOWDEN PK

HIGH ST
PARK LA

Kingston House

Aston Park Stud

Home Farm
CHURCH LA
ASTON GDNS

OX49

ASTON PK

99

Hope Lodge

Aston Rowant

CHINNOR RD

Woodway Farm

Woodway Cottages

The Croft

Ridgeway

1

NETHERCOTE LA

M40

BUTTS WAY
B4009
A40

Hotel

Swan's Way

98

71 A 72 B 73 C

187 168

167   149

A   B   C

HP27

B4445

THAME RD

B4445

B4009 LOWER RD

Lane Farm

ELDERDENE

MCLAND CL

LOWER ICKNIELD WAY

B4009

SPRINGFIELD GDNS

LEYBOURNE GDNS

MALYNS CL

New Farm

DOVELEAT

GRAFTON HO

Lower Wainhill

LC

Mill Lane Cty Prim Sch

BENTON DR

STATION RD

St Andrew's CE Prim Sch

PH

HIGH ST

RECTOR MDW

MUSGRAVE RD

Chinnor

Hempton Wainhill

Icknield Line

01

Middle Farm

MILL LA

DIEMENS WAY

Liby

DUCK SQ

LEVERKUS CT 1

LEVERKUS HO 2

Bledlow Cross

FORESTERS WAY

CHERRY TREE RD

BEECH RD

CHURCH RD

LIME GR

HILL FARM

KEENS LA

PO

LC

CLEAVERS

MILLERS TURN

CONIGRE

ESTOVER WAY

HAILEY CFT

HEDGERLEY

LACEMAKERS

BENWELLS

RANNAL DR

ST ANDREWS HO

PH

CHURCH LA

THE AVENUE

COXLEA

ROBINS PLATT

ASHRIDGE LA

OAKLEY LA

PENLEY

RIDERS WAY

HUNTERS POINT

FOX CL

ORCHARD WAY

DRUIDS WLK

GUYSCROFT

RAVENSMEAD

GREENWOOD MDW

Saw Mill

WYCHAM RISE

GOLDEN HILLS

Chinnor Hill Nature Reserve

3

FLINT HOLLOW

OAKLEY RD

ST ANDREW'S RD

ELM DR

GREENWOOD AVE

ELM CL

TIMBER WAY

WHEELWGHTS

WOODNVILLE

HILL RD

Chinnor

P

HILL TOP LA

CHINNOR RD

Oakley

Crowell End Farm

Quarry

Chinnor Hill

Works

Woodlands Farm

00

OX39

Ridgeway

Quarry

Crowell Farm

CHINNOR RD

Crowell

Quarry

ICKNIELD CL

HIGH ST

B4009

PH

Oakley Hill

CHINNOR HILL

Manor Farm

2

99

Sunley Wood

Swan's Way

Race Course

Venus Wood

Venus Wood

Bledlow Circular Ride

Crowellhill Wood

Crowell Hill

Sprig's Alley

1

Grove Farm

KINGSTON HILL

Crowellhill Farm

SPRIGS HOLLY LA

Kingston Wood

HP14

98

74   A   75   B   76   C

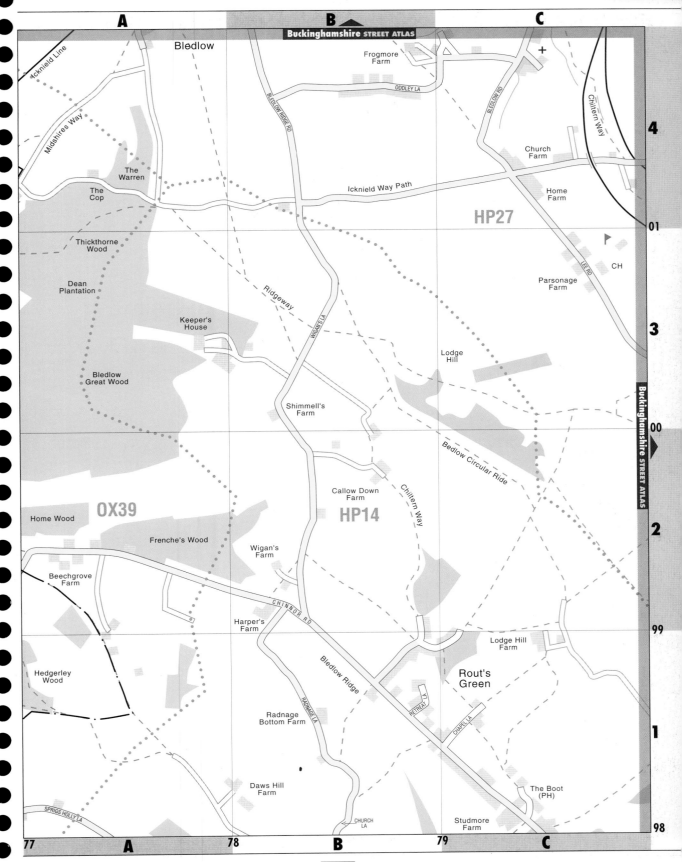

A   B   C

Bledlow

Frogmore Farm

ODDLEY LA

BLEDLOW RIDGE RD

BLEDLOW RD

Chiltern Way

4

Church Farm

Ickield Line

Midshires Way

The Warren

The Cop

Icknield Way Path

HP27

Home Farm

01

Thickthorne Wood

Dean Plantation

Ridgeway

WIGAN'S LA

LEE RD

CH

Parsonage Farm

Keeper's House

Lodge Hill

3

Bledlow Great Wood

Shimmell's Farm

00

OX39

Home Wood

Frenche's Wood

Callow Down Farm

HP14

Chiltern Way

Bedlow Circular Ride

2

Wigan's Farm

Beechgrove Farm

CHINNOR RD

Harper's Farm

Lodge Hill Farm

99

Hedgerley Wood

Bledlow Ridge

RADNAGE LA

Rout's Green

RETREAT LA

CHAPEL LA

Radnage Bottom Farm

The Boot (PH)

1

Daws Hill Farm

CHURCH LA

Studmore Farm

98

SPRIGS HOLLY LA

77   A   78   B   79   C

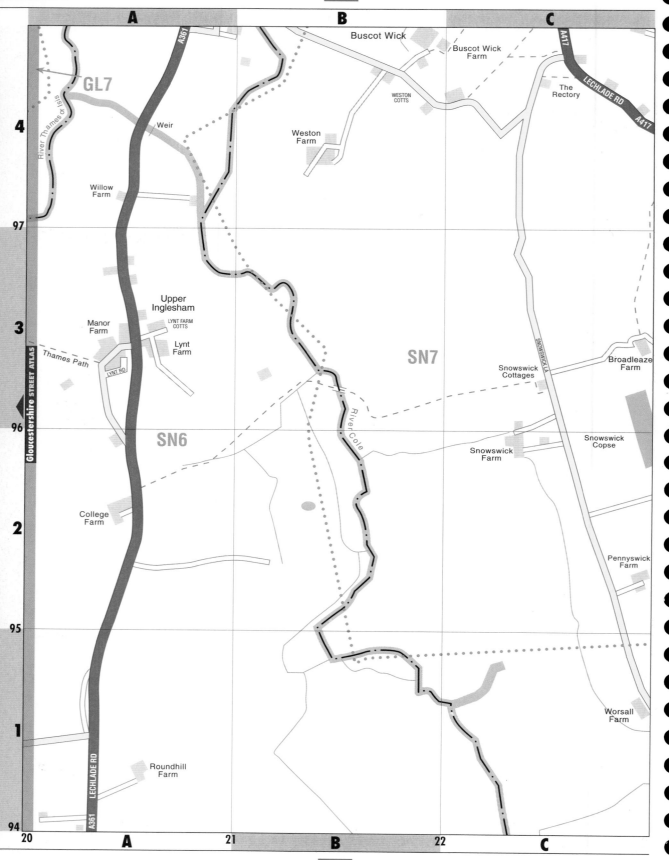

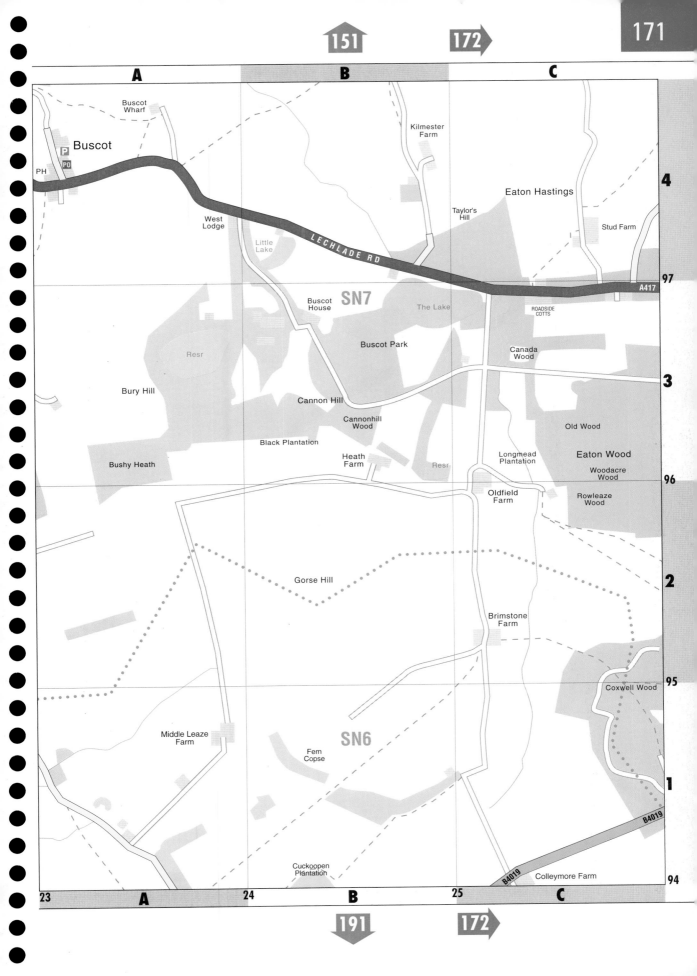

171
152

A B C

4

Thrupp Turn

Hatton Farm

Crabbe-Tree Farm

Northfield Farm

Tudor Farm

Northfield New Covert

Northfield Old Covert

Northfield Farm Cottages

A4095

97

A417

Manor Farm

Eaton Wood

RADCOT RD

Sewage Works

3

Badbury Forest

Step Farm Cottages

Nursery Cottage

LECHLADE RD

Edmonds's Pen

Step Farm

Collins's Ground

Faringdon Park

96

Oak Wood

SN7

Faringdon House

CORNMARKET 1
EASTFIELD CT 2
SOUTHAMPTON ST 3
GLOUCESTER MEWS 4
WHITE HART WLK 5
GOODLAKE AVE 6
BLISSETT TERR 7
ST CHRISTOPHER COTTS 8
GREENGATES 9
CADEL'S ROW 10
LIDDIARD'S ROW 11

WOODVIEW

A4095

Faringdon Inf Sch

Faringdon Jun Sch

Liby

Faringdon

CHURCH ST

2

Wood House

CANADA LA

FARINGDON

CEDAR RD

MAPLE COTTS

GRAVEL WLK

STATION RD

GLOUCESTER ST

MARLBOROUGH ST

PO

MARKET

LONDON ST

FERNDALE

THE PIRES

CHESTNUT AVE

ASH CL

MEND

PARK RD

BENNETT

Smallgains Copse

Badbury Hill House

ORCHARD HILL

BEECH CL

HAWTHORN RD

ELM RD

COXWELL RD

B4019

COXWELL GDNS

MARLBOROUGH CL

EAGLES

WALNUT CT

REGAL WAY

OLD

95

Highden Farm

HIGHWORTH RD

MARLBOROUGH RD

A417

Badbury Hill

WESTLAND RD

MARLB GDNS

MARLB GDNS

CLOCK CL

FOLLY VIEW CRES

FOLLY VIEW RD

MARINERS DR

MEADOW WAY

SAND

TOWN VIEW

TOWER VIEW

TOWN END RD

Badbury

P

THE SETTS

COLESVILLE DR

CA JNS

BADBURY CL

EATON CL

LEAMINGTON DR

CARTER CRES

FERNHAM RD

Faringdon Com Coll

L Ctr

1

B4019

Badburyhill Copse

THE HOLLOW RD

TOLLINGTON CT

COXWELL HALL MEWS

Works

SN6

Gipsy La

Steeds Farm

FERNHAM RD

Great Barn

A420

A420

94

26 A 27 B 28 C

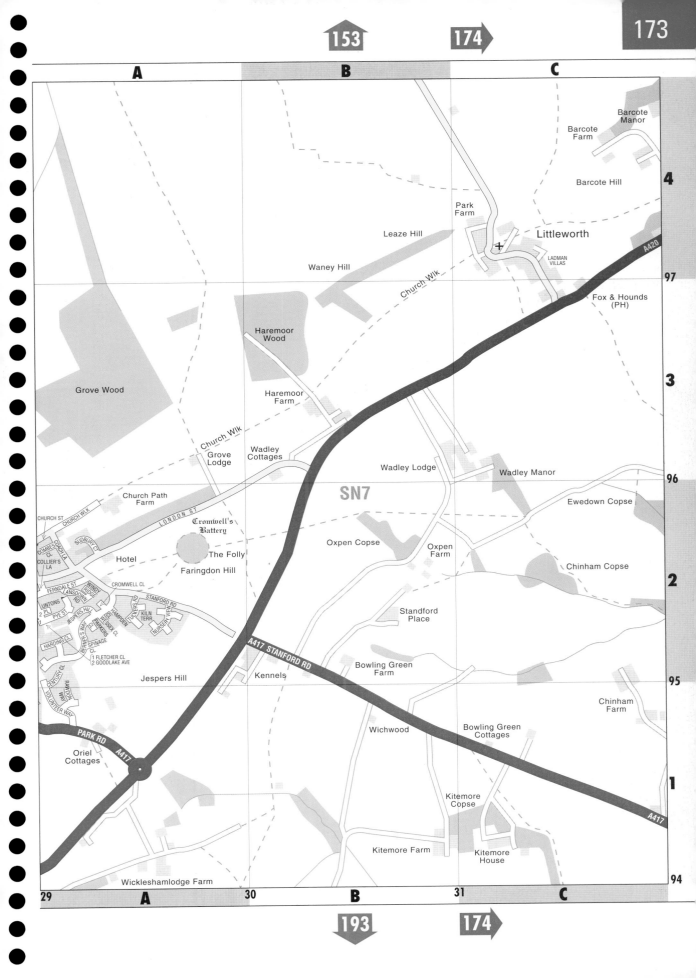

153
174
174

A   B   C

Barcote Manor
Barcote Farm
Barcote Hill
4

Park Farm
Leaze Hill
Littleworth
LADMAN VILLAS
A420
97
Waney Hill
Church Wlk
Fox & Hounds (PH)

Haremoor Wood
3
Grove Wood
Haremoor Farm

Church Wlk
Grove Lodge
Wadley Cottages
Wadley Lodge
Wadley Manor
96
Ewedown Copse

SN7
Church Path Farm
CHURCH WLK
CHURCH ST
LONDON ST
Cromwell's Battery
SUDBURY CL
COMBES CL
COACH LA
COLLIER'S LA
Oxpen Copse
Oxpen Farm
Chinham Copse

Hotel
The Folly
Faringdon Hill
2
FERNDALE ST
WINDY RIDGE
LANSDOWN
CROMWELL CL
STANFORD RD
KILN TERR.
NURSERY VIEW
HAMPDEN
WESSEX CL
TUCKERS RD
STANFORD RD
Standford Place
UNTONS PL
PYE ST
JESPERS WAY
BERNER'S WAY
BARKERS CL
SPINAGE CL
1 FLETCHER CL
2 GOODLAKE AVE
HARDING CL
Jespers Hill
Kennels
A417 STANFORD RD
Bowling Green Farm
95
CENTURY CL
RAWDON
VOLUNTEER WAY
Wichwood
Bowling Green Cottages
Chinham Farm

PARK RD
A417
Oriel Cottages
A417
Kitemore Copse
1
Kitemore Farm
Kitemore House
Wickleshamlodge Farm
94
29   30   31
A   B   C

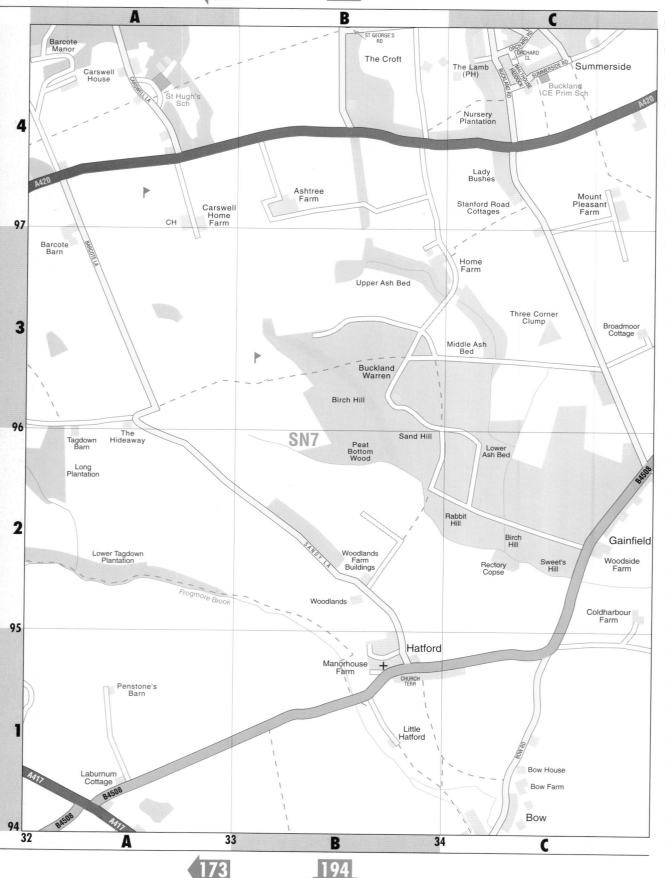

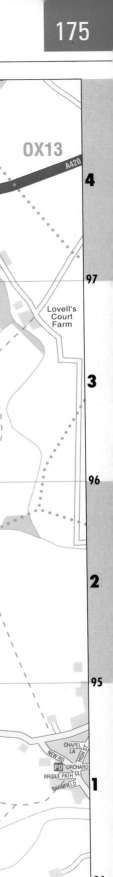

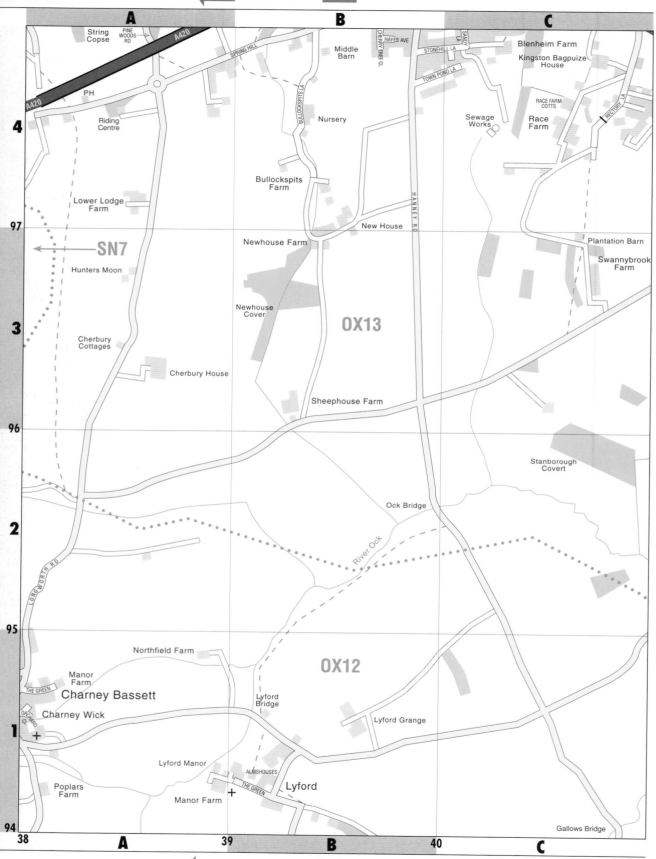

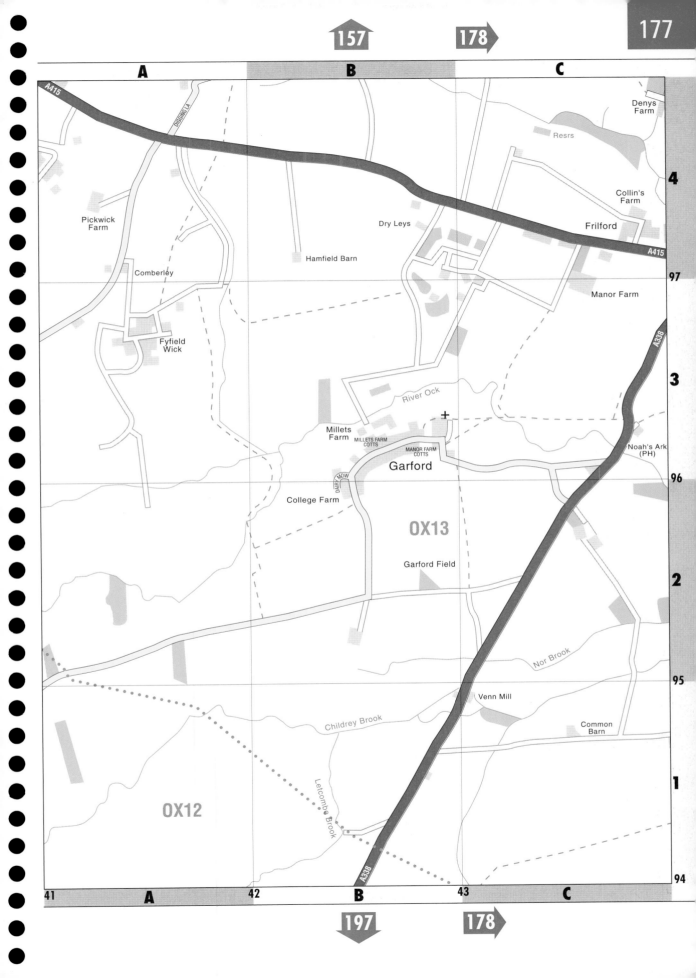

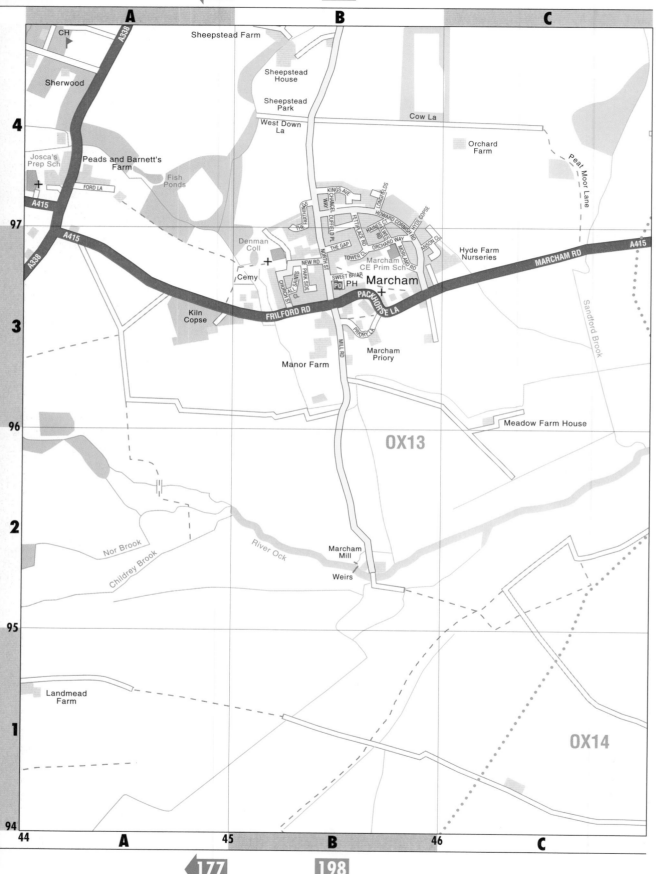

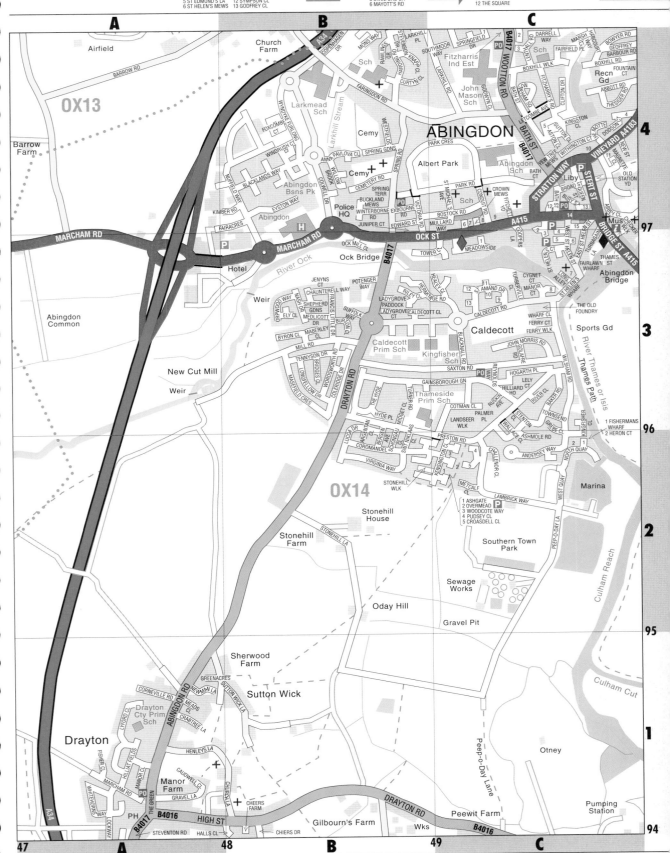

C3
1 MEADOWSIDE CT
2 BREWERS CT
3 WINSMORE LA
4 HIVE MEWS
5 ST EDMUND'S LA
6 ST HELEN'S MEWS
7 BRICK ALLEY
8 MILL PADDOCK
9 BAILIE CL
10 MUSSON CL
11 THURSTON CL
12 SYMPSON CL
13 GODFREY CL

159

C4
1 THORNHILL WLK
2 BOROUGH WLK
3 FINMORE CL
4 THE HOLT
5 STANFORD DR
6 MAYOTT'S RD

180

C4
7 CARSWELL CT
8 TOMKIN'S ALMSHOUSES
9 OCK MEWS
10 BANBURY CT
11 THE VINES
12 THE SQUARE
13 MARKET PL
14 HIGH ST
15 LOMBARD ST

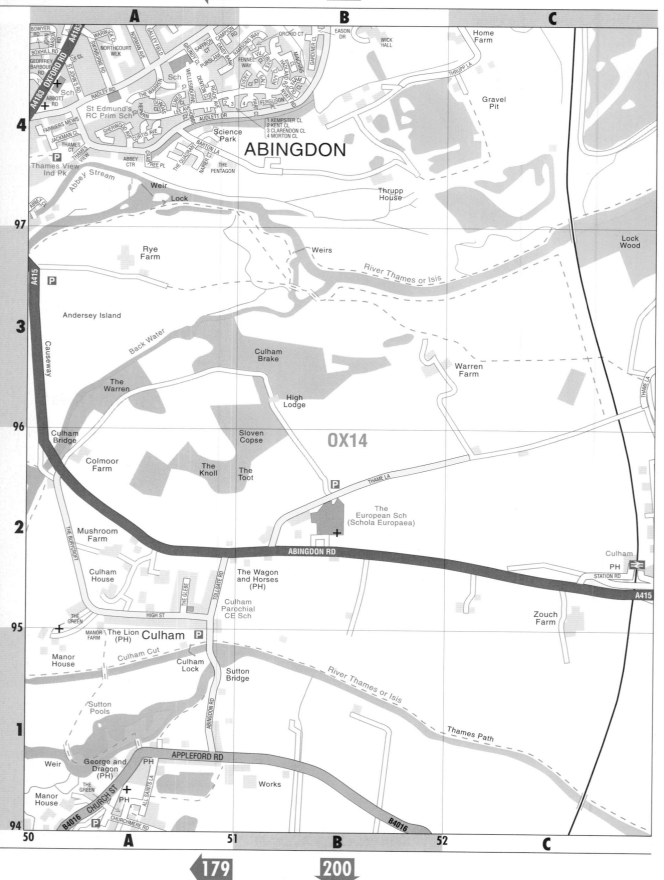

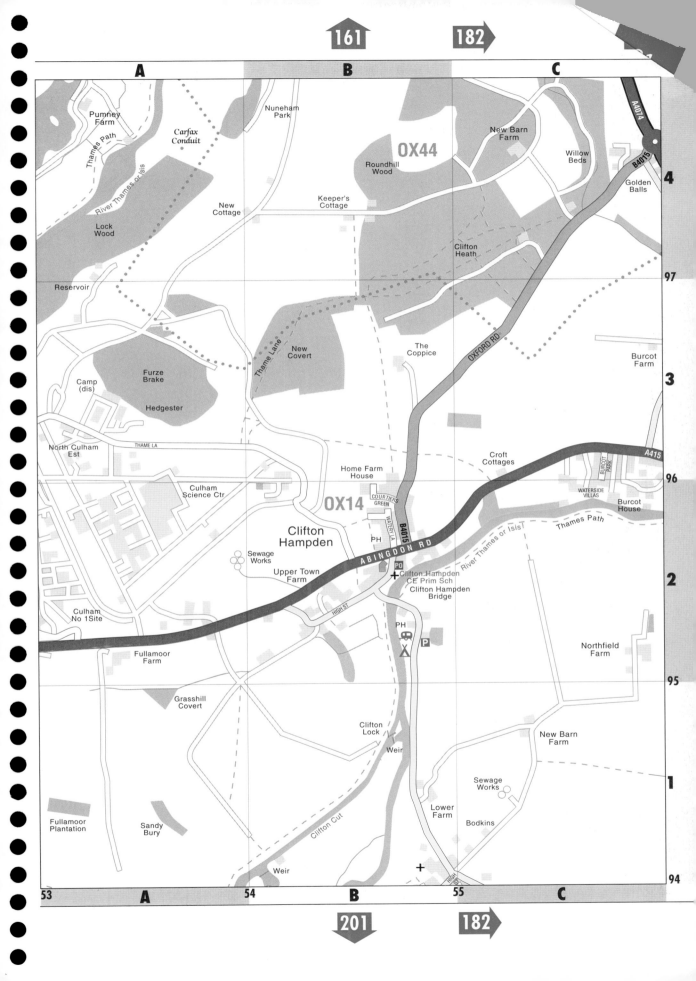

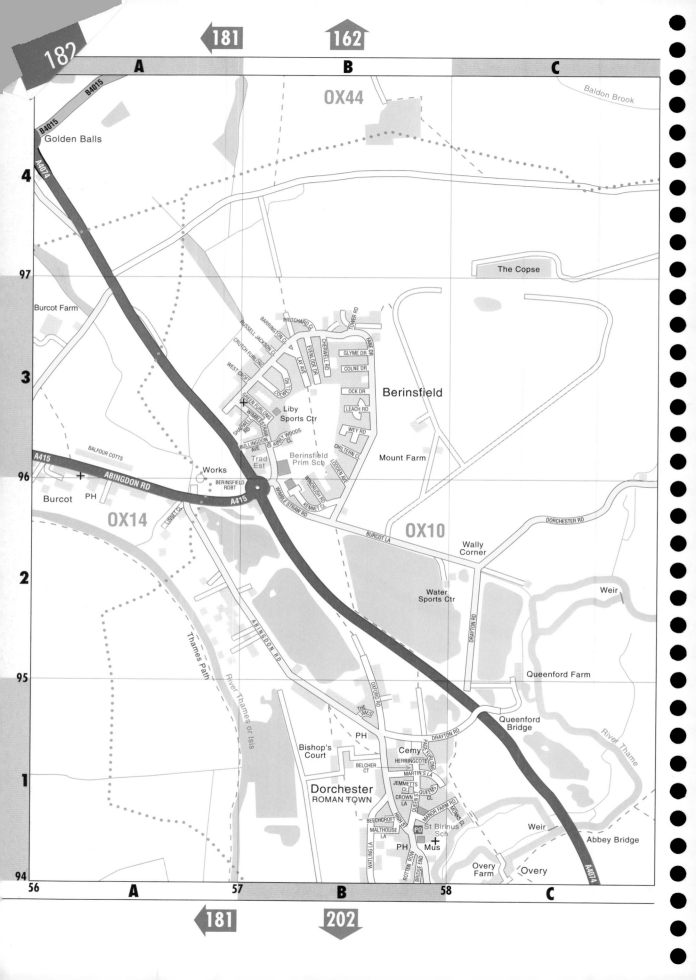

OX44

Baldon Brook

Golden Balls

B4015

B4015

A4074

4

The Copse

97

Burcot Farm

RUSSELL JACKSON CL
BARRINGTON CL
PRITCHARD CL
TOWER RD
FANE DR
CRUTCH FURLONG
CHERWELL RD
EVENLODE DR
GLYME DR
WEST CROFT
COLNE DR
GREEN FURLONG
OCK DR
Berinsfield
3
WIMBLESTRAW RD
SHARWELL RD
LEACH RD
Liby
Sports Ctr
ABBEY WOODS CL
WEY RD
BULLINGDON AVE
CHILTERN CL
A415
BALFOUR COTTS
Trad
Est
Berinsfield
Prim Sch
Mount Farm
WINDRUSH RD
LOUDEN AVE
DORCHESTER RD
96
Works
PH
BERINSFIELD
RDBT
Burcot
A415
WIMBLE STRAW RD
KENNET CL
OX14
LINNET CL
A415
BURCOT LA
OX10
Wally
Corner

Weir

2
DRAYTON RD
Water
Sports Ctr

95
Thames Path
ABINGDON RD
Queenford Farm

River Thames or Isis
OXFORD RD
DRAYTON RD
Queenford
Bridge
River Thame

THE LIMES
PH
Bishop's
Court
PAGE FURLONG
Cemy
HERRINGCOTE
1
BELCHER
CT
MARTIN'S LA
MANOR FARM RD
JEMMETTS
CL
QUEENS
CL
WYNNS CL
Dorchester
ROMAN TOWN
CROWN
LA
QUEEN ST
HIGH ST
BEECHCROFT
PO
St Birinus
Sch
Weir
MALTHOUSE
LA
Mus
Abbey Bridge
WATLING LA
PH
A4074
ROTTEN ROW
BRIDGE END
Overy
Farm
Overy

94
56
A
57
B
58
C

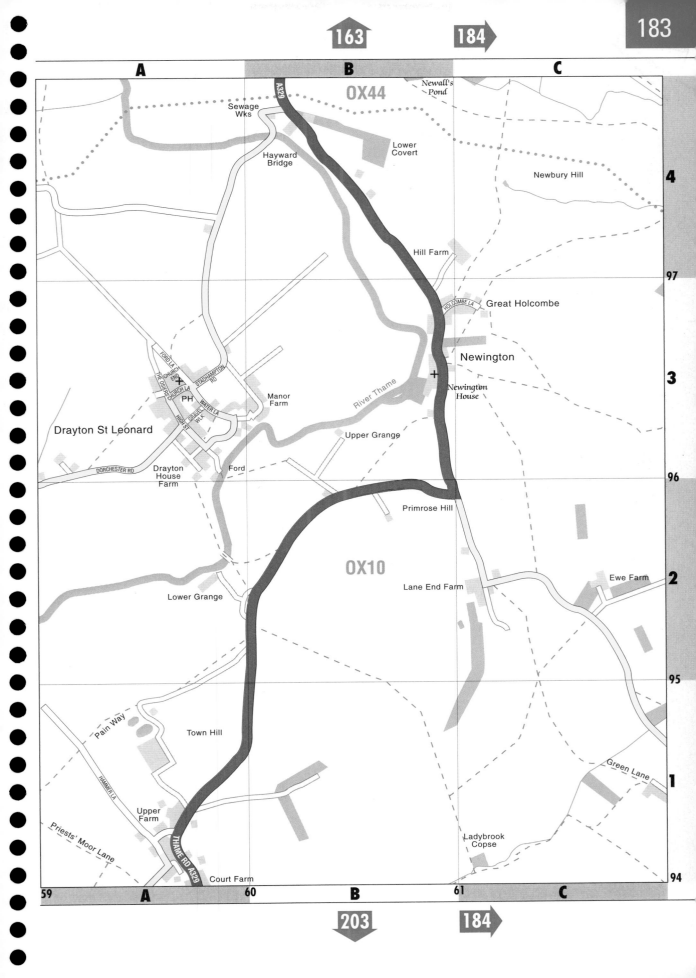

A   **B**   **C**

B480

Chalgrove
Airfield

Hitchcox
Poultry
Farm

Newberry
Hill

Monument
Ind Pk

4

Chalgrove
Field

Fox
Covert

MARLEY LA
BOWER END
BROOKSIDE EST
CINNAMON CL
POPLAR FARM RD

Hampden's
Monument

The Lamb
(PH)

ORCHARD RD
HIGH ST
SAGE CL

97

Little Holcombe
Covert

GRASS CL
FLEMMING AVE
MILLERS CL
ADEANE RD
QUARTERMAIN RD
BRUNSFIELD RD
PADDOCK CL
LANGLEY RD
PO
HAMPDEN LA
LODON RD
FRENCH LAURENCE WAY
SIXPENNY LA
BEVERLEY CL

Manor
Farm

Mill
House
THE RICKYARD
Langley
Hall

SWINSTEAD CT
THE GREEN
CHAPEL LA
MATTOCK
FAIRFAX RD
MONUMENT RD
CHILTERN CL

Chalgrove
Com Prim Sch

IRETON
ARGOSY CL
FARM CL

Langley Field
Farm

OX44

BACONSHURST DR
RUPERT
DB

Chalgrove

3

CHINNALL CL
WILLOW MC
CHURCH LA
FRANKLIN CL
+ ST MARY'S
BERRICK RD
CROMWELL CL

Church
Farm

Chalgrove
Farm

96

Southfield
Barn

Hares Leap

Cadwell La

Hollandstide
House

Cadwell
Farm

Cadwell
Covert

2

OX10

OX49

Whitehouse
Farm

95

Lonesome
Farm

Manor
Farm

Rumbolds Lane

1

Green Lane

Berrick
Prior

Hollandtide Bottom

PH
Ivyhouse
Farm +

Rumbolds
Farm

Berrick
Salome

94

62   **A**   63   **B**   64   **C**

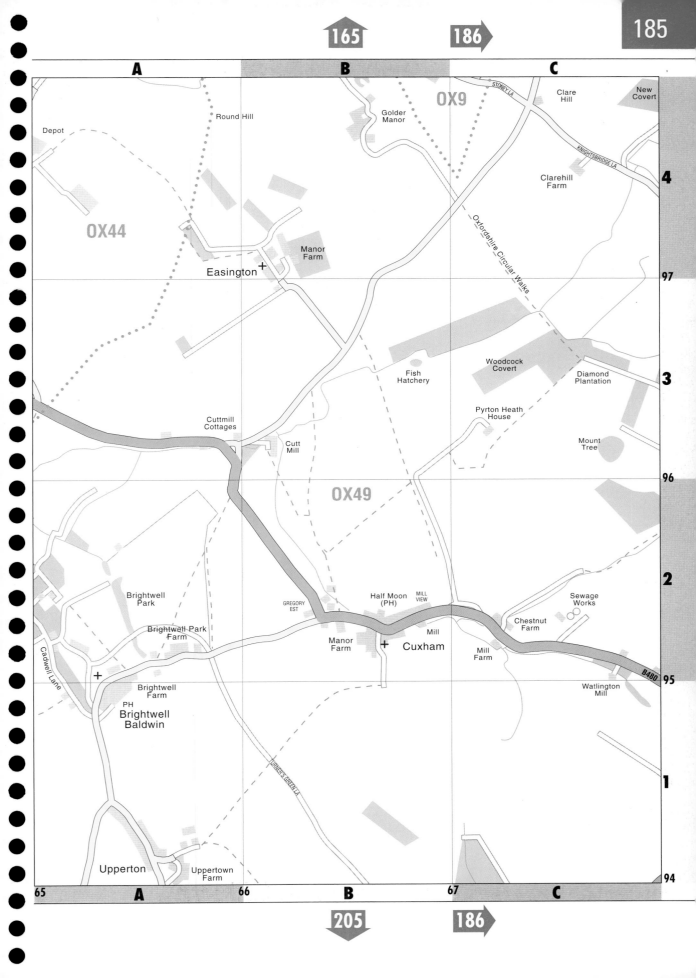

165
186

A   B   C

Depot

Round Hill

OX9

Golder
Manor

STONEY LA

Clare
Hill

New
Covert

KNIGHTSBRIDGE LA

Clarehill
Farm

4

OX44

Manor
Farm

Easington

Oxfordshire Circular Walks

97

Fish
Hatchery

Woodcock
Covert

Diamond
Plantation

3

Cuttmill
Cottages

Cutt
Mill

Pyrton Heath
House

Mount
Tree

OX49

96

Brightwell
Park

Half Moon
(PH)

MILL
VIEW

Sewage
Works

2

GREGORY
EST

Chestnut
Farm

Brightwell Park
Farm

Manor
Farm

Cuxham

Mill

Cadwell Lane

Mill
Farm

B480

95

Brightwell
Farm

PH
Brightwell
Baldwin

Watlington
Mill

TURNER'S GREEN LA

1

Upperton

Uppertown
Farm

94

65   A   66   B   67   C

205
186

185
166

A **B** **C**

Stokefield Farm

OX9

Weston Rd

Moor Court

4

Brookside Covert

Knightsbridge Farm

Model Farm

B4009

97

Field Farm House

Knightsbridge La

Watlington Rd

3

Oxfordshire Way

Shirburn Farm

New Farm

Home Farm

The Plough (PH)

Shirburn Castle

Hall Cl

96

Cemy

OX49

Castle Rd

Blenheim Rd

Church La

Pyrton

Shirburn

Mafeking Row

Lower Farm

Pyrton Manor

2

Ridgeway

Pyrton Field Farm

Middle Way Plantation

Swan's Way

95

B480

Icknield Com Sch

Eastfield Farm

Oxfordshire Way

Willow Ct

Ash Cl 3

Shirburn Rd

Pyrton La

St Edwards Cl

Love La

Watlington Ind Est

Cuxham Rd

Prospect Pl

New Rd

Church St

Pauls Way

Saunders

Orchard Walk

Shirburn St

The Home Cl

Brook Side

Chapel St

Letts Alley

Sheldons Piece 1
Beech Cl 2
Sycamore Cl 3

Hurdlers Gn

Goswell

High St

PO

Watlington

Carriers Arms (PH)

1

Liby

Chestnut Cl

Couching St

P

Britwell Rd

Brook St B4009

The Goggs

Avenue Cl

Barnacre

Watcombe Rd

Springs La

Springfield Cl

Parslow Ho

Hill Rd

White House Farm

Watcombe Manor Ind Est

Home Rd B480

Chiltern Gdns

Stonor Gn

94

B4009

Farmhouse Mews 4
Davenport Pl 5
Ingham La 6

Watcombe Manor

Chiltern Farm

Watlington H

Pyrton Hill House

68 **A** **69** **B** **70** **C**

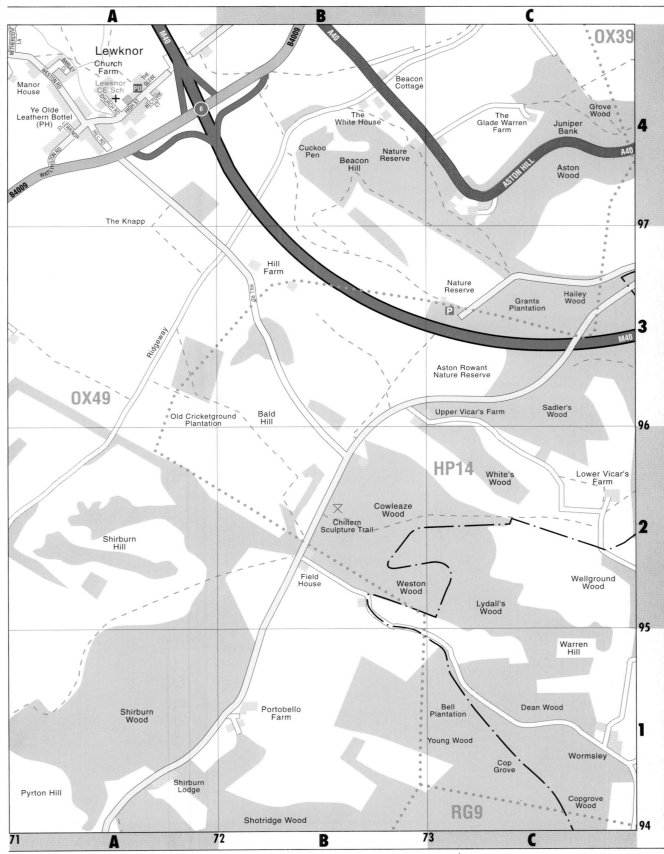

OX39

A

Lewknor
Church
Farm
Manor
House
Ye Olde
Leathern Bottel
(PH)
Lewknor
CE Sch
PO
NETHERCOTE LA
BARLEY CL
WESTON RD
CHURCH RD
HILL RD
CL LEWKNOR
WATLINGTON RD
THE GLEBE
HIGH ST
RECTORY CT
M40
6
B4009

B
B4009
A40
Beacon
Cottage
The
White House
Cuckoo
Pen
Beacon
Hill
Nature
Reserve

The Knapp

Hill
Farm

HILL RD

Ridgeway

OX49

Old Cricketground
Plantation

Bald
Hill

Nature
Reserve
P

Aston Rowant
Nature Reserve

Upper Vicar's Farm

HP14

Chiltern
Sculpture Trail

Cowleaze
Wood

Field
House

Weston
Wood

Shirburn
Hill

Shirburn
Wood

Portobello
Farm

Pyrton Hill

Shirburn
Lodge

Shotridge Wood

The
Glade Warren
Farm

Grove
Wood

Juniper
Bank

Aston
Wood

ASTON HILL

A40

Grants
Plantation

Hailey
Wood

M40

Sadler's
Wood

White's
Wood

Lower Vicar's
Farm

Wellground
Wood

Lydall's
Wood

Warren
Hill

Bell
Plantation

Dean Wood

Young Wood

Cop
Grove

Wormsley

Copgrove
Wood

RG9

4

97

3

96

2

95

1

94

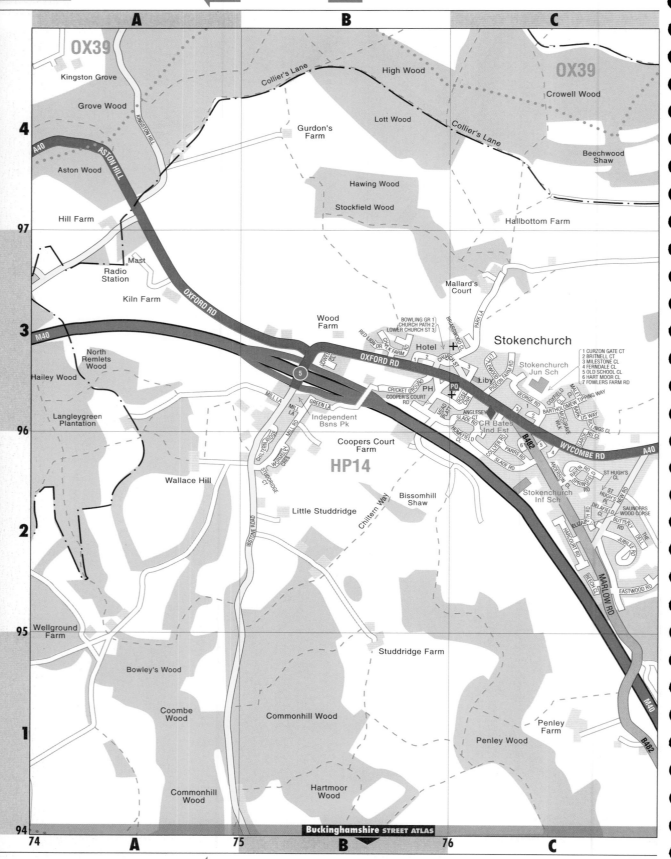

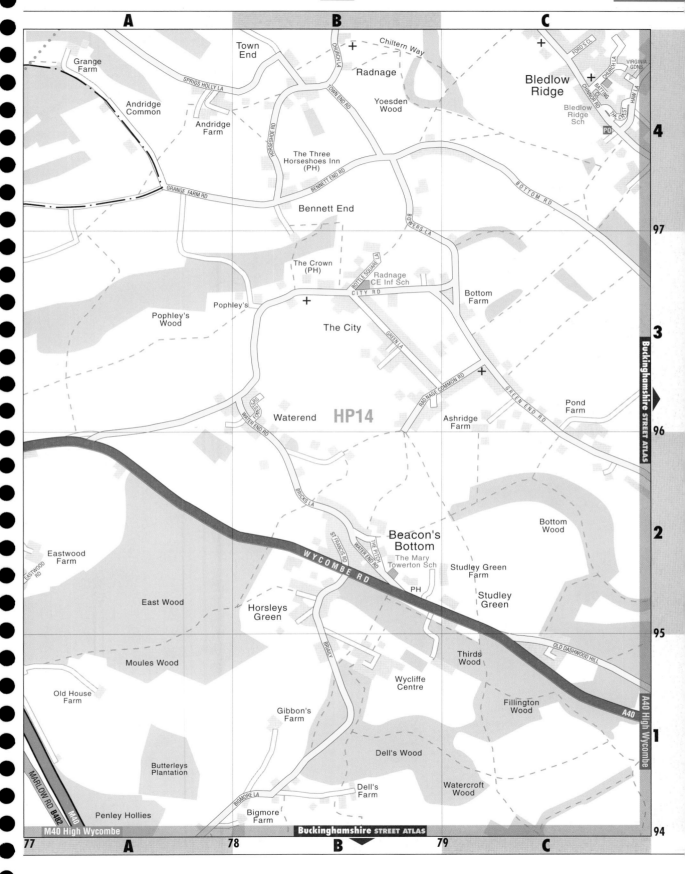

A   **B**   **C**

Town End

Radnage

Chiltern Way

Grange Farm

Andridge Common

SPRIGS HOLLY LA

Yoesden Wood

Bledlow Ridge

FORD'S CL

VIRGINIA GDNS

CHURCH LA

Bledlow Ridge Sch

HAW TY LA

PO

4

Andridge Farm

HORSESHOE RD

TOWN END RD

CHURCH LA

BATTING

CHINNOR RD

TPK CRST

The Three Horseshoes Inn (PH)

BENNETT END RD

BOTTOM RD

GRANGE FARM RD

Bennett End

BOWERS LA

97

The Crown (PH)

BOTTLE SQUARE LA

Radnage CE Inf Sch

Bottom Farm

Pophley's

CITY RD

Pophley's Wood

The City

GREEN LA

3

RADNAGE COMMON RD

GREEN END RD

Pond Farm

Buckinghamshire STREET ATLAS

WATER END RD

Waterend

HP14

Ashridge Farm

96

BRICKS LA

Bottom Wood

Eastwood Farm

ST FRANCIS RD

THE PITCH

WATER END RD

WYCOMBE RD

Beacon's Bottom

The Mary Towerton Sch

PH

Studley Green Farm

Studley Green

2

EASTWOOD RD

East Wood

Horsleys Green

Thirds Wood

OLD DASHWOOD HILL

95

Moules Wood

BRIARLY

Wycliffe Centre

Fillington Wood

A40 High Wycombe

Old House Farm

Gibbon's Farm

Dell's Wood

Watercroft Wood

1

MARLOW RD B482

M40

Butterleys Plantation

BIGMORE LA

Dell's Farm

Penley Hollies

Bigmore Farm

94

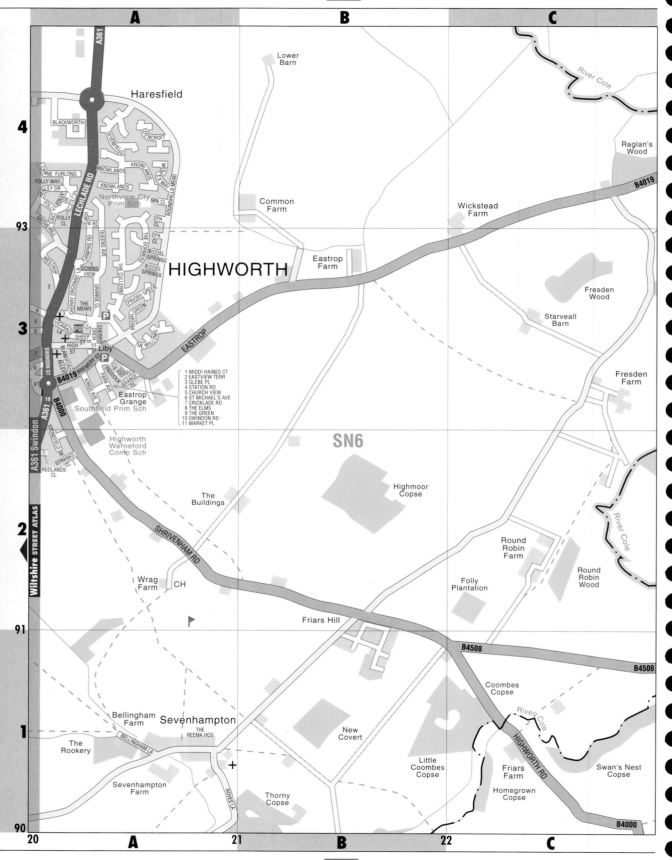

A   B   C

4

93

HIGHWORTH

3

2

91

1

Wiltshire STREET ATLAS

Haresfield

BLACKWORTH

Lower
Barn

River Cole

Raglan's
Wood

B4019

Common
Farm

Wickstead
Farm

Eastrop
Farm

Fresden
Wood

Starveall
Barn

EASTROP

Liby

1 MIDDI HAINES CT
2 EASTVIEW TERR
3 GLEBE PL
4 STATION RD
5 CHURCH VIEW
6 ST MICHAEL'S AVE
7 CRICKLADE RD
8 THE ELMS
9 THE GREEN
10 SWINDON RD
11 MARKET PL

Fresden
Farm

Eastrop
Grange

Southfield Prim Sch

SN6

Highworth
Warneford
Comp Sch

Highmoor
Copse

River Cole

The
Buildings

Round
Robin
Farm

Round
Robin
Wood

SHRIVENHAM RD

Wrag
Farm

CH

Folly
Plantation

Friars Hill

B4508

B4508

Coombes
Copse

River Cole

Bellingham
Farm

Sevenhampton

THE
REEMA HOS

New
Covert

The
Rookery

BELLINGHAM LA

Little
Coombes
Copse

Friars
Farm

HIGHWORTH RD

Swan's Nest
Copse

Sevenhampton
Farm

ROVES LA

Thorny
Copse

Homegrown
Copse

B4000

A361 Swindon

B4000

A361

B4019

STONEFIELD DR

STRANKS
CL

REDLANDS
CL

20   A   21   B   22   C

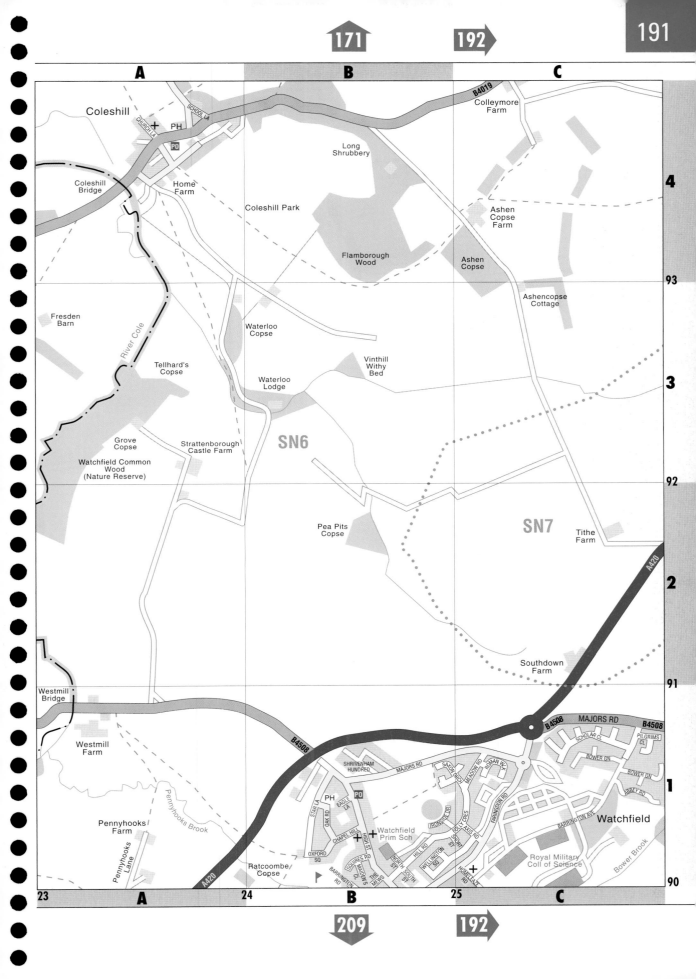

A   B   C

Coleshill

B4019   Colleymore Farm

CHURCH LA   SCHOOL LA   PH   PO

Long Shrubbery

Coleshill Bridge   Home Farm

Coleshill Park

Ashen Copse Farm

Flamborough Wood

Ashen Copse   4

Ashencopse Cottage   93

Fresden Barn

River Cole

Waterloo Copse

Tellhard's Copse

Vinthill Withy Bed

Waterloo Lodge

SN6   3

Grove Copse

Strattenborough Castle Farm

Watchfield Common Wood (Nature Reserve)   92

Pea Pits Copse

SN7

Tithe Farm

A420   2

Southdown Farm   91

Westmill Bridge

MAJORS RD   B4508   B4508

Westmill Farm   B4508   SCHOLAR CL   PILGRIMS CL

SHRIVENHAM HUNDRED   MAJORS RD   BOWER GN   BOWER GN

SAXON INCH   MEADOW CL   ROSAN WAY   ABBEY RD

PH   PO   1

STAR LA   EAGLE LA   FARRINGDON RD   BARRINGTON AVE   Watchfield

Pennyhooks Farm   OAK RD   CHAPEL HILL   Watchfield Prim Sch   IRONSIDE RD   FOLLY CRES   AXIS RD   Royal Military Coll of Science

Pennyhooks Brook   OXFORD SQ   HIGH ST   HILL RD   WELLINGTON SQ   Bower Brook

Pennyhooks Lane   A420   SQUIRES RD   THE MEWS   NORTH ST   SOUTH ST   HOMELEAZE RD

Ratcoombe Copse   BARRINGTON RD   90

191
172

A **B** **C**

4

Court House

CHERRY ORCH

GIPSY LA

Oakfield

PUDDLEDUCK LA

THE HOLLOWAY RD

THE LAURELS

DARK LA

CH

Bury Hill

Great Coxwell

Chowle Cottages

A420

1 GROVE COTTS
2 EAGLE SQ

FERNHAM RD

Galley Hill

Coxwell House

PH

Little Coxwell

Manor Farm

Gorse Farm

Sewage Works

Chowle Farm

Little Coxwell Furze

Onetree Hill

93

Plough Barn

Pry Lane

Broadleaze Barn

COXWELL LA

Ringdale Manor

3

Plough (PH)

St Mary's Priory

Ashen Copse

Fernham Manor

Raspberry Copse

92

SN7

Field Farm

A420

River Ock

B4508

Manor Farm

Burnt Shed

2

Wellington Farm

Henleaze Farm

Nightingale Farm

91

SN6

The Homestead

KING'S LA

HUGHES CRES

King's Farm

MALLINS LA

Longcot House

DOWNLANDS

FERNHAM RD

MEAD LA

B4508

MAJORS RD

Longcot & Fernham CE Prim Sch

CHURCH CL

PRIORY MEAD

1

PH

SHRIVENHAM RD

Longcot

Cleveland Farm

Bower Copse

Stone Farm

City Bridge

LONGCOT RD

OLD WHARF RD

90

26 **A** 27 **B** 28 **C**

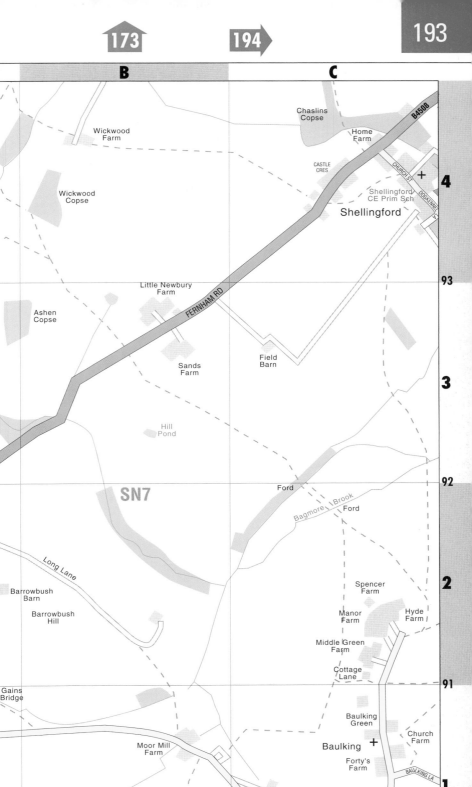

173
194

A
B
C

4

93

3

92

2

91

1

90

Chaslins
Copse

Home
Farm

B4508

CASTLE
CRES

CHURCH ST

DOGKANE

Shellingford
CE Prim Sch

Shellingford

+

Wickwood
Farm

Wickwood
Copse

Cole's
Pits

Lyde
Copse

Ashen
Copse

Little Newbury
Farm

FERNHAM RD

Sands
Farm

Field
Barn

Celia's
Coppice

South Farm
House

Hill
Pond

Ford

Bagmore Brook

Ford

Fernham
Farm

ELMSIDE
CHAPEL LA

PH
CHURCH LA
MANOR FARM
CL
THE GREEN

HIGH ST

+

SILVER ST

BAKERS
SQ

Fernham

SN7

Long Lane

Barrowbush
Barn

Barrowbush
Hill

Spencer
Farm

Manor
Farm

Hyde
Farm

Middle Green
Farm

Cottage
Lane

Gains
Bridge

Baulking
Green

Church
Farm

Alfred's
Hill

River Ock

Moor Mill
Farm

Baulking

+

Forty's
Farm

BAULKING LA

Oldland
Copse

Uffington
Trad Est

Vicarage
Farm

29
A
30
B
31
C

211
194

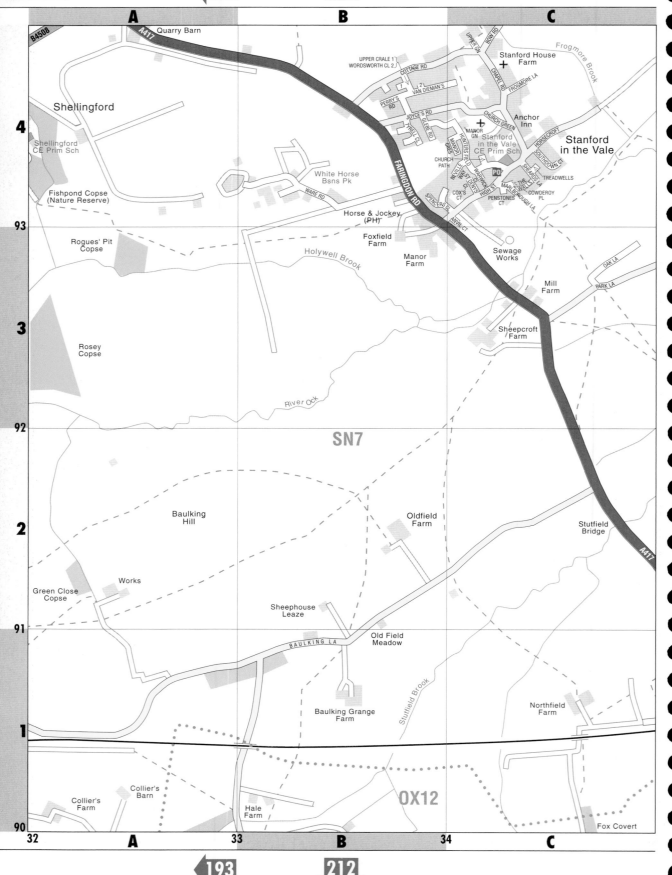

A   **B**   **C**

B4508

A417   Quarry Barn

Shellingford

Shellingford
CE Prim Sch

Fishpond Copse
(Nature Reserve)

Rogues' Pit
Copse

Rosey
Copse

River Ock

Green Close
Copse

Works

Baulking
Hill

Sheephouse
Leaze

BAULKING LA

Old Field
Meadow

Baulking Grange
Farm

Collier's Farm

Collier's
Barn

Hale
Farm

White Horse
Bsns Pk

WARE RD

Holywell Brook

UPPER CRALE 1
WORDSWORTH CL 2

COTTAGE RD

2
VAN DIEMAN'S

PERRY'S
RD

JOYCE'S RD

GLEBE RD

PRELL CT

FARINGDON RD

SPENCERS CL

ANVIL CT

Horse & Jockey
(PH)

Foxfield
Farm

Manor
Farm

SN7

Oldfield
Farm

Stutfield Brook

OX12

Northfield
Farm

Fox Covert

UPPER LN

BOW RD

Stanford House
Farm

CHAPEL RD

FROGMORE LA

Frogmore Brook

CHURCH GREEN

Anchor
Inn

MANOR
GN

Stanford
in the Vale
CE Prim Sch

CHURCH
PATH

NEVILLE

HUNTERS FIELD

WARWICK CL

W ST DENYS

MANOR GRES

COX'S
CT

PO

HIGH ST

PENSTONES
CT

HORSECROFT

SOUTHDOWN CL

THE
WALLS

SHEARES LA

MARLBOROUGH LA

COWDEROY
PL

Stanford
in the Vale

TREADWELLS

Sewage
Works

Mill
Farm

OAK LA

PARK LA

Sheepcroft
Farm

Stutfield
Bridge

A417

A   **B**   **C**

4   93   3   92   2   91   1   90

32   33   34

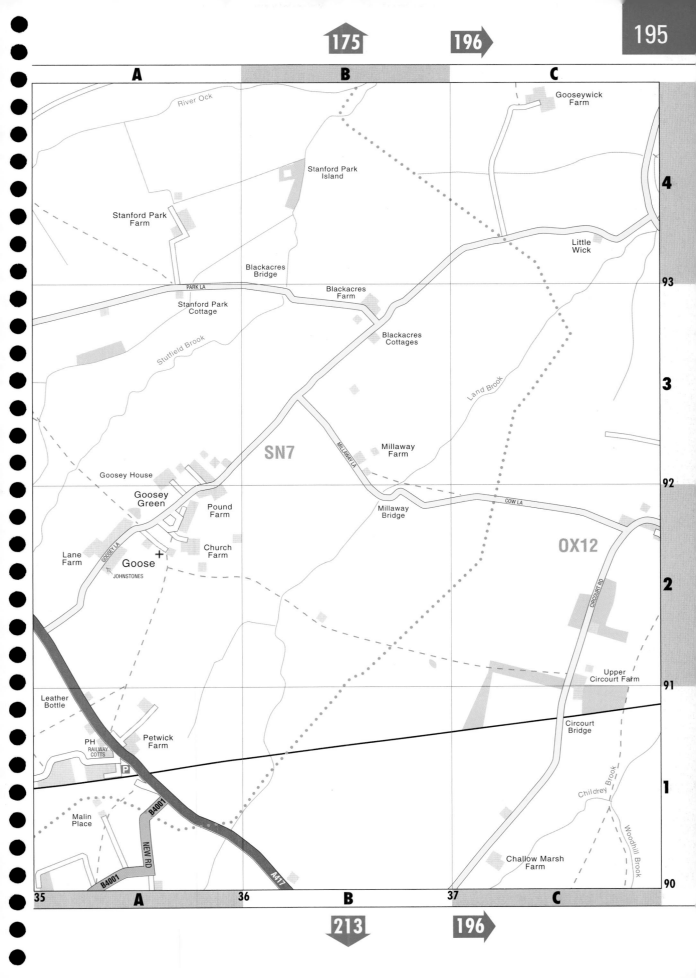

A
B
C

River Ock

Gooseywick Farm

Stanford Park Island

Stanford Park Farm

Little Wick

Blackacres Bridge

PARK LA

Blackacres Farm

Stanford Park Cottage

Blackacres Cottages

Stutfield Brook

Land Brook

SN7

MILLAWAY LA

Millaway Farm

Goosey House

Goosey Green

Pound Farm

Millaway Bridge

COW LA

OX12

Lane Farm

GOOSEY LA

Church Farm

CIRCOURT RD

Goose

JOHNSTONES

Upper Circourt Farm

Leather Bottle

Circourt Bridge

PH
RAILWAY COTTS

Petwick Farm

P

Childrey Brook

B4001

Malin Place

NEW RD

Woodhill Brook

B4001

A417

Challow Marsh Farm

35
A
36
B
37
C

4

93

3

92

2

91

1

90

A B C

4

Land Brook

Hedges Farm

Flapp's Barn

NORTHMEAD LA

Bailey's Mead Copse

Botney Meadows

RECTORY FARM CL
WINTER LA
6TH CN
THE MEADS
Lamb (PH)
THE CROFT
Main St
MONKS CL
THE GREEN
SCHOOL RD
West Hanney
CHURCH ST

93

Grange Farm

Hyde Farm

Lydbrook Farm

Manor Farm

3

HYDE RD

Childrey Brook

Pike's Barn

Cow La

South Denchworth Farm

92

OX12

KIMBERS CL
Denchworth
BROOK LA
CIRCOURT RD
BYRN

Brooklane Bridge

Hill Barn

Sewage Works

COW LA

Bradfield Grove Farm

2

Hanney Bridge

Works

A338

Grove Wick Farm

91

Denchworth Road Bridge

DENCHWORTH RD

Monk's Farm

Townsend

TULWICK LA

Grove CE Sch
The Green
NORTH DR

Little Woodhill

1

FULMAR PL 1
HAWKSWORTH CL 2

THE KESTRELS
NEWLANDS DR
SHEPHERDS
CO LLETT WAY
NOBLES CL
STEPLOE CL
WICK GN
WESTBROOK
FARMS LEA
CHURCH VIEW
St John's CT
ST JOHN'S RD
OXFORD LA
GODFREYS CL
SHANNON CL
Grove

Liby

Woodhill Lane

CARLTON CL 1
HUNTERS CL 2
GROVELANDS CTR 3
BROADMARSH CL 4
FAIRFIELD CL 5

SAVILE WAY

STATION RD
Gipsy Lane

90

38 A 39 B 40 C

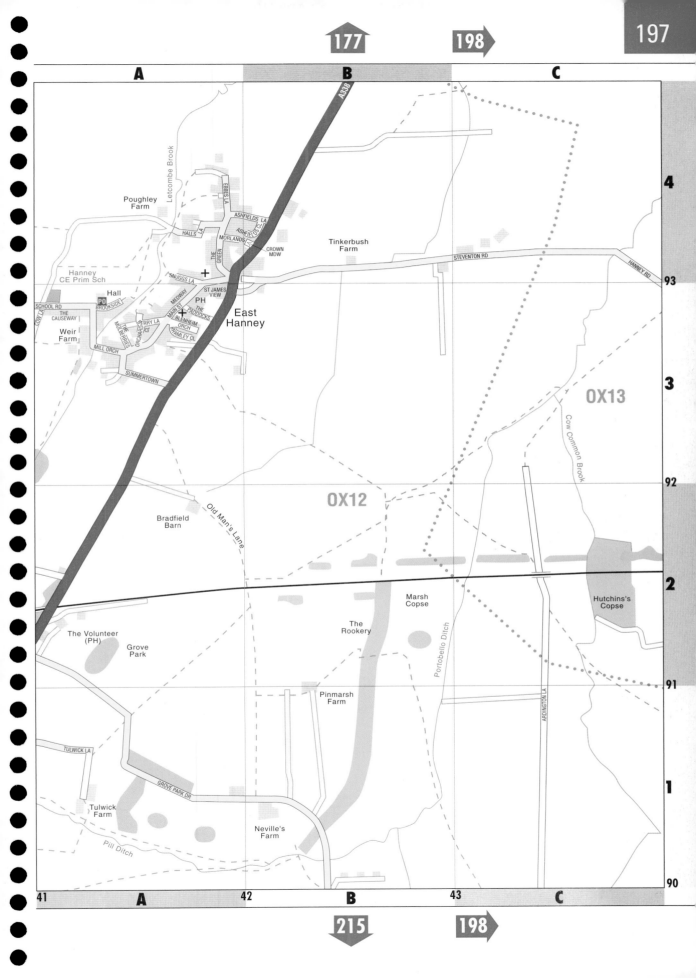

A B C

4

93

OX13

3

92

OX12

2

91

1

90

Letcombe Brook

Poughley Farm

EBBES LA

ASHFIELDS LA

ASHFIELDS CL

HALLS LA

MORLANDS

CROWN MDW

Tinkerbush Farm

STEVENTON RD

HANNEY RD

Hanney CE Prim Sch

SNUGGS LA

ST JAMES VIEW

THE GREEN

MEDWAY

Hall

PO

BROOKSIDE

PH

THE PADDOCKS

East Hanney

SCHOOL RD

COW LA

THE CAUSEWAY

THE MULBERRIES

THE ORCHARD

PERRY LA

MAIN ST

BLENHEIM ORCH

BRAMLEY CL

Weir Farm

MILL ORCH

SUMMERTOWN

A338

Cow Common Brook

Bradfield Barn

Old Man's Lane

Marsh Copse

Hutchins's Copse

The Volunteer (PH)

Grove Park

The Rookery

Portobello Ditch

Pinmarsh Farm

ARDINGTON LA

TULWICK LA

GROVE PARK DR

Tulwick Farm

Neville's Farm

Pill Ditch

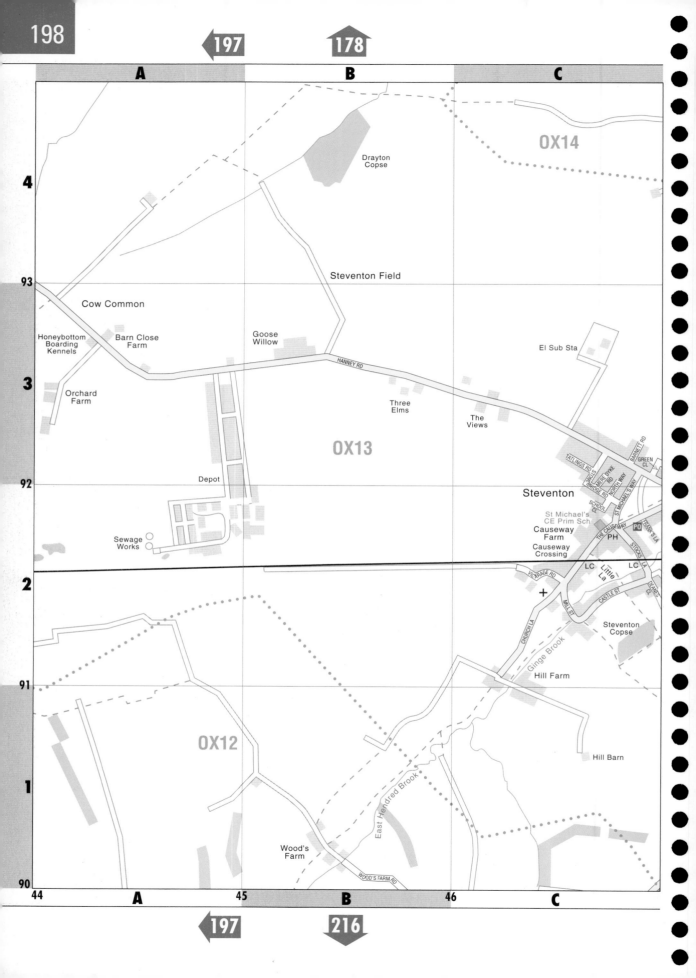

197
178

A
B
C

4

93

OX14

Steventon Field

Cow Common

Honeybottom
Boarding
Kennels

Barn Close
Farm

Goose
Willow

El Sub Sta

HANNEY RD

Orchard
Farm

Three
Elms

The
Views

OX13

TATLINGS RD S

GREEN
CL

BARNETT RD

MERE DYKE RD

NORTH WAY

BRIDGE RD

ST MICHAEL'S WAY

3

Depot

Steventon

SCHOOL
CL

St Michael's
CE Prim Sch

PO

FRANK'S LA

92

Causeway
Farm

THE CAUSEWAY

PH

Causeway
Crossing

STOCKS LA

Sewage
Works

LC

LC

Little
La

DEANE'S

VICARAGE RD

CASTLE ST

2

+

Steventon
Copse

MILL ST

CHURCH LA

Ginge Brook

Hill Farm

91

OX12

East Hendred Brook

Hill Barn

1

Wood's
Farm

WOOD'S FARM RD

90

44

A

45

B

46

C

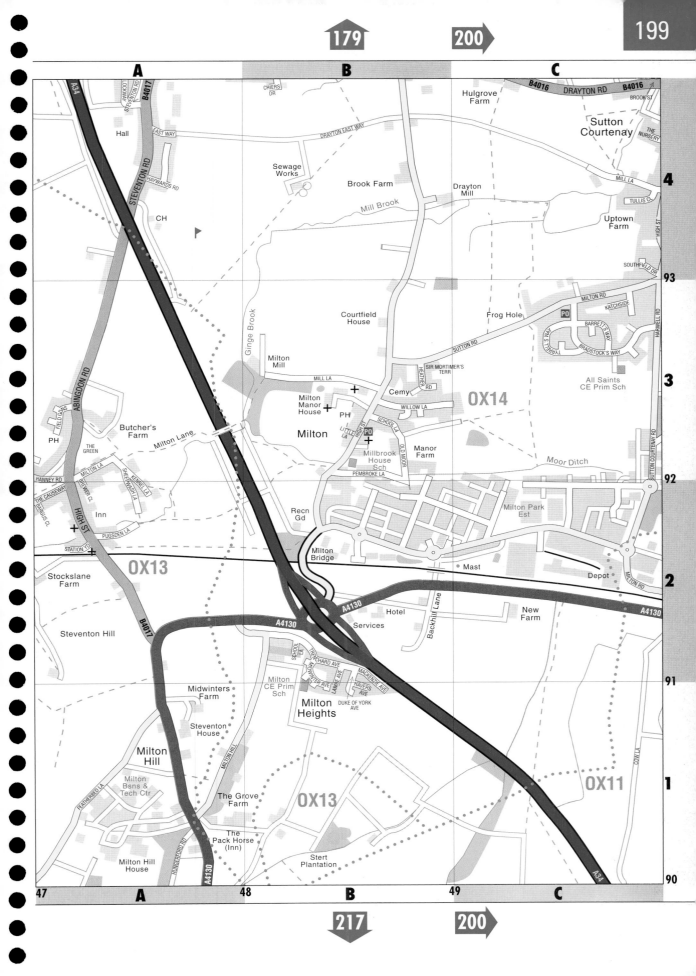

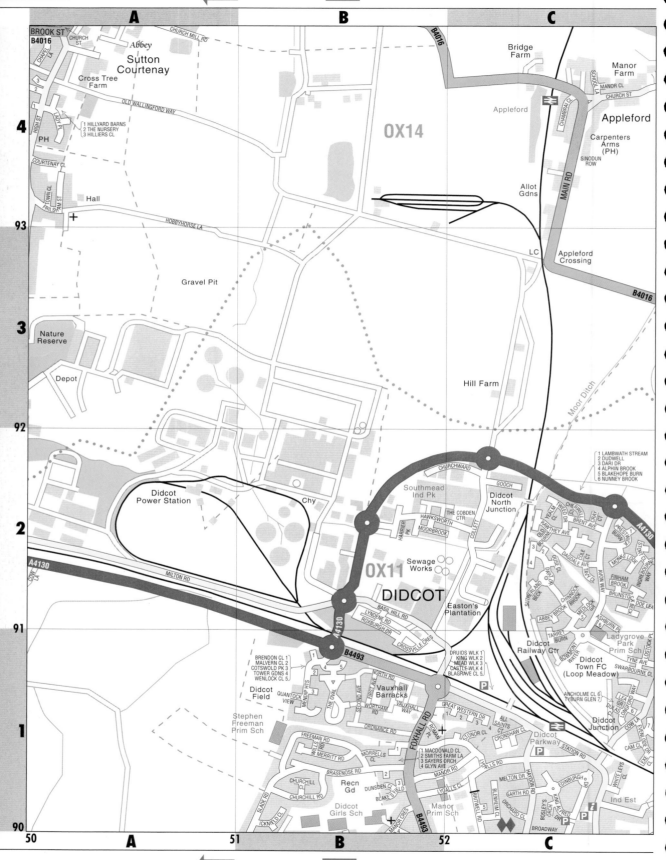

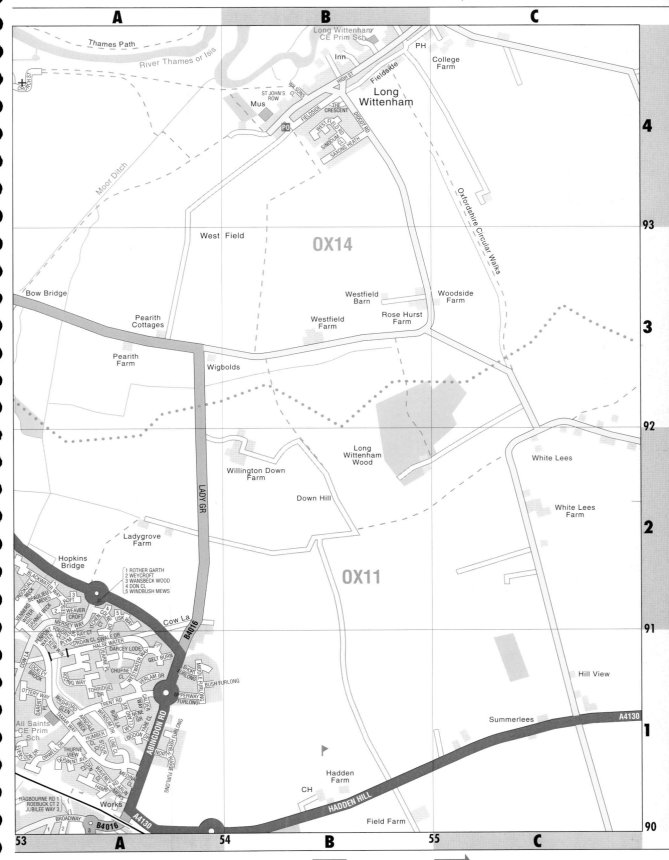

201
182

A **B** **C**

Samian Way
Watling La
Dorchester Bridge
Overy
Bridge End
Tenpenny
Bridge End
Haven Cl
Orchard Haven
Wittenham La
Dyke Hills
River Thame
Sewage Works
Meadside
Henley Rd
A4074

Weir
Day's Lock
Little Wittenham Bridge
Thames Path
River Thames or Isis

4

Little Wittenham

Little Wittenham Wood

93

OX14

Little Wittenham
Nature Reserve
Star Walk
Lowerhill Farm

Wittenham Clumps

Felmore Copse

Hill Farm
North Farm

3

Castle Hill
P
Sinodun Hills

92

Brightwell Barrow
OX10

Redgate Farm
Sires Hill

Highlands Farm

2
Sinodun Hill
Style Acre

OX11
Watermans Lane
High Road Cotts
High Rd
Greenmere
Kings Orch

Didcot Rd
Grove Cotts
West End
Church La
Brightwell CE Prim Sch
Wellsprings
Datchet Gn
Bell La
A4130

91
Frog's Island Farm
PO
Greenmere Path
Monks Mead
Sotwell St
Slade End

North Farm
Brightwell-cum-Sotwell
Brightwell Manor
Brightwell St
PH
Pennygreen La
Croft Path

Frogs' Island
Kibble Ditch

1
A4130
Slade End
Mackney La

Park Farm
Mackney Court Farm

90
56 **A** 57 **B** 58 **C**

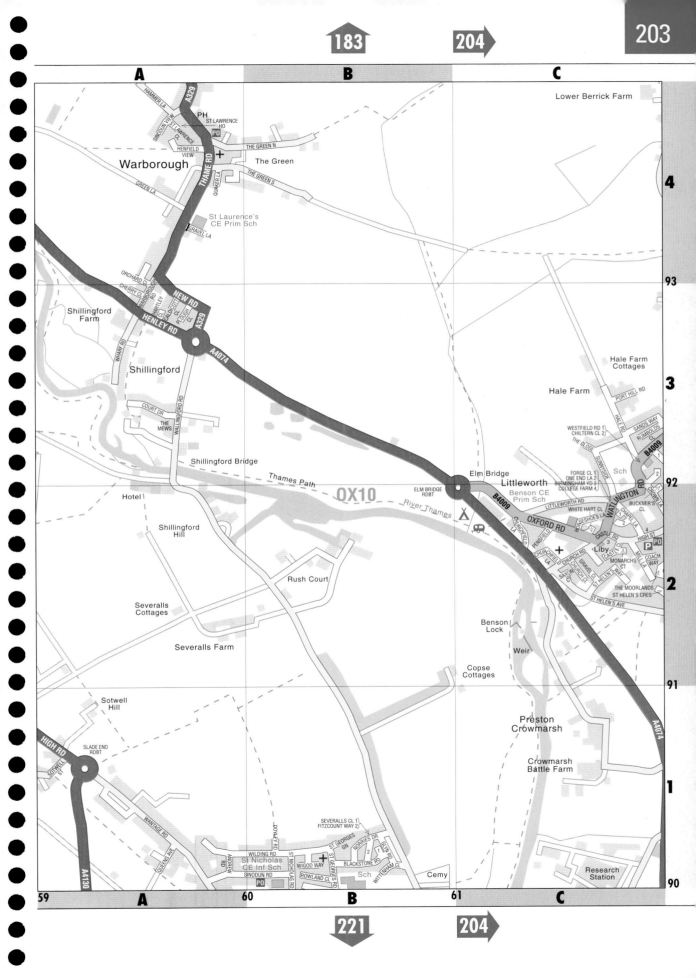

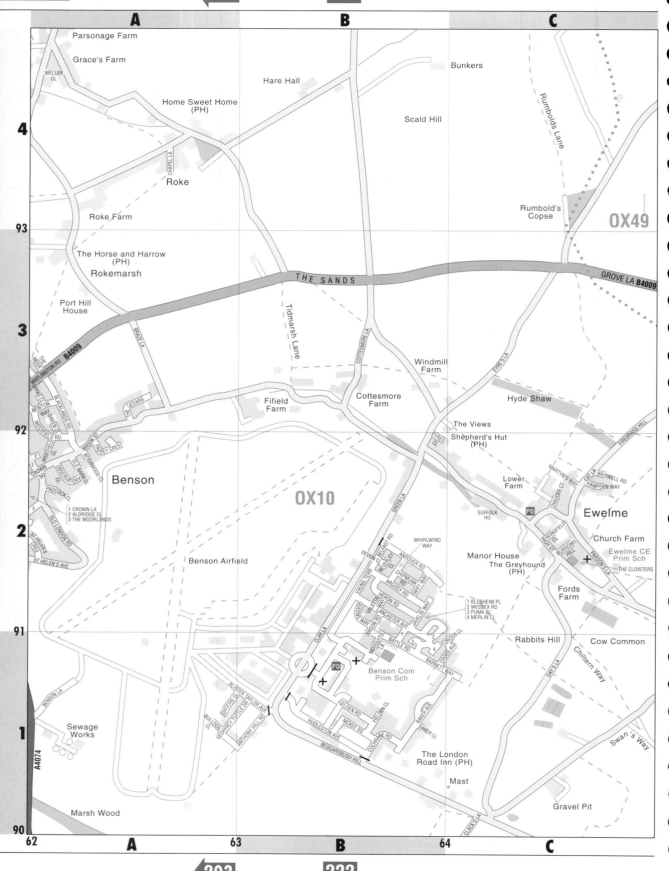

203
184

A   B   C

Parsonage Farm

Grace's Farm

WELLER CL

Home Sweet Home (PH)

Hare Hall

Bunkers

Scald Hill

Rumbolds Lane

4

CHAPEL LA

Roke

Rumbold's Copse

OX49

93

Roke Farm

The Horse and Harrow (PH)

Rokemarsh

THE SANDS

GROVE LA B4009

Port Hill House

B4009

BRAZIL LA

Tidmarsh Lane

Windmill Farm

EYRES LA

3

THE MEER

WATLINGTON RD

UPLANDS CL

BLACKLANDS RD

THE CEDARS

Fifield Farm

Cottesmore Farm

Hyde Shaw

EYRES LA

NEWTON WAY

GREEN WAY

WESTFIELD RD

BROOK ST

PASSEY CRES

The Views

Shepherd's Hut (PH)

FIREBRASS HILL

92

WYCHWOOD CL

OLD BARN CL

OBSERVATORY LA

PADDOCK LA

CROWN SQ

Benson

1 CROWN LA
2 ALDRIDGE CL
3 THE MOORLANDS

OX10

Lower Farm

MARTYN'S WAY

CHAUCER CT

CAT LA

BRITWELL RD

HAMPDEN WAY

PO

Ewelme

OLD LONDON RD

ST HELEN'S CRES

ST HELEN'S AVE

SUFFOLK HO

WINGFIELD CL

HIGH ST

BURROWS HILL

PARSON'S LA

Church Farm

Ewelme CE Prim Sch

THE CLOISTERS

2

Benson Airfield

WHIRLWIND WAY

Manor House

The Greyhound (PH)

Fords Farm

1 BLENHEIM PL
2 WESSEX RD
3 PUMA CL
4 MERLIN CL

BELFAST RD

DEVON CL

BEVERLEY RD

ANDOVER RD

CHIPMUNK RD

ARGOSY RD

SWIFT WAY

JAVELIN WAY

VALETTA RD

HERON RD

LANCASTER AVE

CROSS AVE

GREEN LA

91

GLEN LA

VIKING TERR

PARSON RD

MOSQUITO LA

BATTLE RD

BARNETT WAY

Rabbits Hill

Cow Common

DAY'S LA

Chiltern Way

PO

Benson Com Prim Sch

BAKER AVE

BAKER CL

1

A4074

BENSON LA

Sewage Works

ALISTER TAYLOR AVE

STATURE CL

GEOFFREY TUTTLE DR

ANTHONY HILL RD

BULLDOG CL

FIELDEN RD

FIELDEN CL

McKEE SQ

HUDLESTON AVE

COCHRANE RD

BEGGARSBUSH HILL

The London Road Inn (PH)

Mast

Swan's Way

Gravel Pit

Marsh Wood

CLACK'S LA

90

62   A   63   B   64   C

203
222

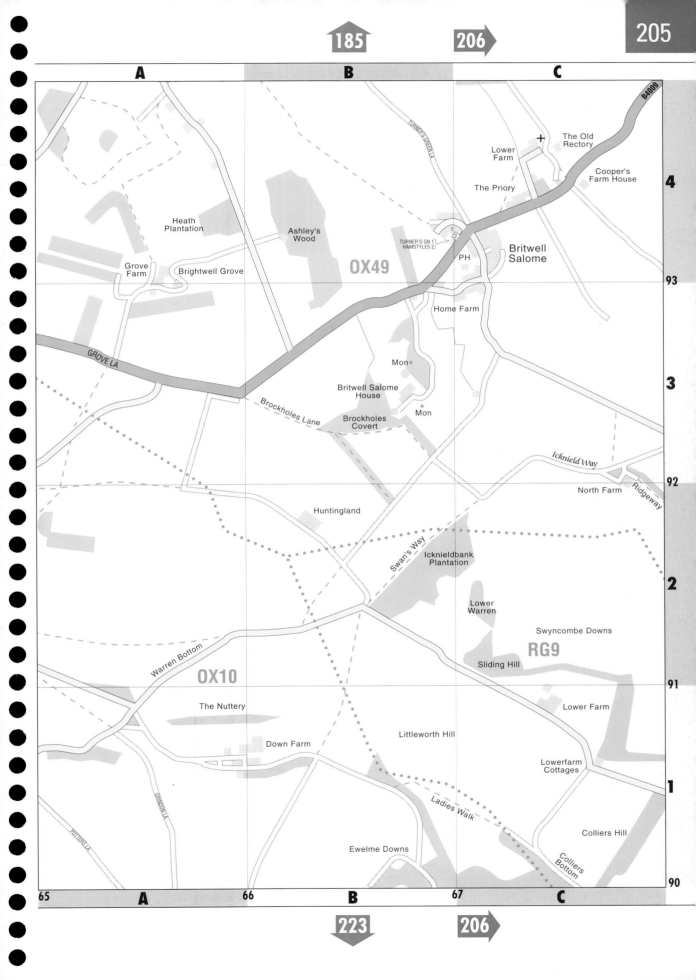

185
206

A   B   C

B4009

TURNER'S GREEN LA

The Old
Rectory

Lower
Farm

Cooper's
Farm House

The Priory

4

Heath
Plantation

Ashley's
Wood

Grove
Farm

Brightwell Grove

OX49

TURNER'S GN 1
HAMSTYLES 2

1
2

PH

Britwell
Salome

93

GROVE LA

Home Farm

Mon

3

Brockholes Lane

Britwell Salome
House

Mon

Brockholes
Covert

Icknield Way

North Farm

Ridgeway

92

Huntingland

Swan's Way

Icknieldbank
Plantation

Lower
Warren

Swyncombe Downs

2

Warren Bottom

RG9

OX10

Sliding Hill

91

The Nuttery

Lower Farm

Down Farm

Littleworth Hill

Lowerfarm
Cottages

1

GRINDON LA

POTTERS LA

Ladies Walk

Colliers Hill

Ewelme Downs

Colliers
Bottom

90

65   A   66   B   67   C

223
206

205
186

A **B** **C**

B4009

Watlington

White Mark
Farm

White Mark

Springfield
Farm

HILL RD

HOWE RD

Cobditch
Hill

Watlington Hill

P

4

Swan's Way

Ridgeway

Icknield House

Piggery

93

Lys Farm
House

Lower
Dean

Lower Deans
Wood

OX49

Dumble
Dore

Watlington
Park

3

Dame Alice
Farm

The
Howe

Greenfield
Copse

Howe
Combe

Howe
Farm

92

Britwell Hill

Britwell Hill
Farm

Howe Wood

Ridgeway

Woods
Farm

Dean
Wood

Greenfield
Manor

2

Mast

Westernend
Shaw

Ploughmans

Lower Greenfield
Farm

91

Coates
Farm

B481

COATES LA

Coates Copse

PATEMORE LA

Grove
Farm

RG9

RED LA

B480

1

Wr
Twr

White
Hill

CHURCH LA

The Rectory

Cookley
Green

RECTORY HILL

Church
Wood

Colliers
Hill

LADIES WALK

Reading Lane

Van
Diemans

Swyncombe
House

Cookley
Farm

B481

90

68 **A** 69 **B** 70 **C**

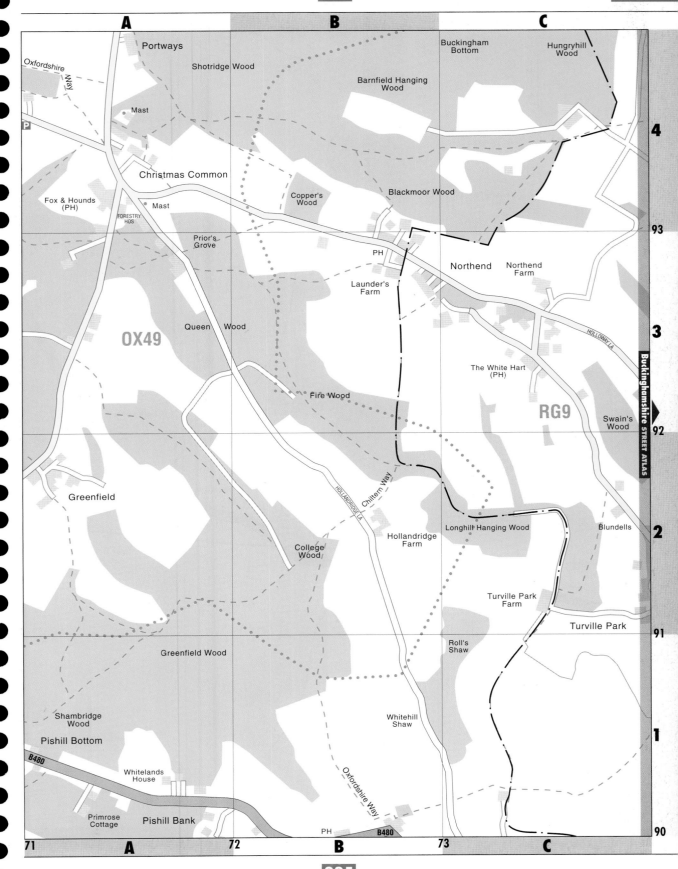

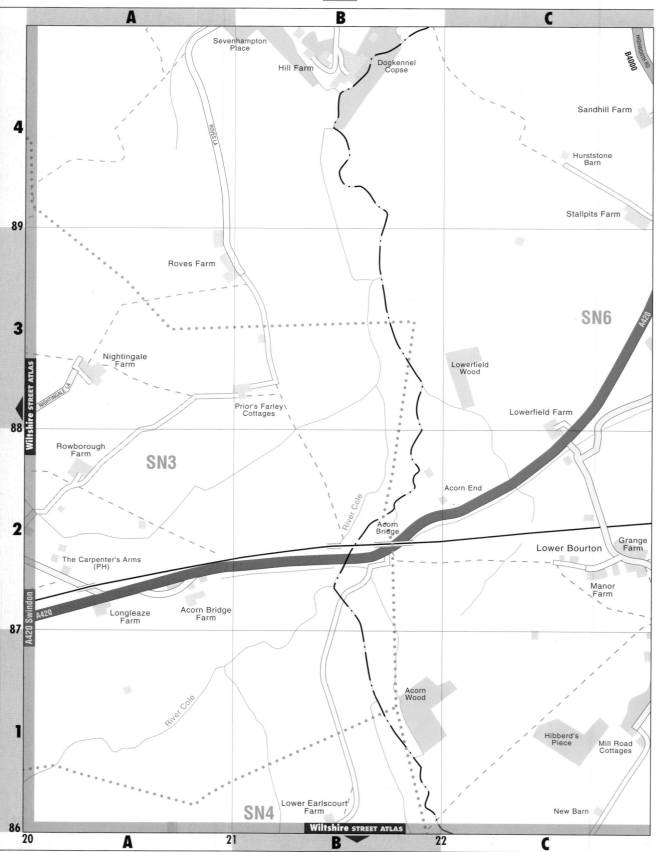

Sevenhampton Place

Hill Farm

Dogkennel Copse

B4000

HIGHWORTH RD

Sandhill Farm

Hurststone Barn

4

ROVES LA

Stallpits Farm

89

Roves Farm

SN6

A420

3

Lowerfield Wood

Wiltshire STREET ATLAS

NIGHTINGALE LA

Nightingale Farm

Lowerfield Farm

Prior's Farley Cottages

88

Rowborough Farm

SN3

Acorn End

River Cole

Acorn Bridge

2

Lower Bourton

Grange Farm

The Carpenter's Arms (PH)

A420 Swindon

A420

Manor Farm

Longleaze Farm

Acorn Bridge Farm

87

River Cole

Acorn Wood

1

Hibberd's Piece

Mill Road Cottages

SN4

Lower Earlscourt Farm

New Barn

86

20   **A**   21   **B**   22   **C**

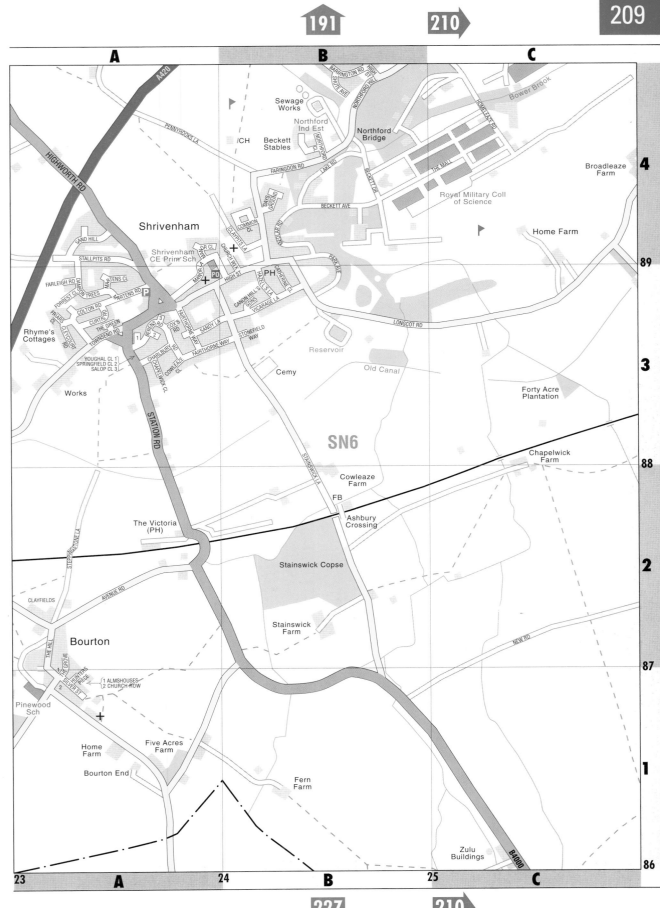

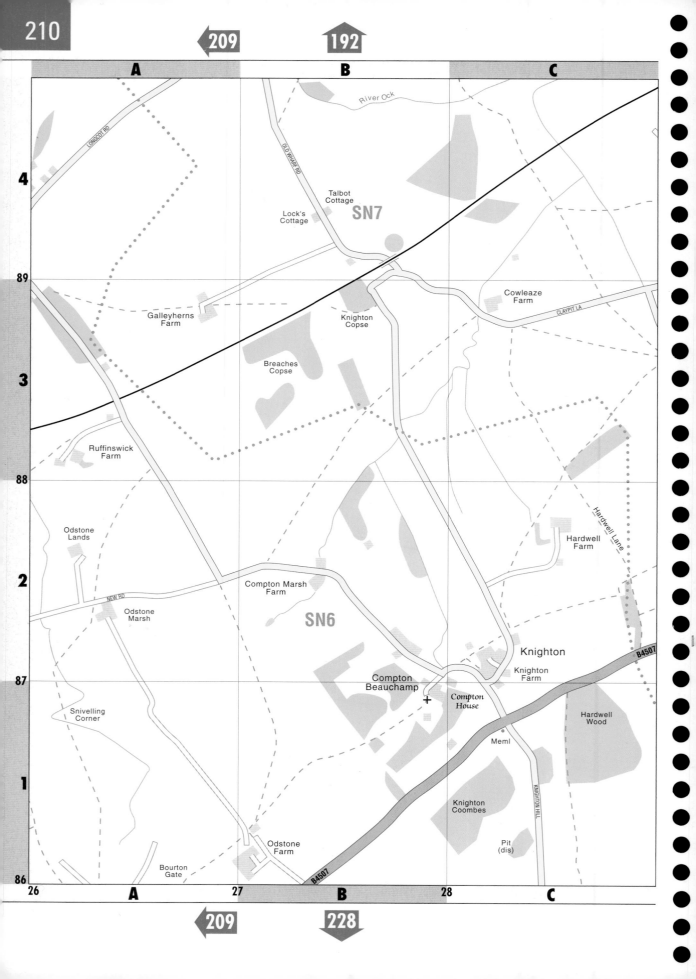

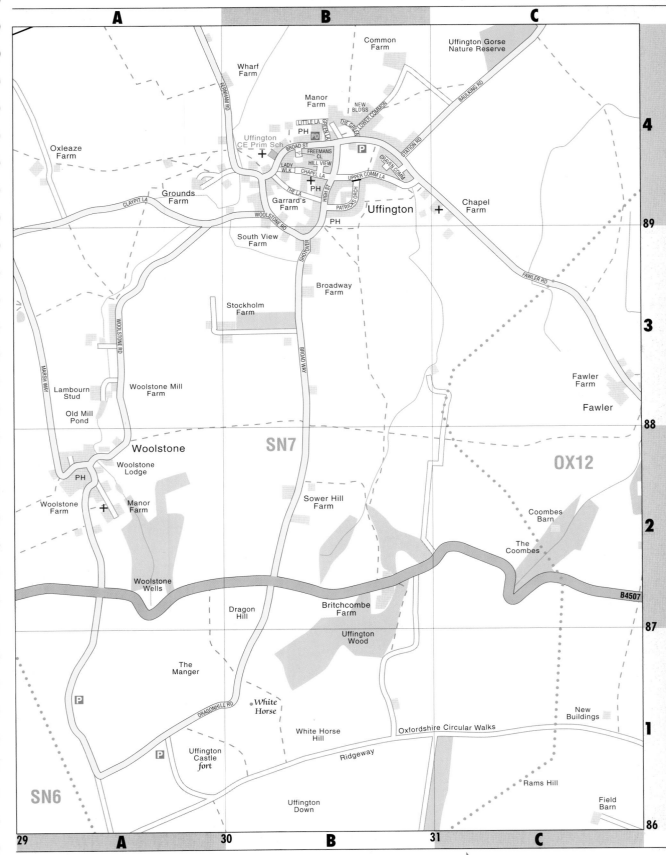
A
B
C

Common Farm

Uffington Gorse Nature Reserve

Wharf Farm

Manor Farm

NEW BLDGS

BAULKING RD

THE GREEN

LOWER COMMON

FEGNHAM RD

LITTLE LA

GREEN LA

PH

PO

STATION RD

Oxleaze Farm

Uffington CE Prim Sch

BROAD ST

FREEMANS CL

HILL VIEW

LADY WLK

P

Grounds Farm

CLAYPIT LA

CHAPEL LA

THE LA

PH

HIGH ST

UPPER COMM LA

CRAVEN COMM

Uffington

Chapel Farm

Garrard's Farm

WOOLSTONE RD

PATRICKS ORCH

PH

South View Farm

SHOTOVER

89

Broadway Farm

Stockholm Farm

WOOLSTONE RD

BROAD WAY

3

MARSH WAY

Lambourn Stud

Woolstone Mill Farm

Fawler Farm

Fawler

Old Mill Pond

88

Woolstone

SN7

OX12

Woolstone Lodge

PH

Manor Farm

Sower Hill Farm

Coombes Barn

Woolstone Farm

The Coombes

2

Woolstone Wells

B4507

Dragon Hill

Britchcombe Farm

87

The Manger

Uffington Wood

P

DRAGONHILL RD

White Horse

White Horse Hill

Oxfordshire Circular Walks

New Buildings

1

P

Uffington Castle fort

Ridgeway

Rams Hill

SN6

Uffington Down

Field Barn

86

29
30
31

A
B
C

SN7

Ladycroft
Pond

Church's
Copse

Stutfield Brook

Long Spinney
Copse

Round Spinney
Copse

Cross Bargain
Farm

Gabbits Copse

Featherbed Lane

Fox Covert

Westcot Lane

South
Farm

Broadleaze
Farm

Kingston Common
Farm

Westcot La

Fawler
Manor

Fawler

Cemy

Kingston Lisle

HILL VIEW

DROVE WAY

The Plough
(PH)

Manor Farm

North
Park

OX12

Georgesgreen
Farm

Hall
Place

Home
Farm

Star
(PH)

WATERY LA

Sparsholt

West St

SPARSHOLT ST

BROADBROOK LA

Kingston Lisle
Farm

Kingston Lisle
House

Green
Park

Kingston Lisle Park

Westcot
Farm

Westcot

CHURCH WAY

BLACKLANDS

Sparsholt Park

EASTMANTON LA

B4507

Blowing Stone

The Warren

BLOWINGSTONE HILL

Oakbank
Plantations

Oakbank Barn

Seven Acre Hill

B4507

The Rides

Oxfordshire

Ridgeway

Circular Walks

Kingstonhill Barn

Sparsholt Field

Field Barn

Sheephouse Bottom

Clements Cottages

Lodge Farm

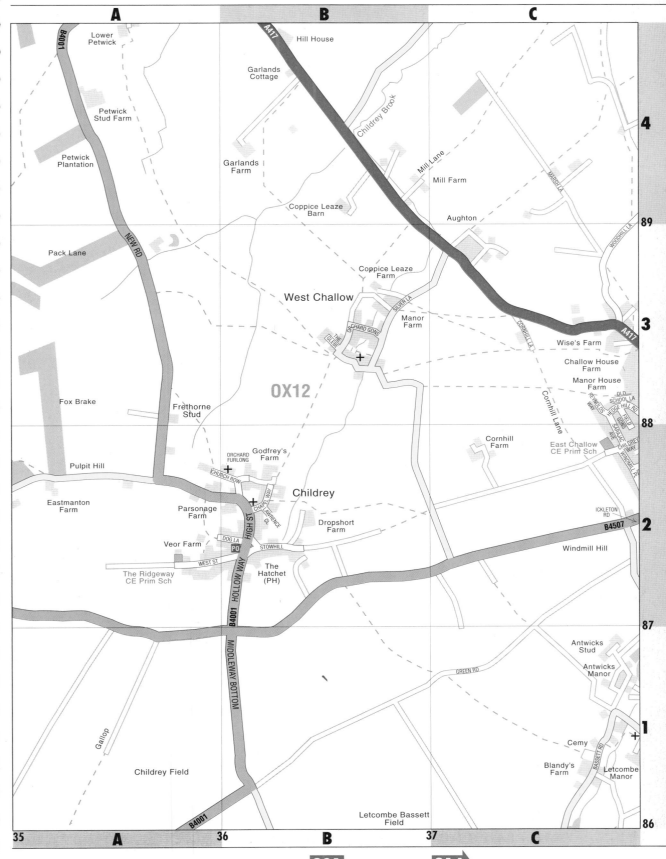

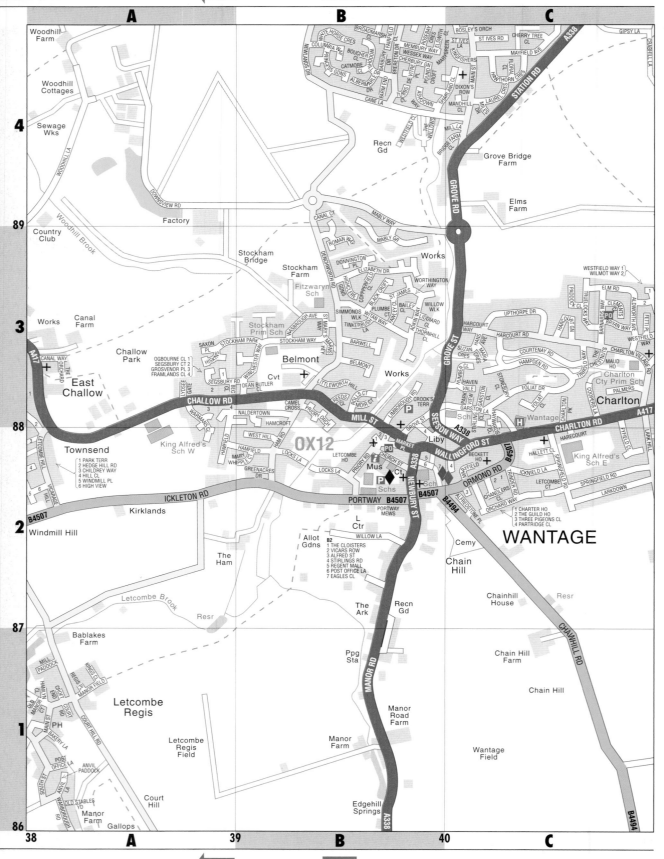

A   B   C

4

89

3

88

2

87

1

86

38   A   39   B   40   C

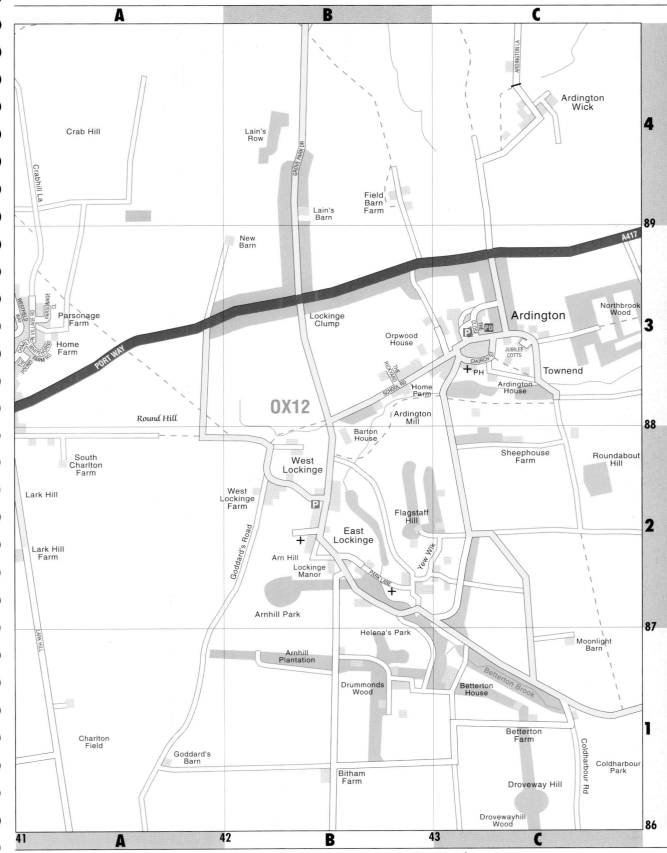

A   B   C

4

89

3

88

2

87

1

86

Crab Hill

Crabhill La

Lain's Row

GROVE PARK DR

Lain's Barn

Field Barn Farm

Ardington Wick

ARDINGTON LA

A417

New Barn

Lockinge Clump

Orpwood House

Ardington

Northbrook Wood

WESTFIELD WAY

PARSONAGE CL

THE CHARLTON VILLAGE RD

WHITECROSS RD

THE POUND

HOME FARM RD

Parsonage Farm

Home Farm

PORT WAY

THE RICKYARD

SCHOOL RD

THE CLOSE

P

PO

THE
CHURCH ST

JUBILEE COTTS

Townend

Home Farm

+ PH

Ardington House

Round Hill

OX12

Barton House

Ardington Mill

South Charlton Farm

West Lockinge

Sheephouse Farm

Roundabout Hill

Lark Hill

West Lockinge Farm

P

+

Flagstaff Hill

Lark Hill Farm

Goddard's Road

East Lockinge

Arn Hill

Lockinge Manor

PARK LANE

+

YEW WLK

Arnhill Park

Helena's Park

Moonlight Barn

LARK HILL

Arnhill Plantation

Drummonds Wood

Betterton Brook

Betterton House

Charlton Field

Goddard's Barn

Bitham Farm

Betterton Farm

Coldharbour Rd

Coldharbour Park

Droveway Hill

Drovewayhill Wood

41   A   42   B   43   C

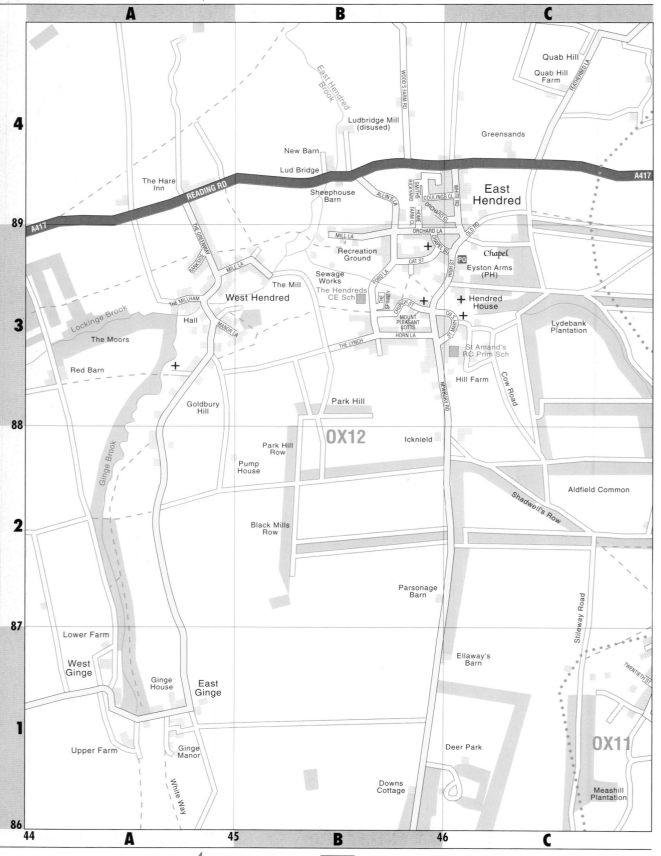

215
198
215
234

A   B   C

4

89

3

88

2

87

1

86

44   A   45   B   46   C

Quab Hill
Quab Hill Farm
FEATHERBED LA

Greensands

A417

East Hendred

Ludbridge Mill (disused)

East Hendred Brook

WOOD'S FARM RD

New Barn

Lud Bridge

The Hare Inn

READING RD

Sheephouse Barn

ALLIN'S LA

SMITHS RICKYARD

HOME FARM CL

ORCHARD CL

COULINGS CL

WHITE RD

OLD RD

Chapel

ORCHARD LA

CHAPEL SQ

CAT ST

HIGH ST

PO

Eyston Arms (PH)

A417

THE GREENWAY

BANKSIDE

MILL LA

MILL LA

The Mill

West Hendred

Recreation Ground

Sewage Works

The Hendreds CE Sch

FORD LA

THE SPINNEY

CHURCH ST

Hendred House

Lydebank Plantation

Lockinge Brook

THE MILLHAM

Hall

MANOR LA

The Moors

Red Barn

Goldbury Hill

THE LYNCH

MOUNT PLEASANT COTTS

HORN LA

NEWBURY RD

ST MARY'S LA

Hill Farm

St Amand's RC Prim Sch

Cow Road

Ginge Brook

Park Hill

Park Hill Row

Pump House

OX12

Icknield

Aldfield Common

Shadwell's Row

Black Mills Row

Parsonage Barn

Stileway Road

Lower Farm

West Ginge

Ginge House

East Ginge

Ellaway's Barn

TWENTIETH ST

OX11

Upper Farm

Ginge Manor

White Way

Deer Park

Downs Cottage

Meashill Plantation

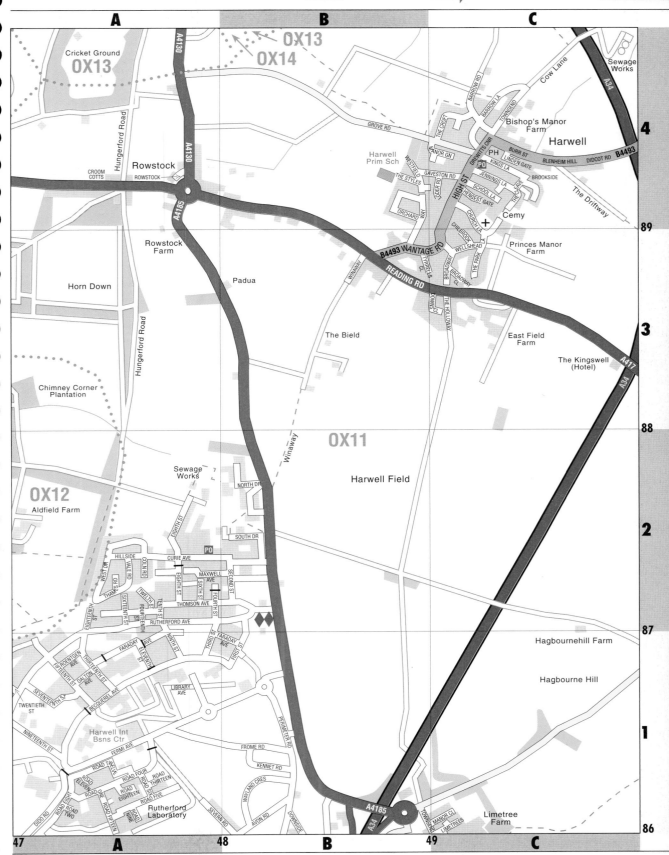

OX13
OX14

Cricket Ground
OX13

A4130

Hungerford Road

CROOM
COTTS

Rowstock
ROWSTOCK

A4185

Rowstock
Farm

Padua

Horn Down

Hungerford Road

Chimney Corner
Plantation

OX12

Aldfield Farm

HILLSIDE
VALE RD
COLN RD
CURIE AVE
MAXWELL
AVE
WEST DR
THAMS DR
EIGHTH ST
SIXTH ST
SECOND ST
TWELFTH ST
SIXTEENTH ST
TENTH ST
FOURTH ST
THOMSON AVE
FOURTEENTH ST
RUTHERFORD AVE
EIGHTEENTH ST
NINTH ST
THIRD ST
FARADAY
AVE
FIRST ST
FARADAY AVE
ROENTGEN AVE
THIRTEENTH ST
DALTON AVE
ELEVENTH ST
FIFTEENTH ST
SEVENTEENTH ST
BECQUEREL AVE
LIBRARY
AVE
TWENTIETH
ST
NINETEENTH ST
Harwell Int
Bsns Ctr
FERMI AVE
ROAD TWELVE
ROAD FOUR
ROAD FIVE
ROAD ELEVEN
ROAD THIRTEEN
ROAD EIGHTEEN
ROAD EIGHT
ROAD ONE
ROAD FIFTEEN
ROAD TWO
ROAD NINE
DIDO RD
Rutherford
Laboratory

PO

NORTH DR

SOUTH DR

Sewage
Works

Winaway

Winaway

The Bield

OX11

Harwell Field

GROVE RD

Harwell
Prim Sch

MANOR GN
WESTFIELD
THE STYLES
LODER RD
ORCHARD
WAY
THE CROFT
BARROW LA
BARROW RD
TOWNSEND
DREWITTS CNR
PH
BURR ST
LINDEN GATE
KINGS LA
PO
GAVESTON RD
JENNINGS LA
HENGEST GATE
SCHOOL LA
CHURCH LA
HIGH ST
CHILBROOK
WELLSHEAD
TYRRELLS CL
DOWNS CL
THE HOLLOW
BROADWAY
BROADWAY CL
THE PARK LA
Bishop's Manor
Farm
Harwell
Cow Lane
BLENHEIM HILL
DIDCOT RD
B4493
A34
Sewage
Works
The Driftway
Cemy
+
Princes Manor
Farm
East Field
Farm
The Kingswell
(Hotel)
A417
A34

B4493 WANTAGE RD
READING RD

Hagbournehill Farm

Hagbourne Hill

FROME RD
KENNET RD
PERIMETER RD
AVON RD
SEVERN RD
WAY AND CRES
DOWNSIDE
A4185
A34
TOWNSEND
MANOR CL
LIMETREES
Limetree
Farm

47
48
A
B
49
C

89
88
87
86
4
3
2
1

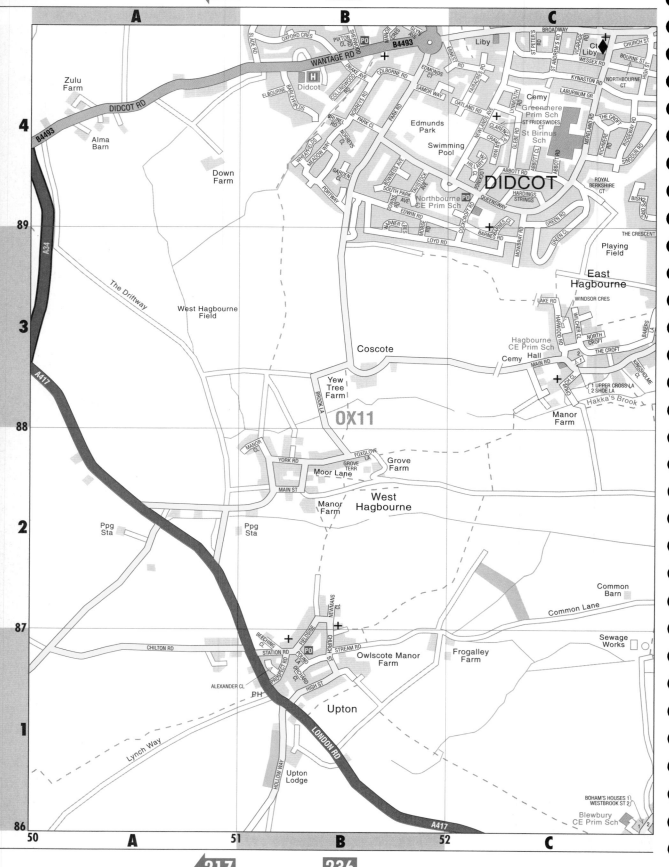

217
200

A **B** **C**

4

89

3

88

2

87

1

86

50 **A** 51 **B** 52 **C**

217
236

Zulu Farm
Alma Barn
DIDCOT RD
B4493
A34
A417

Oxford Cres
Pixton Cl
Sherwood
Slade Rd
Elbourne
Barleyfields
WANTAGE RD
B4493
Manor Cres
Glyn
PO
Liby
St Peter's Rd
Broadway
St Andrew's Rd
Church St
Vicarage
Ct Liby
Bourne St
Drake Ave
Colborne Rd
Edmonds Ct
Ernest Rd
Wessex Rd
Northbourne
Kynaston Rd
Laburnum Gr
Collingwood
Didcot
H

Down Farm

Meadow Way
Brunel Rd
Mothers
Park Rd
Park Ave
Downs Ave
Wheatfields
Portway
Garden Cl
South Park Ave
Queensway
Edwin Rd
Warner Cres
Morse Cl
Samor Way
Oatland Rd
Newlands Ave
Glebe Rd
Hilary
Craig Way
Clarence
Abbott Rd
Abbott Cl
Cemy
Greenmere Prim Sch
St Frideswides Ct
St Birinus Sch
Meredith Rd
Richmere
Ridgeway Rd
The Croft
Royal Berkshire Ct
Bish

Edmunds Park
Swimming Pool
Northbourne CE Prim Sch
PO
Hardings Strings
DIDCOT
Barnes Rd
Barnes Cl
Mowbray Rd
Green Rd
Green Cl
The Crescent
Playing Field

Loyd Rd
Cockcroft Rd

The Driftway
West Hagbourne Field

East Hagbourne
Lake Rd
Windsor Cres
Harwell Rd
Wilcher Cl
North Croft
Bakers Rd
The Croft

Coscote

OX11

Yew Tree Farm
Brook La

Hagbourne CE Prim Sch
Cemy
Hall
Main Rd
Church Cl
Kingsholme Cl
Manor Farm
Hakka's Brook
1 Upper Cross La
2 Shoe La

Manor Cl
York Rd
Grove Terr
Main St
Moor Lane
Foxglove La
Grove Farm

Manor Farm
West Hagbourne

Ppg Sta
Ppg Sta

Common Barn
Common Lane

Chilton Rd
Beeching Cl
Station Rd
Pound
Orchard
Prospect Rd
Newnham Cl
Feldside
Church St
Stream Rd
High St
Alexander Cl
PH
Owlscote Manor Farm
Frogalley Farm
Sewage Works

Upton
LONDON RD
Lynch Way
Hollow Way
Upton Lodge
A417
Boham's Houses 1
Westbrook St 2
Blewbury CE Prim Sch

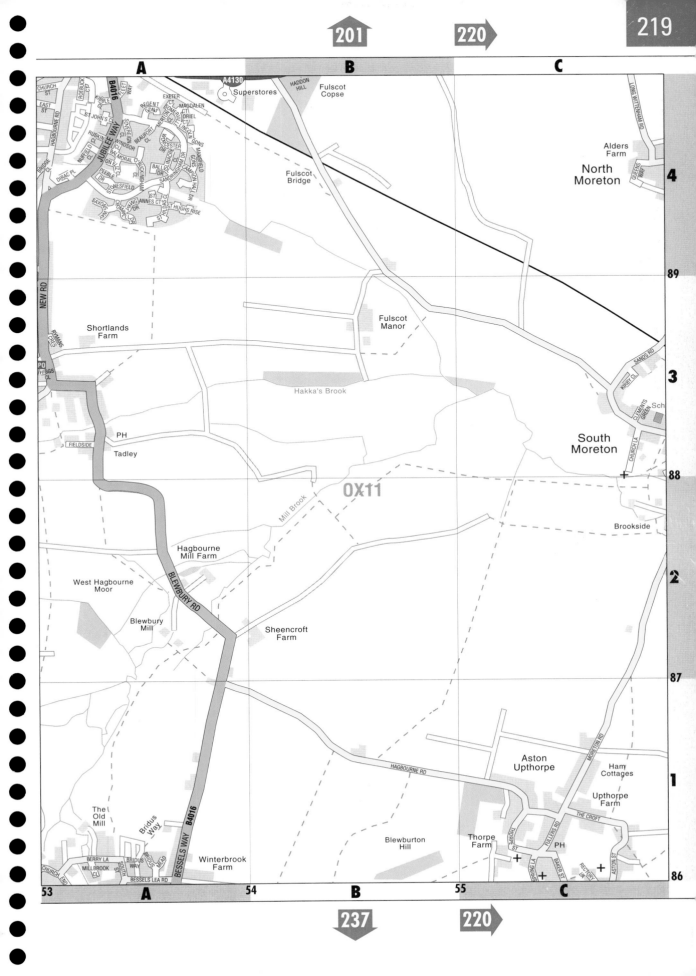

201
220
237
220

A   **B**   **C**

CHURCH ST
ROEBUCK CTP
B4016
KIBBLE CL
EAST ST
ST JOHN'S C
HAGBOURNE RD
NUFFIELD CL
RUSKIN RD
JUBILEE WAY
BRIDGE CL
DIBAC PL
PEEBLE
FLEET WAY
EXETER CT
REGENT GDNS
SOVEREIGN CL
WINDSOR CL
BEAUFORT CL
MERTON
HOMEWORTH
BALMORAL DR
CHESNEFIELD
SANDRINGHAM DR
CAMPION HALL DR
MAGDALEN
ORIEL
LINCOLN GDNS
WORCESTER CL
MANSFIELD GDNS
SAXONS WAY
ON ELIZ CL
CROMAC DR
ANNES CTS CL
ST MILDAS CL
HUGHS RISE
NEW RD
ROMANS CRES
PO
HIGGS CL
FIELDSIDE
PH
Tadley

A4130
Superstores
HADDON HILL
Fulscot Copse
Fulscot Bridge
Fulscot Manor
Hakka's Brook
Mill Brook
OX11

LONG WITTENHAM RD
Alders Farm
North Moreton
QUEENS WAY
SANDS RD
KIRBY CL
CLEMENTS GREEN
Sch
South Moreton
CHURCH LA
Brookside

4

89

3

88

Shortlands Farm

Hagbourne Mill Farm
West Hagbourne Moor
BLEWBURY RD
Blewbury Mill
Sheencroft Farm

HAGBOURNE RD

MORETON RD
Aston Upthorpe
Ham Cottages
Upthorpe Farm
THE CROFT
THORPE ST
FULLERS RD
PH
BAKER ST
RECTORY LA
ASTON ST

2

87

1

The Old Mill
Bridus Way
BESSELS WAY
B4016
BERRY LA
MILLBROOK CL
SOUTH
BRIDUS WAY
BRIDUS MEAD
Winterbrook Farm
CHURCH END
BESSELS LEA RD

Blewburton Hill
Thorpe Farm

86

53   54   55

A   **B**   **C**

219
202

A   **B**   **C**

Mackney

Sherwood Farm

MACKNEY LA

Kibble Ditch

ELM RD

LONG WITTENHAM RD

HIGH ST

The Bear (PH)

BEAR LA

DUNSOMER HILL

Mill Brook

89

Glebe Cottage

Hithercroft Farm

HITHERCROFT

3

The Crown (PH)

GROVE LA

PAPER MILL LA

MILL LA

OX11

Pumping Station

OX10

88

Cholsey Hill

ANCHOR LA

MORETON RD

Hillgreen Farm

2

Poultry Farm

The Manor

Sewage Works

Manor Farm

Cholsey and Wallingford Rly

CHURCH RD

87

GOLDFINCH LA

The Lees

Red Lion (PH)

Cholsey Prim Sch

MARYMEAD

WALLINGFORD RD

CROSS RD

Lees Cottages

THE FORTY

PO

CHEQUERS PL

THE POUND

ILGES LA

1

West End

POUND LA

FAIRFIELD

WEST END

ASHBY

SANDY LA

FORD CL

STATION RD

DROVESIDE

ST GEORGE'S

CL

BROOKSIDE

CRESCENT

KENTWOOD CL

HONEY LA

COLLEGE CL

PATERNOSTER

AMWE PL

RESTWOOD

QUEENS RD

WEXLEY

CRES

Pancroft Farm

THE ROWANS

BUCKTHORN LA

The Elms

WESTFIELD RD

PAPIST WAY

Cholsey

86

56   **A**   **57**   **B**   **58**   **C**

219
238

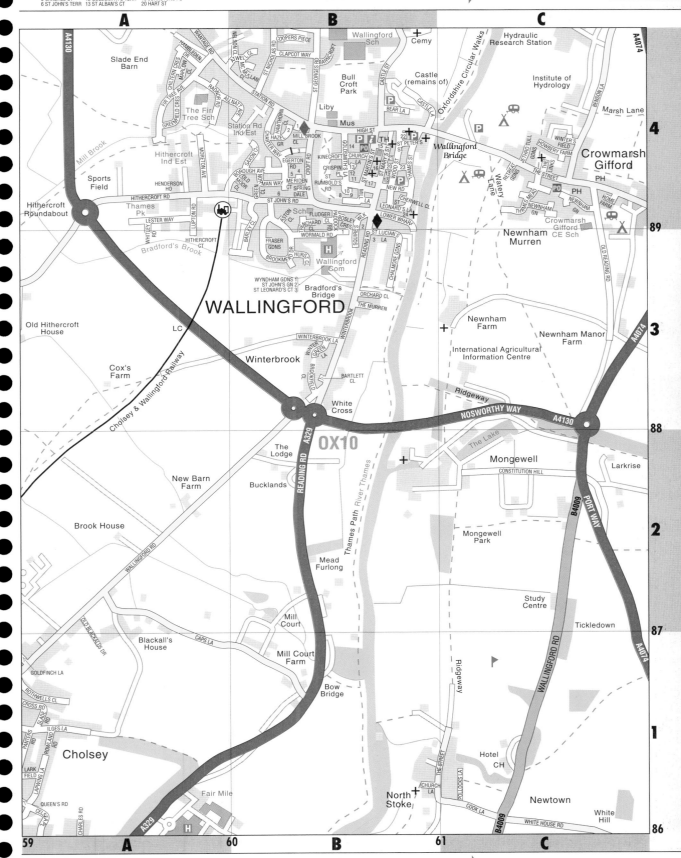

B4
1 WEEDON CT
2 COMPTON TERR
3 CROFT VILLAS
4 SOUTH VIEW
5 OAKDALE CT
6 ST JOHN'S TERR
7 BROOKSIDE
8 CROFT TERR
9 BEANSHEAF TERR
10 ST RUALD'S CL
11 MARIOT CT
12 GOLDSMITH'S TERR
13 ST ALBAN'S CT
14 THE MINT
15 MARKET PL
16 THE ARCADE
17 ST LEONARD'S SQ
18 OLD BLDGS
19 JOHNSTONE PL
20 HART ST
21 MOUSEY LA
22 ST PETER'S PL
23 PRIORY MEWS
24 SEYER MILWARD TERR

203   222

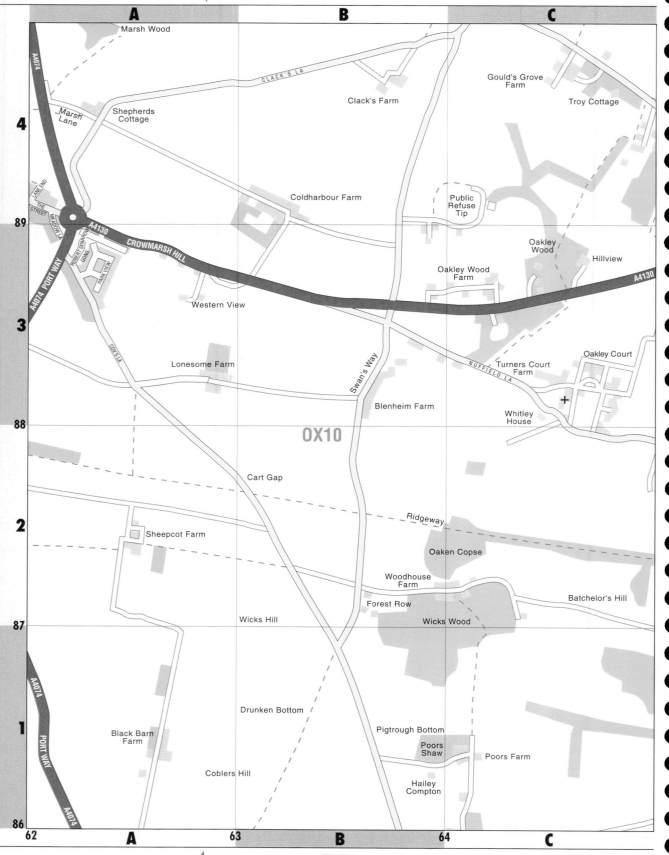

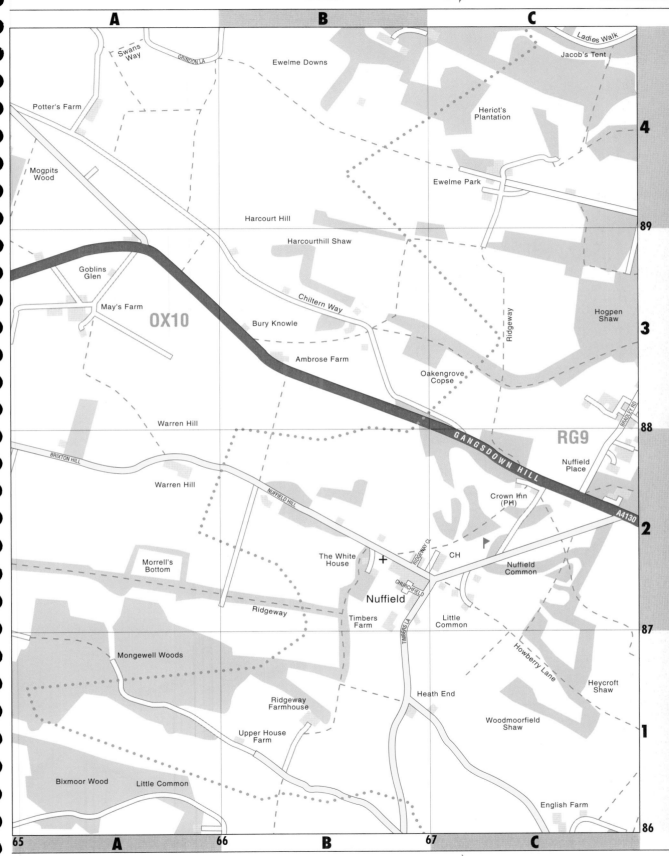

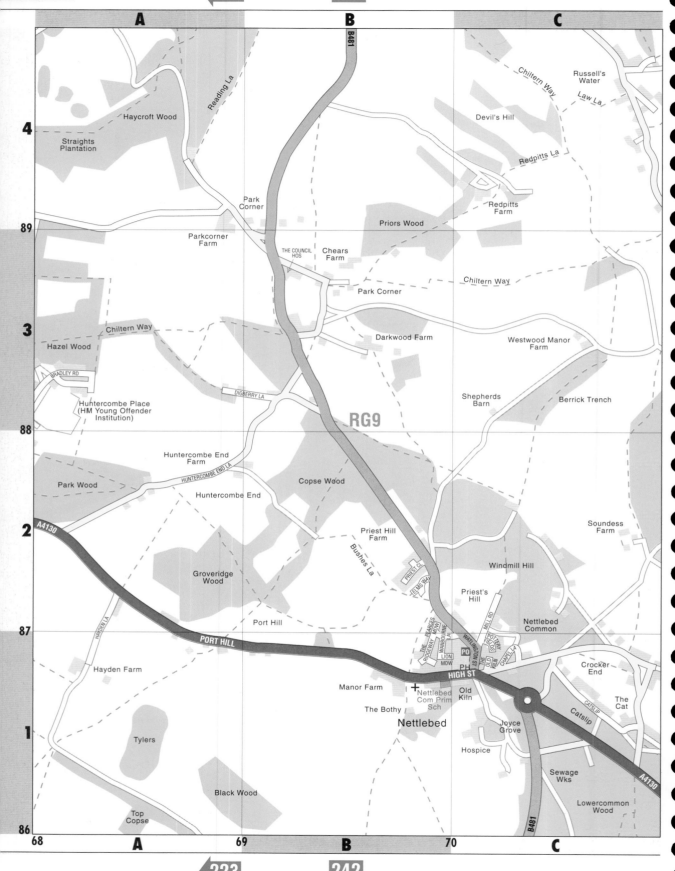

A   B   C

B481

Reading La

Haycroft Wood

Straights
Plantation

4

Chiltern Way

Russell's
Water

Devil's Hill

Law La

Redpitts La

Park
Corner

Priors Wood

Redpitts
Farm

89

Parkcorner
Farm

THE COUNCIL
HOS

Chears
Farm

Chiltern Way

Park Corner

3

Chiltern Way

Hazel Wood

Darkwood Farm

Westwood Manor
Farm

BRADLEY RD

DIGBERRY LA

Huntercombe Place
(HM Young Offender
Institution)

Shepherds
Barn

Berrick Trench

88

RG9

Huntercombe End
Farm

HUNTERCOMBE END LA

Park Wood

Copse Wood

Huntercombe End

Soundess
Farm

A4130

2

Priest Hill
Farm

Windmill Hill

Groveridge
Wood

Bushes La

Priest's
Hill

Nettlebed
Common

PRIEST CL

Port Hill

ELMS WAY

HAYDEN LA

87

PORT HILL

THE RIDGEWAY

WARBOURNE LA

LION MDW

MILL RD

THE OLD KILN

POTTERY

CHAPEL LA

Crocker
End

Hayden Farm

HIGH ST

PH

PO

Manor Farm

Old
Kiln

The
Cat

CATSLIP

Nettlebed
Com Prim
Sch

The Bothy

Catslip

1

Nettlebed

Joyce
Grove

Tylers

Hospice

A4130

Sewage
Wks

B481

Black Wood

Lowercommon
Wood

Top
Copse

86

68   69   70

A   B   C

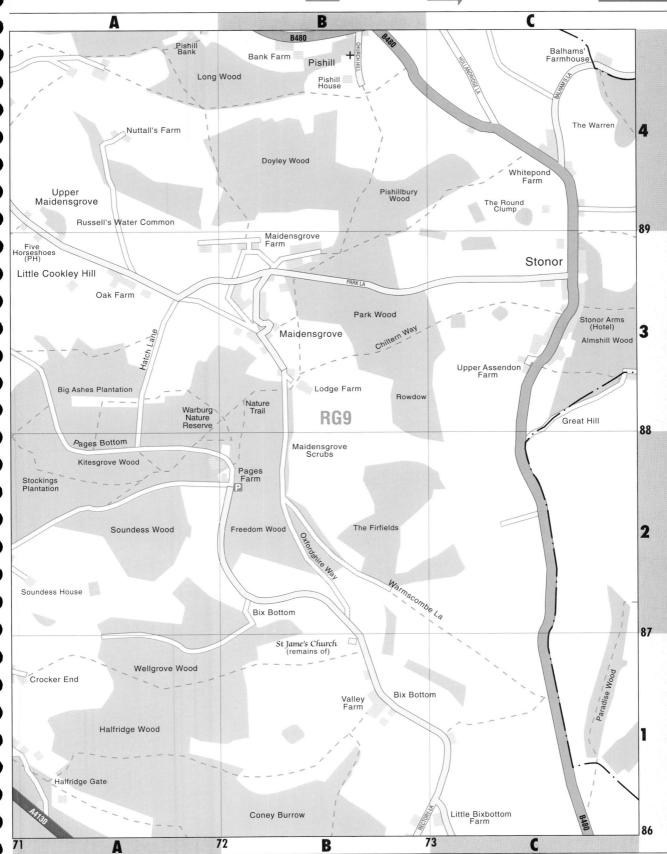

B480

B480

Pishill
Bank

Bank Farm

Pishill

CHURCH HILL

HOLLANDRIDGE LA

Balhams'
Farmhouse

BALHAMS LA

Long Wood

Pishill
House

The Warren

4

Nuttall's Farm

Doyley Wood

Pishillbury
Wood

Whitepond
Farm

Upper
Maidensgrove

The Round
Clump

89

Russell's Water Common

Maidensgrove
Farm

Five
Horseshoes
(PH)

Stonor

Little Cookley Hill

PARK LA

Park Wood

Oak Farm

Stonor Arms
(Hotel)

3

Maidensgrove

Chiltern Way

Almshill Wood

Hatch Lane

Upper Assendon
Farm

Big Ashes Plantation

Lodge Farm

Rowdow

Nature
Trail

RG9

Great Hill

88

Warburg
Nature
Reserve

Maidensgrove
Scrubs

Pages Bottom

Kitesgrove Wood

Pages
Farm

P

Stockings
Plantation

Soundess Wood

Freedom Wood

The Firfields

2

Oxfordshire Way

Soundess House

Warmscombe La

Bix Bottom

87

St Jame's Church
(remains of)

Paradise Wood

Crocker End

Wellgrove Wood

Bix Bottom

Valley
Farm

Halfridge Wood

1

Halfridge Gate

A4130

RECTORY LA

Coney Burrow

Little Bixbottom
Farm

B480

86

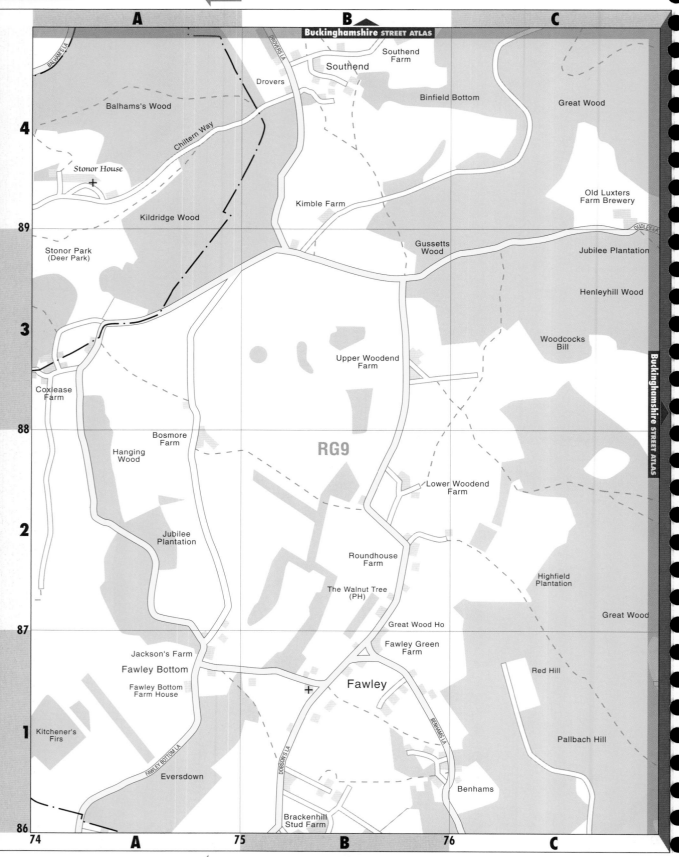

Buckinghamshire STREET ATLAS

Buckinghamshire STREET ATLAS

A B C

Southend
Southend
Farm
Drovers
Binfield Bottom
Great Wood

Balhams's Wood

Chiltern Way

Stonor House

Old Luxters
Farm Brewery

Kimble Farm

Kildridge Wood

Gussetts
Wood

DUDLEY LA

Jubilee Plantation

Stonor Park
(Deer Park)

Henleyhill Wood

Woodcocks
Bill

Upper Woodend
Farm

Coxlease
Farm

Bosmore
Farm

Hanging
Wood

RG9

Lower Woodend
Farm

Jubilee
Plantation

Highfield
Plantation

Roundhouse
Farm

Great Wood

The Walnut Tree
(PH)

Great Wood Ho

Jackson's Farm

Fawley Green
Farm

Red Hill

Fawley Bottom

Fawley

Fawley Bottom
Farm House

Kitchener's
Firs

FAWLEY BOTTOM LA

Pallbach Hill

BENHAMS LA

DOBSON'S LA

Eversdown

Benhams

Brackenhill
Stud Farm

74 75 76

4

89

3

88

2

87

1

86

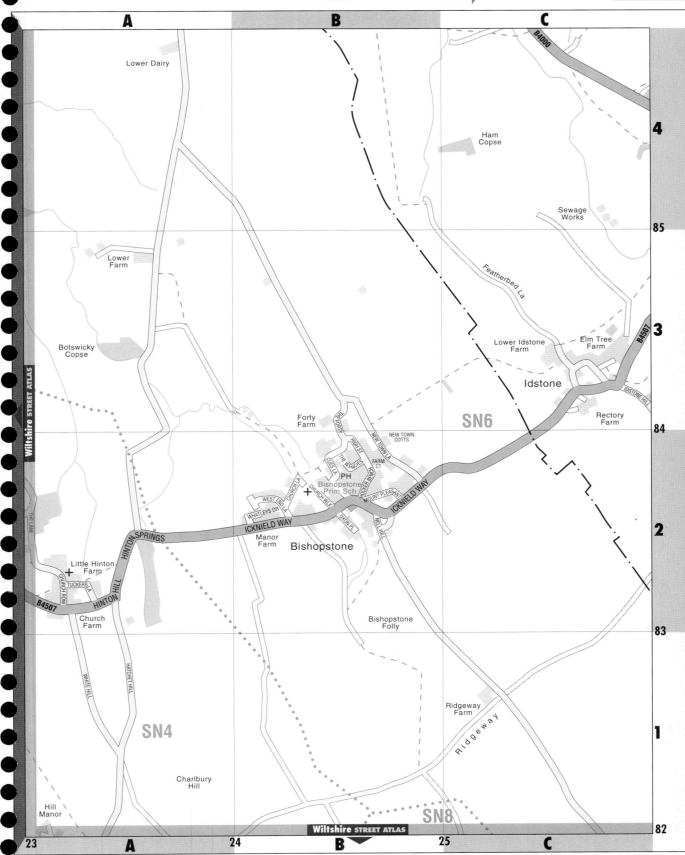

227 210

A B C

Kingstone
Winslow

B4507

Odstone Hill

Winslow
Bank

Kingstone
Farm

Wayland's
Smithy

Ridgeway

B4000

4

Ashbury

Odstone
Coombes

Knighton
Barn

STATION RD

POUND
PIECE

MALTHOUSE CL

WALNUT TREES HILL

Berrycroft

BERRYCROFT RD

CHAPEL LANE

KINGS
CL

Sch

MALTHOUSE

THE
MALTHOUSES

Kingstone Coombes

Odstone Barn

85

PH

PO

HIGH ST

Lertwell

IDSTONE RD

ASHBURY HILL

Resr

Kingstone
Barn

Kingstone Coombes

Ashbury
Folly

Odstone Barn

B4507

3

SN6

Down
Folly

Ridgeway

Compton
Bottom

IDSTONE HILL

Idstone
Plantation

84

Tower Hill

2

Honeybunch
Corner

Odstone Down

83

Hailey Wood

RG17

Crowberry
Tump

Kingstone Down

1

Middle Wood

P

B4000

Alfred's Castle

82

Starveall
Farm

Ashdown
House

26 A 27 B 28 C

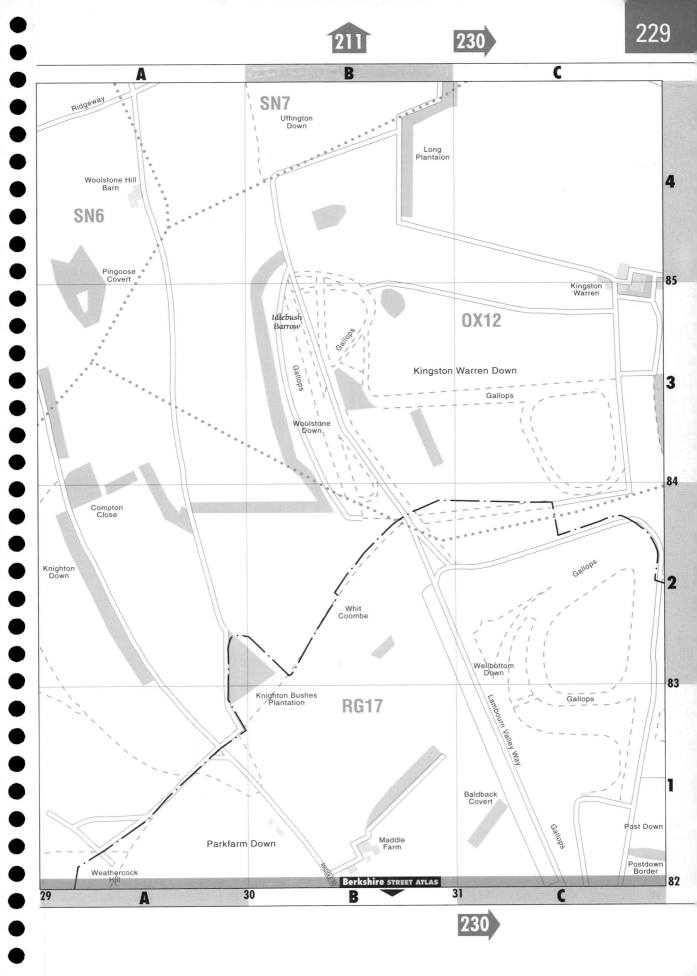

A
B
C

Ridgeway

SN7

Uffington
Down

Long
Plantaion

4

Woolstone Hill
Barn

SN6

Pingoose
Covert

85

Kingston
Warren

Idlebush
Barrow

OX12

Gallops

Gallops

Kingston Warren Down

3

Gallops

Gallops

Woolstone
Down

84

Compton
Close

Gallops

Knighton
Down

Gallops

2

Whit
Coombe

Wellbottom
Down

83

Knighton Bushes
Plantation

RG17

Gallops

Lambourn Valley Way

Baldback
Covert

1

Post Down

Parkfarm Down

Maddle
Farm

Gallops

Postdown
Border

Weathercock
Hill

82

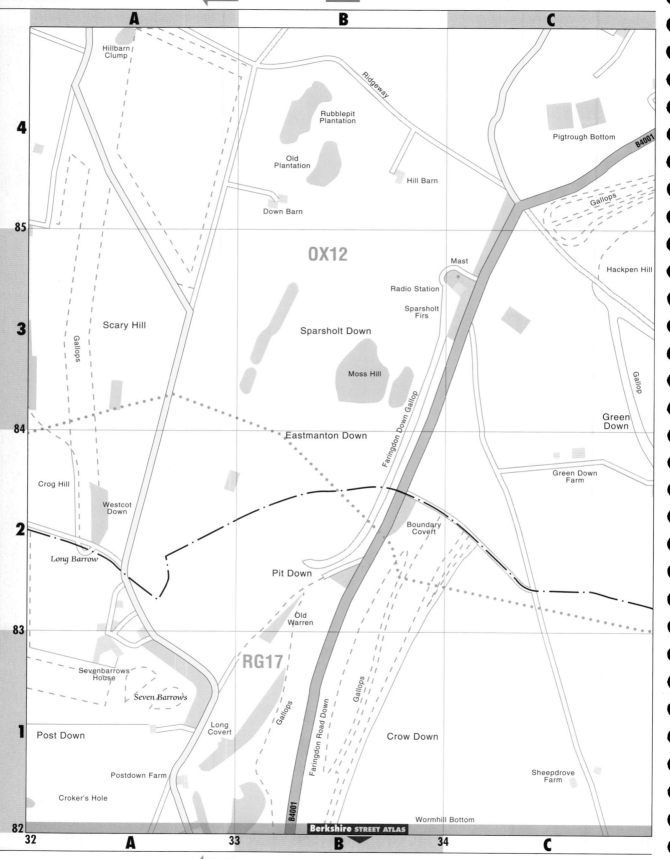

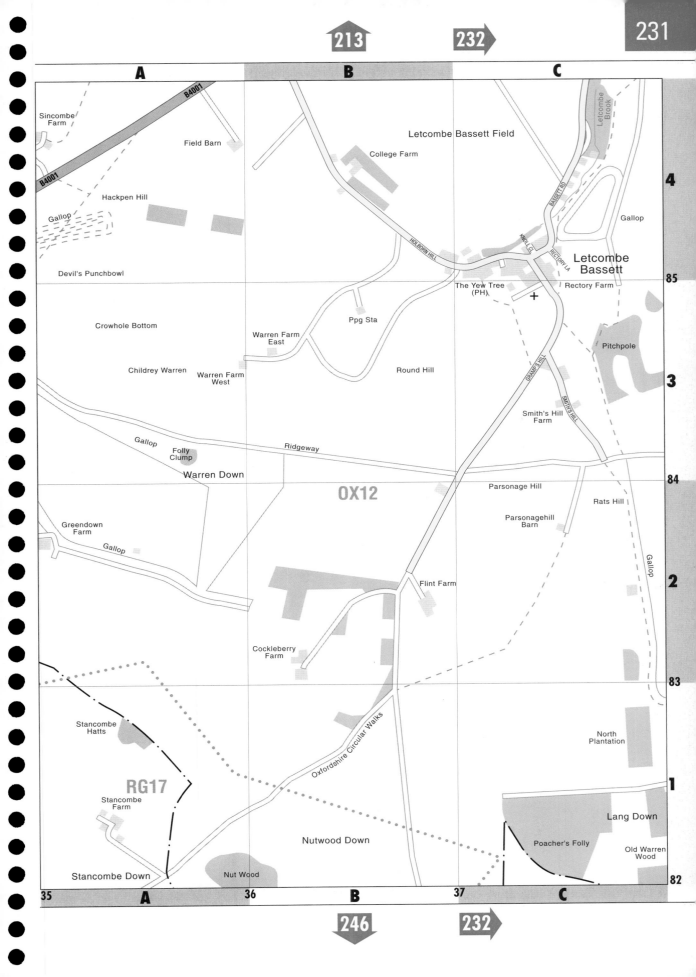

A

B

C

B4001

Sincombe Farm

Field Barn

4

B4001

Hackpen Hill

Gallop

Letcombe Bassett Field

College Farm

Letcombe Brook

HOLBORN HILL

BASSETT RD

KNOLL CL

RECTORY LA

Gallop

Letcombe Bassett

Devil's Punchbowl

Rectory Farm

85

The Yew Tree (PH)

+

Crowhole Bottom

Ppg Sta

Warren Farm East

Round Hill

Pitchpole

Childrey Warren

Warren Farm West

GRAMP'S HILL

SMITH'S HILL

Smith's Hill Farm

3

Gallop

Ridgeway

Folly Clump

Warren Down

OX12

Parsonage Hill

84

Rats Hill

Greendown Farm

Gallop

Parsonagehill Barn

Gallop

2

Flint Farm

Cockleberry Farm

83

Stancombe Hatts

Oxfordshire Circular Walks

North Plantation

RG17

1

Stancombe Farm

Lang Down

Poacher's Folly

Nutwood Down

Old Warren Wood

Stancombe Down

Nut Wood

82

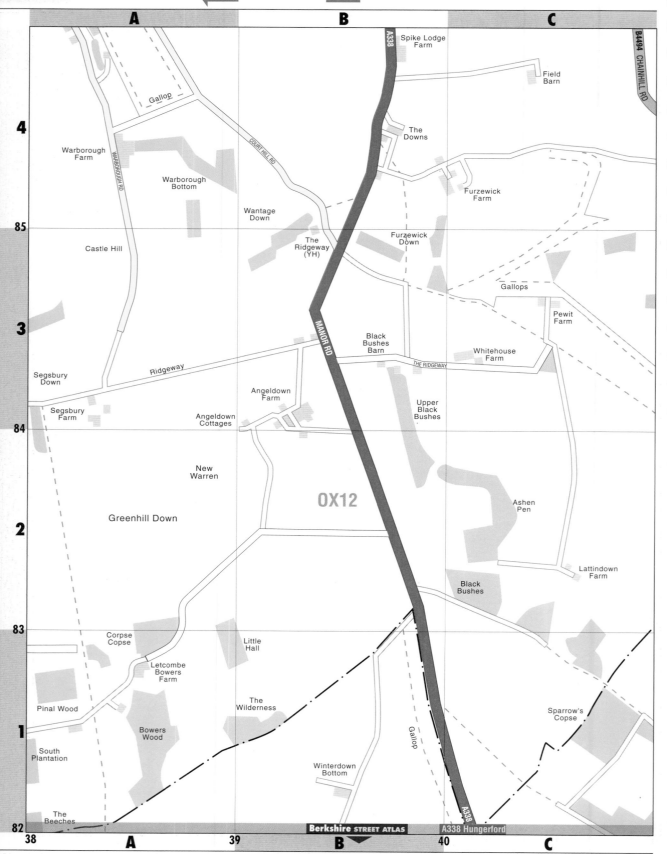

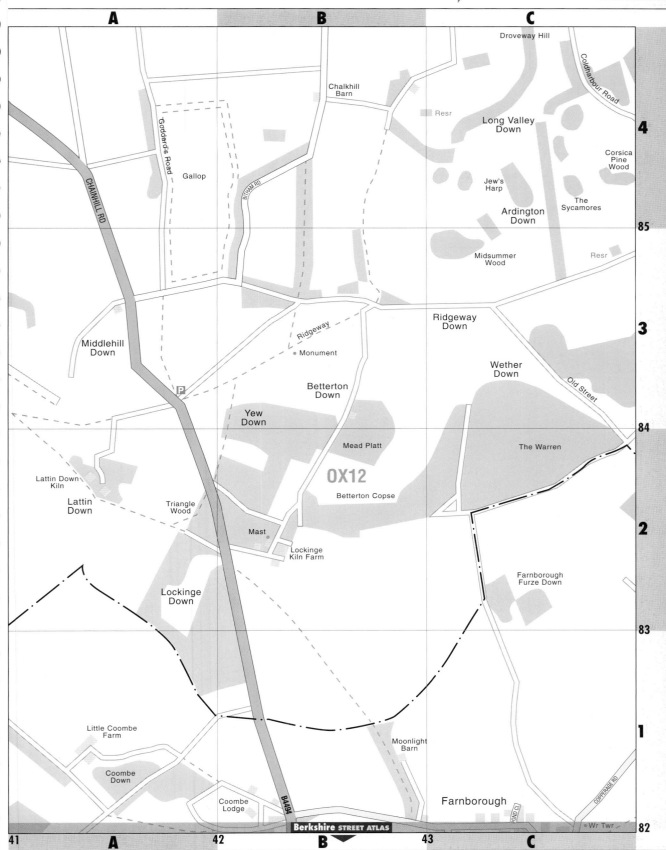

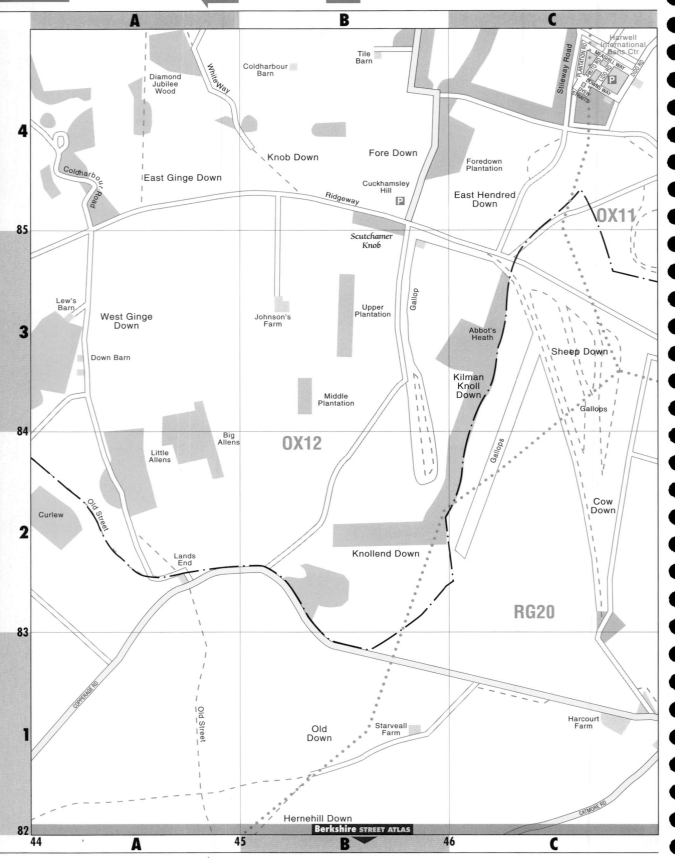

Harwell
International
Bsns Ctr

Tile
Barn

Coldharbour
Barn

Diamond
Jubilee
Wood

WhiteWay

Coldharbour Road

East Ginge Down

Knob Down

Fore Down

Foredown
Plantation

Cuckhamsley
Hill

Ridgeway

East Hendred
Down

OX11

Scutchamer
Knob

Lew's
Barn

West Ginge
Down

Johnson's
Farm

Upper
Plantation

Gallop

Abbot's
Heath

Sheep Down

Down Barn

Kilman
Knoll
Down

Gallops

Middle
Plantation

Big
Allens

OX12

Little
Allens

Gallops

Cow
Down

Curlew

Old Street

Lands
End

Knollend Down

RG20

COPPERAGE RD

Old Street

Old
Down

Starveall
Farm

Harcourt
Farm

CATMORE RD

Hernehill Down

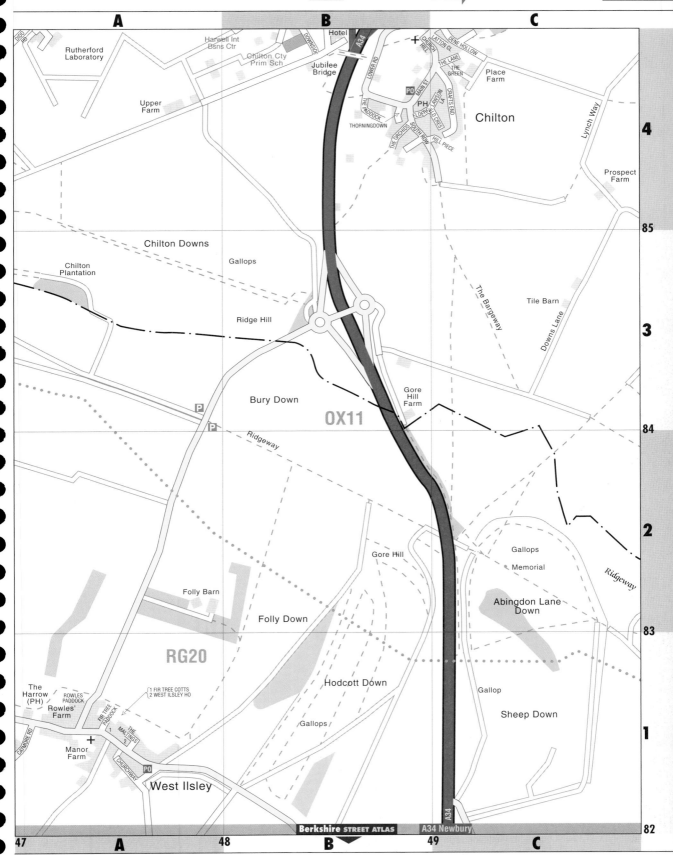

Berkshire STREET ATLAS · A34 Newbury

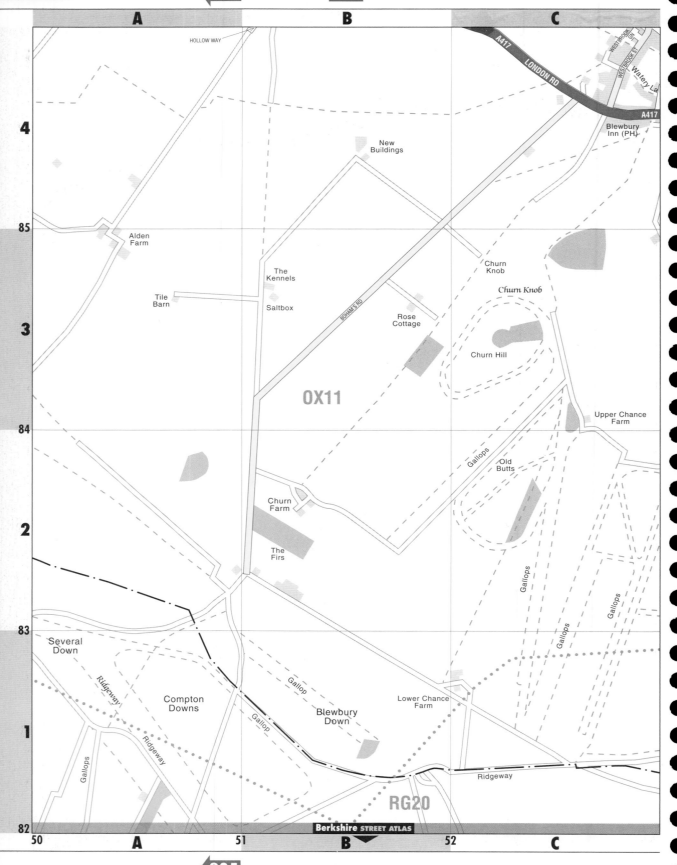

A B C

HOLLOW WAY

A417

LONDON RD

WESTBROOK ST

WESTBROOK GN

Watery La

A417

4

New Buildings

Blewbury Inn (PH)

85

Alden Farm

Churn Knob

The Kennels

Churn Knob

Tile Barn

Saltbox

Rose Cottage

Churn Hill

3

ROMAN'S RD

OX11

Upper Chance Farm

84

Gallops

Old Butts

Churn Farm

2

The Firs

Gallops

Gallops

Gallops

83

Several Down

Gallop

Ridgeway

Compton Downs

Lower Chance Farm

Blewbury Down

1

Gallop

Ridgeway

Ridgeway

Gallops

82

RG20

50 A 51 B 52 C

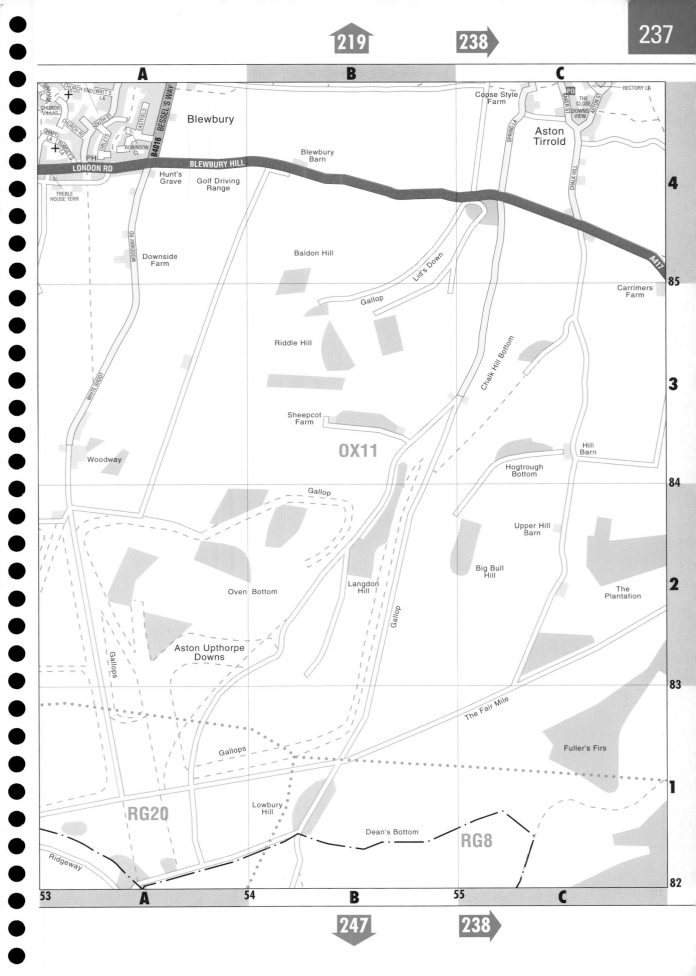

A
B
C

CHURCH END
WATT'S LA
GRAHAM CL
CHURCH RD
CHURCH VILLAS
SOUTH ST
EASTFIELD
BESSEL'S WAY
Blewbury
Copse Style Farm
PO
BAKER'S ST
THE CLOSE
DOWNS VIEW
ASTON ST
RECTORY LA

CHAPEL LA
TRUSSELS LA
DIBLE'S
ROBINSON CL
B4016
SPRING LA
Aston Tirrold

PH
LONDON RD
BLEWBURY HILL
Blewbury Barn
CHALK HILL

TREBLE HOUSE TERR
Hunt's Grave
Golf Driving Range

WOODWAY RD
Downside Farm
Baldon Hill
Lid's Down
A417

4

Gallop
Carrimers Farm

85

WHITE SHOOT
Riddle Hill
Chalk Hill Bottom

3

Woodway
Sheepcot Farm
Hill Barn

OX11
Hogtrough Bottom

84

Gallop
Upper Hill Barn

Oven Bottom
Langdon Hill
Big Bull Hill
The Plantation

2

Gallops
Aston Upthorpe Downs
Gallop

83

The Fair Mile

Gallops
Fuller's Firs

1

RG20
Lowbury Hill

Dean's Bottom
RG8

Ridgeway

82

53
A
54
B
55
C

A

B

C

PAPIST WAY

Westfield
Farm

Lollingdon
Farm

4

The
Lynch

Lollingdon
Hill

85

A417

Bowslade

WESTFIELD RD

Offlands
Farm

OX11

Sheephouse
Farm

3

Breach
House

HALFPENNY LA

Breach
Farm

Cranford
House Sch

A329

Stormerbank
Kennels

OX10

WILLOW COURT LA

Westfield
Stables

WILLOW
COTTS

GLEBE CL

THE STREET

84

Kingstanding
Hill

Moulsford

SHORTLANDS HILL

MEADOW CL

Cholsey
Downs

NORTH RD

UNDERHILL

North Unhill
Bank

2

Moulsford
Bottom

Starveall
Farm

Greenlands
Farm

Unhill
Bottom

COW LA

83

South Unhill
Bank

Lingley
Knoll

Moulsford
Downs

1

Well
Barn

WANTAGE RD

Unhill
Wood

RG8

Ridge
Roads

A417

82

56

A

57

B

58

C

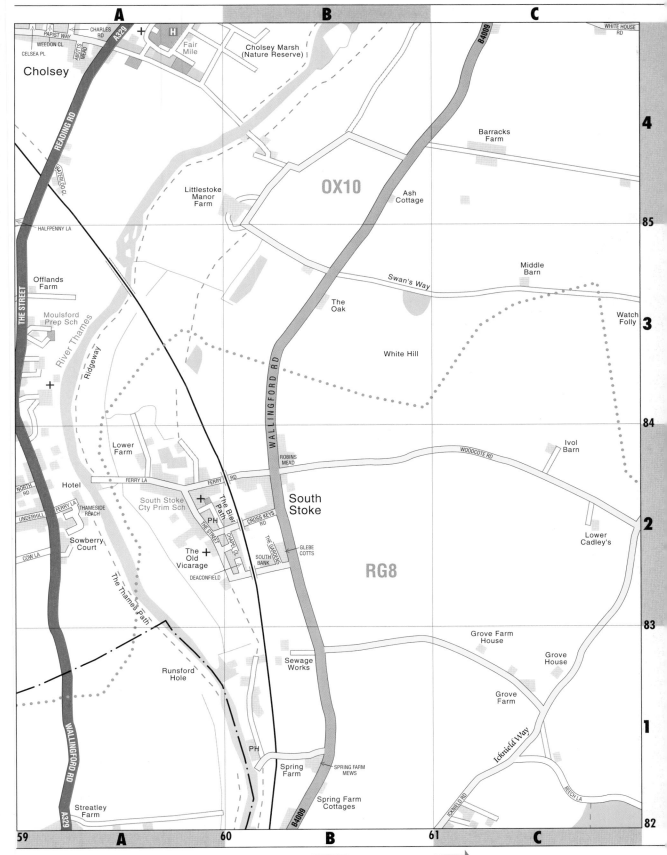

A   B   C

CHARLES RD
PAPIST WAY
WEEDON CL
CELSEA PL
AKOTTS MEAD
A329
H
Fair Mile

Cholsey

Cholsey Marsh
(Nature Reserve)

WHITE HOUSE RD

B4009

READING RD

WATERLOO CL

Barracks
Farm

4

OX10

Littlestoke
Manor
Farm

Ash
Cottage

85

HALFPENNY LA

Swan's Way

Middle
Barn

Offlands
Farm

THE STREET

Moulsford
Prep Sch

The
Oak

Watch
Folly

3

River Thames

Ridgeway

WALLINGFORD RD

White Hill

84

Lower
Farm

ROBINS
MEAD

WOODCOTE RD

Ivol
Barn

NORTH RD

FERRY LA

Hotel

FERRY LA

South Stoke
Cty Prim Sch

FERRY RD

South
Stoke

UNDERHILL

THAMESIDE
REACH

The Bier
Path

PH

CROSS KEYS
RD

Lower
Cadley's

2

COW LA

FERRY LA

Sowberry
Court

THE STREET

CHAPEL CL

THE GARDENS

GLEBE
COTTS

RG8

The
Old
Vicarage

SOUTH
BANK

DEACONFIELD

83

The Thames Path

Grove Farm
House

Grove
House

Runsford
Hole

Sewage
Works

Grove
Farm

1

WALLINGFORD RD

PH

Icknield Way

Spring
Farm

SPRING FARM
MEWS

ICKNIELD RD

BEECH LA

A329

Streatley
Farm

B4009

Spring Farm
Cottages

82

59   60   61

A   B   C

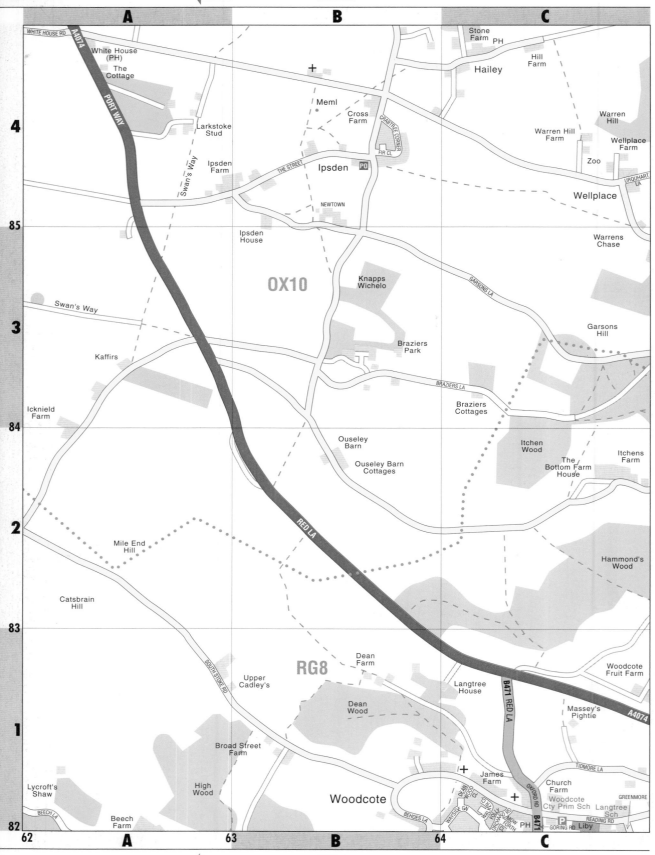

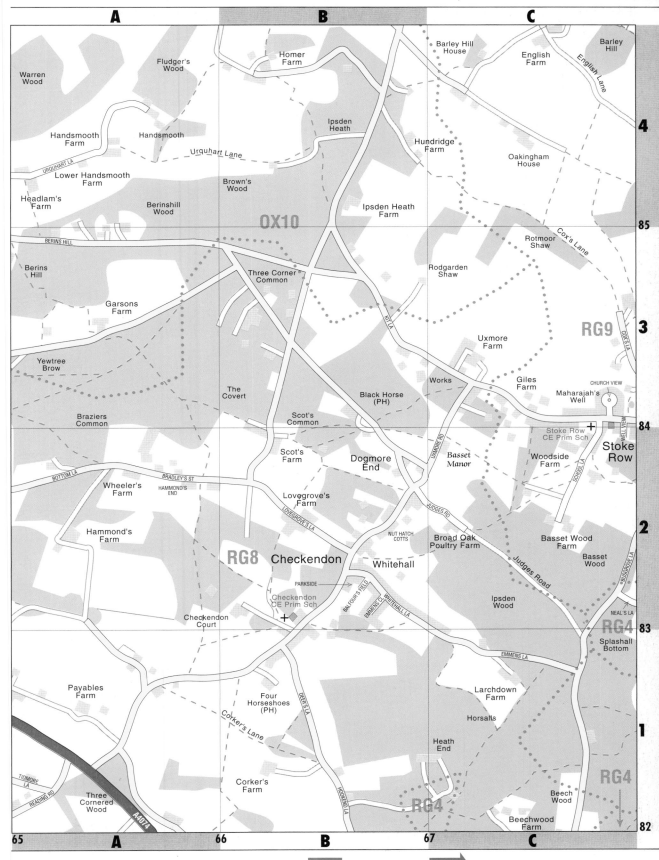

223

242

A   B   C

4

85

OX10

RG9

3

84

Stoke
Row

2

RG8   Checkendon

RG4

83

RG4

1

RG4

82

65   66   67

A   B   C

251

242

Warren
Wood

Fludger's
Wood

Homer
Farm

Barley Hill
House

English
Farm

English Lane

Barley
Hill

Handsmooth
Farm

Handsmooth

Ipsden
Heath

Hundridge
Farm

Oakingham
House

Urquhart Lane

URQUHART LA

Lower Handsmooth
Farm

Brown's
Wood

Headlam's
Farm

Berinshill
Wood

Ipsden Heath
Farm

Cox's Lane

BERINS HILL

Berins
Hill

Three Corner
Common

Rotmoor
Shaw

Rodgarden
Shaw

COX'S LA

Garsons
Farm

KIT LA

Uxmore
Farm

Yewtree
Brow

Works

Giles
Farm

CHURCH VIEW

WELL VIEW

Maharajah's
Well

The
Covert

Black Horse
(PH)

Braziers
Common

Scot's
Common

Stoke Row
CE Prim Sch

Scot's
Farm

Dogmore
End

UXMORE RD

Basset
Manor

Woodside
Farm

SCHOOL LA

BOTTOM LA

BRADLEY'S ST

Wheeler's
Farm

HAMMOND'S
END

Lovegrove's
Farm

LOVEGROVE'S LA

JUDGES RD

Hammond's
Farm

NUT HATCH
COTTS

Broad Oak
Poultry Farm

Basset Wood
Farm

Basset
Wood

BUSGROVE LA

Checkendon

Whitehall

Judges Road

Ipsden
Wood

NEAL'S LA

PARKSIDE

BALFOUR'S FIELD

Checkendon
CE Prim Sch

EMMENS CL

WHITEHALL LA

Checkendon
Court

EMMENS LA

Splashall
Bottom

Payables
Farm

Four
Horseshoes
(PH)

DEER'S LA

Larchdown
Farm

Corker's Lane

Horsalls

TIOMORE
LA

Heath
End

READING RD

Corker's
Farm

HOOKEND LA

A4074

Three
Cornered
Wood

RG4

Beech
Wood

Beechwood
Farm

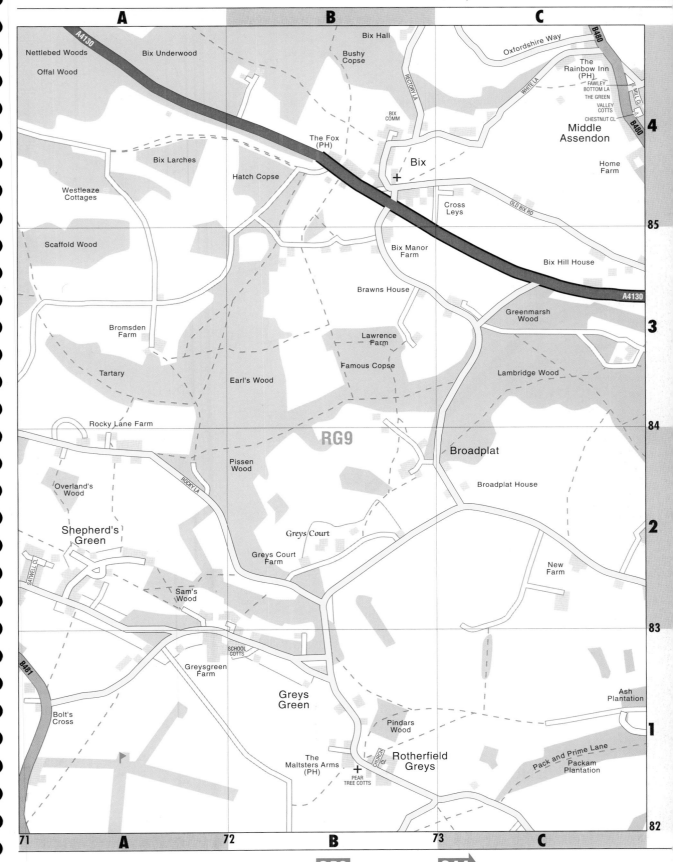

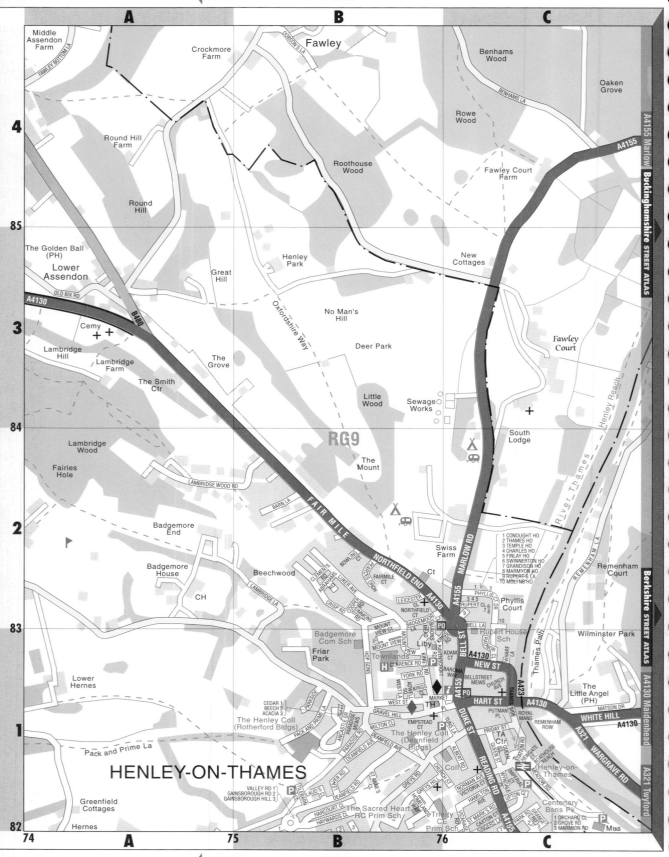

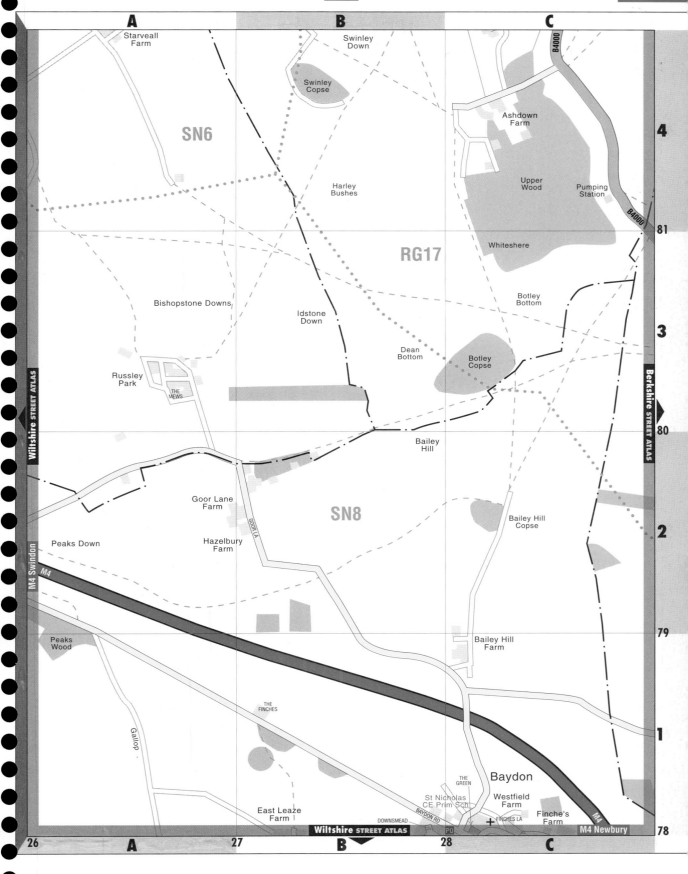

Starveall Farm

Swinley Down

Swinley Copse

B4000

SN6

Ashdown Farm

Harley Bushes

Upper Wood

Pumping Station

B4000

4

81

RG17

Whiteshere

Botley Bottom

Bishopstone Downs

Idstone Down

Dean Bottom

Botley Copse

3

Russley Park

THE MEWS

Bailey Hill

80

Berkshire STREET ATLAS

Wiltshire STREET ATLAS

Goor Lane Farm

GOOR LA

SN8

Bailey Hill Copse

2

Peaks Down

Hazelbury Farm

M4 Swindon

M4

Bailey Hill Farm

79

Peaks Wood

THE FINCHES

Gallop

1

Baydon

THE GREEN

Westfield Farm

St Nicholas CE Prim Sch

Finche's Farm

M4

M4 Newbury

East Leaze Farm

DOWNSMEAD

BAYDON RD

FINCHES LA

PO

78

26

A

27

B

28

C

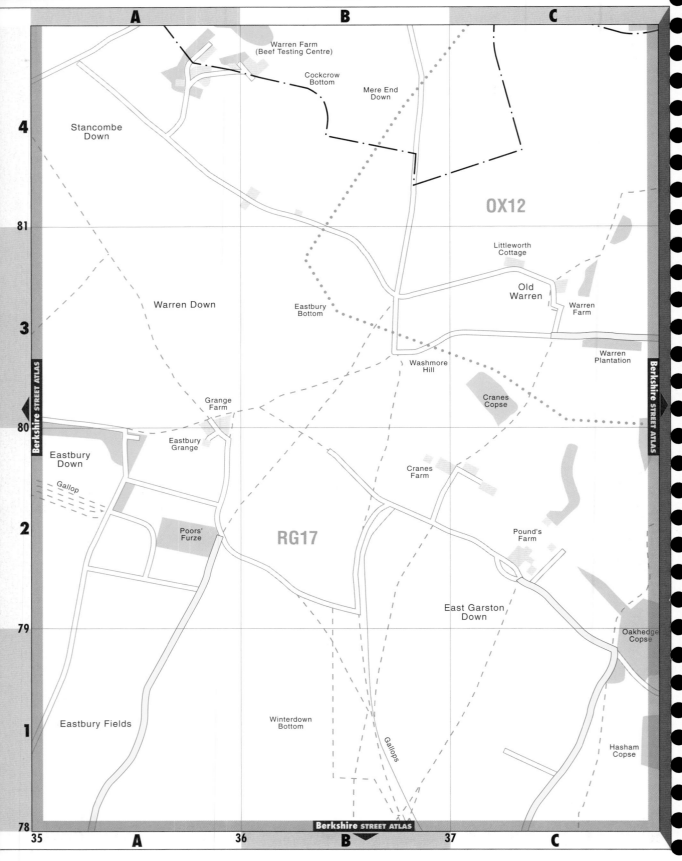

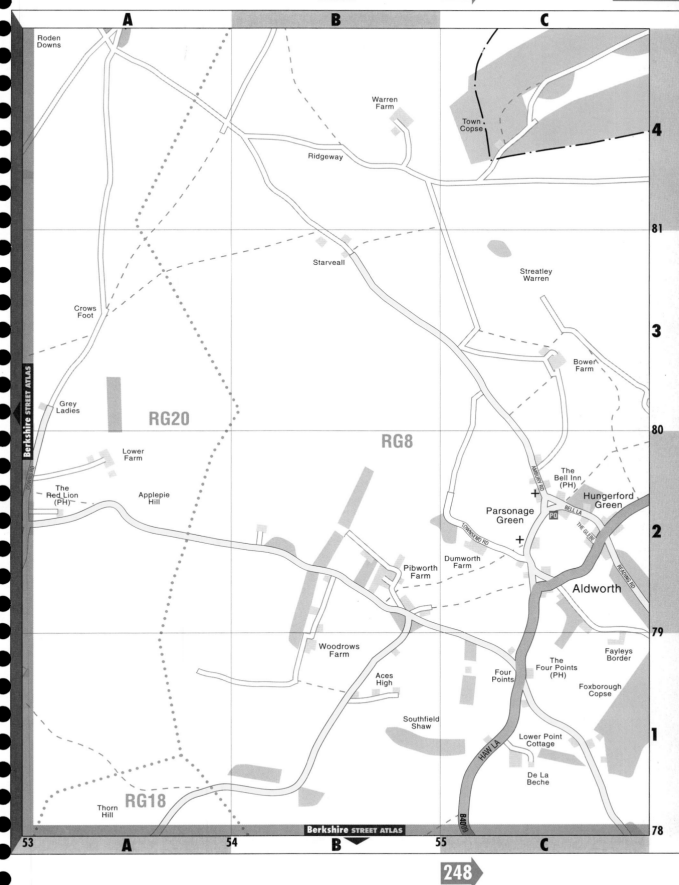

A B C

Roden Downs

Warren Farm

Town Copse

Ridgeway

4

81

Starveall

Streatley Warren

3

Crows Foot

Bower Farm

Grey Ladies

RG20

RG8

80

Lower Farm

The Bell Inn (PH)

Ambury Rd

Parsonage Green

PO

Bell La

Hungerford Green

The Red Lion (PH)

Applepie Hill

Townsend Rd

The Glebe

2

Reading Rd

Pibworth Farm

Dumworth Farm

Aldworth

79

Woodrows Farm

Fayleys Border

Four Points

The Four Points (PH)

Aces High

Foxborough Copse

Southfield Shaw

Haw La

Lower Point Cottage

1

De La Beche

RG18

Thorn Hill

B4009

Berkshire STREET ATLAS

78

53 A 54 B 55 C

Berkshire STREET ATLAS

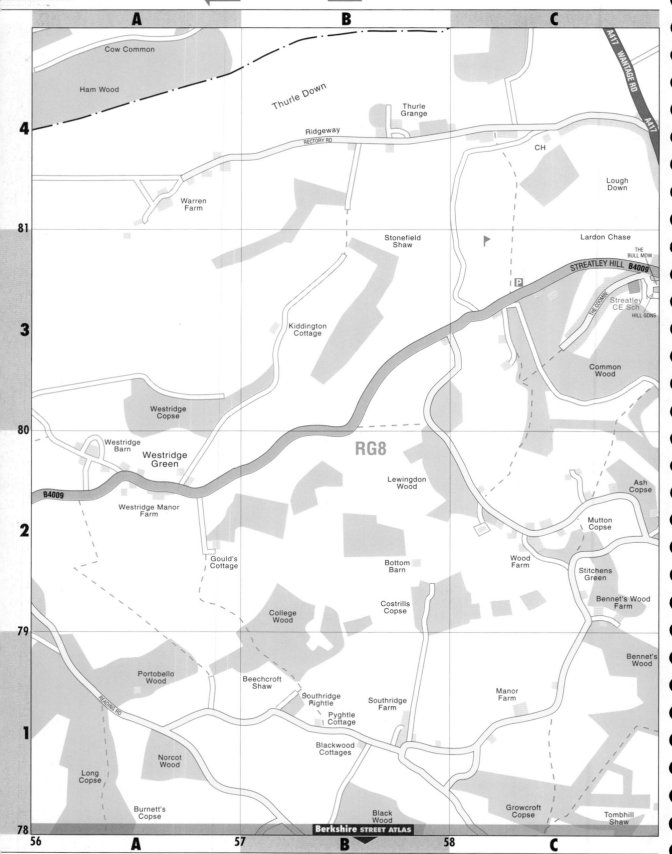

A B C

Cow Common

Ham Wood

Thurle Down

Thurle Grange

Ridgeway
RECTORY RD

CH

A417 WANTAGE RD

4

Lough Down

Warren Farm

81

Stonefield Shaw

Lardon Chase

THE BULL MDW

STREATLEY HILL B4009

THE COOMBE

Streatley CE Sch

HILL GDNS

P

Kiddington Cottage

3

Common Wood

Westridge Copse

80

Westridge Barn

Westridge Green

RG8

Lewingdon Wood

Ash Copse

B4009

Westridge Manor Farm

Mutton Copse

2

Gould's Cottage

Bottom Barn

Wood Farm

Stitchens Green

Bennet's Wood Farm

Costrills Copse

79

College Wood

Bennet's Wood

Portobello Wood

Beechcroft Shaw

Southridge Rightle

Manor Farm

READING RD

Southridge Farm

1

Pyghtle Cottage

Norcot Wood

Blackwood Cottages

Long Copse

Growcroft Copse

Tombhill Shaw

Burnett's Copse

Black Wood

78

56 A 57 B 58 C

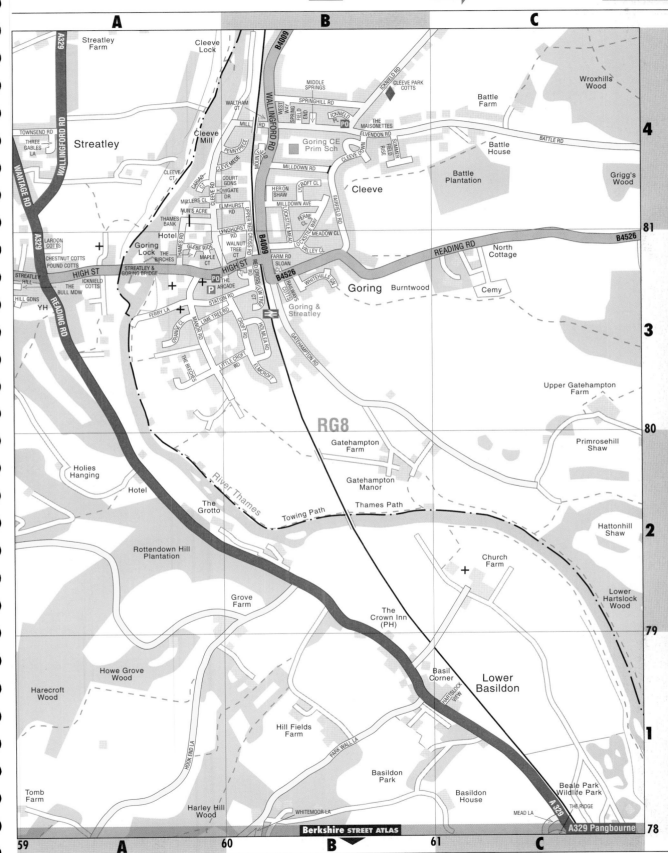

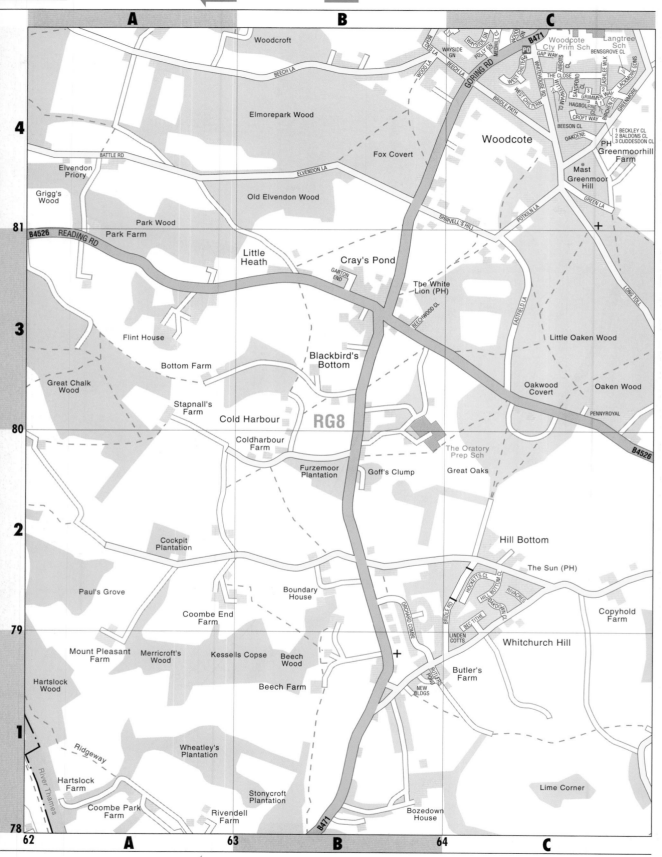

249
240

Woodcroft

BEECH LA

Elmorepark Wood

Fox Covert

ELVENDON LA

Old Elvendon Wood

BATTLE RD

Elvendon
Priory

Grigg's
Wood

Park Wood

Park Farm

B4526 READING RD

Little
Heath

Cray's Pond

GARTON
END

The White
Lion (PH)

Flint House

Bottom Farm

Blackbird's
Bottom

BEECHWOOD CL

Great Chalk
Wood

Stapnall's
Farm

Cold Harbour

RG8

Coldharbour
Farm

Furzemoor
Plantation

Goff's Clump

The Oratory
Prep Sch

Great Oaks

Cockpit
Plantation

Paul's Grove

Coombe End
Farm

Boundary
House

Hill Bottom

The Sun (PH)

Mount Pleasant
Farm

Merricroft's
Wood

Kessells Copse

Beech
Wood

ORCHARD COMBE

BRIDLE RD

Whitchurch Hill

Copyhold
Farm

Butler's
Farm

Hartslock
Wood

Beech Farm

LINDEN
COTTS

NEW
BLDGS

BUTTS
POND

Ridgeway

Wheatley's
Plantation

River Thames

Hartslock
Farm

Coombe Park
Farm

Rivendell
Farm

Stonycroft
Plantation

B471

Bozedown
House

Lime Corner

GORING RD

B471

BEECH LA

WAYSIDE
GN

FOLLY GN

MEDHILL CL

BEECH LA

WOOD LA

Woodcote Cty Prim Sch

Langtree
Sch

BENSGROVE CL

PO

GAP WAY

WEST CHILTERN

WHITEHOUSE RD

WEST CHILTERN

THE CLOSE

BRIDLE PATH

SANDFORD
CL

GRIMMER
WAY

3

ASHLEE WLK

LACKMORE GDNS

GREENMORE

HAGBOURNE
CL

BIRDHILL

CROFT WAY

Woodcote

BEESON CL

OAKDENE

1 BECKLEY CL
2 BALDONS CL
3 CUDDESDON CL

PH
Greenmoorhill
Farm

Mast
Greenmoor
Hill

SHIRVELL'S HILL

POTKILN LA

GREEN LA

EASTFIELD LA

LONG TOLL

Little Oaken Wood

Oakwood
Covert

Oaken Wood

PENNYROYAL

B4526

HOCKETTS CL

HILL BOTTOM CL

RIVACRES

OAKDOWN

BEECH TITHE

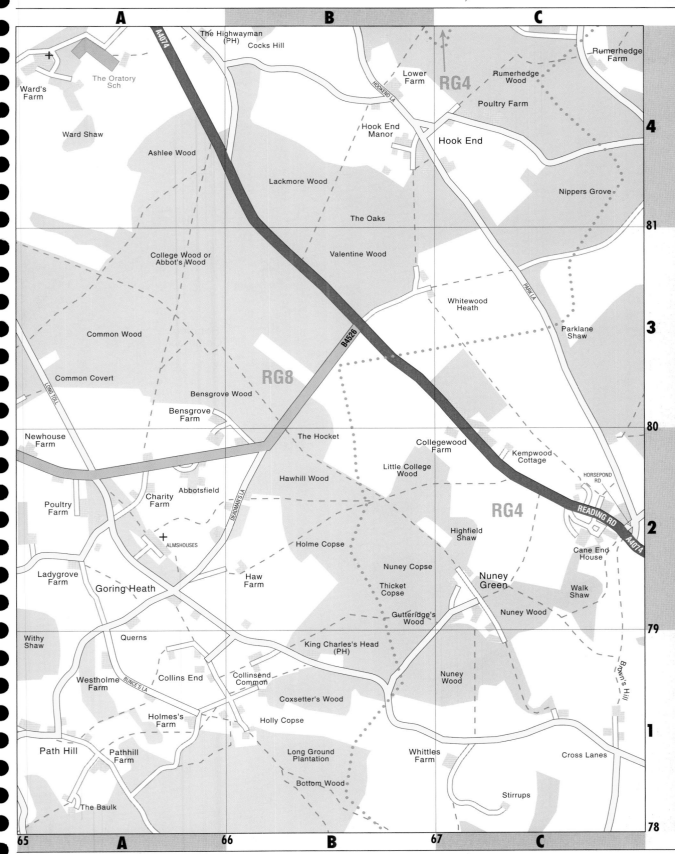

251
242

A **B** **C**

Manor Farm

Park Farm

STEVENS LA
ESTER CARLING LA
DOVE LA

COLMORE LA

COLLIERS LA

Peppard Hill

CHURCH LA

B481

WYFOLD LA

RG9

Peppard Common

Wyfold Grange

STOKE ROW RD

CHILTERN RD

PEPPARD HILL

SPRINGWOOD LA

4

CHILTERN BANK

GALLOWSTREE RD

Shiplake Bottom

HILLCREST LA

81

Wyfold Wood

New Copse

SHIPLAKE BOTTOM

GRAVEL HILL

BLOUNTS COURT RD

PRIORY COPSE

CRES

CHURCH

OLD COPSE
GDN

CARLING RD

BEECH RD

GRAVEL RISE

PEPPARD RD B481

Bishopswood Sch

NEWFIELD RD

SEDGEWELL RD

SEDGEFIELD

WOODLANDS RD

Withy Copse

WYFOLD RD

Common Farm

WOODSIDE LA

Gallowstree Common

Bishopswood Farm

Sonning Common

SEDGEWELL RD

JOSCT CL

HAZEL GDNS

WOOD LANE

3

HEARNS LA

THE HAMLET

ORCHARD AVE

APPLETREE

SMITH CL

WYCHWOOD CL

GREEN LA

WOOD LA

Council Cotts

HORSEPOND RD

LAMBOURNE RD

RUSSET CL

BRAMLEY CRES

WALNUT CL

BASKERVILLE

ILSLEY RD

PO

Liby

The Crown & Anchor (PH)

ASHFORD AVE

PAGES ORCH

CROMSLEY WAY

Sonning Common Prim Sch

ELM CT

80

READE'S LA

RG4

FARM CL

GROVE RD

CHERITON RD

ROWAN CL

LEA RD

SCH CL

WESTLEIGH DR

ILEX CL

Coldnorton Wood

HAZELMOOR LA

Chiltern Edge Com Sch

KENNYLANDS RD

Coldnorton Shaw

WOOD LA

Oakridge Farm

KIDMORE LA

Holly Tree Farm

2

Cane End Farm

GRAVEL EAZE

Kidmore End CE Prim Sch

READING RD A4074

Kidmore End

PH

Vines Farm

Curtis Farm

COOPERS PIGHTLE

BUTLERS ORCH

Cemy

Stocking Shaw

79

Madge Gray's Wood

Highland Wood

Cross Farm

CHALKHOUSE GREEN RD

Green Dean Wood

GREEN DEAN HILL

Tankers Table Farm

MILL LA

Bardolph's Wood

Kidmore House

1

Hodmore Farm

SHEEPWAYS LA

The Pack Horse (PH)

TOKERS GREEN RD

Dyson's Wood

DYSONSWOOD LANE

CHALKHOUSE GREEN LA

TANNERS

KIDMORE END RD

Hodmore Farm Cottage

Tinker's Green

A4074

78

68 **A** 69 **B** 70 **C**

251
258

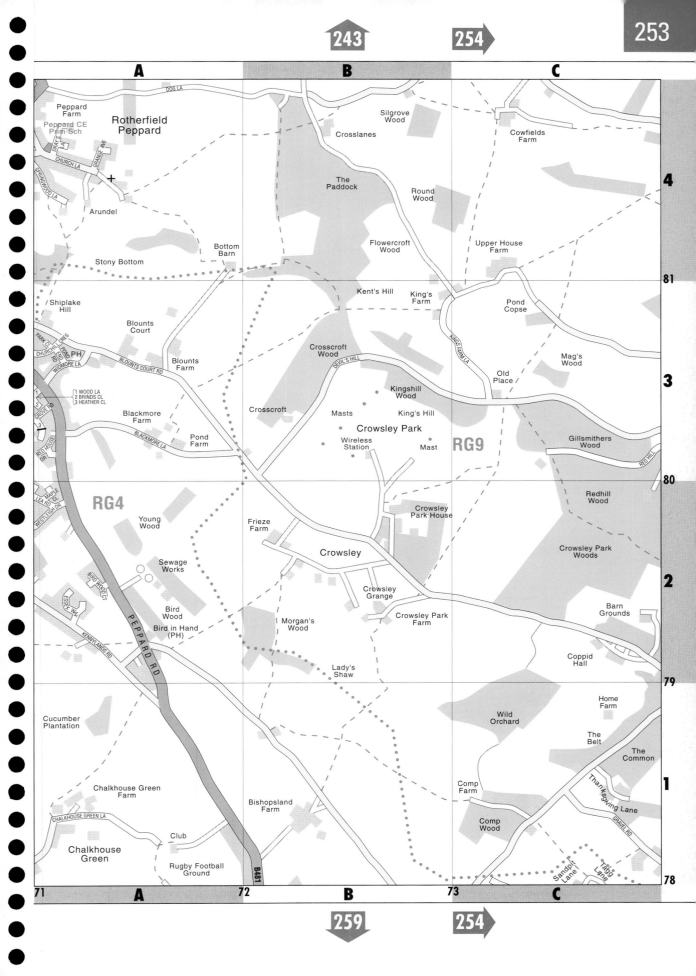

A B C

4
81
3
80
2
79
1
78

Peppard Farm
Peppard CE Prim Sch
Rotherfield Peppard
DOG LA
DRAY'S LA
GRANGE AVE
CHURCH LA
SPRINGWOOD LA
Arundel
Stony Bottom
Bottom Barn
Silgrove Wood
Crosslanes
The Paddock
Round Wood
Flowercroft Wood
Cowfields Farm
Upper House Farm

Shiplake Hill
Blounts Court
Kent's Hill
King's Farm
Pond Copse
PARK CL
CHURCHILL CRES
POND END RD
PH
WIDMORE LA
BLOUNTS COURT RD
Blounts Farm
Crosscroft Wood
DEVIL'S HILL
KINGS FARM LA
Old Place
Mag's Wood
1 WOOD LA
2 BRINDS CL
3 HEATHER CL
Blackmore Farm
BLACKMORE LA
Pond Farm
Crosscroft
Kingshill Wood
King's Hill
Masts
Crowsley Park
RG9
Gillsmithers Wood
GROVE RD
RED HOUSE DR
Wireless Station
Mast
RED HILL
Redhill Wood

RG4
MAPLE LEA RD CL
WESTLEIGH DR
Young Wood
Frieze Farm
Crowsley Park House
Crowsley Park Woods

Sewage Works
Crowsley
Crowsley Grange
Crowsley Park Farm
Barn Grounds
BIRD WOOD CT
ESSEX WAY
Bird Wood
Bird in Hand (PH)
Morgan's Wood
Coppid Hall
KENNYLANDS RD
PEPPARD RD
Lady's Shaw

Cucumber Plantation
Wild Orchard
Home Farm
The Belt
The Common
Comp Farm
Thanksgiving Lane

Chalkhouse Green Farm
Bishopsland Farm
Comp Wood
GRAVEL RD
CHALKHOUSE GREEN LA
Club
B481
Sandpit Lane
Tabb Lane
Chalkhouse Green
Rugby Football Ground

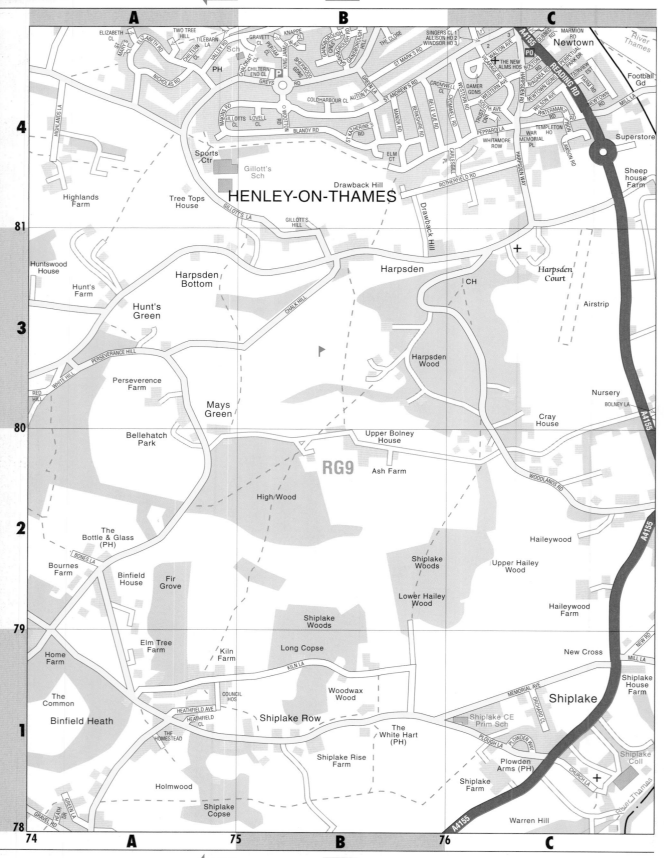

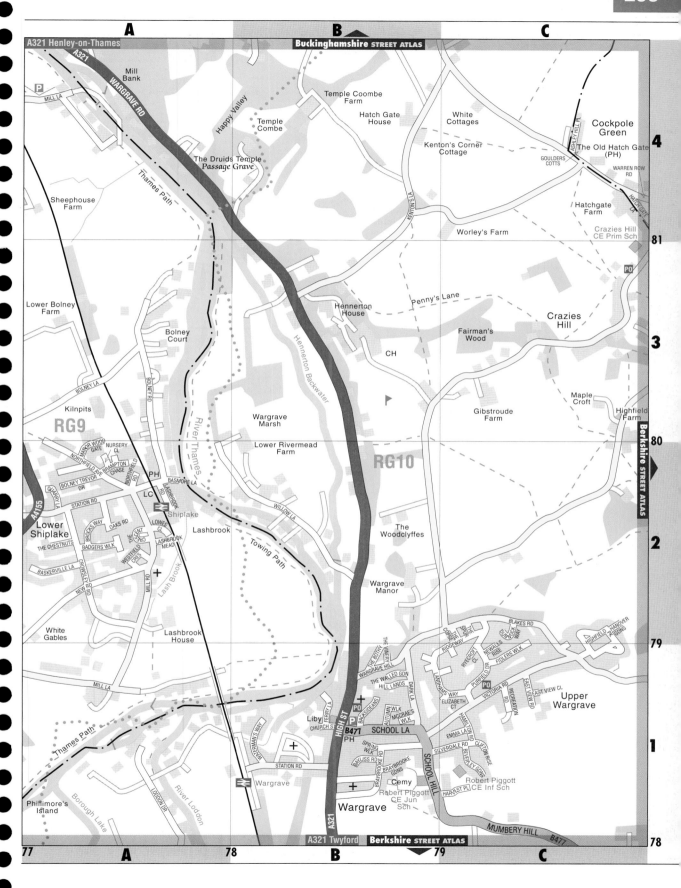

Buckinghamshire STREET ATLAS

A321 Henley-on-Thames

Mill Bank

WARGRAVE RD

A321

P

MILL LA

Happy Valley

Temple Coombe Farm

Hatch Gate House

Temple Coombe

White Cottages

Cockpole Green

ASHLEY HILL PL

The Old Hatch Gate (PH)

Kenton's Corner Cottage

GOULDERS COTTS

WARREN ROW RD

4

The Druids Temple
Passage Grave

Thames Path

Sheephouse Farm

HATCHGATE

Hatchgate Farm

Worley's Farm

Crazies Hill CE Prim Sch

81

Penny's Lane

PO

Lower Bolney Farm

Hennerton House

Crazies Hill

Bolney Court

BOLNEY LA

BOLNEY RD

Fairman's Wood

CH

Maple Croft

Highfield Farm

3

Kilnpits

RG9

Wargrave Marsh

Gibstroude Farm

Berkshire STREET ATLAS

River Thames

Lower Rivermead Farm

RG10

80

MANOR WOOD GATE

NURSERY CL

NORTHFIELD AVE

BRAMPTON CHASE

NORTHFIELD RD

BOLNEY TREVOR DR

PH

BASMORE LA

LASHBROOK RD

LC

A4155

QUARRY LA

STATION RD

Shiplake

LOWES CL

WILLOW LA

The Woodclyffes

2

Lower Shiplake

BROOKS WAY

OAKS RD

THE CRESCENT

LASHBROOK MEAD

Lashbrook

THE CHESTNUTS

WESTFIELD CRES

BADGERS WLK

Towing Path

BASKERVILLE LA

CROWSLEY RD

NEW RD

MILL RD

Lash Brook

Wargrave Manor

79

White Gables

Lashbrook House

BLAKES RD

THE COPSE

HANOVER GDNS

HIGHFIELD

MILL LA

WARGRAVE HILL

THE BOTHY

THE VINERY

HILL LANDS

DARK LA

RIDGEWAY

LANGHAMS WAY

RYECROFT CL

NEWALLS RISE

FIDLERS WLK

PURFIELD DR

VICTORIA RD

RECREATION

EAST VIEW RD

EAST VIEW CL

Upper Wargrave

1

Thames Path

WATERMANS WAY

STATION RD

Liby

FERRY LA

CHURCH ST

HIGH ST

PO

P

BACKSIDANS

AUTUMN WLK

MCCRAE'S WLK

SCHOOL LA

HAMILTON RD

EMMA LA

SILVERDALE RISE

CLIFTON RISE

BEVERLEY GDNS

SCHOOL HILL

Robert Piggott CE Inf Sch

Phillimore's Island

Borough Lake

River Loddon

LODDON DR

Wargrave

B471

PH

SPRING WLK

BAYLISS RD

BRAYBROOKE RD

BRAYBROOKE GDNS

Cemy

Robert Piggott CE Jun Sch

HARVEST PLACE

Wargrave

A321

A321 Twyford

Berkshire STREET ATLAS

MUMBERY HILL

B477

78

250

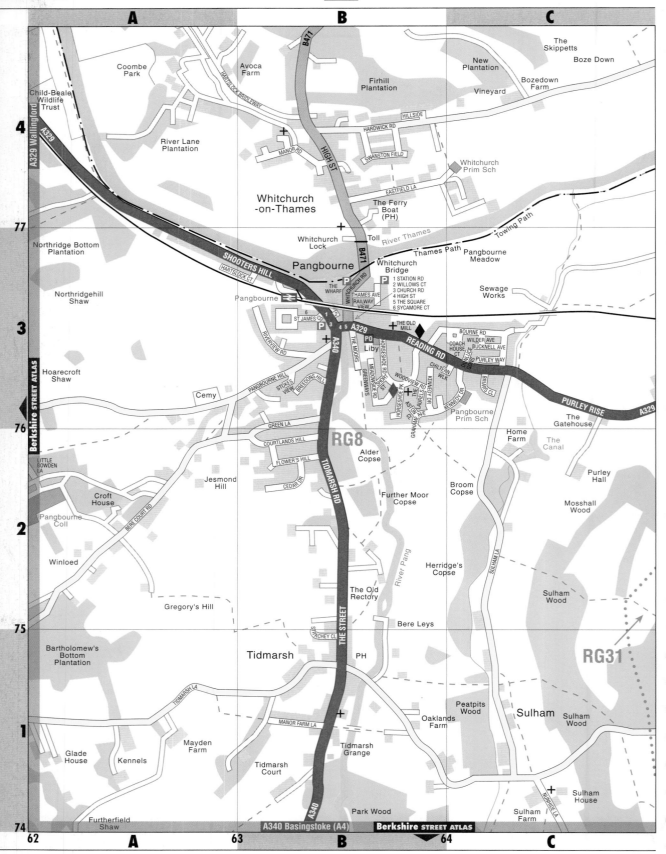

A | B | C

4

The Skippetts
Boze Down

New Plantation
Bozedown Farm
Vineyard

Coombe Park

Avoca Farm

HARTSLOCK BRIDLEWAY

Firhill Plantation

HILLSIDE

HARDWICK RD

Whitchurch Prim Sch

River Lane Plantation

MANOR RD

HIGH ST

B471

SWANSTON FIELD

EASTFIELD LA

A329 Wallingford

Child-Beale Wildlife Trust

Whitchurch -on-Thames

The Ferry Boat (PH)

77

Northridge Bottom Plantation

SHOOTERS HILL

HARTSLOCK CT

Whitchurch Lock

Toll

River Thames

Towing Path

Thames Path

Pangbourne Meadow

Pangbourne

Whitchurch Bridge

THE WHARF

WHITCHURCH RD

1 STATION RD
2 WILLOWS CT
3 CHURCH RD
4 HIGH ST
5 THE SQUARE
6 SYCAMORE CT

THAMES AVE
RAILWAY VIEW

Sewage Works

Northridgehill Shaw

Pangbourne

ST JAMES CT

A329

READING RD

The Old Mill

BOURNE RD

WILDER AVE

BUCKNELL AVE

COACH HOUSE CT

PURLEY WAY

3

A340

RIVERVIEW RD

PANGBOURNE HILL

STOKES VIEW

BREDONS HILL

THE MOORS

Liby

GREENWAYS

HORSESHOE RD

WOODVIEW RD

MEADOWSIDE

THE ASTON AVE

THE LAURELS

KENNEDY DR

CHILTERN WLK

LINK CL

BRIARS CL

Home Farm

PURLEY RISE

A329

Hoarecroft Shaw

Cemy

GREEN LA

COURTLANDS HILL

FLOWER'S HILL

CEDAR DR

HORSESHOE PK

GRAHAME AVE

KENNEDY DR

Pangbourne Prim Sch

The Gatehouse

The Canal

76

RG8

Alder Copse

Broom Copse

Purley Hall

LITTLE BOWDEN LA

Croft House

BERE COURT RD

Jesmond Hill

TIDMARSH RD

Further Moor Copse

Mosshall Wood

2

Pangbourne Coll

Winloed

River Pang

Herridge's Copse

SULHAM LA

Sulham Wood

Gregory's Hill

The Old Rectory

Bere Leys

75

RG31

Bartholomew's Bottom Plantation

STRACHEY CL

THE STREET

Tidmarsh

PH

Peatpits Wood

Sulham

Sulham Wood

TIDMARSH LA

MANOR FARM LA

Oaklands Farm

Sulham House

1

Glade House

Kennels

Mayden Farm

Tidmarsh Grange

Tidmarsh Court

Park Wood

A340

NUNHIDE LA

Sulham Farm

Furtherfield Shaw

74

62 | A | 63 | B | 64 | C

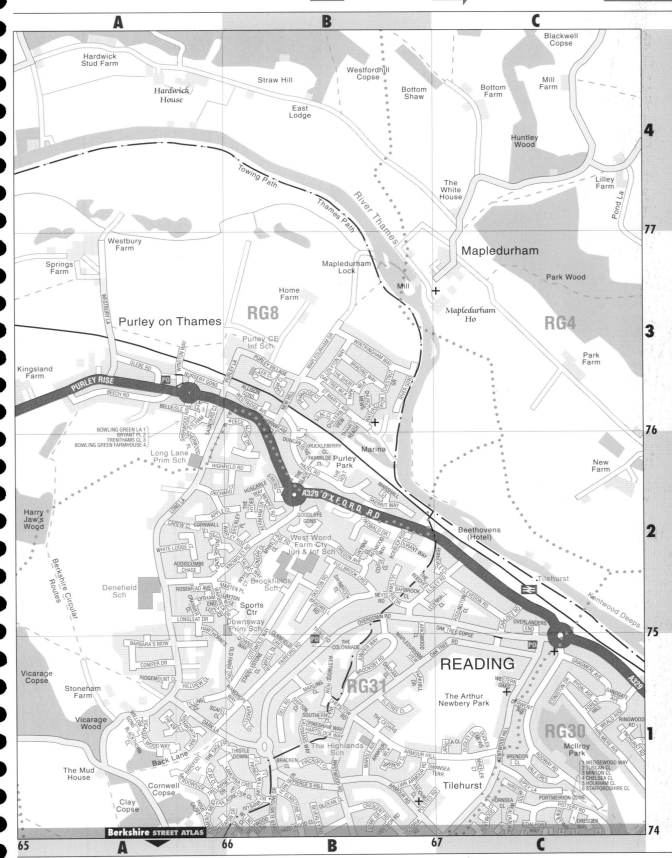

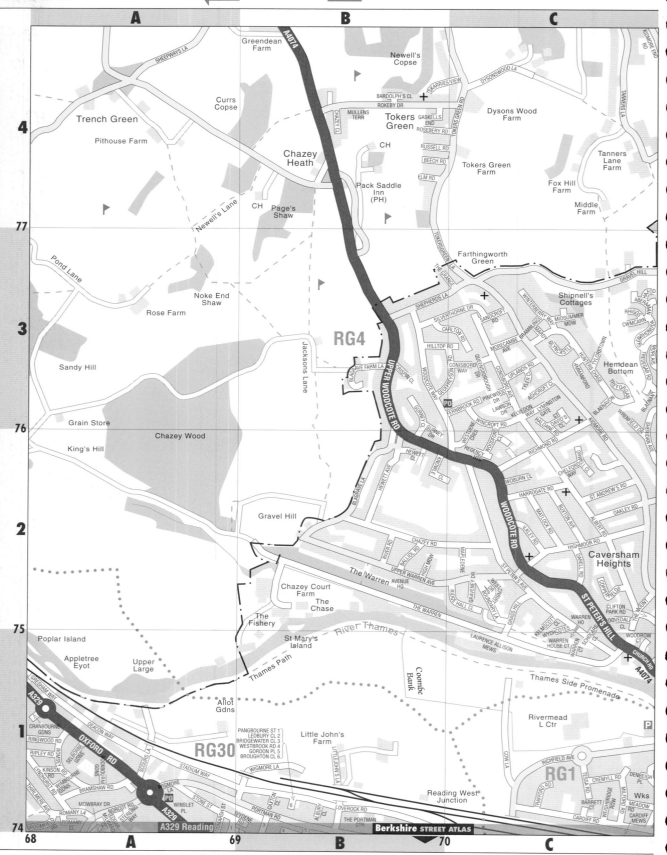

257
252

A B C

Greendean Farm

SHEEPWAYS LA

Newell's Copse

Currs Copse

Trench Green

Pithouse Farm

CARRIES VIEW

DYSONSWOOD LA

BARDOLPH'S CL
ROKEBY DR

CHAZEY CL

Dysons Wood Farm

Chazey Heath

MULLENS TERR

Tokers Green

GASKELLS END
ROSEBERY DR

CH

RUSSELL RD

BEECH RD

ELM RD

Tokers Green Farm

TOKERS GREEN RD

4

Fox Hill Farm

Tanners Lane Farm

TANNERS LA

Pack Saddle Inn (PH)

Middle Farm

77

CH Page's Shaw

Newell's Lane

Farthingworth Green

THE GRANGE

TOKERS GREEN LA

SHEPHERDS LA

GRAVEL HILL

Pond Lane

Shipnell's Cottages

SILVERTHORNE DR

SANDCROFT RD

WINTERBERRY WAY

MIDSUMMER MDW

BRAMBLINGS

CWMCARN

RHIGOS

ABERDARE

HAFOD

Noke End Shaw

RG4

CARLTON RD

HILLTOP RD

WOODCOTE WAY

MORECAMBE AVE

MANDY CT

BLAGRAVE FARM LA

HUNTERS CHASE

ALMANORD

Hemdean Bottom

TRECYCH

Rose Farm

3

Sandy Hill

Jacksons Lane

UPPER WOODCOTE RD

GURNEY CL
SURREY DR

GEOFFREYS

FERNBROOK RD

PINEWOOD LA
DR

CONISBOROUGH
DR

QUEENSBOROUGH
DR

CONISBORO RD

UPLANDS RD

TYLER CL

ASHCROFT CL

HALDANE RD

DAVID'S HILL

KOMORE RD

WRENFIELD DR

BLAENAVON

PO

CL

LAWSON DR

KELVEDON WAY
LYMINGTON GATE

WINCROFT RD

WOODCROFT

REGENCY

RICHMOND RD

CHELFORD
WAY

ORRELL CL

Grain Store

76

Chazey Wood

HEWETT CL

HEWETT AVE

BLAGRAVE LA

KENWE CL

WOODBURN CL

St ANDREW'S RD

OAKLEY RD

King's Hill

HARROGATE RD

BUXTON AVE

ALBERT RD

Gravel Hill

2

CHAZEY RD

RIVER RD

BALLIOL RD

HILL MDW

MAPLEDENE

UCKLEY RD

MATLOCK RD

HIGHMOOR RD

Caversham Heights

UPPER WARREN AVE

The Warren

AVENUE HO

GRAVENEY CL

RIDGE HALL CL

St PETER'S AVE

WESTFIELD RD

DARELL RD

COPPICE

CLIFTON PARK RD

Chazey Court Farm

The Chase

THE WARREN

GRASS HILL

KELMSCOTT CL

WYCHCOTES

WARREN HO

WOODROW CT

75

The Fishery

St Mary's Island

River Thames

LAURENCE ALLISON MEWS

WARREN HOUSE CT

SCHOLARS CL

St PETER'S HILL

CHURCH RD

A4074

Poplar Island

Coombe Bank

Appletree Eyot

Upper Large

Thames Path

Thames Side Promenade

P

Allot Gdns

Little John's Farm

Rivermead L Ctr

1

A329

GRESHAM WAY

DEACON WAY

OXFORD RD

SCOURS LA

STADIUM WAY

WIGMORE LA

RG30

PANGBOURNE ST 1
LEDBURY CL 2
BRIDGEWATER CL 3
WESTBROOK RD 4
GORDON PL 5
BROUGHTON CL 6

LITTLEJOHN'S LA

RICHFIELD AVE

RG1

CRANBOURNE GDNS

RINGWOOD RD

RIPLEY RD

ROMSEY

SELBORNE GDNS

BROOKBOURNE GDNS

BRAMSHAW RD

KINSON RD

LYNDHURST RD

WIMBOURNE GDNS

MOWBRAY DR

NORCOT RD

STERLING WAY

WINSLET PL

STONE ST

CAXTON

PORTMAN RD

ALBURY

LOVEROCK RD

Reading West Junction

TRAFFORD RD

BARRETT
CT

TESSA RD

WEIGHBRIDGE

CREMYLL RD

MILFORD RD

MEADOW

DENBEIGH PL

Wks

CARDIFF MEWS

THIRLMERE AVE

GROOMEFIELD

ROMANY LA

A329

PO

WIGMORE LA

IVYDENE

UDMARSH RD

THE PORTMAN CTR

CARDIFF RD

74

A329 Reading

68 A 69 B 70 C

257

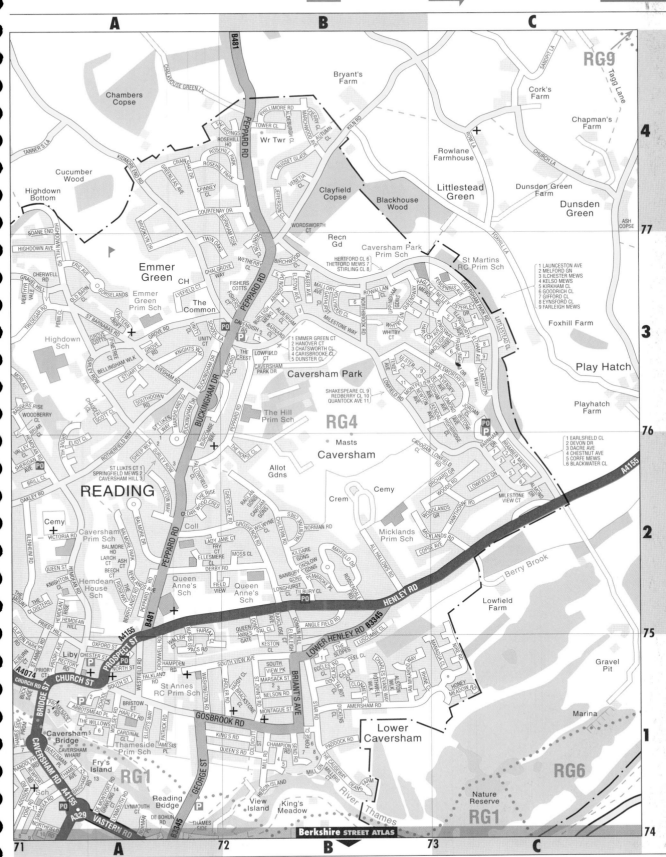

Berkshire STREET ATLAS

A1
1 SHORT ST
2 ARCHWAY RD
3 RIVERSIDE CT
4 CRENDON CT
5 CLAYDON CT
6 ST STEPHENS CL
7 RICHFIELD AVE
8 CARDIFF RD
9 BARRY PL

10 MONMOUTH CT
11 ROSS RD
12 THAMES SIDE
13 REGENTS RIVERSIDE
14 HALLSMEAD CT

B1
1 FLAMBARDS
2 RICHARD NEVILL CT
3 WALEYS PL
4 PIGGOTT'S RD
5 MONKLEY CT
6 GOSBROOK HO
7 BROOK LEA
8 GLIFFARD HO
9 PEMBROKE HO

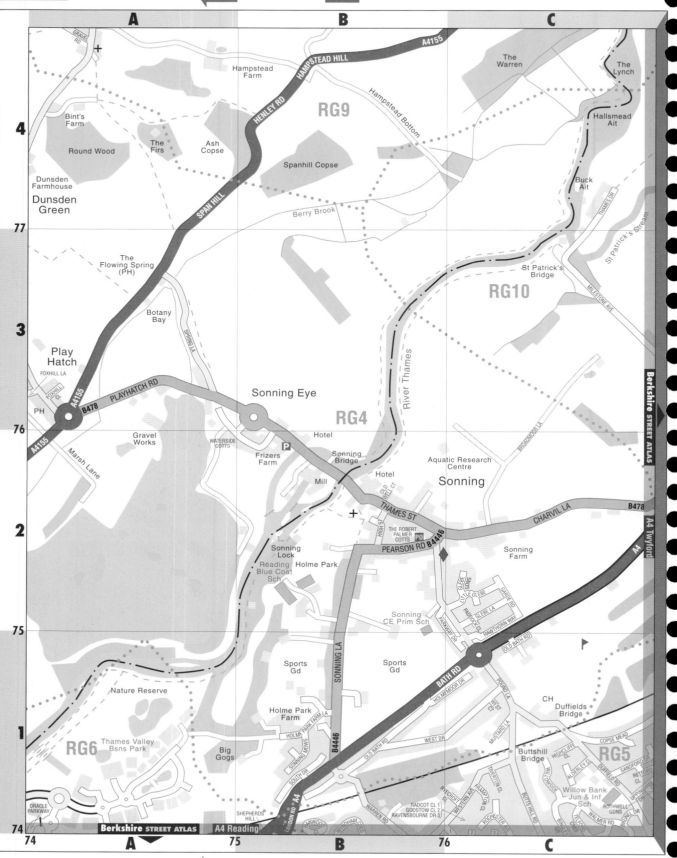

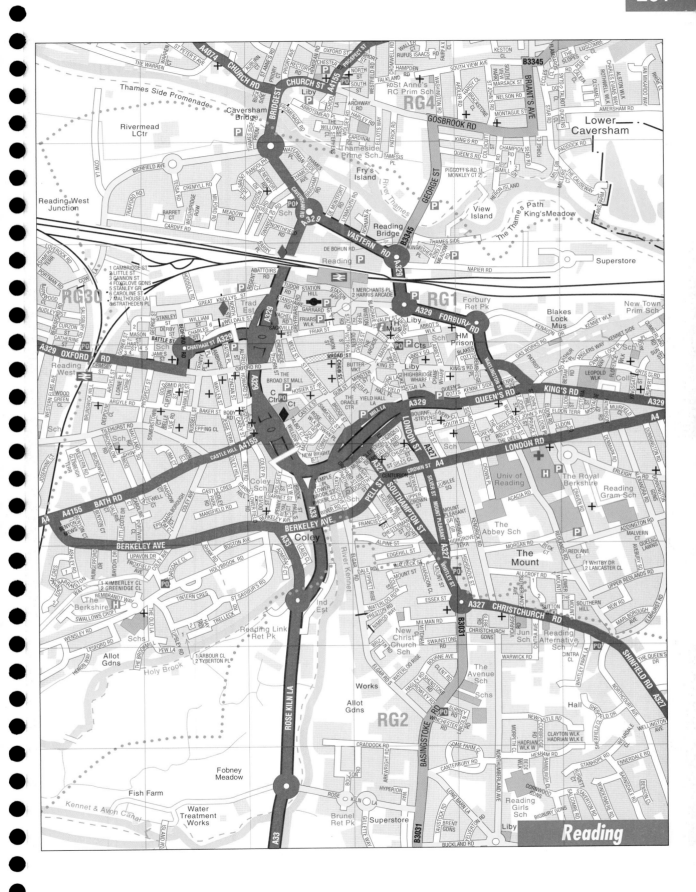

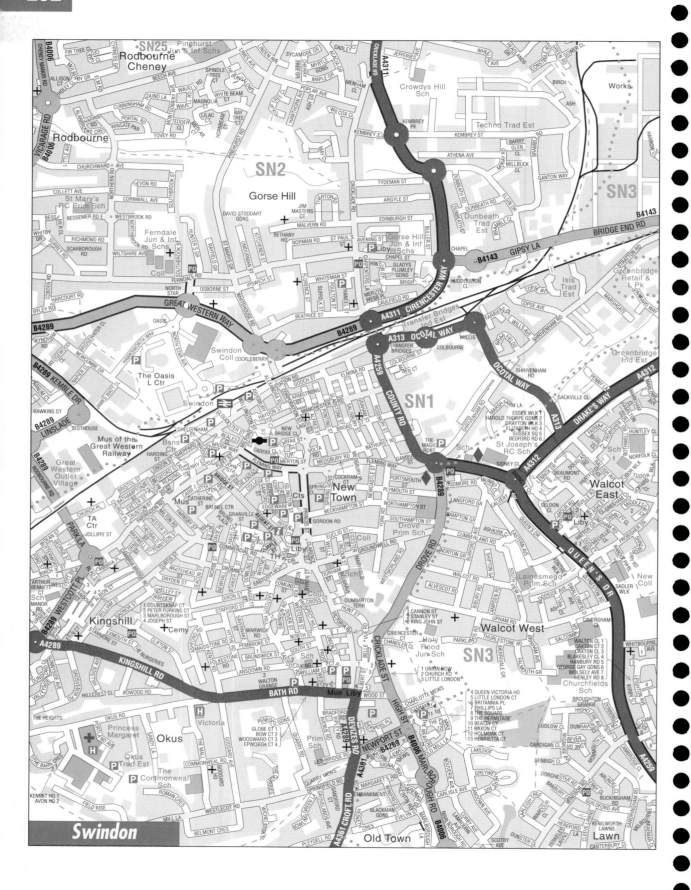

Swindon

Index

Church Rd 6 Beckenham BR2.........**53** C6

Place name	Location number	Locality, town or village	Postcode district	Page and grid square
May be abbreviated on the map	Present when a number indicates the place's position in a crowded area of mapping	Shown when more than one place has the same name	District for the indexed place	Page number and grid reference for the standard mapping

Public and commercial buildings are highlighted in magenta   **Places of interest** are highlighted in blue with a star★

Abbreviations used in the index

Acad	Academy	Comm	Common	Gd	Ground	L	Leisure	Prom	Prom
App	Approach	Cott	Cottage	Gdn	Garden	La	Lane	Rd	Road
Arc	Arcade	Cres	Crescent	Gn	Green	Liby	Library	Recn	Recreation
Ave	Avenue	Cswy	Causeway	Gr	Grove	Mdw	Meadow	Ret	Retail
Bglw	Bungalow	Ct	Court	H	Hall	Meml	Memorial	Sh	Shopping
Bldg	Building	Ctr	Centre	Ho	House	Mkt	Market	Sq	Square
Bsns, Bus	Business	Ctry	Country	Hospl	Hospital	Mus	Museum	St	Street
Bvd	Boulevard	Cty	County	HQ	Headquarters	Orch	Orchard	Sta	Station
Cath	Cathedral	Dr	Drive	Hts	Heights	Pal	Palace	Terr	Terrace
Cir	Circus	Dro	Drove	Ind	Industrial	Par	Parade	TH	Town Hall
Cl	Close	Ed	Education	Inst	Institute	Pas	Passage	Univ	University
Cnr	Corner	Emb	Embankment	Int	International	Pk	Park	Wk, Wlk	Walk
Coll	College	Est	Estate	Intc	Interchange	Pl	Place	Wr	Water
Com	Community	Ex	Exhibition	Junc	Junction	Prec	Precinct	Yd	Yard

Index of localities, towns and villages

Castle St *continued*
Deddington OX15 33 C2
Oxford OX1 123 B1
Steventon OX13 198 C2
Wallingford OX10 221 B4
Castle Wlk OX11 200 C1
Caswell La OX18 116 C3
Cat La Ewelme OX10 204 C2
Stadhampton OX44 163 B1
Cat St OX12 216 B3
Catharine Cl OX14 160 C2
Catherine Cl SN6 209 B3
Catherine St OX4 142 A4
Catkins Cl SN7 172 C1
Catmore Cl OX12 214 B4
Catmore Rd RG20 234 C1
Catsham La
Chadlington OX7 72 B3
Chilson OX7 72 B3
Catslip RG9 224 C1
Catte St OX1 123 B1
Cattle Mkt OX7 42 C2
Catwell Cl OX4 142 A3
Caudwell Cl
Drayton OX14 179 A1
Grove OX12 196 C1
Causeway Banbury OX16 16 C3
Bicester OX26 65 C1
Bletchingdon OX5 93 A4
Causeway The
East Hanney OX12 197 A3
Reading RG4 259 B1
Steventon OX13 198 C2
Woodstock OX20 91 A3
Causmans Way RG31 257 B1
Cavalier Rd OX9 130 A1
Cave St OX4 123 C1
Cavell Rd OX4 142 A3
Cavendish Dr OX3 123 C3
Cavendish Pl OX27 52 B1
Cavendish Rd
Cutteslowe OX2 123 A4
Reading RG4 259 B3
Cavendish Wlk OX9 130 A1
Caversham Hill RG4 259 A2
Caversham Park Dr
RG4 259 B3
Caversham Park Prim Sch
RG4 259 B3
Caversham Park Rd
RG4 259 C3
Caversham Prim Sch
RG4 259 A2
Caversham Rd RG4 259 A1
Caversham Wharf RG1 259 A1
Cawley Rd OX17 23 A3
Cawsam Gdns RG4 259 B2
Caxton Cl RG30 258 B1
Caxton Ct RG9 244 C1
Cecil Aldin Dr RG31 257 B2
Cecil Sharpe Cl OX3 124 B1
Cedar RG9 244 B1
Cedar Cl OX16 16 B1
Cedar Cres OX9 147 B4
Cedar Ct OX4 142 B3
Cedar Dr Bicester OX26 65 C2
Pangbourne RG8 256 B2
Cedar Rd Faringdon SN7 172 C2
N Hinksey Village OX2 140 B4
Cedar Villa OX16 16 A3
Cedar Wood Cres RG4 259 A2
Cedars The Benson OX10 204 A3
Reading RG31 257 B1
Celandine Pl [12] OX4 142 C1
Celsea Pl OX10 221 A1
Cemetery Rd
Abingdon OX14 179 B4
Bicester OX26 65 C1
Centaury Pl OX4 143 A1
Centenary Bsns Pk RG9 244 C1
Centre Rise OX33 143 B3
Centre St OX16 16 C4
Centremead OX2 141 A4
Century Cl SN7 173 A2
Chacombe CE Prim Sch
OX17 10 C2
Chacombe Rd OX17 10 C1
Chadlington CE Prim Sch
OX7 57 B1
Chadlington Rd
Oxford OX2 123 B3
Spelsbury OX7 72 C4
Chaffinch Wlk OX4 142 C1
Chainhill Rd OX12 214 C1
Chalcraft Cl RG9 254 B4
Chalfont Rd OX2 123 A3
Chalford Cl OX7 42 C2
Chalford Rd OX9 167 A2
Chalgrove Com Prim Sch
OX44 184 B3
Chalgrove Rd OX9 130 A1
Chalgrove Way RG4 259 A3
Chalk Farm Rd HP14 188 B3
Chalk Hill
Aston Tirrold OX11 237 C4
Henley-on-T RG9 254 B3
Chalkhouse Green La
RG4 253 A1
Chalkhouse Green Rd
RG4 252 C1
Chalkhousegreen La
RG4 259 A4
Challenor Cl OX14 179 C2
Challow Rd OX12 214 A3
Chalmore Gdns OX10 221 B3
Chalvey Cl OX26 65 B1
Chalvey Rd OX26 65 B1
Chamberlain Pl OX5 92 B1
Chamberlaine Ct [1]
OX16 16 B3
Chambrai Cl OX14 200 C4
Champion Rd RG4 259 B1
Champion Way OX4 142 A2
Champs Cl OX14 160 B1
Chancel Way
Lechlade GL7 150 B2
Marcham OX13 178 B4
Chandler Cl OX18 134 C2
Chandlers Cl
Abingdon OX14 160 B1
Wantage OX12 214 C2
Chandlings Manor Sch
OX1 160 A4
Chapel & Pope's Twr★
OX29 138 A4
Chapel Cl
Deddington OX15 34 C2
Leafield OX29 86 C2
South Stoke RG8 239 B2
Chapel Dr OX25 81 B2
Chapel End
Croughton NN13 36 B4
Great Rollright OX7 29 A2
Chapel Hill
Brize Norton OX18 116 A2
Swerford OX7 30 C2
Watchfield SN6 191 B1
Chapel La Adderbury OX17 23 A2
Benson OX10 203 C2
Berrick Salome OX10 204 A4
Bledington OX7 54 B1
Bledlow Ridge HP14 169 C1
Blewbury OX11 237 A4
Bodicote OX15 22 C4
Chalgrove OX44 184 B3
Charney Bassett OX12 175 C1
Cropredy OX17 4 C1
Enstone OX7 58 C3
Fernham SN7 193 A3
Great Bourton OX17 9 B3
Hailey OX29 104 A3
Kingham OX7 55 A4
Little Tew OX7 45 A3
Milton (Banbury) OX15 22 B2
Nettlebed RG9 224 C1
North Leigh OX29 105 A4
Northmoor OX29 138 B2
Oxford OX4 142 A1
Ratley OX15 2 A2
Salford OX7 41 C3
Shipton-u-W OX7 85 B4
Shotteswell OX17 8 B4
Standlake OX29 137 B2
Sutton Courtenay OX14 200 A4
Turweston NN13 24 A4
Uffington SN7 211 B4
Chapel Rd Ashbury SN6 228 A4
South Leigh OX29 119 A3
Stanford in the V SN7 194 C4
Chapel Row OX17 4 C1
Chapel Sq
Deddington OX15 33 C2
East Hendred OX12 216 B3
Chapel St Bicester OX26 65 C1
Bloxham OX15 21 C2
Hook Norton OX15 30 A4
Oxford OX4 141 C4
Warmington OX17 3 A2
Watlington OX49 186 A1
Chapel Way
Childrey OX12 213 B2
N Hinksey Village OX2 122 B1
Chapelwick Cl SN6 209 A3
Chapmans La OX15 34 A2
Chapmans Piece OX18 100 C3
Charbridge La OX26 66 A1
Charbridge Way OX26 66 B1
Charcroft Cl OX29 118 A3
Charlbury Cl OX5 92 B1
Charlbury Prim Sch OX7 73 B2
Charlbury Rd Finstock OX7 88 B4
Oxford OX2 123 B3
Shrivenham SN6 209 A3
Charlbury Sta OX7 73 A2
Charles Ct OX16 16 B3
Charles Dr OX9 130 A1
Charles Evans Way RG4 259 B1
Charles Ho RG9 244 C2
Charles Rd OX10 239 A4
Charles St OX4 142 A4
Charlton Cty Prim Sch
OX12 214 C3
Charlton Pk OX12 214 C3
Charlton Rd Aynho OX17 35 B4
Wantage OX12 214 C3
Charlton Village Rd
OX12 214 C3
Charlton-on-Otmoor CE Prim
Sch OX5 95 A2
Charney Ave OX14 160 B1
Charter Ho OX12 214 C2
Charter Way OX10 221 B4
Charterville Cl OX29 102 C1
Chartwell Dr OX7 73 B2
Charvil La RG4 260 C2
Chase Barn OX27 37 A2
Chastleton Ho★ GL56 40 B4
Chatham Rd OX1 141 B3
Chatsworth Cl RG4 259 B3
Chatsworth Dr OX16 16 C2
Chatterpie La OX29 89 C3
Chaucer Cl Bicester OX26 65 B2
Reading RG4 259 A3
Chaucer Ct OX10 204 C2
Chaucer's La OX20 91 A3
Chaundy Rd OX5 77 B3
Chaunterell Way OX14 179 B3
Chawley La OX2 140 A3
Chazey Cl RG4 258 B4
Chazey Rd RG4 258 B2
Cheapside OX18 134 C2
Chearsley Rd HP18 129 C4
Cheatle Cl OX18 100 C2
Checkendon CE Prim Sch
RG8 241 B2
Checker Wlk OX14 179 C4
Chedworth Dr OX28 117 C4
Cheers Farm OX14 179 B1
Chelford Way RG4 258 C2
Chelmscote Row OX17 10 C4
Chelsea Cl RG30 257 C1
Chenderit Sch OX17 11 A1
Cheney Ct OX17 10 C1
Cheney Gdns OX17 10 C1
Cheney La OX3 124 A1
Cheney Rd OX16 16 C4
Cheney Sch OX3 124 A1
Cheney Wlk OX14 159 C1
Chepstow Gdns OX16 15 C3
Chepstow Rd RG31 257 B1
Chequers Pl
Cholsey OX10 220 C1
Oxford OX3 124 C2
Cherbury Gn OX12 214 B4
Cheriton Pl RG4 252 C2
Cherry Cl Kidlington OX5 108 C4
Reading RG4 259 B4
Sandford-on-T OX4 142 C1
Stratton Audley OX27 52 B1
Warborough OX10 203 A3
Cherry Fields OX17 4 C1
Cherry Orch
Great Coxwell SN7 192 B4
Highworth SN6 190 A3
Cherry Orchard La SN6 190 A3
Cherry Rd OX16 16 A4
Cherry St OX27 52 B1
Cherry Tree Cl
Grove OX12 214 C4
Kingston Bagpuize OX13 176 B4
Stoke Row RG9 242 A3
Cherry Tree Dr OX13 159 B1
Cherry Tree Rd OX39 168 B3
Cherrys Cl OX15 21 B2
Cherwell Ave OX5 109 A4
Cherwell Bank OX25 62 C3
Cherwell Bsns Ctr OX5 92 B1
Cherwell Cl
Abingdon OX14 160 A1
Bicester OX26 65 B1
Didcot OX11 200 C2
Wallingford OX10 221 B4
Cherwell Dr OX3 123 C3
Cherwell Lodge OX2 123 B4
Cherwell Rd
Berinsfield OX10 182 B3
Reading RG4 259 A3
Cherwell Sch The OX2 123 B3
Cherwell st Banbury OX16 16 B4
Oxford OX4 123 C1
Cherwood House Cotts
OX27 66 A4
Cheshire Dr OX25 63 B4
Cheshire Rd OX9 148 B4
Chester St Oxford OX4 141 C4
Reading RG4 259 A1
Chester Way OX16 15 C3
Chesterton CE Prim Sch
OX26 79 C4
Chestnut Ave
Faringdon SN7 172 C2
Oxford OX3 124 B2
Radley OX14 160 C2
Reading RG4 259 C2
Thame OX9 147 B4
Chestnut Cl Bix RG9 243 C4
Brize Norton OX18 116 B2
Chesterton OX26 80 A4
Launton OX26 66 B1
Witney OX28 104 A1
Chestnut Cotts RG8 249 A3
Chestnut Ct [5] OX4 142 B2
Chestnut Dr OX7 71 A1
Chestnut End OX26 65 C2
Chestnut Gr RG8 257 B3
Chestnut Pl OX49 186 A1
Chestnut Rd
Mollington OX17 4 A2
N Hinksey Village OX2 140 B4
Chestnut Tree Cl OX13 159 B1
Chestnuts The
Abingdon OX14 160 B1
Deddington OX15 34 C2
Kirtlington OX5 78 A2
Shiplake RG9 255 A2
Wantage OX12 214 C3
Chetwode Banbury OX16 16 A4
Banbury, Overthorpe OX17 17 B3
Chetwyn Mead OX18 134 C2
Cheviot Way OX16 8 C1
Cheyne La OX18 134 C2
Chibnall Cl OX44 184 B3
Chichester Cl OX26 65 C1
Chichester Pl OX18 116 B2
Chichester Wlk OX16 9 A1
Chiers Dr OX14 179 B1
Chilbridge Rd OX29 120 B4
Chilbrook OX11 217 C3
Childrey Way
Abingdon OX14 160 A1
East Challow OX12 213 C2
Chilgrove Dr OX25 49 C1
Chillingworth Cres OX3 142 C4
Chillingworth Ct OX3 142 C4
Chilswell La
Sunningwell OX1 141 A1
Wootton (Oxford) OX1 140 C2
Chilswell Rd OX1 141 B4
Chiltern App OX26 65 C2
Chiltern Bank RG9 252 C4
Chiltern Bsns Ctr OX4 142 C2
Chiltern Cl Benson OX10 203 C3
Berinsfield OX10 182 B3
Chalgrove OX44 184 C3
Henley-on-T RG9 254 A4
Chiltern Cres OX10 221 A4
Chiltern Ct RG4 259 A3
Chiltern Edge Com Sch
RG4 252 C2
Chiltern End Cl RG9 254 B4
Chiltern Gdns OX49 186 B1
Chiltern Gr OX9 148 A4
Chiltern Nursery Training
Coll RG4 259 A2
Chiltern Rd Reading RG4 259 B2
Rotherfield Peppard RG9 252 C4
Chiltern Ridge HP14 188 B2
Chiltern Sculpture Trail★
HP14 187 B2
Chiltern View
Little Milton OX44 164 A4
Purley on T RG8 257 B3
Tetsworth OX9 166 A4
Chiltern Wlk RG8 256 C3
Chilton Cl OX14 160 A1
Chilton Cty Prim Sch
OX11 235 B4
Chilton Park Rd RG4 259 A1
Chilton Rd
Long Crendon HP18 129 B4
Upton OX11 218 A1
Chilworth Rd OX44 145 B2
Chinalls Cl MK18 39 B3
Chinnock Brook OX11 200 C2
Chinnor Hill OX39 168 C2
Chinnor Hill Nature
Reserve★ OX39 168 C3
Chinnor Rd
Aston Rowant OX49 167 B1
Bledlow Ridge HP14 169 B2
Thame OX9 148 B3
Towersey OX9 148 C3
Chipmunk Rd OX10 204 B2
Chipperfield Park Rd
OX15 21 C3
Chipping Norton Hospl
OX7 42 C2
Chipping Norton Mus★
OX7 42 C2
Chipping Norton Rd
Chadlington OX7 57 A2
Hook Norton OX15 30 A4
Chipping Norton Sch
OX7 42 C1
Chipping Warden Prim Sch
OX17 5 C4
Choicehill Rd OX7 42 C3
Cholesbury Grange
OX3 124 A2
Cholsey & Wallingford Rly★
OX10 220 C2
Cholsey Cl OX4 142 B2
Cholsey Prim Sch OX10 220 C1
Cholsey Sta OX10 220 C1
Cholswell Ct OX13 159 B2
Cholswell Rd OX13 159 B1
Chorefields OX5 92 B1
Choswell Spring OX4 142 C1
Chowns Cl OX9 148 A4
Christ Church OX1 123 B1
Christ Church Cath Sch
OX1 141 B4
Christ Church Old Bldgs [4]
OX1 123 A1
Christchurch Cath★
OX1 123 B1
Christchurch Ct OX16 16 B3
Christopher Rawlins CE Prim
Sch OX17 23 A2
Church Ave
Henley-on-T RG9 244 C1
Kings Sutton OX17 23 C3
Church Cl Adderbury OX17 23 A2
Ascott-u-W OX7 71 B1
Benson OX10 203 C2
Black Bourton OX18 133 C3
Charlbury OX7 73 A2
Cuddesdon OX44 144 B2
Cumnor OX2 121 B1
East Hagbourne OX11 218 C3
Fringford OX27 52 B4
Great Bourton OX17 9 B4
Islip OX5 93 C1
Longcot SN7 192 B1
Merton OX25 95 B4
Rotherfield Greys RG9 243 B1
South Hinksey OX1 141 A3
Wardington OX17 5 C1
Weston-on-the-G OX25 79 A1
Church Cotts OX44 161 C2
Church Cowley Rd OX4 142 A3
Church Cowley St James CE
Fst Sch OX4 142 B2
Church End
Blewbury OX11 219 A1
Croughton NN13 36 B4
Drayton St L OX10 183 A3
Great Rollright OX7 29 A2
South Leigh OX29 119 B3
Standlake OX29 137 B2
Church Furlong OX15 20 B4
Church Gn
Long Crendon HP18 129 B4
Stanford in the V SN7 194 C4
Witney OX28 118 A4
Church Hill Chilton OX11 235 B4
Great Haseley OX44 164 C4
Little Milton OX44 163 C3
Stonor RG9 225 B4
Tackley OX5 77 A3
Warmington OX17 3 A2
Church Hill Rd OX4 142 A2
Church La Adderbury OX17 23 A2
Aston Rowant OX49 167 B2
Banbury OX16 16 B3
Bicester OX26 65 C1
Bishopstone SN6 227 B2
Bledington OX7 54 B1
Bledlow Ridge HP14 189 C4
Bledlow Ridge, Radnage
HP14 189 B4
Brightwell-cum-S OX10 202 C2
Burford OX18 100 C3
Cassington OX29 107 B1
Chacombe OX17 10 C2
Chalgrove OX44 184 B3
Charlbury OX7 73 A2
Charlton-on-O OX5 95 A2
Chinnor OX39 168 B3
Chipping Norton OX7 42 C2
Claydon OX17 1 B1
Coleshill SN6 191 A4
Croughton NN13 36 B4
Crowmarsh G OX10 221 B1
Drayton OX14 179 B1
Drayton St L OX10 183 A3
Ewelme RG9 206 A1
Fernham SN7 193 A2
Fringford OX27 52 B4
Fulbrook OX18 100 C3
Hailey OX29 104 A3
Hampton Poyle OX5 93 A2
Hanwell OX17 8 C2
Harwell OX11 217 C4
Hornton OX15 7 B3
Horton-cum-S OX33 112 A3
Islip OX5 93 C1
Kirtlington OX5 78 A2
Langford GL7 132 B1
Longworth OX13 156 A2
Lower Heyford OX25 62 B3
Ludgershall HP18 98 B4
Marston OX3 123 C3
Middle Barton OX7,OX25 61 A4
Middleton Cheney OX17 10 C1
Milcombe OX15 21 A1
Mixbury NN13 38 C4
Mollington OX17 4 A2
Reading RG4 259 C4
Rotherfield Peppard RG9 253 A4
Shilton OX18 115 A3
Shiplake RG9 254 C1
Shotteswell OX17 8 B4
South Moreton OX11 219 C3
Spelsbury OX7 72 C4
Steventon OX13 198 C2
Towersey OX9 148 C4
Wallingford OX10 221 B4
Watlington OX49 186 A2
Wendlebury OX26 80 A2
Weston-on-the-G OX25 79 A1
Witney OX28 118 B4
Yarnton OX5 108 A2
Church Mdw OX7 70 A1
Church Mews RG8 257 B3
Church Mill Cl OX29 137 B2
Church Pas [4] OX16 16 B3
Church Path
Stanford in the V SN7 194 C4
Stokenchurch HP14 188 B3
Church Pl GL56 54 A4
Church Rd
Appleton OX13 158 A4
Ardley OX27 50 B2
Benson OX10 203 C2
Blewbury OX11 237 A4
Brackley NN13 24 A4
Chadlington OX7 57 B1
Chinnor OX39 168 B3
Cholsey OX10 220 C2
Great Milton OX44 145 A1
Hinton Waldrist SN7 155 C1
Horspath OX33 143 B3
Ickford HP18 127 C2
Lewknor OX49 187 A4
Long Hanborough OX29 106 B4
Lower Odington GL56 54 A4
Milton-u-W OX7 70 A1
North Leigh OX29 105 A4
Pangbourne RG8 256 B3
Radley OX14 160 C2
Reading RG4 259 A1
Sandford-on-T OX4 161 A4
Thame OX9 129 C1
Weston-on-the-G OX25 79 A1
Wheatley OX33 144 A4
Church Rise OX7 88 B3
Church Row
Bishopstone SN4 227 A2
Bourton SN6 209 A1
Childrey OX12 213 B2
Langford GL7 132 B1
Church Sq OX5 93 C1
Church St
Ardington OX12 215 C3
Bampton OX18 134 C2

Croft Terr **8** OX10 . . . . .221 B4
Croft The
  Aston Tirrold OX11 . . . . . .219 C1
  Didcot OX11 . . . . .218 C4
  East Hagbourne OX11 . . . .218 C3
  Haddenham HP17 . . . . . . .130 C3
  Harwell OX11 . . . . .217 C4
  Nuneham Courtenay OX44 162 A2
  Oxford OX3 . . . . .124 B2
  West Hanney OX12 . . . . . .196 C4
Croft Villas **3** OX10 . . . . .221 B4
Croft Way RG8 . . . . .250 C4
Croft's La OX15 . . . . .30 A3
Crofts The OX14 . . . . .118 A4
Cromer Cl RG31 . . . . .257 B1
Cromwell Ave OX9 . . . . . .130 A1
Cromwell Cl
  Chalgrove OX44 . . . . . . .184 C3
  Faringdon SN7 . . . . .173 A2
  Henley-on-T RG9 . . . . . . .254 C4
  Marston OX3 . . . . .123 C2
Cromwell Ct OX16 . . . . .16 A4
Cromwell Dr OX11 . . . . . . .219 A4
Cromwell Pk OX7 . . . . .42 C2
Cromwell Rd
  Banbury OX16 . . . . .16 A3
  Henley-on-T RG9 . . . . . . .254 C4
  Reading RG4 . . . . .259 A1
Cromwell St **12** OX1 . . . . .141 B4
Cromwell Way OX5 . . . . . .109 A4
Cronshaw Cl OX11 . . . . . . .200 C1
Crook's Terr OX12 . . . . . . .214 B3
Crookdale Beck OX11 . . . . .201 A2
Croom Cotts OX11 . . . . . . .217 A4
Cropredy CE Prim Sch
  OX17 . . . . .4 C1
Cross Ave OX10 . . . . .204 C4
Cross Cl OX10 . . . . .204 C1
Cross Hill Rd OX17 . . . . . . .22 C2
Cross Keys Rd RG8 . . . . . .239 B2
Cross Leys OX7 . . . . .42 C1
Cross Rd OX10 . . . . .220 C1
Cross St OX4 . . . . .141 C4
Cross Tree La GL7 . . . . . . .132 A3
Cross's La OX7 . . . . .56 C1
Crosslands OX27 . . . . .52 B3
Crosslands Dr OX14 . . . .159 C1
Crossville Cres OX11 . . . . .200 B1
Crossway OX7 . . . . .60 C4
Crotch Cres OX3 . . . . .124 A2
Crouch Hill Rd OX16 . . . . .16 A4
Crouch St OX16 . . . . .16 B3
Croughton All Saints' CE
  Prim Sch NN13 . . . . .36 A4
Croughton Elementary Sch
  NN13 . . . . .36 C3
Croughton Mid Sch
  NN13 . . . . .36 C4
Croughton Rd OX17 . . . . . .35 B4
  Wootton OX20 . . . . .75 B4
Crow La Great Bourton OX17 **9** B4
Crowberry Rd OX4 . . . . . . .142 C1
Crowell Rd OX4 . . . . .142 B2
Crowmarsh Gifford CE Sch
  OX10 . . . . .221 C4
Crowmarsh Hill OX10 . . . .222 A3
Crowmarsh Rd OX27 . . . . . .64 C3
Crown La Benson OX10 . . .203 C2
  Dorchester OX10 . . . . . . .182 B1
  South Moreton OX11 . . . .220 A3
Crown Mdw OX12 . . . . . . .197 B2
Crown Mews OX14 . . . . . . .179 C4
Crown La Kidlington OX5 . .108 B4
  Wheatley OX33 . . . . .144 A4
Crown Sq Benson OX10 . . .204 A4
  Wheatley OX33 . . . . .144 A4
Crown St OX4 . . . . .141 C4
Crown Wlk OX26 . . . . .65 C1
Crowsley Rd RG9 . . . . .255 A2
Crowsley Way RG4 . . . . . .252 C3
Croxford Gdns OX5 . . . . . .108 C4
Crozier Cl OX2 . . . . .140 B4
Crumps Butts OX26 . . . . . .65 C1
Crutch Furlong OX10 . . . .182 B3
Cuckamus La OX29 . . . . . .105 A3
Cuckoo Cl OX27 . . . . .65 C3
Cuckoo La
  Eynsham OX29 . . . . .106 A2
  Freeland OX29 . . . . .106 A2
Cuddesdon Cl RG8 . . . . . .250 C4
Cuddesdon Rd OX33 . . . . .143 C3
Cuddesdon Way OX4 . . . . .142 C1
Cues La SN6 . . . . .227 B2
Culham Cl OX14 . . . . .160 A1
Culham Parochial CE Sch
  OX14 . . . . .180 A2
Culham Sta OX14 . . . . .180 C2
Cullerne Cl OX14 . . . . .160 A1
Cullerns The SN6 . . . . .190 A3
Cullum Rd OX33 . . . . .144 B4
Cullum Ho OX33 . . . . .144 B4
Culworth Rd OX17 . . . . .5 C1
Cumberford OX15 . . . . .21 B2
Cumberford Cl OX15 . . . . . .21 B2
Cumberford Hill OX15 . . . . .21 B2
Cumberland Rd OX4 . . . . . .142 A4
Cumberlege Cl OX3 . . . . . .123 C4
Cummings Cl OX3 . . . . .124 C1
Cumnor CE Prim Sch
  OX2 . . . . .139 C2
Cumnor Hill Cumnor OX2 140 A4
  N Hinksey Village OX2 . . .140 A4
Cumnor Rd Cumnor OX2 . .139 C4
  Wootton (Oxford) OX1 . . .159 A4
Cumnor Rise Rd OX2 . . . . .140 B4
Cunliffe Cl OX2 . . . . .123 B3
Cup & Saucer OX17 . . . . . . .4 C1

Curbridge Rd
  Ducklington OX29 . . . . . .118 A2
  Witney OX28 . . . . .117 C4
Curie Ave OX11 . . . . .217 C2
Cursus The GL7 . . . . .150 B3
Curtis Ave OX14 . . . . .180 A4
Curtis Rd Kidlington OX5 . .92 C1
  Shrivenham SN6 . . . . . . .209 A3
Curtiss Cl OX26 . . . . .66 A3
Curtyn Cl OX14 . . . . .179 B4
Cuthwine Pl GL7 . . . . .150 B3
Cuttewine Way OX4 . . . . . .142 B2
Cutteslowe Fst Sch OX2 109 B1
Cutteslowe Rdbt OX2 . . . .109 A1
Cuttle Brook Gdns OX9 . . .129 C3
Cuxham Rd OX49 . . . . .186 A1
Cwmcarn RG4 . . . . .258 C3
Cygnet Cl OX9 . . . . .166 A4
Cygnet Ct OX14 . . . . .179 C3
Cypress Gdns OX26 . . . . . .65 C3
Cyprus Terr OX2 . . . . .122 C4

North Rd *continued*
Moulsford OX10 238 C2
North Side OX25 48 A1
North St Aston OX18 135 C2
Banbury OX16 16 C4
Bicester OX26 65 C1
Fritwell OX27 49 C4
Islip OX5 93 C1
Marcham OX13 178 B3
Middle Barton OX7 60 C4
Oxford OX2 123 A1
Reading RG4 259 A1
Thame OX9 129 C1
Watchfield SN6 191 B1
North Way
Cutteslowe OX2 109 A1
Oxford OX3 124 C2
Steventon OX13 198 C2
Northampton Rd OX1 141 B3
Northbourne CE Prim Sch OX11 218 C4
Northbourne Ct OX11 218 C4
Northbrook Ho 29 OX4 142 C1
Northbrook Rd RG4 259 B3
Northcot La OX16 16 A4
Northcourt La OX14 160 A1
Northcourt Rd OX14 159 C1
Northcourt Wlk OX11 180 A4
Northern By-pass Rd
Cutteslowe OX2 108 C1
Oxford OX3 124 B3
Northern Ho Sch OX2 123 A4
Northfield Ave RG9 255 A2
Northfield Cl OX4 142 B1
Northfield Ct RG9 244 B2
Northfield End RG9 244 B2
Northfield Rd
Abingdon OX14 160 A2
Oxford OX3 124 C2
Reading RG1 259 A1
Shiplake RG9 255 A2
Northfield Sch OX4 142 B1
Northford Cl SN6 209 B4
Northford Hill SN6 209 B4
Northford Ind Est SN6 209 B4
Northmead La OX12 196 A4
Northmoor Pk OX29 138 B1
Northmoor Rd OX2 123 B3
Northolt Rd OX18 115 C2
Northumberland Ct 4 OX16 16 C3
Northview Cty Prim Sch SN6 190 A4
Northwood Cres OX18 115 C2
Northwood Rd OX29 103 B1
Norton Cl OX3 124 B1
Norton Pk OX7 42 C2
Norton Terr OX29 102 B4
Norton Way OX18 115 C2
Norwood Ave OX13 156 C1
Nosworthy Way OX10 221 C3
Nottwood La RG9 242 A3
Nourse Cl OX3 110 A3
Nowell Rd OX4 141 C2
Nuffield Cl Bicester OX26 65 C2
Didcot OX11 219 A4
Nuffield Coll Oxford OX1 123 A1
Oxford OX1 123 B1
Nuffield Dr OX16 16 A4
Nuffield Hill RG9 223 B2
Nuffield Ind Est OX4 142 B1
Nuffield La OX10 222 C3
Nuffield Orthopaedic Ctr OX3 124 B1
Nuffield Rd OX3 124 C1
Nuffield Way OX14 179 B4
Nun's Acre RG8 249 A4
Nuneham Courtenay Arboretum OX44 161 C1
Nuneham Sq OX14 179 C4
Nunhide La RG8 256 C1
Nunnery Cl OX4 142 B1
Nunney Brook OX11 200 C2
Nurseries Rd OX5 108 B4
Nursery Cl Oxford OX3 124 B1
Shiplake RG9 255 A2
Nursery Dr OX16 16 B4
Nursery Gdns RG8 257 A3
Nursery La OX16 16 B4
Nursery Rd OX29 105 B4
Nursery The OX14 200 A4
Nursery View SN7 173 A2
Nut Hatch Cotts RG8 241 B2
Nuthatch Cl 1 OX4 142 C1
Nyatt Rd OX14 180 B4
Nye Bevan Cl OX4 142 A4

O

O'Connors Rd OX29 102 C1
Oak Ave OX14 160 C3
Oak Cl OX26 65 C2
Oak Dr OX5 92 C1
Oak End Way OX39 168 B3
Oak Farm Cl OX9 166 A4
Oak La Ambrosden OX25 81 B2
Stanford in the V SN7 194 C3
Oak Rd SN6 191 B1
Oak St GL7 150 B2
Oak Tree Copse RG31 257 C2
Oak Tree Rd RG31 257 B1
Oak Tree Wlk RG8 257 B3
Oakdale Ct 5 OX10 221 B4
Oakdene RG8 250 C4
Oakdown Cl RG8 250 C2
Oakes La OX2 121 B1
Oakey Cl OX18 133 B3
Oakfield Ind Est OX29 120 B3
Oakfield Pl OX28 118 A4
Oakfield Rd OX18 115 B1
Oakham Cl RG31 257 B1
Oakham Rd GL56 27 A1
Oakland Cl OX29 105 C4
Oakland Rd OX16 16 B1
Oaklands OX2 121 A2
Oakley Ho OX13 158 B1
Oakley La OX39 168 A3
Oakley Rd Chinnor OX39 168 B3
Horton-cum-S OX33 112 B3
Reading RG4 258 C2
Oaks Rd RG9 255 A2
Oaksmere OX13 158 A3
Oakthorpe Pl OX2 123 A3
Oakthorpe Rd OX2 123 A3
Oasis Pk OX29 120 B3
Oathurst Est OX18 134 C2
Oatland Rd OX11 218 C4
Oatlands Rd OX2 122 C1
Observatory Cl OX10 204 A2
Observatory St OX2 123 A2
Ock Dr OX10 182 B3
Ock Mews 9 OX14 179 C4
Ock Mill Cl OX14 179 B3
Ock St OX14 179 C3
Ockley Brook OX11 201 A1
Octavian Way NN13 24 A4
Oddley La HP27 169 B4
Odiham Ave RG4 259 C3
Odiham Cl OX18 115 C2
Offas Cl OX10 204 A3
Ogbourne Cl OX12 214 A3
Old Arncott Rd OX25 81 B2
Old Bakery The 2 OX1 123 A1
Old Barn Cl Benson OX10 204 A2
Reading RG4 259 A3
Old Barn Gnd OX3 124 C4
Old Bath Rd RG4 260 B1
Old Bix Rd RG9 243 C4
Old Blackalls Dr OX10 221 A2
Old Bldgs 18 OX10 221 B4
Old Bourne OX11 200 C2
Old Bridge Rd OX15 21 C2
Old Burford Rd OX7 54 B1
Old Chapel Cl OX5 92 C1
Old Coachyard The OX28 104 A1
Old Copse Gdns RG4 252 C3
Old Council Hos The
Horley OX15 8 A2
South Newington OX15 31 C4
Old Croft Cl OX39 167 C2
Old Dashwood Hill HP14 189 C1
Old Farm Cl
Abingdon OX14 180 B4
Worminghall HP18 127 B3
Old Farm Cres RG31 257 B1
Old Field OX44 164 A4
Old Forge Cl OX7 54 B1
Old Forge Rd OX7 29 A2
Old Foundry The OX14 179 C3
Old George Yd OX18 100 C3
Old Glebe OX15 20 B4
Old Greyfriars St OX1 141 B4
Old Grimsbury Rd OX16 16 C4
Old High St OX3 124 B2
Old Kiln★ RG9 224 C1
Old Kiln The RG9 224 C1
Old London Rd
Benson OX10 204 A2
Tiddington OX9 145 C2
Wheatley OX33 144 B4
Chipping Norton OX7 56 B4
Old Luxters Farm Brewery★ HP14 226 C4
Old Maltings The 2 OX9 129 C1
Old Manor Ct OX12 214 A1
Old Marston Rd OX3 123 C2
Old Mill Cl OX12 196 C1
Old Mill The RG8 256 B3
Old Moor OX14 199 B3
Old Moor Cl OX10 221 B4
Old Nursery View OX1 141 B2
Old Orch OX39 149 C1
Old Parr Cl OX16 16 B3
Old Parr Rd OX16 16 B3
Old Place Yd OX26 65 C1
Old Plough Wlk OX15 33 A2
Old Pound The OX13 159 A3
Old Rd
East Hendred OX12 216 C3
Great Tew OX7 45 B4
Oxford OX3 124 C1
Ratley OX15 2 A2
Wheatley OX33 143 C4
Old Reading Rd OX10 221 C3
Old Rectory OX25 48 C1
Old Rectory Ct OX26 80 A2
Old Sawmills Rd SN7 172 C1
Old School Cl
Bicester OX27 65 C4
Stokenchurch HP14 188 C2
Old School End OX15 30 A4
Old School Ho The OX7 70 A1
Old School La OX12 213 C3
Old School Pl OX16 16 C3
Old School The OX4 142 B3
Old Stables The OX3 124 B2
Old Stables Yd OX12 214 A1
Old Station Yd OX14 179 C4
Old Town NN13 24 A4
Old Wallingford Way OX14 200 A4
Old Warehouse Flats The OX28 104 B1
Old Well Ct RG4 260 B2
Old Wharf Rd SN7 210 B4
Old Windmill Way HP18 129 B4
Old Witney Rd OX29 120 B4
Oldean Cl RG31 257 B1
Oliver Rd OX4 142 C3
One End La OX10 203 C2
Onley Ct 26 OX1 141 B4
Onslow Dr OX9 130 A1
Onslow Gdns RG4 259 B2
Oracle Parkway RG6 260 A1
Orange Cl SN6 190 A3
Oratory Prep Sch The RG8 250 B3
Oratory Sch The RG8 251 A4
Orchard Ave RG4 252 C3
Orchard Cl
Abingdon OX14 160 A1
Banbury OX16 16 A3
Buckland SN7 174 C4
Cassington OX29 107 B1
Chalgrove OX44 184 B4
Charney Bassett OX12 175 C1
Combe OX29 90 A2
Didcot OX11 200 C1
East Hanney OX12 197 A3
East Hendred OX12 216 B4
Eynsham OX29 120 C4
Henley-on-T RG9 244 C1
Lechlade GL7 150 B2
Purley on T RG31 257 B2
Salford OX7 41 C2
Shiplake RG9 254 C1
Thame OX9 148 A4
Upton OX11 218 B1
Wallingford OX10 221 B3
Warborough OX10 203 A4
Wheatley OX33 144 A4
Orchard Combe RG8 250 B2
Orchard Cotts OX7 57 A1
Orchard Ct OX4 142 A2
Orchard Field RG4 252 B3
Orchard Field La OX20 91 B2
Orchard Furlong OX12 213 B2
Orchard Gdns OX12 213 B3
Orchard Gr Bloxham OX15 21 B2
Reading RG4 259 C2
Orchard Ground OX7 69 B1
Orchard Haven OX10 202 B4
Orchard Hill SN7 172 C2
Orchard La Cropredy OX17 4 C1
East Hendred OX12 216 B3
Upper Heyford OX25 62 C4
Wootton (Oxford) OX1 140 B1
Orchard Meadow Fst Sch OX4 142 C1
Orchard Piece OX17 4 A2
Orchard Pl
Upper Heyford OX25 62 C4
Westbury NN13 25 A2
Orchard Rd Ardley OX27 50 A2
Buckland SN7 174 C4
Hook Norton OX15 30 A4
N Hinksey Village OX2 140 A4
Orchard Rise
Burford OX18 100 C2
Chesterton OX26 79 C4
Orchard Row OX18 100 C3
Orchard The
Appleton OX13 158 A4
East Challow OX12 214 A3
Merton OX25 95 B4
Orchard View OX17 4 C1
Orchard Way
Banbury OX16 16 A3
Bicester OX26 65 B2
Chinnor OX39 168 B3
Harwell OX11 217 B4
Kidlington OX5 108 C4
Kingham OX7 54 C2
Marcham OX13 178 B3
Middle Barton OX7 46 C1
Oxford OX4 142 B2
Wantage OX12 214 C2
Witney OX28 118 A4
Orchard Wlk OX49 186 B1
Orchid Cl OX26 65 C3
Orchid Ct OX14 180 B4
Orchids The OX11 235 B4
Ordnance Rd OX11 200 B1
Oregon Ave RG31 257 B2
Oriel Coll OX1 123 B1
Oriel Ct OX11 219 A4
Oriel Sq OX1 123 B1
Oriel St OX1 123 B1
Oriel Way OX26 65 C2
Orkney Pl OX28 117 C4
Ormerod Sch OX3 125 A2
Ormond Rd Thame OX9 130 A1
Wantage OX12 214 C2
Orpine Cl OX26 65 B3
Orpwood Way OX14 179 B3
Orwell Cl RG4 258 C2
Orwell Dr OX11 201 A1
Osberton Rd OX2 123 A4
Osborne Cl Bicester OX26 65 B2
Cutteslowe OX2 122 C4
Kidlington OX5 108 B4
Osiers The OX10 183 A3
Osler Rd OX3 124 B2
Osney Cl OX15 30 A4
Osney La OX1 123 A1
Osney Mead OX2 141 A4
Osney Mead Ind Est OX2 141 A4
Osney Mews OX2 123 A1
Osprey Cl OX26 81 A4
Osterley Dr RG4 259 C3
Osterley Gr OX16 16 A2
Oswestry Rd OX1 141 B3
Otmoor La Beckley OX3 111 A2
Charlton-on-O OX5 95 A2
Otters Reach OX1 141 C1
Ottery Way OX11 201 A1
Otwell Cl OX14 160 A1
Our Lady's Convent Senior Sch OX14 180 A4
Our Lady's RC Fst Sch OX4 142 B3
Ouse Cl OX11 200 C2
Ouseley Cl OX3 123 C2
Outmoor View OX25 95 B4
Outram Rd OX4 142 A3
Oval The Bicester OX26 65 B2
Didcot OX11 200 B1
Oxford OX4 142 A2
Over Norton Rd OX7 42 C2
Overbrooke Gdns OX4 143 A1
Overdale Cl OX3 124 C2
Overdown Rd RG31 257 B1
Overlanders End RG31 257 C2
Overmead OX14 179 C2
Overmead Gn OX4 142 C1
Overstrand Cl OX26 66 A2
Overthorpe Prep Sch OX17 17 B4
Overthorpe Rd OX16 16 C3
Overton Dr OX9 130 A1
Owlington Cl OX2 122 B1
Ox Cl OX14 180 A4
Oxen Piece OX44 145 B1
Oxeye Ct OX4 161 C4
Oxford Brookes Univ OX3 124 A1
Oxford Brookes Univ Sch of Occupational Therapy OX3 124 B1
Oxford Bsns Ctr The OX1 141 A4
Oxford Bsns Pk OX2 109 A1
Oxford Bsns Pk N OX4 142 B3
Oxford Bsns Pk S OX4 142 B2
Oxford Cl OX5 77 C2
Oxford Coll of F Ed OX1 141 A4
Oxford Cres OX11 218 B4
Oxford High Sch For Girls OX2 123 B3
Oxford Hill OX28,OX29 118 B4
Oxford La OX12 196 C1
Oxford Rd
Abingdon OX13, OX14 160 A3
Adderbury OX17 23 A2
Banbury OX15,OX16 16 B2
Benson OX10 203 C2
Bicester OX25,OX26 80 B4
Bletchingdon OX5 93 A4
Burford OX18 100 C2
Clifton Hampden OX14 181 C3
Cumnor OX2 139 C3
Cutteslowe OX2 109 A2
Deddington OX15 33 C1
Dorchester OX10 182 B1
Enstone OX7 58 C3
Eynsham OX29 120 C4
Garsington OX4,OX44 143 B1
Hampton Poyle OX5 93 A2
Kennington OX1 160 A3
Kidlington OX5 108 C4
Kirtlington OX5 77 C2
Marston OX3 123 C3
Middleton Stoney OX25 64 A2
North Aston OX25 47 C3
Oxford OX4 142 C2
Oxford, Littlemore OX4 142 A2
Oxford, Temple Cowley OX4 142 B3
Reading RG30 258 A1
Stokenchurch HP14 188 B3
Thame OX9 147 C4
Tiddington OX9 145 C3
Woodcote RG8 240 C1
Woodstock OX20 91 B3
Oxford Science Pk OX4 142 A1
Oxford Spires Bsns Pk OX5 92 A2
Oxford Sq SN6 191 B1
Oxford St Reading RG4 259 A1
Woodstock OX20 91 A3
Oxford Utd FC OX4 142 B1
Oxford Univ Botanic Gdns★ OX1 123 B2
Oxford Univ Inst Of Experimental Psychology OX1 123 B1
Oxford Upper Sch OX4 142 A4
Oxhey Hill OX17 4 B2
Oxhey Rise OX15 31 A4
Oxlease OX28 118 B4
Oxlip Cl OX26 65 B2
Oxon Pl SN6 227 B2
Oxpens Rd OX1 141 A4

P

Pack & Prime La RG9 244 B1
Pack La OX7 61 A4
Packhorse La OX13 178 B3
Paddock Cl Benson OX10 204 A2
Chalgrove OX44 184 B4
Sonning RG4 260 C2
Wantage OX12 214 C3
Paddock Farm La OX15 22 B4
Paddock Mews OX13 156 B1
Paddock Rd Ardley OX27 50 A2
Paddock Rd *continued*
Reading RG4 259 B1
Wallingford OX10 221 B4
Paddock The
Chilton OX11 235 B4
Highworth SN6 190 A3
Kennington OX1 160 C4
Longworth OX13 156 B1
Somerton OX25 48 C3
Paddocks The
Bampton OX18 134 C1
Deddington OX15 33 C2
East Hanney OX12 197 A3
Mollington OX17 3 C2
Souldern OX6 35 C2
Yarnton OX5 108 A3
Paddox Cl OX2 123 A4
Paddox The OX2 123 A4
Page Furlong OX10 182 B1
Pages La OX15 7 B3
Pages Orch RG4 252 C3
Paget Rd OX4 142 C3
Pagisters Rd OX14 160 B1
Paines Hill OX25 62 A4
Painswick Cl OX28 103 C1
Painters Cl OX15 21 B2
Palmer Ave OX25 96 C4
Palmer Pl OX14 179 C3
Palmer Rd OX3 124 C1
Palmers OX12 214 C3
Pampas Cl OX18 115 C1
Panbourne Hill RG8 256 B3
Pangbourne Coll RG8 256 A2
Pangbourne Prim Sch RG8 256 C3
Pangbourne St RG30 258 A1
Panters Rd OX10 221 A1
Paper Mill Cotts OX18 99 B3
Paper Mill La OX11 220 A3
Papist Way OX10 238 C4
Parade The
Kidlington OX5 108 C3
Oxford OX3 124 B2
Paradise La OX15 21 A1
Paradise Mews RG9 244 B1
Paradise Rd RG9 244 B1
Paradise Sq OX1 123 A1
Paradise St OX1 123 A1
Paradise Terr OX7 42 B1
Park Ave Highworth SN6 190 A3
Kidlington OX5 92 B1
Shrivenham SN6 209 B4
Park Cl Avon Dassett CV47 2 C4
Banbury OX16 16 B3
Bladon OX20 91 A2
Cutteslowe OX2 109 A1
Didcot OX11 218 B4
Hanwell OX17 8 C2
Hook Norton OX15 30 A3
Kirtlington OX5 77 C3
Middleton Stoney OX25 64 A2
North Leigh OX29 105 B3
Sonning Common RG4 253 A3
Yarnton OX5 108 A2
Park Cres OX14 179 C4
Park Ct Banbury OX16 16 A3
Thame OX9 148 A4
Park End Bodicote OX15 16 C1
Croughton NN13 36 B4
Park End Cl OX15 16 C1
Park End Ct OX15 16 C1
Park End St OX1 123 A1
Park End Works NN13 36 B4
Park Hill
Hook Norton OX15 30 A4
Wheatley OX33 126 A1
Park Hospl For Children OX3 124 B1
Park La Appleton OX13 158 A4
Ardington OX12 215 B2
Aston Rowant OX39 167 C2
Bladon OX20 91 A1
Checkendon RG8,RG4 251 C3
Long Hanborough OX29 90 B1
North Newington OX15 15 B2
Stanford in the V SN7 195 A3
Stokenchurch HP14 188 C3
Stonor RG9 225 B3
Swalcliffe OX15 19 C4
Woodstock OX20 91 A3
Park Rd Abingdon OX14 179 C4
Banbury OX16 16 A3
Chipping Norton OX7 42 C2
Combe OX29 90 A3
Didcot OX11 218 B4
Ducklington OX29 118 A2
Faringdon SN7 172 C2
Henley-on-T RG9 244 C1
Hook Norton OX15 30 A4
North Leigh OX29 105 A3
Witney OX28 103 C1
Park Rise OX25 81 B2
Park Side Marcham OX13 178 B3
Woodstock OX20 91 B3
Park St Bladon OX20 91 A1
Charlbury OX7 73 A2
Thame OX9 148 A4
Woodstock OX20 91 A3
Park Terr
East Challow OX12 214 A3
Thame OX9 148 A4
Park The Cumnor OX2 139 C2
Harwell OX11 217 C3
Park Town OX2 123 B2

Rea – St K 279

Reading Rd *continued*
Harwell OX11 . . . 217 B3
Kidmore End RG4 . . . 252 A2
Pangbourne RG8 . . . 256 B3
Streatley RG8 . . . 249 A3
Wallingford OX10 . . . 221 B2
Woodcote RG8 . . . 240 C1
Recreation Rd
Wargrave RG10 . . . 255 C1
Woodstock OX20 . . . 91 B3
Rectory Cl
Marsh Gibbon OX27 . . . 67 C2
Warmington OX17 . . . 3 A2
Wendlebury OX26 . . . 80 A2
Rectory Cres OX7 . . . 60 C4
Rectory Ct OX49 . . . 187 A4
Rectory Farm Cl OX12 . . . 196 C4
Rectory Gdns OX15 . . . 15 B4
Rectory Hill RG9 . . . 206 A1
Rectory La
Aston Tirrold OX11 . . . 237 C4
Bix RG9 . . . 225 B1
Fringford OX27 . . . 52 B3
Kingston Bagpuize OX13 . . . 176 C4
Letcombe Bassett OX12 . . . 231 C4
Lewknor OX9 . . . 166 C1
Longworth OX13 . . . 156 A2
Middleton Cheney OX17 . . . 10 C1
Woodstock OX20 . . . 91 A3
Rectory Mdw OX39 . . . 168 B4
Rectory Rd
Great Haseley OX44 . . . 164 C4
Hook Norton OX15 . . . 30 A4
Oxford OX4 . . . 141 C4
Reading RG4 . . . 259 A1
Streatley RG8 . . . 248 B4
Red Bridge Hollow OX1 141 B2
Red Copse Rd OX1 . . . 140 C1
Red Cross Rd RG8 . . . 249 B3
Red Hill RG9 . . . 253 C3
Red House Dr RG4 . . . 253 A3
Red House Rd OX15 . . . 22 C4
Red La Ewelme RG9,OX49 206 B1
Woodcote RG8 . . . 240 B2
Red Lion Dr HP14 . . . 188 B3
Red Lion Sq OX1 . . . 123 B1
Red Lion St Cropredy OX17 . 4 C1
Kings Sutton OX17 . . . 23 C3
Red Poll Cl OX16 . . . 16 A4
Redberry Cl RG4 . . . 259 B3
Rede Cl OX3 . . . 124 C1
Redland Rd OX3 . . . 124 A3
Redlands Cl SN6 . . . 190 A2
Redmoor Cl OX4 . . . 142 B1
Redmoor Ct OX26 . . . 65 B2
Redwing Cl OX26 . . . 66 A1
Redwood Cl
Kingston Bagpuize OX13 . . 156 C1
Oxford OX4 . . . 143 A1
Redwood Way RG31 . . . 257 B2
Reedmace Cl OX4 . . . 143 A1
Reedmace Rd OX26 . . . 65 C2
Reeds Cl OX12 . . . 214 B3
Reema Hos The SN6 . . . 190 A1
Regal Ct 13 OX26 . . . 65 C1
Regal Way SN7 . . . 172 C2
Regency Hts RG4 . . . 258 C2
Regent Gdns OX11 . . . 219 A4
Regent Mall 5 OX12 . . . 214 B2
Regent Mews SN7 . . . 172 C2
Regent St OX4 . . . 141 C4
Regents Park Coll OX1 . 123 B1
Regents Riverside 13
RG1 . . . 259 A1
Regis Pl OX12 . . . 214 A1
Reid Cl OX16 . . . 16 A3
Reid Pl OX25 . . . 63 A4
Remenham La RG9 . . . 244 C2
Remenham Row RG9 . . . 244 C1
Remus Gate NN13 . . . 24 A3
Remy Pl OX4 . . . 141 C3
Renault Ho OX4 . . . 141 C3
Rest Harrow 32 OX4 . . . 142 C1
Retford Cl RG5 . . . 260 C1
Retreat Gdns OX10 . . . 221 C4
Retreat La HP14 . . . 169 B1
Rewley Abbey Ct OX1 . 123 A1
Rewley Rd OX1 . . . 123 A1
Reynard Ct 3 OX26 . . . 65 C1
Reynolds Cl OX7 . . . 70 B1
Reynolds Way
Abingdon OX14 . . . 179 C3
East Challow OX12 . . . 213 C3
Rhigos RG4 . . . 258 C3
Rhine Cl RG4 . . . 259 B1
Rhodes Ho OX1 . . . 123 B1
Richard Gray Ct OX1 . . 123 A1
Richard Nevill Ct 2
RG4 . . . 259 B1
Richards La OX2 . . . 123 A4
Richards Way OX3 . . . 124 C1
Richardson Ct OX4 . . . 123 C1
Richens Dr OX18 . . . 115 B1
Richfield Ave RG1 . . . 258 C1
Richman Gdns OX16 . . . 15 C4
Richmere Rd OX11 . . . 218 C4
Richmond Rd
Oxford OX1 . . . 123 A1
Reading RG4 . . . 258 C2
Richmond St OX17 . . . 23 C3
Rickyard Cl OX1 . . . 123 A1
Rickyard The
Ardington OX12 . . . 215 B3
Chalgrove OX44 . . . 184 B3
Fulbrook OX18 . . . 100 C3
Shutford OX15 . . . 14 A3
Riddell Pl OX2 . . . 109 A1
Ride The OX13 . . . 158 A3
Riders Way OX39 . . . 168 B3
Ridge Cl OX16 . . . 16 B2
Ridge Hall Cl RG4 . . . 258 C2
Ridge The RG8 . . . 249 C1
Ridgefield Rd OX4 . . . 142 A4
Ridgemont Cl OX2 . . . 123 A4
Ridgemount Cl RG31 . . 257 A1
Ridgeway
Wargrave RG10 . . . 255 C1
Wootton (Oxford) OX1 . . . 140 B1
Ridgeway (YH) The★
OX12 . . . 232 B3
Ridgeway CE Prim Sch The
OX12 . . . 213 A2
Ridgeway Cl RG9 . . . 223 B2
Ridgeway Rd
Didcot OX11 . . . 218 C4
Oxford OX3 . . . 124 C2
Ridgeway The
Bloxham OX15 . . . 21 C2
Nettlebed RG9 . . . 224 B1
Reading RG4 . . . 259 A2
Wantage OX12 . . . 232 B3
Riding La OX29 . . . 103 B4
Riding The OX29 . . . 86 C1
Ridings Bglws OX29 . . . 86 C2
Ridings The Banbury OX16 16 C4
Kidlington OX5 . . . 92 B1
Oxford OX3 . . . 142 C4
Reading RG4 . . . 259 B4
Stonesfield OX29 . . . 89 B4
Ridley Rd OX4 . . . 142 C3
Riely Cl OX29 . . . 90 B1
Riley Cl OX14 . . . 179 B3
Riley Dr OX16 . . . 15 C4
Riley Ho OX4 . . . 142 B2
Rimes Cl OX13 . . . 156 C1
Rimmer Cl OX3 . . . 123 C3
Ringwood Rd
Oxford OX3 . . . 125 A2
Reading RG30 . . . 258 A1
Ripley Ave OX29 . . . 102 C1
Ripley Rd RG30 . . . 258 A1
Ripon Coll OX44 . . . 144 A2
Rippington Dr OX3 . . . 123 C2
Rise The Adderbury OX17 . . 23 A2
Aston Rowant OX39 . . . 167 C2
Islip OX5 . . . 93 C1
Reading RG4 . . . 259 A2
Rising Hill OX25 . . . 48 C1
Rissington Cl RG31 . . . 257 C2
Rissington Dr OX28 . . . 117 C4
Rivacres RG8 . . . 250 C2
River & Rowing Mus★
RG9 . . . 244 C1
River Cl OX14 . . . 179 C3
River Gdns RG8 . . . 257 B3
River Rd RG4 . . . 258 B2
River View
Kennington OX1 . . . 141 C1
Sandford-on-T OX4 . . . 161 A4
Rivermead Rd OX4 . . . 141 C2
Rivermead Rehabilitation Ctr
OX1 . . . 141 C3
Riverside OX16 . . . 16 C3
Riverside Ct Oxford OX1 . 141 B4
3 Reading RG4 . . . 259 A1
Riverside Gdns OX28 . . . 104 A1
Riverside Rd OX2 . . . 122 C1
Riverview Rd RG8 . . . 256 B3
Rivington Glebe GL56 . . . 27 A1
Rivy Cl OX14 . . . 180 B4
Road Eight OX11 . . . 217 A1
Road Eighteen OX11 . . . 217 A1
Road Eleven OX11 . . . 217 A1
Road Fifteen OX11 . . . 217 A1
Road Five OX11 . . . 217 A1
Road Four OX11 . . . 217 A1
Road Nine OX11 . . . 217 A1
Road One OX11 . . . 217 A1
Road Six OX11 . . . 217 A1
Road Thirteen OX11 . . . 217 A1
Road Twelve OX11 . . . 217 A1
Road Two OX11 . . . 217 A1
Roadside Cotts SN7 . . . 171 A3
Robert Palmer Cotts The
RG4 . . . 260 B2
Robert Piggott CE Prim Sch
RG10 . . . 255 B1
Robert Robinson Ave
OX4 . . . 142 B1
Robert Sparrow Gdns
OX10 . . . 222 A3
Roberts Cl OX3 . . . 125 A2
Robin Hill OX29 . . . 90 A2
Robin Pl OX4 . . . 142 C1
Robins Cl
Barford St M OX15 . . . 32 C3
Great Rollright OX7 . . . 29 A2
Robins Mead RG8 . . . 239 B2
Robins Platt OX39 . . . 168 A3
Robins Way OX26 . . . 81 A4
Robinson Cl
Blewbury OX11 . . . 237 A4
Carterton OX18 . . . 115 B2
Robinswood OX16 . . . 16 A2
Robsart Pl OX2 . . . 139 C2
Rochester Ave RG5 . . . 260 C1
Rochester Pl OX7 . . . 73 B2
Rochester Way OX17 . . . 23 A3
Rochford Gdns OX26 . . . 66 A2
Rock Cl OX18 . . . 115 B2
Rock Edge OX3 . . . 124 B1
Rock Farm La OX4 . . . 161 A4
Rock Hill OX7 . . . 42 C2
Rock Rd OX18 . . . 115 B2
Rock The OX15 . . . 32 C3
Rockbourne Gdns RG30 258 A1
Rockhill Farm Ct OX7 . . 42 C2
Rocky La RG9 . . . 243 A2
Roding Way OX11 . . . 201 A1
Rodney Pl OX13 . . . 156 B2
Rodway Rd RG30 . . . 257 C1
Roebuck Ct OX11 . . . 219 A4
Roebuck Rise RG31 . . . 257 B2
Roentgen Ave OX11 . . . 217 A1
Rofford La OX44 . . . 164 A2
Roger Bacon La 2 OX1 141 B4
Roger Dudman Way
OX1,OX2 . . . 123 A1
Rogers St OX2 . . . 123 A4
Rokeby Dr RG4 . . . 258 B4
Rolfe Pl OX3 . . . 124 A2
Rollright Stones★ OX7 . . 28 A1
Rolls Ct OX12 . . . 214 B3
Roman Pl OX11 . . . 200 B1
Roman Rd OX33 . . . 144 B4
Roman Way Beckley OX3 111 A2
Bicester OX26 . . . 65 C1
Brackley NN13 . . . 24 A4
Lechlade GL7 . . . 150 B3
Oxford OX4 . . . 142 C3
Wantage OX12 . . . 214 B3
Roman Wlk SN6 . . . 191 C1
Romany Cl RG30 . . . 258 A1
Romany La RG30 . . . 258 A1
Romney Rd OX16 . . . 8 C1
Romsey Rd RG30 . . . 258 A1
Romulus Way NN13 . . . 24 A3
Rookery Cl
Abingdon OX13 . . . 159 A1
Bodicote OX15 . . . 22 C4
Rookery Ho OX44 . . . 143 C1
Rookery The OX5 . . . 92 B1
Rookery Way OX26 . . . 65 B2
Rooks La OX9 . . . 147 C4
Roosevelt Dr OX3 . . . 124 B1
Roosevelt Rd OX29 . . . 106 A4
Rope Way OX15 . . . 30 A3
Rope Wlk OX16 . . . 16 B3
Roper Rd OX25 . . . 63 B4
Rosamund Dr OX20 . . . 91 A4
Rosamund Rd OX2 . . . 122 C4
Rose Ave OX14 . . . 159 C2
Rose Cl Bucknell OX27 . . . 64 C4
Carterton OX18 . . . 115 B1
Rose Cnr HP14 . . . 188 C3
Rose Ct 6 OX4 . . . 142 A2
Rose Gdns OX2 . . . 140 B4
Rose Hill OX4 . . . 142 A2
Rose Hill Fst Sch OX4 . 142 A2
Rose La OX1 . . . 123 B1
Rose Pl OX1 . . . 141 B4
Rosebay Cres OX12 . . . 214 B4
Rosebery Rd RG4 . . . 258 B4
Rosedale Ave OX16 . . . 9 A1
Rosehill Ho RG4 . . . 259 B4
Rosehill Pk RG4 . . . 259 B4
Rosemary Ct OX4 . . . 141 C4
Rosemary La OX18 . . . 134 C2
Rosemead Ave RG31 . . . 257 A2
Roses La OX7 . . . 41 C3
Rosina Wlk OX16 . . . 9 A1
Ross Rd 11 RG4 . . . 259 A1
Rossendale Rd RG4 . . . 259 B2
Rotha Field Rd OX2 . . . 109 A1
Rother Garth OX11 . . . 201 A2
Rother Rd OX16 . . . 8 C1
Rotherfield Rd RG9 . . . 254 C4
Rotherfield Way RG4 . . . 259 A2
Rothwell Gdns RG5 . . . 260 C1
Rothwell Wlk RG4 . . . 259 B1
Rothwells Cl OX10 . . . 221 A1
Rotten Row OX10 . . . 182 B1
Round Close Rd
Adderbury OX17 . . . 22 C2
Hook Norton OX15 . . . 30 A4
Roundham Cl OX5 . . . 92 B1
Roundhead Dr OX9 . . . 129 C1
Roundhill Rd OX17 . . . 4 A2
Roundhills Mead SN6 . . 190 A4
Roundtown OX17 . . . 35 B4
Roundway The OX3 . . . 124 C2
Rouses La GL7 . . . 132 A3
Rousham Pk★ OX25 . . . 62 A3
Rousham Rd OX5 . . . 77 B4
Routh Rd OX3 . . . 124 C2
Roves La SN6 . . . 208 A4
Row La RG4 . . . 259 C4
Row The Bletchingdon OX5 . 93 A4
Hinton Waldrist SN7 . . . 155 C1
Lechlade GL7 . . . 150 C4
Lyneham OX7 . . . 70 B3
Mollington OX17 . . . 3 C2
Stanton Harcourt OX29 . . 138 A4
Wootton OX20 . . . 75 B4
Rowallan Cl RG4 . . . 259 B3
Rowan Cl Carterton OX18 115 B2
Kidlington OX5 . . . 108 C4
Sonning Common RG4 . . . 252 C2
Rowan Gr OX4 . . . 143 A1
Rowan Rd OX26 . . . 65 C2
Rowans The OX10 . . . 220 C1
Rowel Dr OX5 . . . 92 A1
Rowell Way OX7 . . . 42 C2
Rowland Cl
Cutteslowe OX2 . . . 122 C4
Wallingford OX10 . . . 203 B1
Rowland Rd OX10 . . . 221 A1
Rowlands Ho OX3 . . . 125 A2
Rowles Cl OX1 . . . 141 C1
Rowles Paddock RG20 . 235 A1
Rowney Pl OX4 . . . 142 A2
Rowstock OX11 . . . 217 A4
Roxburgh Dr OX11 . . . 200 B2
Royal Berkshire Ct
OX11 . . . 218 C4
Royal Mans RG9 . . . 244 C1
Royal Military Coll of Science
SN6 . . . 209 C4
Ruck Keene Cl OX26 . . . 65 B1
Rufus Isaacs Rd RG4 . . . 259 A1
Rugge Furlong OX11 . . . 201 A1
Rumbolds Cl OX10 . . . 203 C3
Rumsey's La OX11 . . . 237 A4
Rupert Cl RG9 . . . 244 C2
Rupert House Sch RG9 . 244 C1
Rupert Rd
Chalgrove OX44 . . . 184 B3
Oxford OX4 . . . 142 C3
Rupert Way OX9 . . . 130 A1
Rupert's La RG9 . . . 244 C2
Ruscote Arc OX16 . . . 16 A4
Ruscote Ave OX16 . . . 16 A4
Ruscote Sq OX16 . . . 16 A4
Rush Common Cty Prim Sch
OX14 . . . 160 A1
Rushall Rd OX9 . . . 130 A1
Rushbeds Wood Nature
Reserve★ HP18 . . . 98 B2
Rushmead Copse OX14 . 160 B1
Ruskin Ave OX14 . . . 179 C3
Ruskin Cl OX11 . . . 219 A4
Ruskin Coll Oxford OX1 . 123 A1
Oxford,Headington OX3 . . 124 B2
Ruskin Rd OX16 . . . 16 B2
Ruskin Wlk OX26 . . . 65 C2
Russell Ct OX2 . . . 123 A2
Russell Jackson Cl
OX10 . . . 182 B3
Russell Rd RG4 . . . 258 B4
Russell St OX2 . . . 123 A1
Russet Ave GL7 . . . 150 C2
Russet Cl RG4 . . . 252 C3
Russet Glade RG4 . . . 259 B4
Russet Rd OX27 . . . 50 B2
Rutherfield Cl OX14 . . . 160 A1
Rutherford Ave OX11 . . . 217 A2
Rutherway OX2 . . . 123 A2
Rutten La OX5 . . . 108 A3
Rutters Cl OX5 . . . 108 B4
Rycote La OX9 . . . 146 B3
Rycotewood Coll OX9 . . 129 C1
Rydal Ave RG30 . . . 257 C1
Ryder Cl OX5 . . . 108 A3
Rydes Cl OX15 . . . 22 C4
Rydes The OX15 . . . 22 C4
Rye Cl OX16 . . . 8 C1
Rye Grass OX20 . . . 91 B3
Rye St Antony Sch OX3 124 A2
Ryecote Chapel★ OX9 . 146 B3
Ryecroft Cl Sonning RG5 . 260 C1
Wargrave RG10 . . . 255 C1
Rymans Cres OX11 . . . 219 A3
Rymers La OX4 . . . 142 A3

S

Sackville Cl OX17 . . . 8 C2
Sacred Heart RC Prim Sch
RG9 . . . 244 B1
Sadler Wlk OX1 . . . 141 A4
Sadlers Croft OX44 . . . 143 C1
Sadlers Ct OX14 . . . 160 A2
Sadlers The RG31 . . . 257 A1
Saffron Cl OX26 . . . 65 B3
Saffron Ct OX14 . . . 180 A4
Sage Rd RG31 . . . 257 B2
Sage Wlk 18 OX4 . . . 142 C1
St Alban's Ct 13 OX10 . . 221 B4
St Aldates OX1 . . . 141 B4
St Aloysius RC Fst Sch
OX2 . . . 123 A2
St Amand Dr OX14 . . . 179 C3
St Amand's RC Prim Sch
OX12 . . . 216 C3
St Andrew's CE Inf Sch
OX39 . . . 168 B4
St Andrew's CE Prim Sch
OX39 . . . 168 B4
St Andrew's La OX3 . . . 124 B2
St Andrew's Rd
Chinnor OX39 . . . 168 B3
Didcot OX11 . . . 218 C4
Henley-on-T RG9 . . . 254 B4
Oxford OX3 . . . 124 B2
St Andrews CE Fst Sch
OX3 . . . 124 B2
St Andrews Cl OX14 . . . 160 B1
St Andrews Ct OX9 . . . 147 C4
St Andrews Ho OX39 . . . 168 B3
St Andrews Rd RG4 . . . 258 C2
St Anne's Cl RG9 . . . 244 B1
St Anne's Coll OX2 . . . 123 B2
St Anne's Rd
Banbury OX16 . . . 16 B2
Oxford OX3 . . . 124 B1
St Annes Cl OX26 . . . 65 C2
St Annes Ct OX11 . . . 219 A4
St Annes RC Prim Sch
RG4 . . . 259 A1
St Annes Rd RG4 . . . 259 A1
St Anthony's Wlk OX26 . . 66 A2
St Antonys Coll OX2 . . . 123 A2
St Augustine of Canterbury
RC/CE Upper Sch OX4 141 C3
St Barnabas CE Fst Sch
OX2 . . . 123 A1
St Barnabas Rd RG4 . . . 259 A3
St Barnabas St OX2 . . . 123 A1
St Bernard's Rd OX2 . . . 123 A2
St Birinus Ct GL7 . . . 150 B3
St Birinus Sch
Didcot OX11 . . . 218 C4
Dorchester OX10 . . . 182 B1
St Catherine's Coll OX1 123 C1
St Catherines Ho OX4 . . 123 C1
St Christopher's CE Fst Sch
OX4 . . . 142 B3
St Christopher's CE Prim Sch
GL7 . . . 132 B1
St Christopher's Pl OX4 142 B3
St Clement's St OX4 . . . 123 C1
St Cristopher Cotts SN7 172 C2
St Cross Bldg OX1 . . . 123 B1
St Cross Rd OX1 . . . 123 B1
St David's Ct NN13 . . . 24 A4
St Davids Cl RG4 . . . 258 C3
St Denys Cl SN7 . . . 194 C4
St Ebbe's CE Fst Sch
OX1 . . . 141 B4
St Ebbes St 3 OX1 . . . 141 B4
St Edburg's Cl OX26 . . . 65 B1
St Edburg's Prim Sch
OX26 . . . 65 C1
St Edith's Way OX26 . . . 65 B1
St Edmund's La 5
OX14 . . . 179 C3
St Edmund's RC Prim Sch
OX14 . . . 180 A4
St Edward's Ave OX2 . . . 123 A4
St Edwards Ct OX2 . . . 123 A3
St Edwards Sch OX2 . . . 123 A4
St Francis CE Fst Sch
OX4 . . . 142 C3
St Francis Ct OX3 . . . 142 C4
St Francis Rd HP14 . . . 189 B2
St Frideswides Ct OX11 218 C4
St George's Cl OX10 . . . 220 C1
St George's Cres OX16 . . 16 B2
St George's Pl OX1 . . . 123 B1
St George's Rd SN7 . . . 154 B1
St Georges Gate 6
OX1 . . . 123 A1
St Georges Gn OX10 . . . 203 B1
St Georges Rd OX10 . . . 221 B4
St Giles OX5 . . . 93 A4
St Giles Cl OX26 . . . 80 A2
St Giles' OX1 . . . 123 B1
St Helen's Ave OX10 . . . 203 C2
St Helen's Cres OX10 . . . 204 A2
St Helen's Ct OX14 . . . 179 C3
St Helen's Mews 6
OX14 . . . 179 C3
St Helen's Pas OX1 . . . 123 B1
St Helen's Way OX10 . . . 203 C2
St Helen's Wharf OX14 . 179 C3
St Hilda's Cl OX26 . . . 65 C2
St Hilda's Coll OX4 . . . 141 C4
St Hildas Cl OX11 . . . 219 A4
St Hugh's Cl
Bicester OX26 . . . 65 C2
Stokenchurch HP14 . . . 188 C2
St Hugh's Coll OX2 . . . 123 A2
St Hugh's Pl HP14 . . . 188 C2
St Hugh's Sch SN7 . . . 174 A4
St Hughs Cl OX16 . . . 16 B2
St Hughs Rise OX11 . . . 219 A4
St Ives La OX12 . . . 214 C4
St Ives Rd OX12 . . . 214 C4
St James OX12 . . . 214 B3
St James Cl RG8 . . . 256 B3
St James Ct OX29 . . . 89 B4
St James Rd OX14 . . . 160 C2
St James Terr OX14 . . . 160 C1
St James View OX12 . . . 197 A3
St James' Tutorial Unit
OX4 . . . 142 A2
St John Fisher RC Fst Sch
OX4 . . . 142 B2
St John St OX1 . . . 123 B1
St John's Cl Didcot OX11 219 A4
Fyfield OX13 . . . 157 A1
St John's Coll OX1 . . . 123 B1
St John's Ct
12 Banbury OX16 . . . 16 B3
Grove OX12 . . . 196 C1
St John's Gn OX10 . . . 221 B3
St John's Prim Sch
OX10 . . . 221 B4
St John's RC Prim Sch
OX16 . . . 16 C2
St John's Rd
Abingdon OX14 . . . 180 A4
Banbury OX16 . . . 16 B3
Grove OX12 . . . 196 C1
Reading RG4 . . . 259 B1
Wallingford OX10 . . . 221 B4
St John's Row OX14 . . . 201 B4
St John's St Bicester OX26 65 C1
Lechlade GL7 . . . 150 B2
St John's Terr 6 OX10 . 221 B4
St John's Way OX15 . . . 33 A2
St Johns Dr
Carterton OX18 . . . 115 C2
Kidlington OX5 . . . 92 C1
St Johns Rd OX5 . . . 77 B3
St Joseph's RC Fst Sch
OX3 . . . 124 A2
St Joseph's RC Prim Sch
OX16 . . . 15 C3
St Joseph's RC Prim Sch
OX18 . . . 115 B1
St Joseph's RC Prim Sch
OX9 . . . 147 C4
St Katherine's Rd RG9 . 254 B4

St Kenelm's CE Prim Sch OX29 .102 C1
St Kenelm's Cl OX29 .102 C1
St Laurence's CE Prim Sch OX10 .203 A4
St Lawrence Cl OX10 .203 A4
St Lawrence Ho OX10 .203 A4
St Lawrence Rd
Lechlade GL7 .150 B2
South Hinksey OX1 .141 A3
St Lawrence's CE Prim Sch GL7 .150 B2
St Leonard's CE Prim Sch OX16 .16 C3
St Leonard's Cl OX16 .16 C3
St Leonard's Ct OX10 .221 B3
St Leonard's La OX10 .221 B4
St Leonard's Rd OX3 .124 B2
St Leonard's Sq 17 OX10 .221 B4
St Leonards Cl OX49 .186 A1
St Lucian's La OX10 .221 B3
St Luke's Rd OX4 .142 B3
St Lukes Ct RG4 .259 A2
St Lukes Way RG4 .259 A3
St Margaret's Rd OX2 .123 A2
St Mark's Rd RG9 .254 B4
St Martin's Rd OX4 .142 A2
St Martin's St OX10 .221 B4
St Martins RC Prim Sch RG4 .259 C3
St Mary & John CE Fst Sch OX4 .142 A4
St Mary's CE Inf Sch OX28 .118 A4
St Mary's CE Prim Sch
Banbury OX16 .16 B3
Chipping Norton OX7 .42 C1
St Mary's Cl
3 Banbury OX16 .16 B3
Bicester OX26 .65 B1
Chalgrove OX44 .184 B3
Henley-on-T RG9 .254 A4
Kidlington OX5 .92 C1
Oxford OX4 .142 A1
St Mary's Ct OX28 .118 A4
St Mary's Gn OX14 .159 C1
St Mary's Ho OX33 .144 A4
St Mary's La OX7 .30 C2
St Mary's Mead OX28 .118 A4
St Mary's RC Prim Sch OX26 .65 C1
St Mary's Rd
Adderbury OX17 .22 C1
East Hendred OX12 .216 C3
Oxford OX4 .141 C4
St Mary's Sch OX12 .214 B2
St Mary's St OX10 .221 B4
St Mary's Way OX12 .214 B3
St Mary's Wlk OX27 .50 B2
St Marys Ave RG8 .257 B3
St Marys Cl OX33 .144 A4
St Michael's Ave
Abingdon OX14 .179 C4
Highworth SN6 .190 A3
St Michael's CE Prim Sch OX13 .198 C2
St Michael's Cl OX27 .52 B3
St Michael's La OX5 .107 C4
St Michael's St OX1 .123 B1
St Michael's Way OX13 .198 C2
St Michaels CE Fst Sch OX3 .123 C1
St Michaels Cl OX7 .85 B4
St Nicholas CE Inf Sch OX10 .203 B1
St Nicholas CE Prim Sch SN8 .245 C1
St Nicholas Fst Sch OX3 .123 C3
St Nicholas Rd
Oxford OX4 .142 B1
Tackley OX5 .77 B3
Wallingford OX10 .221 B4
St Nicholas' Gn OX14 .159 C1
St Nicolas CE Sch OX14 179 C4
St Omer Rd OX4 .142 B3
St Paul's Cres OX2 .140 B4
St Pauls Arts Ctr★ OX2 123 A1
St Peter's CE Inf Sch OX18 .133 B3
St Peter's CE Prim Sch OX29 .107 B1
St Peter's Cl
Cassington OX29 .107 B1
Stoke Lyne OX27 .51 A3
Wootton (Oxford) OX13 .159 A3
St Peter's Coll OX1 .123 B1
St Peter's Cres OX26 .65 C2
St Peter's Pl 22 OX10 .221 B4
St Peter's Rd
Abingdon OX14 .160 B1
Brackley NN13 .24 A4
Cutteslowe OX2 .122 C4
Didcot OX11 .218 C4
St Peter's St OX10 .221 B4
St Peters Ave RG4 .258 C2
St Peters Cl OX15 .31 C4
St Peters Gate NN13 .24 A4
St Peters Hill RG4 .258 C2
St Philip & St James CE Fst Sch OX2 .123 A2
St Ruald's Cl 10 OX10 .221 B4
St Rumbold's Rd OX10 .221 B4
St Stephens Cl 6 RG4 .259 A1
St Swithun's CE Prim Sch OX1 .160 C4
St Swithun's Rd OX1 .160 C4
St Thomas Moore RC Sch OX5 .108 C4
St Thomas St OX15 .33 C2
St Thomas' St OX1 .123 A1
St Thomas's Cl SN7 .155 C1
Salegate La OX4 .142 B3
Salesian Gdns OX4 .142 B3
Salesian Ho OX4 .142 B3
Salford Rd OX3 .123 C2
Salisbury Cres OX2 .123 A4
Sallow Cl OX26 .65 C3
Salmon Cl OX15 .21 C3
Salop Cl SN6 .209 A3
Salt La OX9 .166 C1
Salter Cl OX1 .141 B4
Salters La HP18 .98 B4
Salvia Cl OX16 .9 A1
Samian Way OX10 .202 B4
Samor Way OX11 .218 B4
Samphire Rd OX4 .142 C1
Samuelson Ct 25 OX16 .16 B3
Sand Hill SN6 .209 A4
Sand View SN7 .172 C1
Sandcroft Rd RG4 .258 C3
Sandell Cl OX16 .16 B3
Sanderling Cl OX26 .81 A4
Sanderling Wlk OX16 .16 C2
Sandfield Rd OX3 .124 A2
Sandfine Rd OX15 .15 A1
Sandford Cl
Abingdon OX14 .160 A1
Woodcote RG8 .250 C4
Sandford Dr RG5 .260 C1
Sandford Gn OX16 .15 C4
Sandford La OX1 .160 C4
Sandford Mount OX7 .73 B2
Sandford Pk OX7 .73 B2
Sandford Rd OX4 .142 A1
Sandford Rise OX7 .73 B2
Sandford St Martin Rd OX7 .46 B1
Sandgate Ave RG30 .257 C1
Sandhill Rd OX5 .108 A4
Sandhills Prim Sch OX3 125 A2
Sandleigh Rd OX13 .159 A4
Sandpiper Cl OX26 .81 A4
Sandpit Hill MK18 .39 C3
Sandpit La RG4 .259 C4
Sandringham Dr OX11 .219 A4
Sandringham Rd OX17 .23 C3
Sands Cl Bletchingdon OX5 93 A4
Cumnor OX2 .139 C3
Sands La OX15 .31 C4
Sands Rd OX11 .219 C3
Sands The Benson OX10 .204 B3
Milton-u-W OX7 .70 A1
Sands Way OX10 .203 C3
Sandy La Beckley OX3 .111 A1
Cholsey OX10 .220 C1
Kingston Bagpuize OX13 .156 C1
Long Crendon HP18 .129 A3
Oxford OX4 .142 C2
Shrivenham SN6 .209 A3
Stanford in the V SN7 .174 B2
Tiddington OX9 .145 C3
Upper Rissington GL54 .68 A2
Wootton (Oxford) OX1 .140 B1
Yarnton OX5 .108 B4
Sandy La W OX4 .142 B2
Sandy Lane Ct GL54 .68 A2
Sandy Lane Est OX9 .145 C4
Sarajac Ave OX12 .213 C2
Sarsden Cl OX7 .57 A1
Sarum Cl OX18 .115 C2
Satin La OX15 .33 C2
Satwell Cl RG9 .243 A2
Saunders Cl OX49 .186 A1
Saunders Ct RG8 .257 A3
Saunders Rd OX4 .142 A3
Saunders Wood Copse HP14 .188 C2
Savile Rd OX1 .123 B1
Savile Way OX12 .196 B1
Saw Cl OX44 .184 B4
Sawpit Rd OX4 .142 C2
Sawpits La GL56 .40 A1
Saxel Cl OX18 .135 C2
Saxifrage Sq 5 OX4 .142 C1
Saxon Cl OX10 .221 B4
Saxon Ct Benson OX10 .203 C2
Bicester OX26 .65 C1
Saxon Orch SN6 .191 B1
Saxon Pl OX12 .214 A3
Saxon Way Oxford OX3 .124 A2
Witney OX28 .118 A4
Saxons Heath OX14 .201 B4
Saxons Way OX11 .219 A4
Saxton Rd OX14 .179 C3
Sayers Orch OX11 .200 B1
Scafell Cl RG31 .257 B1
Scampton Cl OX26 .66 A2
Schilling St OX25 .63 A4
Schofield Ave OX28 .104 A2
Schofield Gdns OX28 .104 A2
Schofields Way OX15 .21 C3
Scholar Cl SN6 .191 C1
Scholar Pl OX2 .140 B4
Scholars Acre OX18 .115 B2
Scholars Cl RG4 .258 C2
Schongau Cl OX14 .179 B2
School Cl Ickford HP18 .128 A2
Long Compton CV36 .27 C3
Longworth OX13 .156 B2
Steventon OX13 .198 C2
School Cotts RG9 .243 B1
School End OX17 .35 B4
School Hill
Minster Lovell OX29 .102 C2
Mollington OX17 .3 C2
Wargrave RG10 .255 B1
School La
Appleford OX14 .200 C4
Aston Rowant OX49 .167 C2
Banbury OX16 .16 B3
Black Bourton OX18 .133 C3
Chilson OX7 .71 C2
Coleshill SN6 .191 A4
Great Bourton OX17 .9 B4
Harwell OX11 .217 C4
Kingston Bagpuize OX13 .156 C1
Middleton Stoney OX25 .64 A2
Milton OX14 .199 B3
Milton, Milton Heights OX14 .199 B2
Minster Lovell OX29 .102 C2
North Newington OX15 .15 B2
Reading RG4 .259 A1
Reading, Emmer Green RG4 .259 A3
Shabbington HP18 .128 B2
Stadhampton OX44 .163 B1
Stoke Lyne OX27 .51 A3
Stoke Row RG9 .241 C2
Upper Heyford OX25 .62 C4
Wargrave RG10 .255 B1
Warmington OX17 .3 A2
School of St Helen & St Katherine OX14 .179 B4
School Paddock OX27 .64 C4
School Pl OX1 .141 B3
School Rd
Ardington OX12 .215 B3
Finstock OX7 .88 B3
Kidlington OX5 .92 C1
West Hanney OX12 .196 C3
School View OX16 .16 C3
School Yd OX44 .163 B1
Schooler's La GL56 .40 B2
Scotland End OX15 .30 A4
Scotsgrove Cotts OX9 .130 A2
Scott Cl Bicester OX26 .65 B2
Kidlington OX5 .108 B4
Reading RG4 .259 A3
Scott Rd OX2 .123 A4
Scotts Cnr NN13 .25 A2
Scotts La OX27 .67 C1
Scours La RG30 .258 A1
Scrutton Cl OX3 .124 C2
Seacourt Rd OX2 .122 B1
Sealham Rd OX29 .118 A2
Second Ave OX11 .200 B1
Second St
Croughton NN13 .36 C3
Harwell OX11 .217 B2
Sedgefield Cl RG4 .252 C3
Sedgemoor Dr OX9 .130 A1
Sedgewell Rd RG4 .252 C3
Seelscheid Way OX26 .81 A4
Seeson Way OX12 .214 B2
Sefton Pl OX15 .22 C4
Sefton Rd OX3 .124 C2
Segsbury Ct OX12 .214 A3
Segsbury Rd OX12 .214 A3
Selborne Gdns RG30 .258 A1
Sellwood Dr OX18 .115 C2
Sellwood Rd OX14 .159 C1
Selwyn Cres OX14 .160 C1
Send Rd RG4 .259 B1
Sermon Cl OX3 .124 C1
Setler Ho 1 OX16 .16 C3
Setts The SN7 .172 C1
Seven Acres
Long Crendon HP18 .129 A4
Thame OX9 .148 A4
Sevenfields SN6 .190 A4
Seventeenth St OX11 .217 A1
Seventh Ave OX3 .142 C4
Severalls Cl OX10 .203 B1
Severn Cl OX26 .65 A2
Severn Rd
Abingdon OX13 .159 B1
Harwell OX11 .217 A1
Sewell Cl OX14 .160 B1
Sewell's La OX39 .167 C4
Seyer Milward Terr 24 OX10 .221 B4
Shackleton Cl 4 OX26 .66 A2
Shades The OX16 .16 B3
Shadwell Rd OX10 .182 B3
Shaftesbury Rd OX3 .124 C3
Shakenoak OX29 .105 B3
Shakespeare Cl RG4 .259 B3
Shakespeare Dr OX26 .65 B2
Shakespeare Rd OX29 .120 B4
Shannon Cl OX12 .196 C1
Shannon Rd OX26 .65 A1
Sharland Cl OX12 .214 C4
Sharman Beer Ct OX9 .147 C4
Sharpey Cotts OX26 .66 C1
Shaw Cl OX26 .65 B2
Shaw's Copse OX14 .160 C1
Sheards La SN7 .194 C4
Shearings The OX15 .30 A4
Shearwater Dr OX26 .81 A4
Sheen Cl OX27 .65 C3
Sheep St Bicester OX26 .65 C1
Burford OX18 .100 C3
Charlbury OX7 .73 A2
Highworth SN6 .190 A3
Sheep Wlk RG4 .259 A2
Sheepwash La OX13 .199 A3
Sheepway Ct 2 OX4 .142 A2
Sheepways La RG4 .258 A4
Sheerstock HP17 .130 C3
Sheldon Rd HP18 .128 A2
Sheldon Way OX4 .142 B2
Sheldonian★ OX1 .123 B1
Sheldons Piece OX49 .186 A1
Shelford Pl OX3 .124 B1
Shelley Cl
Abingdon OX14 .160 A1
Banbury OX16 .16 A2
9 Bicester OX26 .65 B2
Oxford OX3 .124 C1
Shelley Rd OX4 .142 A3
Shellingford CE Prim Sch SN7 .193 C4
Shenington CE Prim Sch OX15 .6 C1
Shenington Kart Club★ OX15 .6 B1
Shepard Way OX7 .42 C2
Shepherd Gdns OX14 .179 B3
Shepherds Cl
Grove OX12 .196 B1
Sibford Gower OX15 .19 A4
Weston-on-the-G OX25 .79 A1
Shepherds Hill
Sandford-on-T OX4 .142 C1
Sonning RG6 .260 B1
Shepherds La RG4 .258 B3
Sheraton Dr RG31 .257 B1
Sherborne St GL7 .150 B2
Sherbourne Rd OX28 .117 B4
Sheridan Ave RG4 .259 A2
Sheriff's Dr OX2 .122 C4
Sherwood Ave OX14 .180 A4
Sherwood Cl OX26 .66 B1
Sherwood Gdns RG9 .254 B4
Sherwood Pl RG8 .257 A2
Sherwood Rd OX11 .218 B4
Sherwood Rise RG8 .257 A3
Shifford La OX29 .137 B1
Shilbrook Manor OX18 .133 C2
Shillbrook Ave OX18 .115 B3
Shilldeane Dr OX18 .115 B2
Shilson La OX7 .73 A2
Shilton Rd Burford OX18 .100 C2
Carterton OX18 .115 B2
Ship St OX1 .123 B1
Shiplake Bottom RG9 .252 C3
Shiplake CE Prim Sch RG9 .254 C1
Shiplake Coll RG9 .254 C1
Shiplake Sta RG9 .255 A2
Shipston Rd CV36 .27 C4
Shipton Cl RG31 .257 B1
Shipton Rd
Ascott-u-W OX7 .71 A1
Shipton-u-W OX7 .70 A1
Woodstock OX20 .91 B3
Shipton Sta OX7 .70 C1
Shirburn Rd OX49 .186 B1
Shirburn St OX49 .186 B1
Shirelake Cl OX1 .141 B4
Shires Bsns Pk The NN13 .24 A3
Shires Rd NN13 .24 A3
Shirley Pl OX2 .123 A2
Shirvell's Hill RG8 .250 C4
Shoe La
East Hagbourne OX11 .218 C3
Oxford OX1 .123 B1
Shooters Hill RG8 .256 A3
Short Furlong OX11 .201 A1
Short St Pangbourne RG8 256 B3
1 Reading RG4 .259 A1
Watchfield SN6 .191 B1
Short The RG8 .257 B3
Shorte Cl OX3 .142 C4
Shortlands Hill OX10 .238 B2
Shotover SN7 .211 B3
Shotover Ctry Pk★ OX3 125 A1
Shotover Kilns OX3 .124 C1
Shotover Trad Est OX3 .124 C1
Shrewsbury Pl OX18 .134 C2
Shrieves Cl OX14 .160 A1
Shrivenham CE Prim Sch SN6 .209 A4
Shrivenham Hundred SN6 .191 B1
Shrivenham Rd
Highworth SN6 .190 A2
Longcot SN7 .192 B1
Shrubbery The GL7 .150 B2
Shute Ave SN6 .209 B4
Shutford Rd
North Newington OX15 .15 A2
Tadmarton OX15 .20 C4
Sibford Gower Prim Sch OX15 .19 A4
Sibford Rd
Hook Norton OX15 .30 A4
Shutford OX15 .13 C2
Sibford Sch OX15 .19 A4
Sideleigh Rd OX15 .22 C4
Sidings Ind Est The NN13 .24 A4
Sidings Rd OX7 .55 C3
Sidney St OX4 .141 C4
Signet End OX18 .100 C2
Silkdale Cl OX4 .142 B3
Silver Birches OX33 .125 C4
Silver La OX12 .213 B3
Silver Rd OX4 .142 A4
Silver St Bourton SN6 .209 A1
Chacombe OX17 .10 C2
Fernham SN7 .193 A2
Tetsworth OX9 .166 A4
Wroxton OX15 .15 A4
Silverdale Rd RG10 .255 C1
Silvermead HP18 .127 B3
Silverthorne Dr RG4 .258 C3
Simmns Cl OX33 .125 B4
Simmonds Wlk OX12 .214 B3
Simmons Rd RG9 .244 B2
Simmons Way OX9 .129 C1
Simon Ho OX3 .124 B2
Simon's Cl OX33 .144 A4
Simons Cl RG31 .257 B2
Simons La OX7 .85 B4
Simpsons Way OX1 .160 C4
Sinclair Ave OX16 .16 A4
Sinclair Dr OX16 .16 A4
Singers Cl RG9 .254 C4
Singers La RG9 .244 C1
Singletree OX4 .142 A2
Sinnels Field OX7 .85 C4
Sinodum Cl OX14 .201 B4
Sinodun Rd Didcot OX11 .218 C4
Wallingford OX10 .203 B1
Sinodun Row OX14 .200 C4
Sinodun View OX10 .203 A4
Sint Niklaas Cl OX14 .179 B2
Sir Georges La OX17 .23 A2
Sir Mortimer's Terr OX14 .199 B3
Sires Hill OX10 .202 B2
Siskin Rd Bicester OX26 .66 A1
Upper Rissington GL54 .68 A3
Sixpenny La OX44 .184 C3
Sixteenth St OX11 .217 A2
Sixth St Croughton NN13 .36 C4
Harwell OX11 .217 A2
Skarries View RG4 .258 B4
Skelton Ct OX4 .123 C1
Skene Cl OX3 .124 B1
Skerrit Way RG8 .257 B2
Skilton Rd RG31 .257 B2
Skimmingdish La OX27 .65 C3
Skimmingdish Rd OX26 .66 A2
Skinner Rd OX26 .66 B1
Skippett La OX7 .88 A2
Skippon Way 6 OX9 .129 C1
Skittle Alley OX17 .35 B4
Slade Cl OX3 .124 B1
Slade End OX10 .202 C2
Slade End Rdbt OX10 .203 A1
Slade Farm Cotts OX5 .63 A1
Slade Rd Cholsey OX10 .221 A1
Didcot OX11 .200 B1
Stokenchurch HP14 .188 C2
Slade The Charlbury OX7 .73 B2
Oxford OX3 .142 C4
Slaters Ct OX29 .90 A1
Slave Hill HP17 .130 C3
Slaymaker Cl OX3 .124 C1
Sloan Cl RG8 .249 B3
Slopes The RG4 .259 B1
Small Ho OX15 .19 B4
Smith Barry Cir GL54 .68 A2
Smith Barry Cres GL54 .68 A2
Smith Barry Rd GL54 .68 A2
Smith Cl RG4 .252 C3
Smith's Cl OX18 .135 C1
Smith's Hill OX12 .231 C3
Smiths Farm La OX11 .200 B1
Smiths Rickyard OX12 .216 B4
Snakehill La OX15 .33 A2
Snipe Rd GL54 .68 A2
Snowdon Mede OX3 .124 A2
Snows La OX33 .125 B4
Snowshill Dr OX28 .103 B1
Snowsill Dr OX28 .117 B4
Snowswick La SN7 .170 C3
Snuff La OX17 .8 B4
Snuggs La OX12 .197 A4
Soane End RG4 .259 A4
Soden Pl OX13 .156 B1
Soden Rd OX25 .63 B4
Sollershott OX2 .108 C1
Solters Cl HP18 .98 B4
Somerton Rd Ardley OX27 50 A2
North Aston OX25 .48 A4
Upper Heyford OX25 .48 C1
Somerville OX11 .219 A4
Somerville Coll OX2 .123 B2
Somerville Ct OX17 .23 B2
Somerville Dr OX26 .65 C2
Songers Cl OX2 .140 A4
Sonning CE Prim Sch RG4 .260 B2
Sonning Common Prim Sch RG4 .252 C3
Sonning La RG4 .260 B1
Sonning Mdws RG4 .260 B1
Soot La OX17 .3 A2
Sopwith Rd GL54 .68 A3
Sorrel Mead OX26 .65 B2
Sorrel Rd OX4 .143 A1
Sotwell St
Brightwell-cum-S OX10 .202 C1
Brightwell-cum-S OX10 .203 A1
South Ave
Abingdon OX14 .159 C1
Henley-on-T RG9 .254 C4
Kidlington OX5 .108 C3
South Bank RG8 .239 B2
South Bar St OX16 .16 B3
South Bridge Row OX1 .141 B4
South Cl OX5 .108 C3
South Dr Harwell OX11 .217 B2
Sonning RG4 .260 B1
South End
Great Rollright OX7 .29 A2
Haddenham HP17 .130 C3
South Gate Ct GL54 .68 A2
South Hills HP18 .98 A1
South Leigh Rd OX29 .119 A4

South Lodge The 8 OX26 .65 C1
South Mdw OX25 .81 B2
South Mere OX18 .116 B2
South Moreton Sch OX11 .219 C3
South Newington Rd
Barford St M OX15 .32 B3
Bloxham OX15 .21 A1
South Par OX2 .123 A4
South Park Ave OX11 .218 B4
South Park Ct 6 OX4 .141 C4
South Parks Rd OX1 .123 B1
South Row OX11 .235 B4
South Side OX25 .62 A4
South St Banbury OX16 .16 C4
Blewbury OX11 .237 A4
Letcombe Bassett OX12 .214 A1
Lower Heyford OX25 .63 A3
Middle Barton OX7 .60 C4
Oxford OX2 .141 A4
Reading RG4 .259 A1
Watchfield SN6 .191 B1
South Stoke Cty Prim Sch RG8 .239 A2
South Stoke Rd RG8 .240 A1
South View
Great Bourton OX17 .9 B4
4 Wallingford OX10 .221 B4
South View Ave RG4 .259 B1
South View Pk RG4 .259 B1
Southam Rd
Banbury OX16, OX17 .9 B2
Mollington OX17 .4 A2
Southampton St SN7 .172 C2
Southby Cl OX13 .158 A4
Southcroft OX3 .123 C3
Southdale Rd OX2 .123 A4
Southdown Ct SN7 .194 C4
Southdown Rd RG4 .259 A3
Southend OX44 .162 C4
Southend Cotts OX5 .78 A2
Southern By-pass Rd
Kennington OX1 .141 B2
N Hinksey Village OX2 .140 C4
Oxford OX1,OX4 .141 C2
South Hinksey OX1 .141 A2
Southern Rd OX9 .147 C4
Southerndene Cl RG31 .257 B1
Southfield Dr OX14 .199 C4
Southfield La OX27 .49 C4
Southfield Pk OX4 .142 A4
Southfield Prim Sch SN6 .190 A3
Southfield Rd OX4 .142 A4
Southlands OX18 .135 C1
Southlawn OX28 .117 C4
Southmead Ind Pk OX11 .200 B2
Southmoor Pl OX2 .123 A2
Southmoor Rd OX2 .123 A2
Southmoor Way OX14 .179 C4
Southrop CE Prim Sch GL7 .131 A2
Southrop Rd OX15 .30 A3
Southwold 3 OX26 .65 C2
Southwold Cty Prim Sch OX26 .65 C3
Southwood Rd OX29 .103 B1
Sovereign Cl OX11 .219 A4
Spa Cl SN6 .190 A4
Span Hill RG4 .260 A4
Spareacre La OX29 .120 C4
Sparsey Pl OX2 .109 A1
Sparsholt St OX12 .212 C2
Spears The OX5 .108 A3
Speedwell Croft OX26 .65 C3
Speedwell Fst Sch OX4 142 A1
Speedwell St OX1 .141 B4
Spencer Ave OX5 .108 A3
Spencer Cres OX4 .142 A2
Spencer Ct 23 OX16 .16 B3
Spencers Cl SN7 .194 B4
Spendlove Ctr The OX7 .73 A2
Spenlove Cl OX14 .159 C1
Spenser Cl OX26 .65 B2
Spey Rd OX13 .159 B2
Speyside Cl OX18 .115 B3
Spier's La OX27 .67 C1
Spinage Cl SN7 .173 A2
Spindleberry Cl OX4 .142 C1
Spindlers OX5 .92 C1
Spindleside 1 OX26 .65 C2
Spinney Bank OX17 .23 C3
Spinney Cl RG4 .259 A4
Spinney Dr OX16 .16 C2
Spinney Field OX4 .142 C1
Spinney The
Abingdon OX14 .159 B1
East Hendred OX12 .216 B3
Launton OX26 .66 B1
Lechlade GL7 .150 B2
Spinneys Cl OX14 .160 C2
Spinneys The OX7 .58 C3
Spitfire Cl Benson OX10 .204 A1
6 Bicester OX26 .66 A2
Spleen The OX15 .14 A3
Spooner Cl OX3 .124 C2
Sprigs Holly La HP14 .189 A4
Spring Cl OX28 .118 A4
Spring Copse OX1 .141 B2
Spring Farm OX25 .47 B3
Spring Farm Mews RG8 239 B1
Spring Gdns
Abingdon OX14 .179 B4
Lechlade GL7 .150 B2
Spring Hill OX13 .176 B4
Spring Hill Rd OX5 .107 C4
Spring La
Aston Tirrold OX11 .237 C4
Great Bourton OX17 .9 B3
Horspath OX33 .143 B4
Idbury OX7 .69 A2
Oxford OX4 .142 B1
Oxford,Headington Quarry OX3 .124 C1
Reading RG4 .260 A3
Watlington OX49 .186 B1
Spring Path OX9 .147 C4
Spring Pl OX7 .42 C1
Spring Rd OX14 .179 B4
Spring St OX7 .42 C2
Spring Terr OX14 .179 B4
Spring Wlk RG10 .255 B1
Springdale OX10 .221 B4
Springfield OX17 .8 C2
Springfield Ave OX16 .16 B2
Springfield Cl
Shrivenham SN6 .209 A3
Watlington OX49 .186 B1
Springfield Dr OX14 .179 C4
Springfield End RG8 .249 B4
Springfield Gdns OX39 .168 B4
Springfield Mews RG4 .259 A2
Springfield Oval OX28 .103 C1
Springfield Pk OX28 .103 C1
Springfield Rd
Bicester OX27 .65 C4
Kidlington OX5 .108 C4
N Hinksey Village OX2 .140 B4
Stokenchurch HP14 .188 C2
Wantage OX12 .214 C2
Springfield Sch OX28 .103 C1
Springhill Rd RG8 .249 B4
Springs The OX28 .118 A4
Springwell Hill OX5 .78 A1
Springwell Ho 15 OX16 .16 B3
Springwood La RG9 .253 A4
Spruce Dr OX26 .65 C3
Spruce Gdns OX4 .161 C4
Spruce Rd OX5 .108 C4
Spur The RG10 .255 C2
Square Firs OX29 .90 A3
Square The
12 Abingdon OX14 .179 C4
Aston OX18 .135 C2
Aynho OX17 .35 B4
Ducklington OX29 .118 A2
Eynsham OX29 .120 C4
Great Tew OX7 .45 B4
Kings Sutton OX17 .23 C3
Long Crendon HP18 .129 B3
Longworth OX13 .156 A2
N Hinksey Village OX2 .122 B1
2 Oxford OX4 .142 B2
Pangbourne RG8 .256 B3
Swalcliffe OX15 .19 C4
Squire's Wlk OX10 .221 B3
Squires Cl OX18 .116 B2
Squires Rd SN6 .191 B1
Squitchey La OX2 .123 A4
Stable Cl Finmere MK18 .39 B4
Oxford OX1 .123 A1
Stable Cotts GL56 .40 B2
Stable Rd OX26 .65 C2
Staddlestone Cl RG31 .257 B1
Stadhampton Prim Sch OX44 .163 B1
Stadhampton Rd
Drayton St L OX10 .183 A3
LIttle Milton OX44 .163 C3
Stadium Way RG30 .258 A1
Staffordshire Cl RG30 .257 C1
Stainer Pl OX3 .123 C2
Stainfield Rd OX3 .124 A3
Stainswick La SN6 .209 B3
Stallpits Rd SN6 .209 A4
Stanbridge Cl OX16 .16 A3
Standlake CE Prim Sch OX29 .137 B2
Standlake Rd
Ducklington OX29 .118 B2
Northmoor OX29 .138 A1
Standon Ct OX3 .124 B1
Stanford Dr 5 OX14 .179 C4
Stanford in the Vale CE Prim Sch SN7 .194 C4
Stanford Rd SN7 .173 A2
Stanier Pl OX16 .16 C4
Stanley Cl OX2 .140 B4
Stanley Rd OX4 .141 C4
Stanmore Cres OX18 .115 C2
Stansfield Pl OX3 .124 C1
Stansfield Cl OX3 .124 C1
Stanton Cl OX28 .117 C4
Stanton Cotts OX33 .125 B4
Stanton Harcourt CE Prim Sch OX29 .138 A4
Stanton Harcourt Ind Est OX29 .138 A4
Stanton Harcourt Rd
South Leigh OX29 .119 B3
Witney OX28 .118 B4
Stanton Rd
Forest Hill OX33 .125 C2
N Hinksey Village OX2 .140 C3
Stanville Rd OX2 .140 A4
Stanway Cl OX28 .103 B1
Stanway Rd OX3 .125 A2
Stanwell Cl OX17 .11 A1
Stanwell Dr OX17 .11 A1
Stanwell La OX17 .9 B4
Stanwell Lea OX17 .11 A1
Stapleton Rd OX3 .124 B1
Star La SN6 .191 B1
Star Rd RG4 .259 B1
Starina Croft OX16 .9 A1
Starnham Rd OX29 .118 A2
Starwort Path 34 OX4 .142 C1
Station App Bicester OX26 65 C1
Kidlington OX5 .92 B1
Station Field Ind Est OX5 92 B1
Station La OX28 .118 A3
Station Rd Ardley OX27 .50 B2
Ashbury SN6 .228 A4
Aynho OX17 .35 A3
Bampton OX18 .134 C3
Black Bourton OX18 .133 C3
Blackthorn OX25 .82 A2
Bletchingdon OX5 .93 A4
Brize Norton OX18 .116 B2
Chinnor OX39 .168 B3
Chipping Norton OX7 .42 B1
Cholsey OX10 .220 C1
Cropredy OX17 .4 C1
Culham OX14 .180 C2
Didcot OX11 .200 C1
Eynsham OX29 .120 C4
Faringdon SN7 .172 C2
Goring RG8 .249 B3
Grove OX12 .214 C4
Haddenham HP17 .130 C3
Henley-on-T RG9 .244 C1
Highworth SN6 .190 A3
Hook Norton OX15 .30 B4
Kingham OX7 .54 C2
Launton OX26 .66 C2
Lechlade GL7 .150 B3
Lower Heyford OX25 .62 B3
Marsh Gibbon OX27 .67 C2
Pangbourne RG8 .256 B3
Shiplake RG9 .255 A2
Shipton-u-W OX7 .70 C1
Shrivenham SN6 .209 A3
South Leigh OX29 .119 B3
Uffington SN7 .211 B4
Upton OX11 .218 B1
Wallingford OX10 .221 B4
Wargrave RG10 .255 B1
Wheatley OX33 .144 A4
Station Rd Ind Est OX10 221 B4
Station Yard Ind Est
Adderbury OX17 .23 A1
Chipping Norton OX7 .42 B1
Station Yd
Steventon OX13 .199 A2
Thame OX9 .148 A4
Staunton Rd OX3 .124 A2
Staverton Rd OX2 .123 A3
Steady's La OX29 .138 A4
Steep Rise OX3 .124 B3
Steeple Cl OX15 .21 C2
Steepness Hill OX15 .32 C2
Stenton Cl OX14 .179 C3
Stephen Ct OX3 .124 B2
Stephen Freeman Prim Sch OX11 .200 B1
Stephen Rd OX3 .124 B2
Stephenson Ho 14 OX1 .141 B4
Steppingstone La SN6 .209 A2
Steptoe Cl OX12 .196 B1
Sterling Cl
7 Bicester OX26 .66 A2
Kidlington OX5 .108 C4
Sterling Rd OX5 .108 C4
Sterling Road App OX5 .92 C1
Sterling Way RG30 .258 A1
Stert Rd OX39 .167 C2
Stert St OX14 .179 C4
Stevens Cl OX2 .123 A2
Stevens La RG9 .252 B4
Stevenson Cl OX26 .65 B2
Stevenson Dr OX14 .179 B4
Steventon Rd
Drayton OX13,OX14 .199 A4
East Hanney OX12,OX13 .197 C4
Stewart St OX1 .141 B3
Stile Rd OX3 .124 B2
Stimpsons Cl OX2 .122 A1
Stirling Cl
Carterton OX18 .115 B2
Reading RG4 .259 B3
Wantage OX12 .214 C3
Stirling Ct OX16 .15 C3
Stirlings Rd 4 OX12 .214 B2
Stockey End OX14 .160 B1
Stockham Pk OX12 .214 B3
Stockham Prim Sch OX12 .214 B3
Stockham Way OX12 .214 B3
Stocking La OX15 .6 B1
Stockleys Rd OX3 .124 A3
Stockmore St OX4 .141 C4
Stocks La OX13 .198 C2
Stocks The OX7 .57 A1
Stocks Tree Cl OX5 .108 A3
Stoke Lyne Rd OX27 .52 B1
Stoke Pl OX3 .124 B2
Stoke Row CE Prim Sch RG9 .241 C3
Stoke Row Rd RG9 .252 C4
Stokenchurch Inf Sch HP14 .188 C2
Stokenchurch Jun Sch HP14 .188 C3
Stokes View RG8 .256 B3
Stone Cl OX2 .122 A1
Stone Ct 20 Banbury OX16 .16 B3
Great Rollright OX7 .29 A2
Stone Hill OX15 .21 B2
Stone House Cl OX13 .156 C1
Stone Quarry La OX4 .142 A2
Stone St Oxford OX4 .142 A4
Reading RG30 .258 A1
Stonebridge Rd OX13 .198 C3
Stoneburge Cres OX26 .65 C2
Stonebury Cl OX12 .214 C3
Stonecrop Leyes OX26 .65 C3
Stonefield Dr SN6 .190 A2
Stonefield Way SN6 .209 B3
Stonegables OX28 .118 A3
Stonehill La
Abingdon OX14 .179 B2
Kingston Bagpuize OX13 .176 B4
Stonehill Wlk OX14 .179 B2
Stoneleigh Cl OX7 .57 A1
Stoneleigh Dr OX18 .115 B3
Stonesfield OX11 .219 A4
Stonesfield La OX7 .73 B1
Stonesfield Prim Sch OX29 .89 B4
Stonesfield Rd OX29 .90 A3
Stonesfield Riding OX7 .74 B1
Stoney La OX9,OX49 .185 C4
Stonhouse Cres OX14 .160 C1
Stonor Cl OX11 .200 C1
Stonor Gn OX49 .186 A1
Stonor Ho* OX49 .226 A4
Stonor Pl OX3 .124 A1
Stort Cl OX11 .200 C2
Stour Cl OX11 .201 A1
Stoutsfield Cl OX5 .108 A3
Stow Ave OX28 .117 B4
Stow Rd Bledington OX7 .54 B1
Fifield OX7 .69 A1
Stowford Ct OX3 .124 C3
Stowford Rd OX3 .124 C2
Stowhill OX12 .213 B2
Stowood Cl OX3 .124 C2
Strachey Cl RG8 .256 B1
Strafford Way OX9 .148 A4
Strainges Cl OX29 .118 A2
Stranks Cl SN6 .190 A2
Stratfield Rd
Cutteslowe OX2 .123 A3
Kidlington OX5 .108 C3
Stratford Dr OX29 .120 B4
Stratford La OX20 .76 A1
Stratford Rd
Drayton (Banbury) OX15 .15 C4
Shenington OX15 .6 C4
Wroxton OX15 .14 C4
Stratford St OX4 .141 C4
Strathmore Cl OX18 .115 B3
Stratton Audley Manor OX27 .52 B1
Stratton Audley Rd
Fringford OX27 .52 B3
Stoke Lyne OX27 .51 A3
Stratton Way OX14 .179 C4
Strawberry Hill OX15 .21 C3
Strawberry Path OX4 .142 C1
Strawberry Terr OX15 .21 C3
Stream Rd OX11 .218 B1
Streatley & Goring Bridge RG8 .249 A3
Streatley Hill RG8 .248 C3
Streatley Lodge 24 OX1 .141 B4
Streatley CE Sch RG8 .248 C3
Street The
Crowmarsh G OX10 .221 C4
Crowmarsh G, N Stoke OX10 .221 B1
Ipsden OX10 .240 B4
Moulsford OX10 .239 A3
South Stoke RG8 .239 A2
Stoke Lyne OX27 .51 A3
Tidmarsh RG8 .256 B1
Stroud Cl OX16 .16 C4
Stuart Cl RG4 .259 A3
Stuart Way OX9 .130 A1
Stubble Cl OX2 .140 A4
Stubbs Ave OX3 .142 C4
Stud Farm Cl OX17 .5 C1
Studdridge Ct HP14 .188 B2
Sturges Cl OX3 .124 B3
Sturt Cl OX7 .73 B1
Sturt Rd OX7 .73 B2
Styles Cl OX27 .67 C1
Styles The OX11 .217 B4
Sudbury Ct SN7 .173 A2
Sudbury La OX13 .156 B2
Suffolk Ct OX27 .67 C2
Suffolk Ho OX10 .204 C2
Suffolk Way OX14 .179 B3
Sugarswell La OX15 .6 A3
Sugworth Cres OX14 .160 C3
Sugworth La OX14 .160 B3
Sulham La RG8 .256 C2
Summer Fields OX14 .160 A2
Summer Ley OX15 .32 C3
Summerfield OX1 .141 B3
Summerfield Rd OX2 .123 A4
Summerfield Rise RG8 .249 B4
Summerhill Rd OX2 .123 A4
Summers Cl OX17 .23 A3
Summerside Rd SN7 .174 C4
Summerton Pl OX7 .42 C2
Summertown OX12 .197 A3
Summertown Ct OX2 .123 A4
Summertown Ho OX2 .123 A4
Sunderland Ave OX2 .109 A1
Sunderland Dr OX26 .66 A2
Sundew Cl OX4 .143 A1
Sunningwell CE Prim Sch OX13 .159 C3
Sunningwell Rd
Oxford OX1 .141 B3
Sunningwell OX13 .159 C2
Sunny Rise OX33 .143 B3
Sunnymeade Ct 2 OX2 .109 A1
Sunnyside Benson OX10 .203 C3
Sunnyside *continued*
Oxford OX4 .142 B3
Wheatley OX33 .144 B4
Surley Row RG4 .259 A3
Sussex Dr OX16 .15 C4
Sutherland Beck OX11 .200 C2
Sutton Cl OX14 .179 C4
Sutton Courtenay Rd OX14 .199 C3
Sutton La OX29 .120 A1
Sutton Rd Milton OX14 .199 C3
Oxford OX3 .124 A3
Sutton Wick La OX14 .179 B1
Suzan Cres OX12 .214 C3
Swain Ct OX28 .118 A3
Swalcliffe Lea OX15 .14 A1
Swalcliffe Park Sch OX15 .19 C4
Swalcliffe Rd OX15 .20 A4
Swale Dr OX11 .201 A1
Swallow Cl Bicester OX26 .81 A4
21 Sandford-on-T OX4 .142 C1
Swan Cl Grove OX12 .196 B1
Lechlade GL7 .150 B2
Middleton Cheney OX17 .17 C4
Swan Close Rd OX16 .16 B3
Swan Ct 7 Oxford OX1 .123 A1
Witney OX28 .118 A4
Swan Gdns OX9 .166 A4
Swan Ind Est OX16 .16 B3
Swan La Burford OX18 .100 C3
Faringdon SN7 .172 C2
Great Bourton OX17 .9 B4
Long Hanborough OX29 .90 A1
Swan Lane Cl OX18 .100 C3
Swan St Eynsham OX29 .120 C4
Oxford OX2 .123 A1
Swan Wlk OX9 .147 C4
Swanhall La OX29 .104 A3
Swanlands Ho OX29 .120 C4
Swansea Rd RG1 .259 A1
Swansea Terr RG31 .257 B1
Swansfield Bicester OX26 .81 A4
Lechlade GL7 .150 B3
Swanston Field RG8 .256 B4
Swarbourne Cl OX11 .200 C1
Sweeps La OX18 .100 C3
Sweet Briar OX13 .178 B3
Sweetmans Rd OX2 .140 B4
Swerford Rd OX15 .30 A3
Swift Cl Bicester OX26 .65 B2
25 Sandford-on-T OX4 .142 C1
Swift Way OX10 .204 B2
Swin La OX18 .101 C3
Swinbourne Rd OX4 .142 A1
Swinbrook Cl RG31 .257 B2
Swinbrook Ct OX28 .118 A4
Swinbrook Rd
Carterton OX18 .115 B3
Shipton-u-W OX7 .85 C3
Swinburne Rd
Abingdon OX14 .180 A4
Oxford OX4 .141 C3
Swindon Rd SN6 .190 A3
Swindon St SN6 .190 A3
Swingburn Pl OX28 .118 A4
Swinnerton Ho RG9 .244 C2
Swinstead Ct OX44 .184 B3
Sworford La OX44 .144 C3
Sycamore Cl
Abingdon OX13 .159 B1
Long Crendon HP18 .129 B3
Sibford Gower OX15 .19 A4
Watlington OX49 .186 A1
Witney OX28 .104 B1
Sycamore Cres OX1, OX14 .160 C4
Sycamore Ct RG8 .256 B3
Sycamore Dr
Banbury OX16 .16 B1
Carterton OX18 .115 B2
Thame OX9 .147 B4
Sycamore Gdns OX26 .65 C2
Sycamore Pl OX18 .114 B4
Sycamore Rd
Ambrosden OX25 .81 B2
Launton OX26 .66 B1
N Hinksey Village OX2 .140 B4
Sycamore Terr OX15 .21 B2
Sycamore Wlk OX12 .196 B1
Sycamores The OX3 .124 C2
Sydenham Gr OX39 .167 C4
Sylvester Cl OX18 .100 C3
Sympson Cl 12 OX14 .179 C3
Syringa Wlk OX16 .9 A1

T

Tackley CE Prim Sch OX5 .77 B3
Tackley Pl OX2 .123 A2
Tackley Sta OX5 .77 C3
Tacks La HP17 .130 C3
Tadmarton Pk OX15 .21 A3
Tadmarton Rd OX15 .21 A3
Taggs Gate OX3 .124 C3
Tailsman Bsns Ctr The OX26 .80 C4
Tait Dr OX25 .63 A4
Talbot Cl Banbury OX16 .15 C4
Reading RG4 .259 B1
Talbot Fields OX18 .135 A2
Talbot Rd OX2 .109 A1
Talbot Way RG31 .257 B2

Using the Ordnance Survey National Grid

NG	NH	NJ	NK		
NM	NN	NO	NP		
NR	NS	NT	NU		
NX	NY	NZ			
SC	SD	SE	TA		
SH	SJ	SK	TF	TG	
SM	SN	SO	SP	TL	TM
SR	SS	ST	SU	TQ	TR
SW	SX	SY	SZ	TV	

Any feature in this atlas can be given a unique reference to help you find the same feature on other Ordnance Survey maps of the area, or to help someone else locate you if they do not have a Street Atlas.

The grid squares in this atlas match the Ordnance Survey National Grid and are at 1 kilometre intervals. The small figures at the bottom and sides of every other grid line are the National Grid kilometre values (**00** to **99** km) and are repeated across the country every 100 km (see left).

To give a unique National Grid reference you need to locate where in the country you are. The country is divided into 100 km squares with each square given a unique two-letter reference. Use the administrative map to determine in which 100 km square a particular page of this atlas falls.

The bold letters and numbers between each grid line (**A** to **F**, **1** to **4**) are for use within a specific Street Atlas only, and when used with the page number, are a convenient way of referencing these grid squares.

Example   *The railway bridge over DARLEY GREEN RD in grid square A1*

Step 1: Identify the two-letter reference, in this example the page is in **SP**

Step 2: Identify the 1 km square in which the railway bridge falls. Use the figures in the southwest corner of this square: Eastings **17**, Northings **74**. This gives a unique reference: **SP 17 74**, accurate to 1 km.

Step 3: To give a more precise reference accurate to 100 m you need to estimate how many tenths along and how many tenths up this 1 km square the feature is. This makes the bridge about **8** tenths along and about **1** tenth up from the southwest corner.

This gives a unique reference: **SP 178 741**, accurate to 100 m.

Eastings (read from left to right along the bottom) come before Northings (read from bottom to top). If you have trouble remembering say to yourself "Along the hall, THEN up the stairs"!

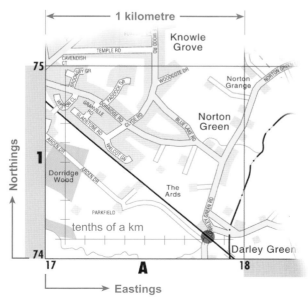

Name and Address	Telephone	Page	Grid reference

Street Atlases from Philip's

Philip's publish an extensive range of regional and local street atlases which are ideal for motoring, business and leisure use. They are widely used by the emergency services and local authorities throughout Britain.

Key features include:

◆ Superb county-wide mapping at an extra-large scale of 3½ inches to 1 mile, or 2½ inches to 1 mile in pocket editions

◆ Complete urban and rural coverage, detailing every named street in town and country

◆ Each atlas available in two handy sizes – standard spiral and pocket paperback

'The mapping is very clear... great in scope and value'
★★★★ BEST BUY   AUTO EXPRESS

1 Bedfordshire
2 Berkshire
3 Birmingham and West Midlands
4 Bristol and Bath
5 Buckinghamshire
6 Cambridgeshire
7 Cardiff, Swansea and The Valleys
8 Cheshire
9 Derbyshire
10 Dorset
11 County Durham and Teesside
12 Edinburgh and East Central Scotland
13 North Essex
14 South Essex
15 Glasgow and West Central Scotland
16 Gloucestershire
17 North Hampshire
18 South Hampshire
19 Hertfordshire
20 East Kent
21 West Kent
22 Lancashire
23 Leicestershire and Rutland
24 London
25 Greater Manchester
26 Merseyside
27 Northamptonshire
28 Nottinghamshire
29 Oxfordshire
30 Somerset
31 Staffordshire
32 Surrey
33 East Sussex
34 West Sussex
35 Tyne and Wear and Northumberland
36 Warwickshire
37 Wiltshire and Swindon
38 East Yorkshire and Northern Lincolnshire
39 North Yorkshire
40 South Yorkshire
41 West Yorkshire

How to order
The Philip's range of street atlases is available from good retailers or directly from the publisher by phoning 01903 828503